MARTIN LUTHER KING, JR.

Dedication

To Marlene, Robin, Paul, Lisa, and Maria, who encouraged me to document the life of Dr. Martin Luther King, Jr.; and to the late Wilson Hicks, former executive editor of *Life* magazine, who taught me to use words and pictures together.

MARTIN LUTHER KING, JR.

A DOCUMENTARY...MONTGOMERY TO MEMPHIS

with an introduction by Coretta Scott King

Editor: FLIP SCHULKE

Associate Editor: Bob Fitch
Text by: Penelope McPhee

W · W · NORTON & COMPANY

New York · London

ACKNOWLEDGEMENTS

A word and picture documentary book like this one could not be done without the gifts of both time and creative works of many people. I am extremely grateful to my editor at W. W. Norton & Company, Starling Lawrence, for giving me the chance to compile this documentary and for his constant help and understanding during the progress of the project. My deepest thanks to Robert Fitch, former staff assistant and photographer for the Southern Christian Leadership Conference (SCLC) who donated both his time, interviewing ability, and photographs to the book. To Susan Greenwood, researcher and interviewer, my thanks, because she cared.

I would like to thank Robert Nemser for his art direction, and Howard Chapnick, Black Star Picture Agency, for his decisive picture editing during the layout sessions spiced by his friendship and sense of humor. To Bill Lyons, director of news pictures, United Press International, for his help in making the complete UPI files on Dr. King available to us. A special thank you to the many photographers who took the photographs credited to UPI, among them: Gary Haynes, Bill Lyons, Phil Sandlin, Hugo Wessels, Bob Gordon, Bill Bryant, Hank Leifermann, Joe Holloway, Jerry Huff, Emile Morone, Pete Fisher, and Sam Parrish.

Bernita Bennett was especially helpful, along with Dora McDonald, in confirming the chronology of Dr. King's life. Thanks also to Stanley Levison, Richard Kaplan, and Barry Ralbag for their help in structuring the narrative.

Thanks are due Herbert Nipson, editor, and John H. Johnson, publisher, of *Jet* and *Ebony,* who gave me my first assignments on Dr. King; Basil Phillips, librarian for *Jet* and *Ebony* magazines; Joan Daves, Dr. King's literary agent; and George Evans and the staff of the Martin Luther King Foundation.

My deep appreciation to Congressman Andrew Young, Georgia State Representative Hosea Williams, Reverend Ralph Abernathy, Mrs. Rosa Parks, Reverend Jesse Jackson, and Reverend Martin Luther King, Sr., for granting me and my associates lengthy personal interviews.

A photography book is dependent on photographic prints of the highest quality. Wolfram Kloetz, Vernon Sigl, and Jorge Figueroa of Modern-Age Custom Labs, New York, took that extra effort in printing most of the photographs in this book.

I am grateful to my fellow Black Star photographers whose works appear, as credited: Charles Moore, Dan McCoy, Declan Haun, Ron McCool, Matt Herron, Lee Lockwood, Ivan Massar, Fred Ward, Vernon Merritt, Mike Mauney, Harry Benson, and Steve Shapiro. Special appreciation goes to the Lyndon Baines Johnson Library, and presidential photographers Cecil Stoughton and Yoichi Okamoto. Special thanks for photographs to James Karales, Joseph Louw, and Reverend Wyatt Tee Walker.

Finally, my deepest appreciation to Coretta Scott King, who made herself personally available to answer many of my questions, and the Martin Luther King, Jr., Center for Social Change, Atlanta, Georgia, which she directs in the furtherance of her husband's life and ideas.

Flip Schulke
Miami, Florida
October, 1975

Designed by Robert S. Nemser, Nemser & Howard, Inc.

W. W. Norton & Company, Inc., 500 Fifth Avenue, New York, N.Y. 10110

ISBN 0-393-07487-0 cloth edition
ISBN 0-393-07492-7 paper edition

7 8 9 0

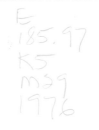

Contents

Prologue
THE PROBLEM

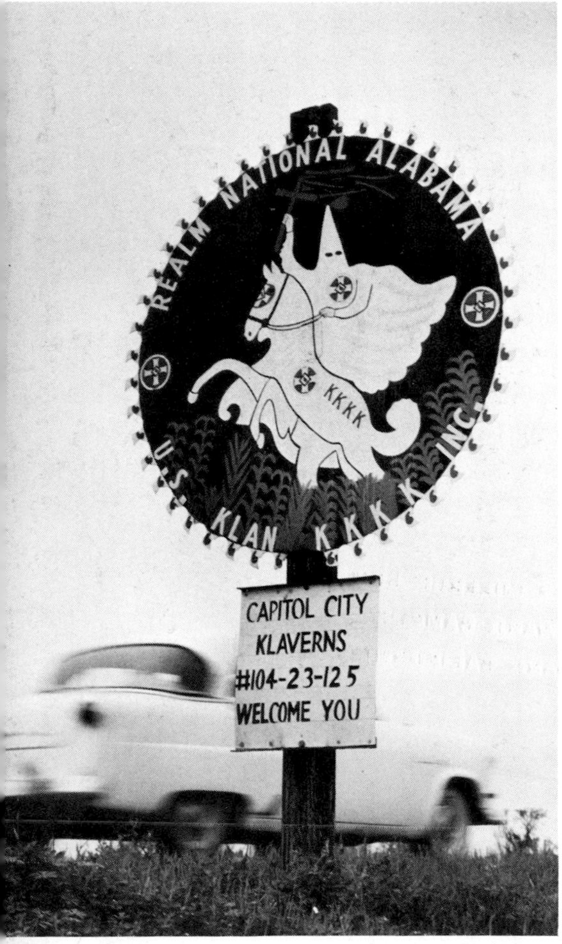
REALM NATIONAL ALABAMA
KKKK
U.S. KLAN KKKK INC.
CAPITOL CITY
KLAVERNS
#104-23-125
WELCOME YOU

Charles Moore

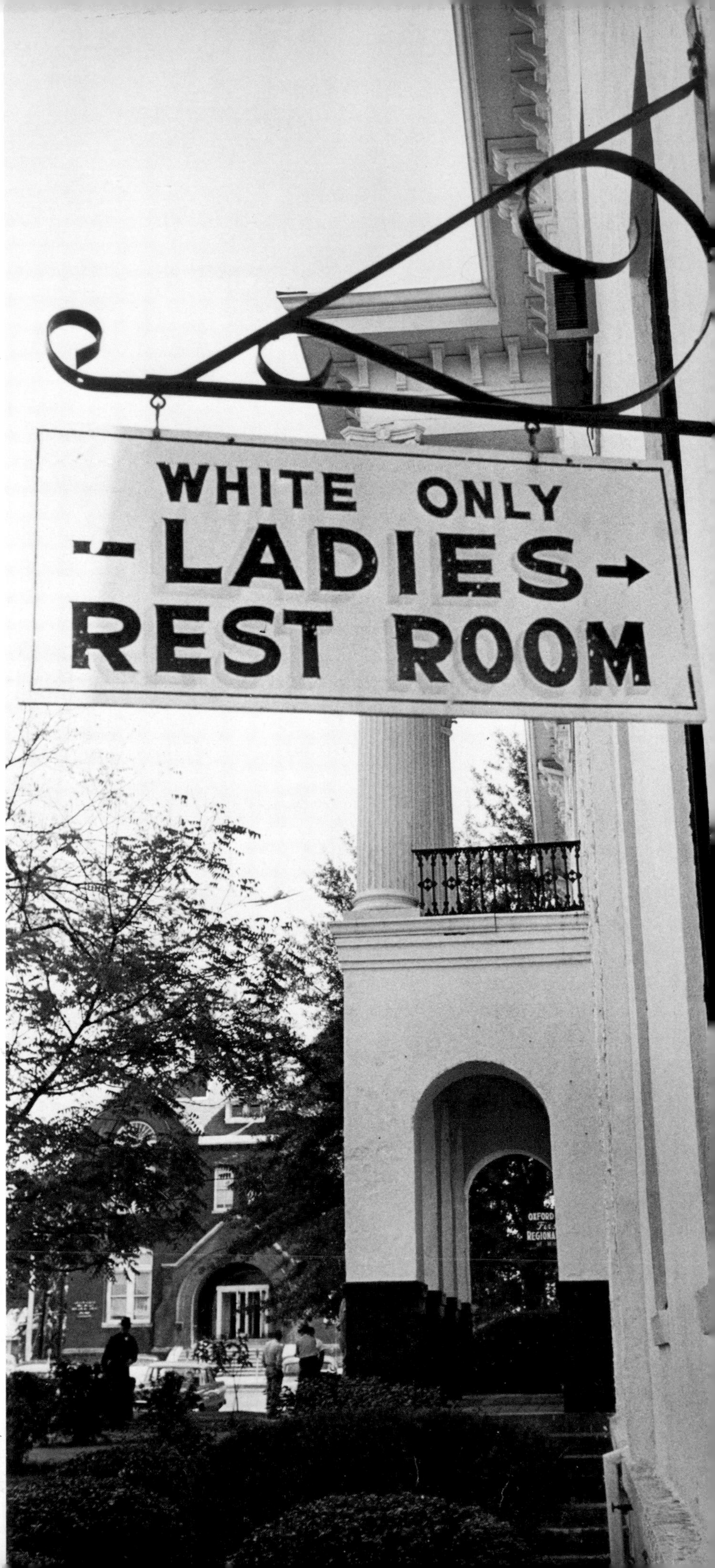
WHITE ONLY
LADIES
REST ROOM

Dan McCoy

Bob Fitch

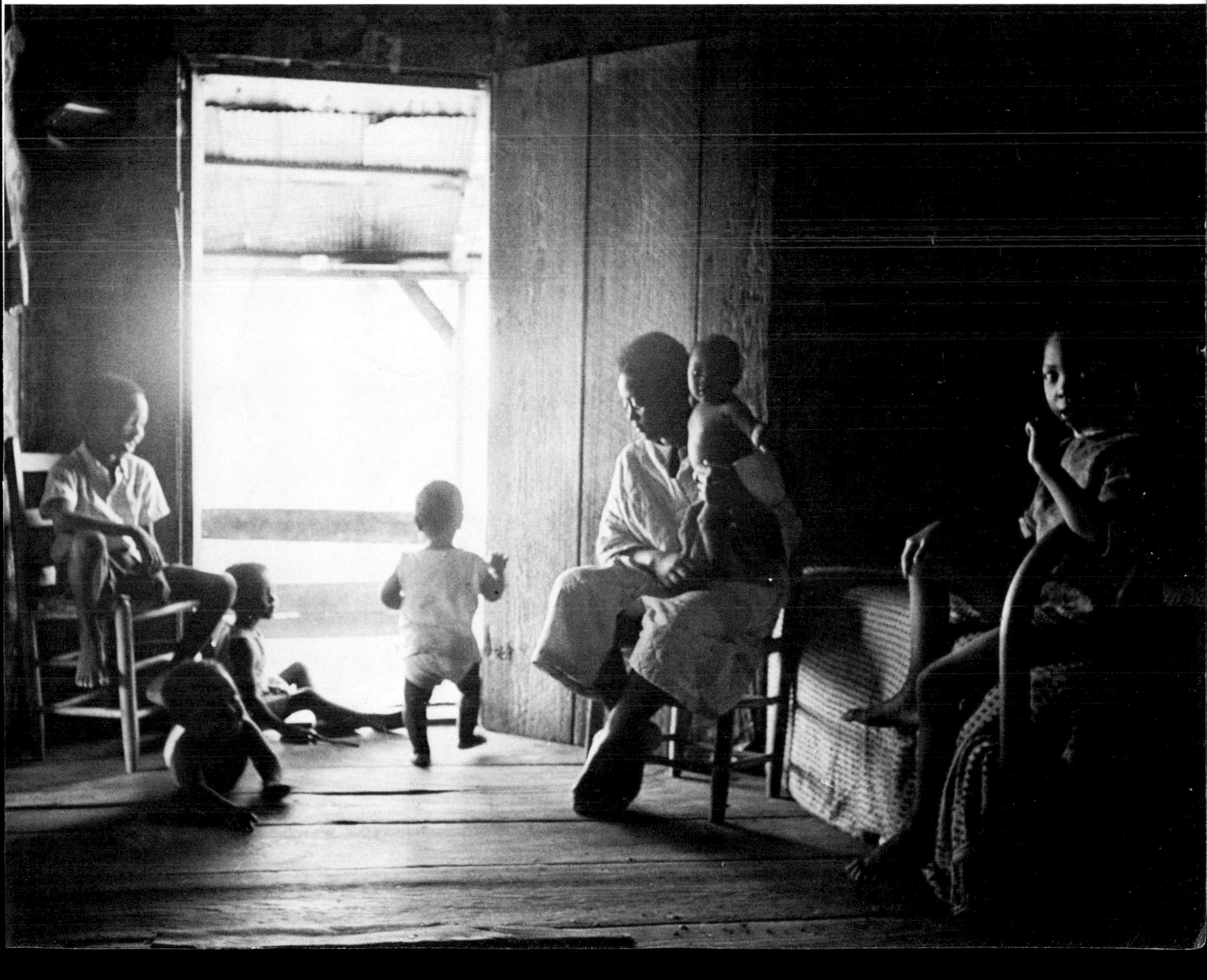

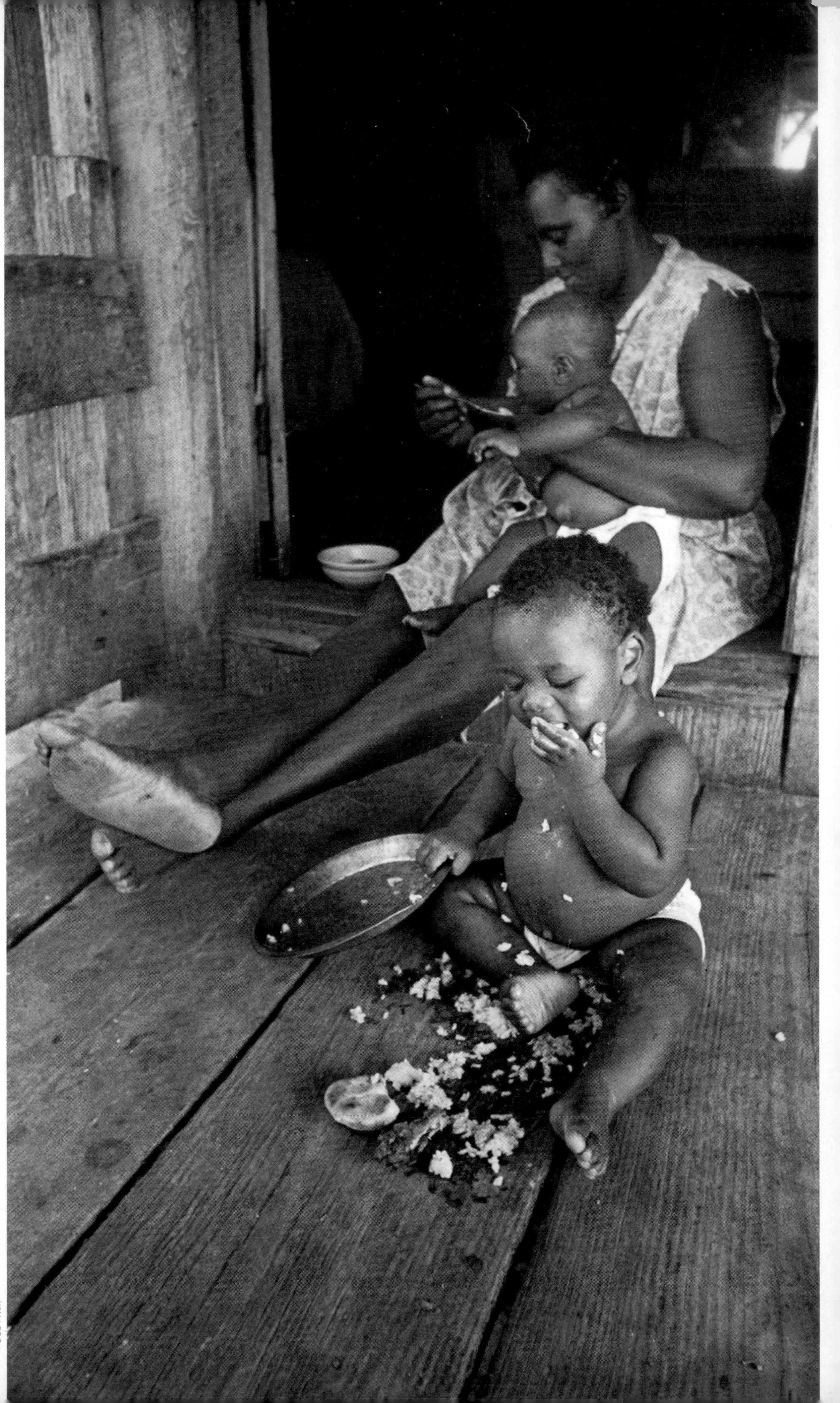

Bob Fitch

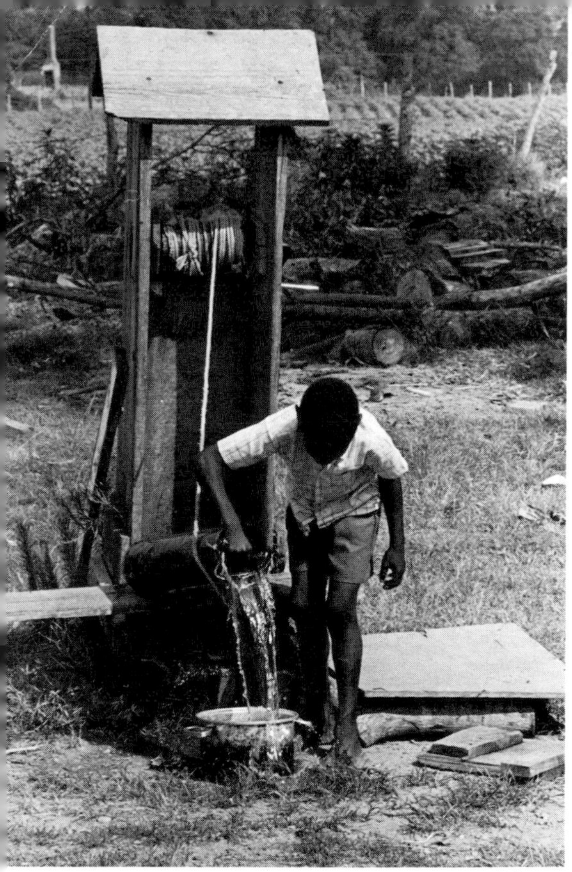

Bob Fitch

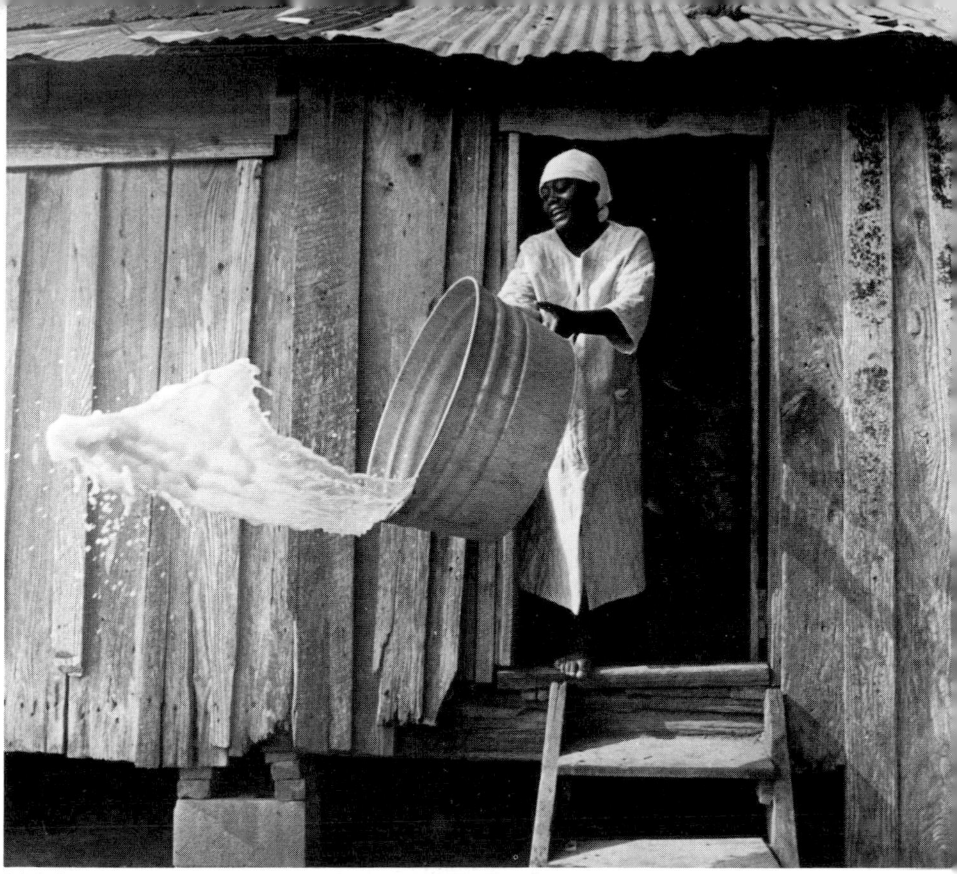

Bob Fitch

Bob Fitch

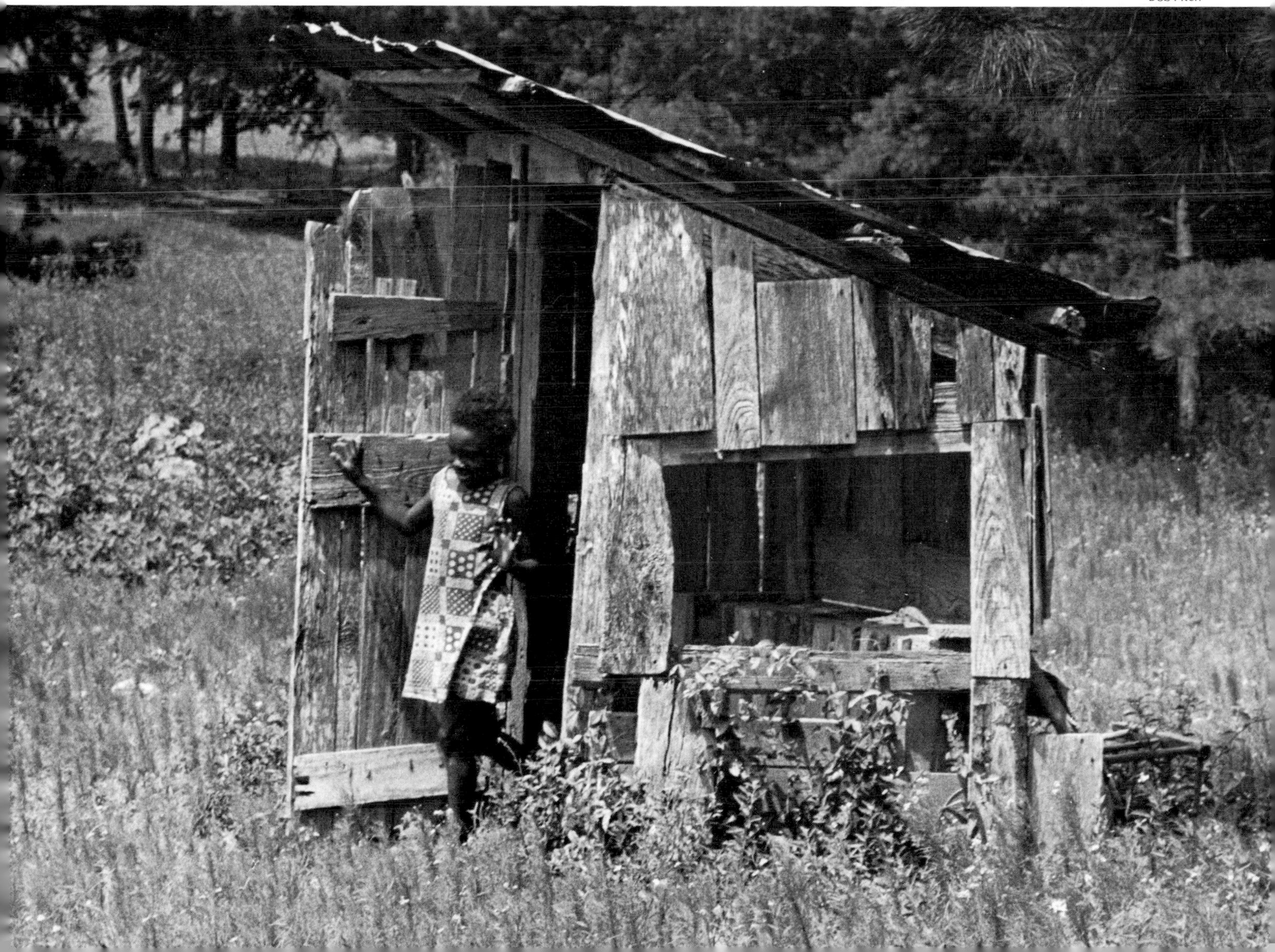

Matt Herron

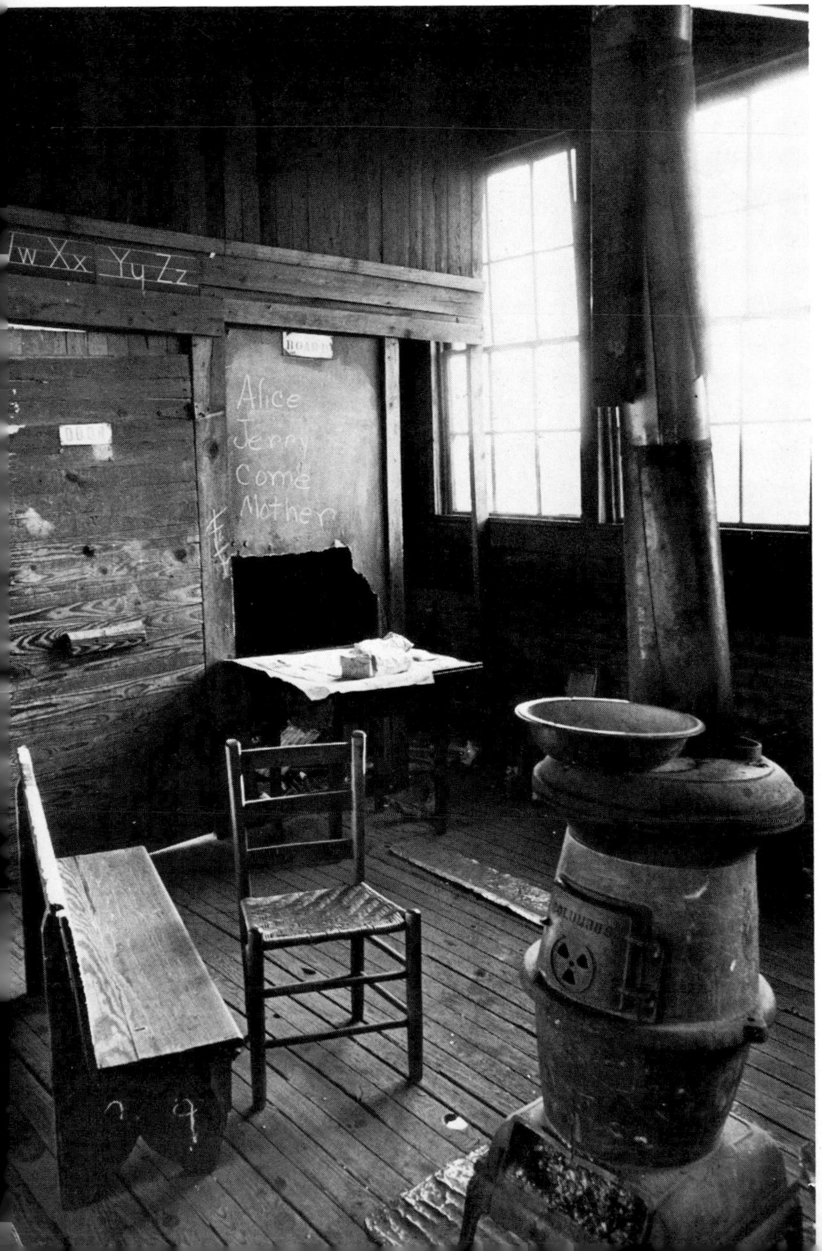
w Xx Yy Zz
Alice
Jerry
Come
Mother

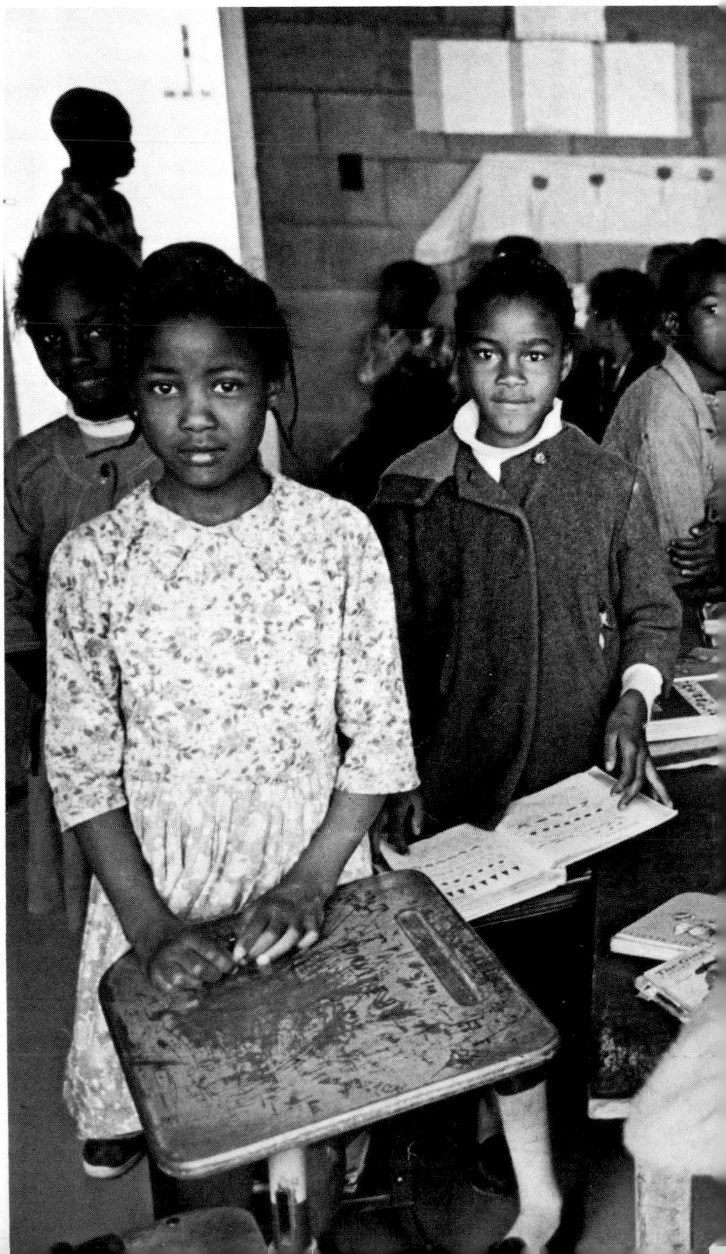

Bob Fitch

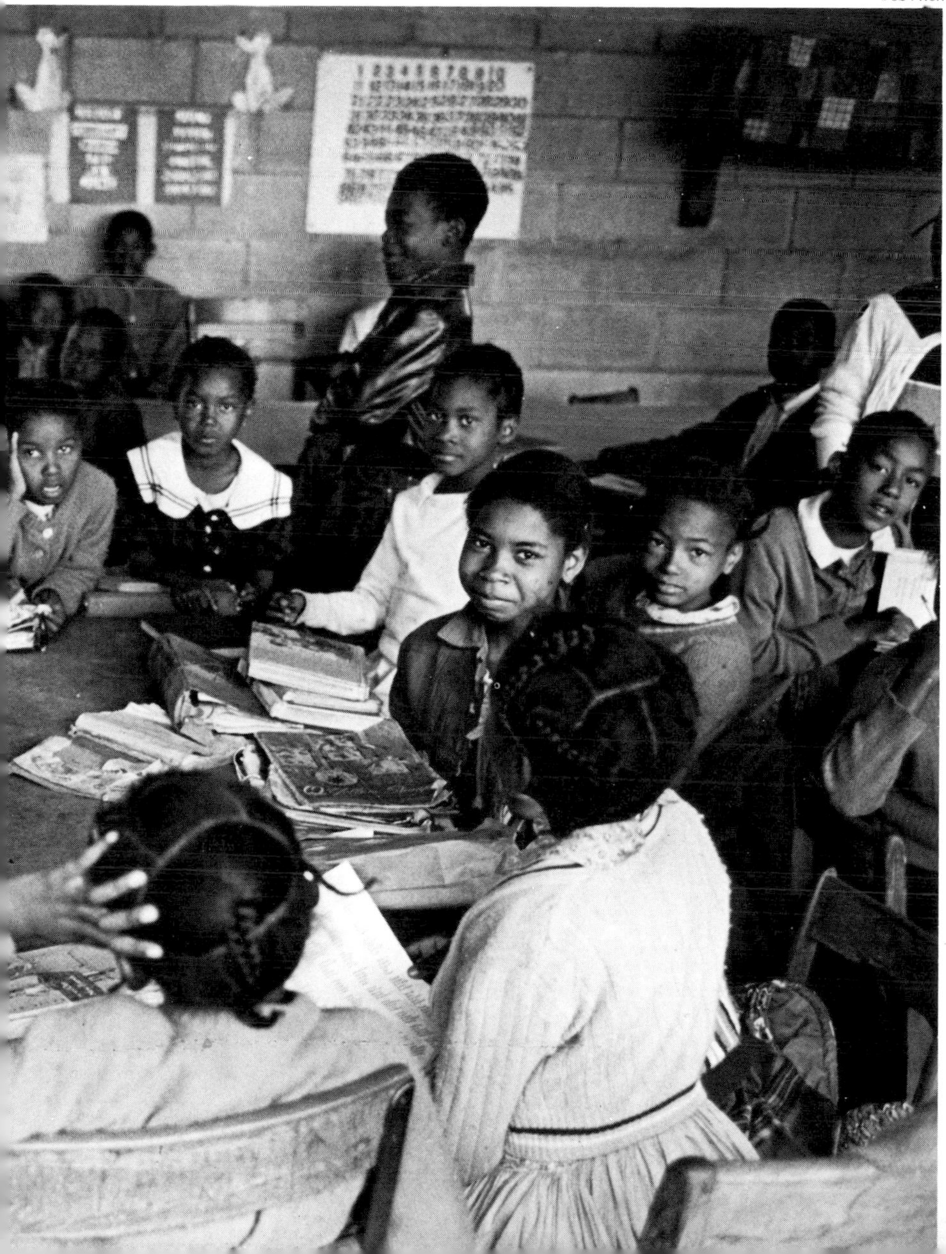

Flip Schulke

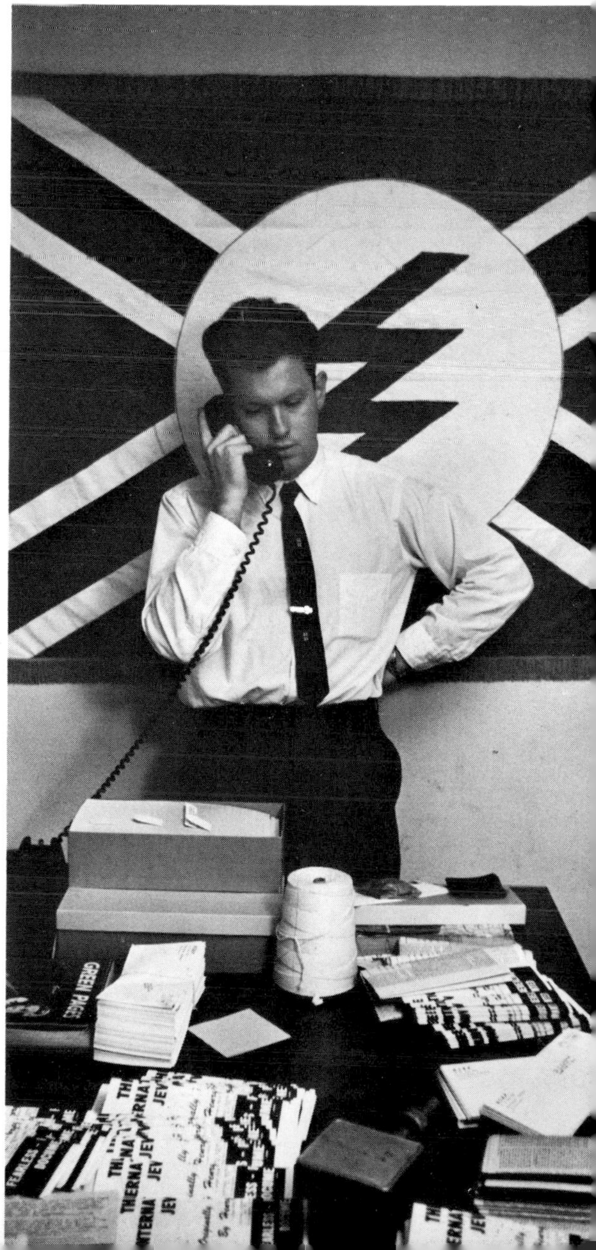

Bob Fitch

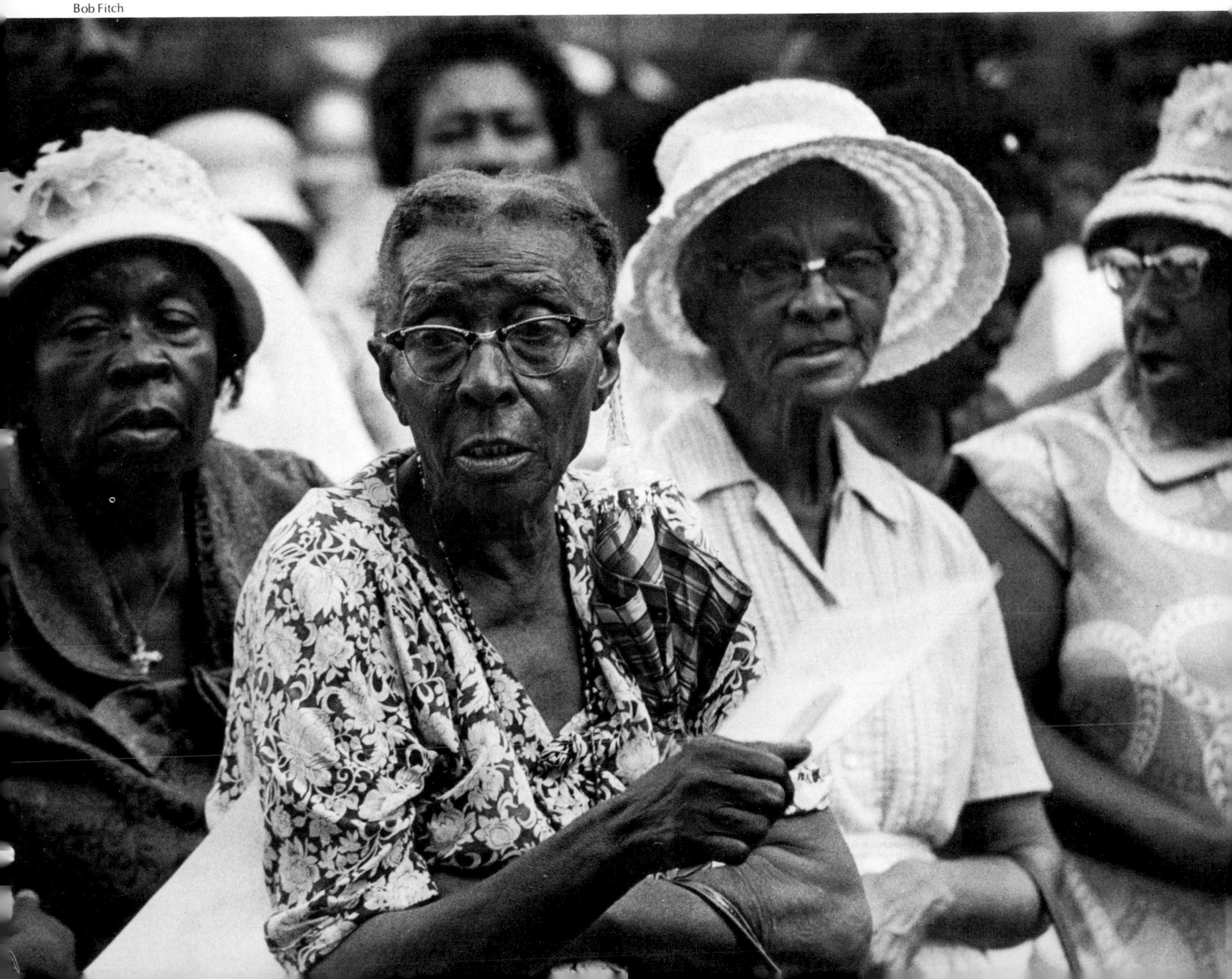

Flip Schulke

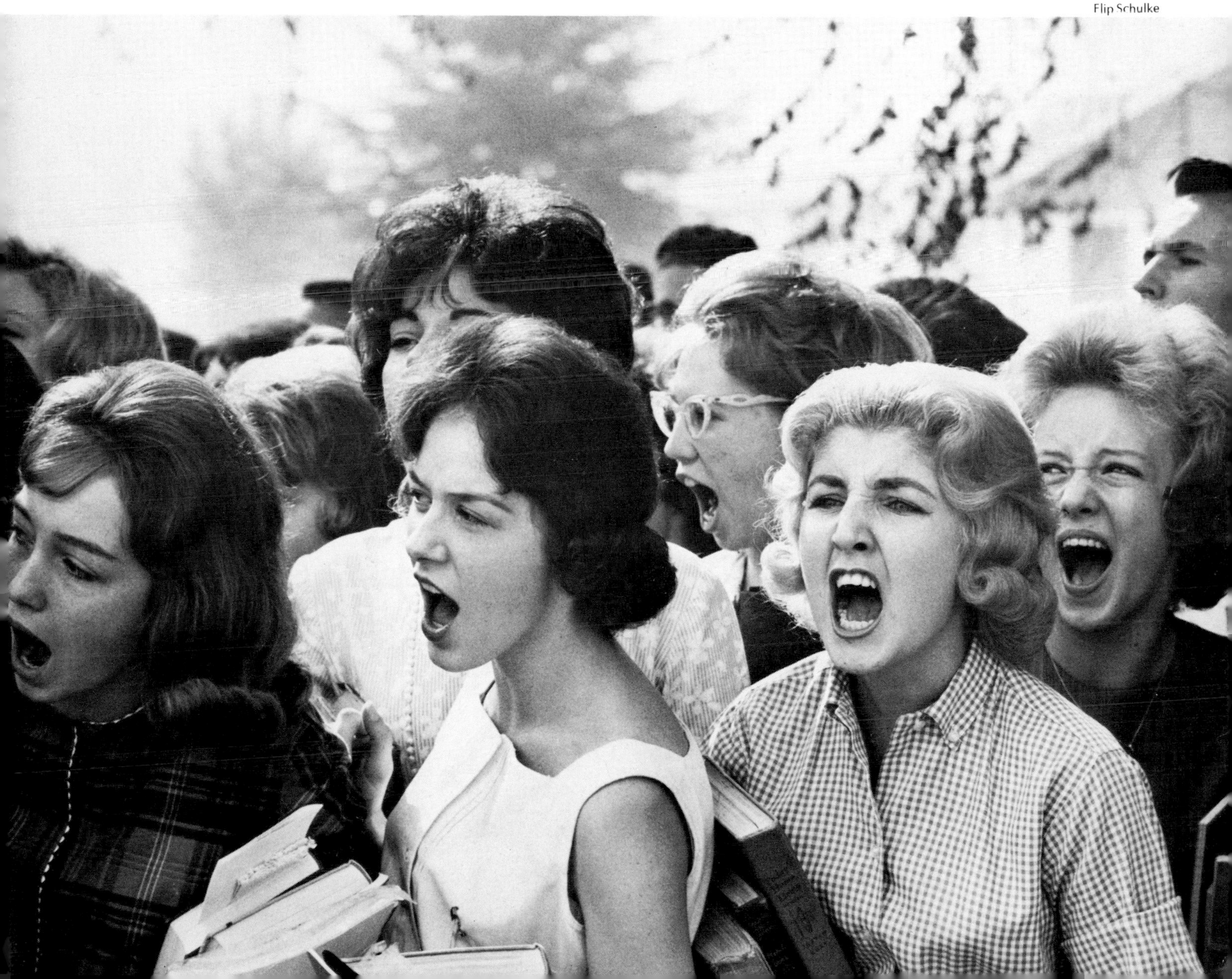

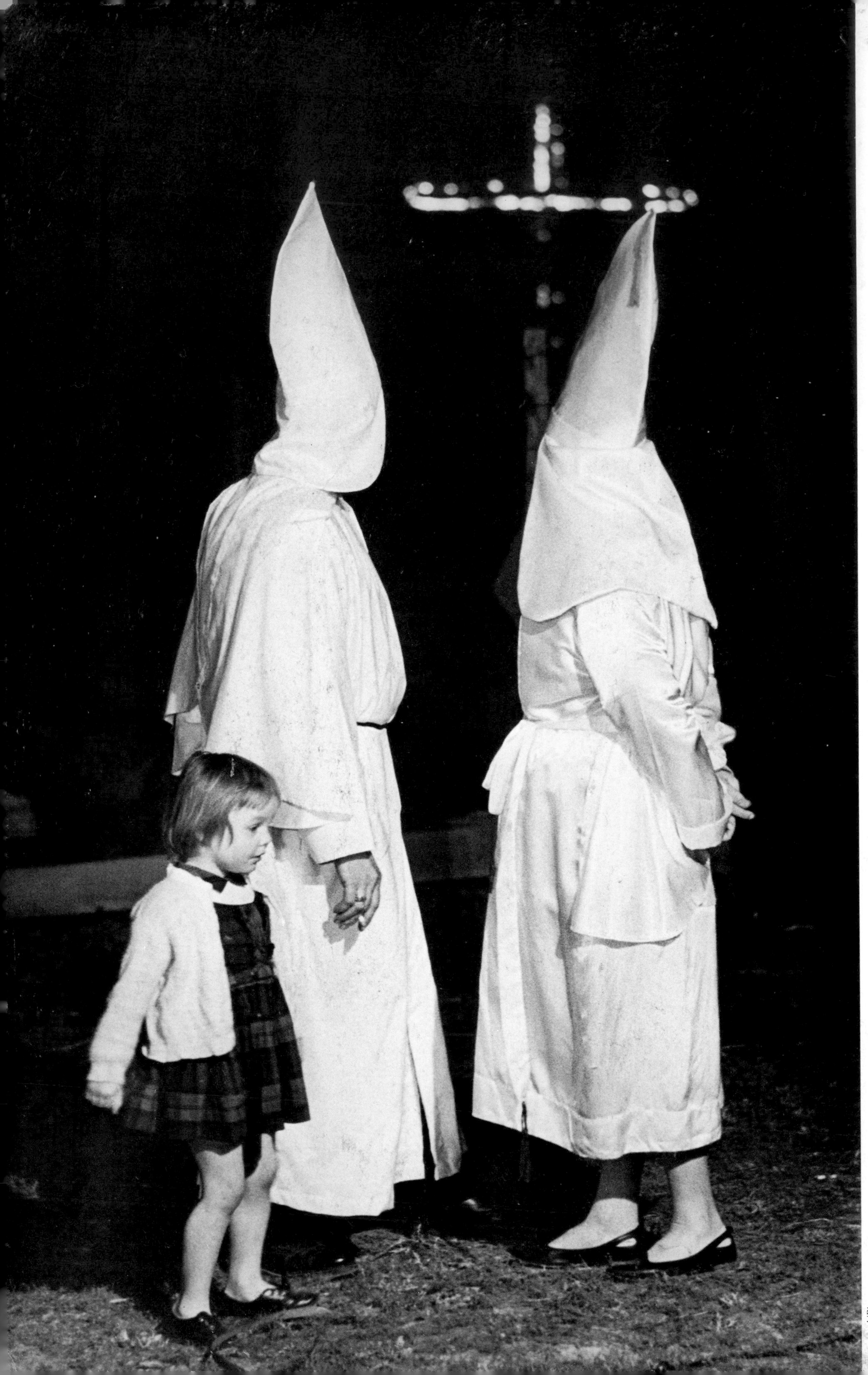

UPI

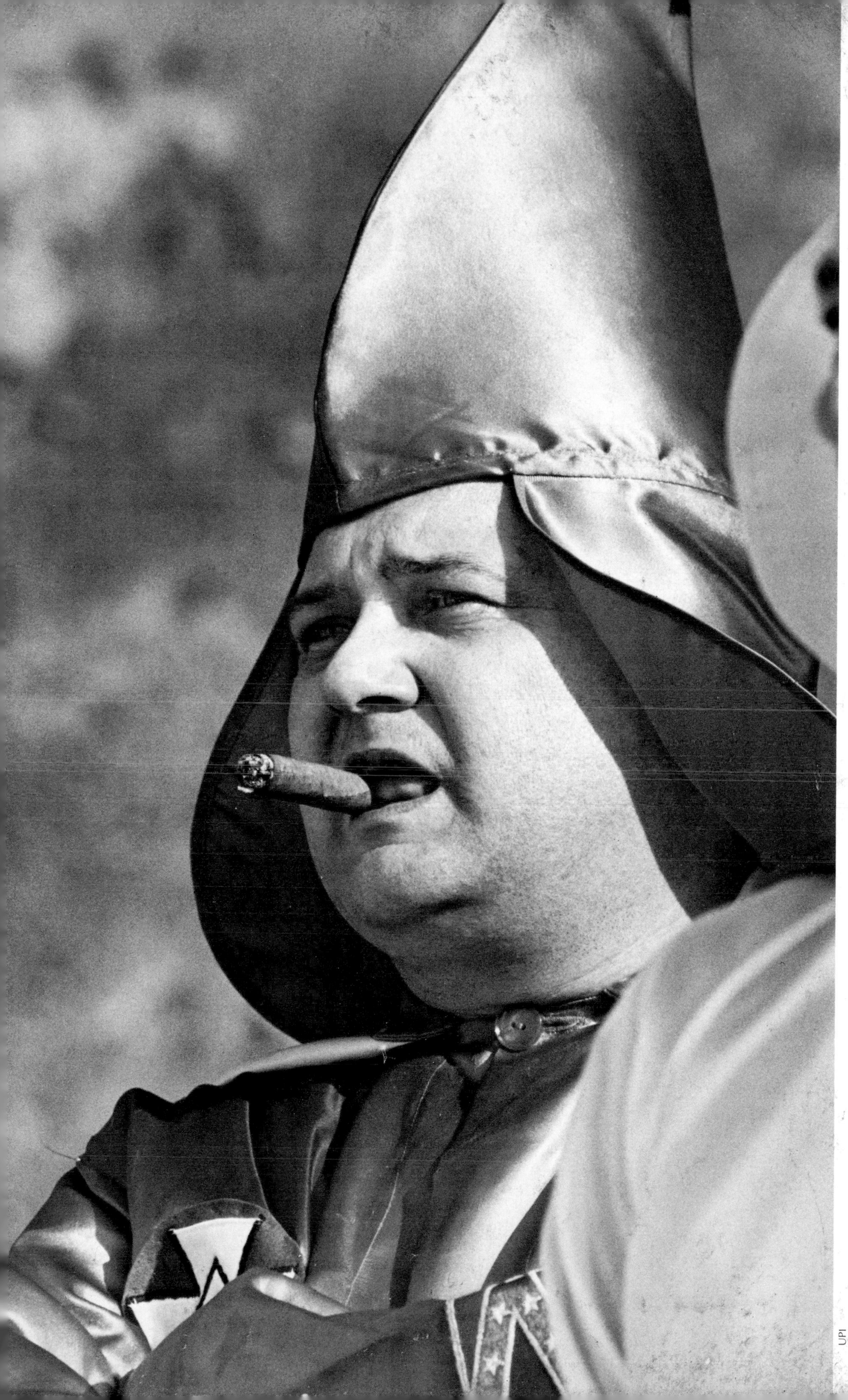
UPI

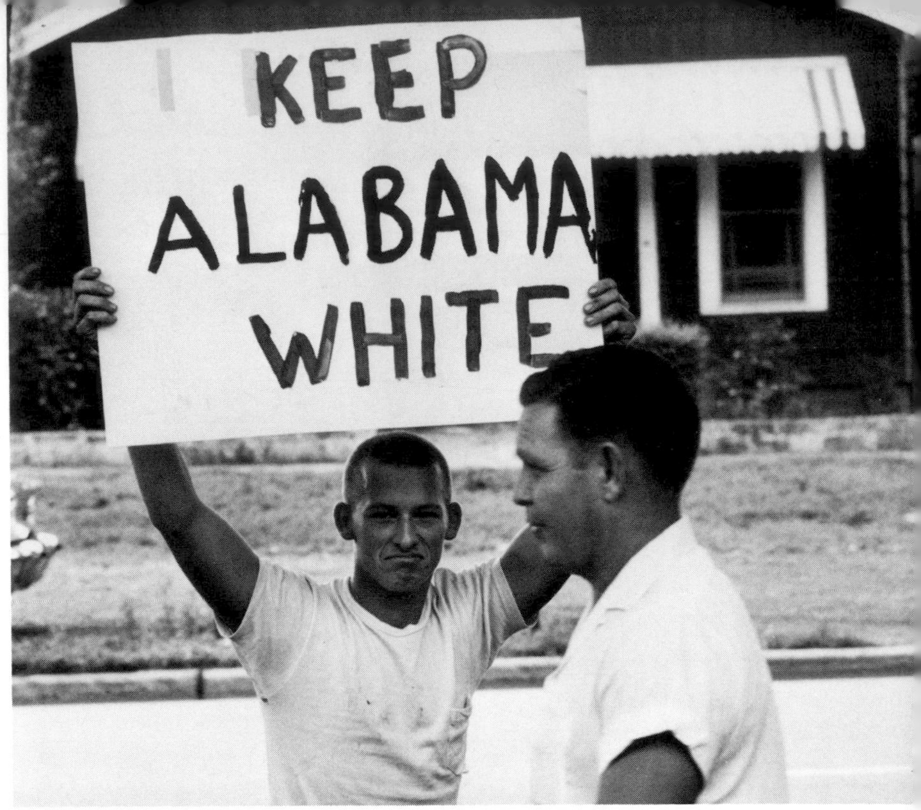
KEEP
ALABAMA
WHITE

Flip Schulke

Charles Moore

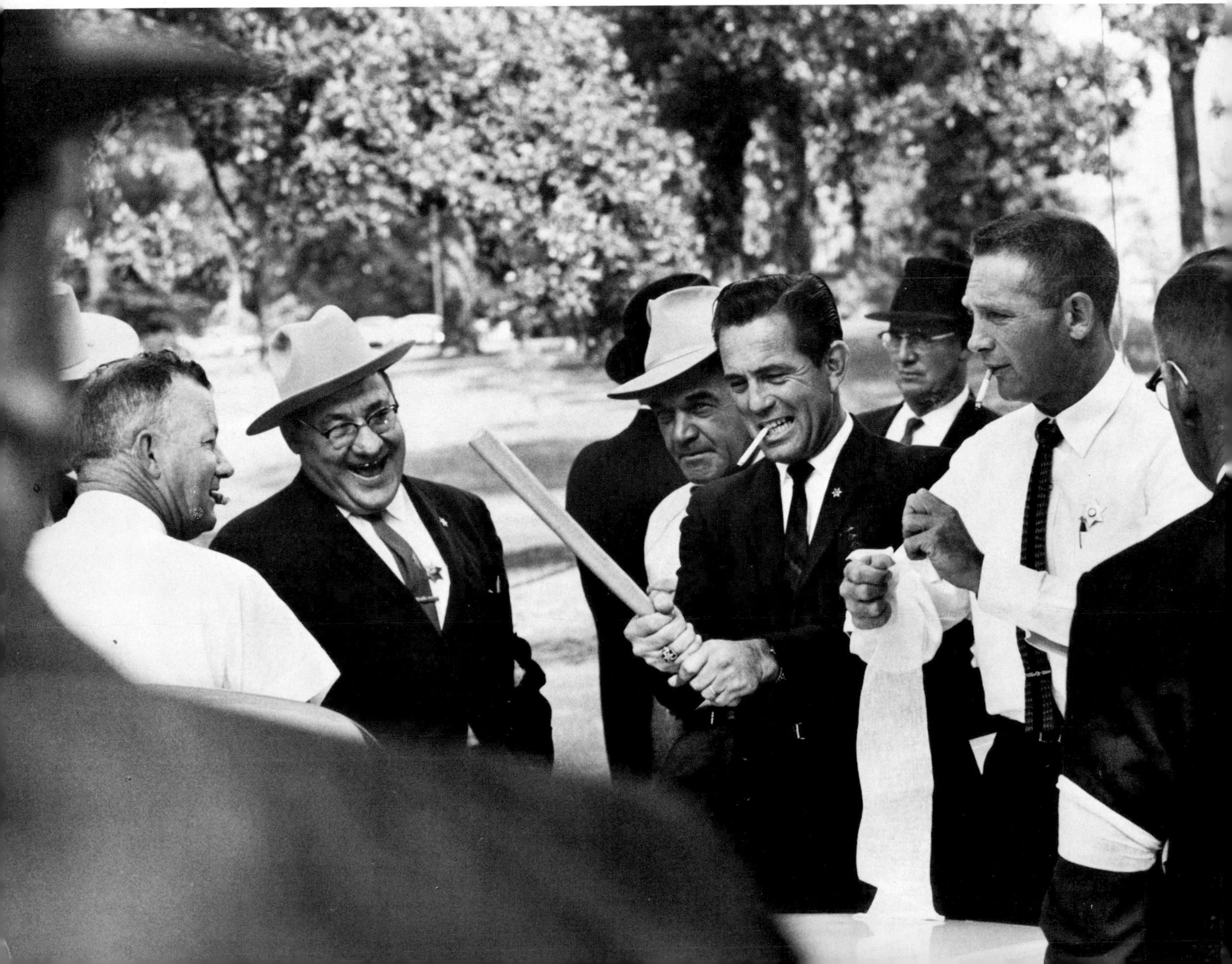

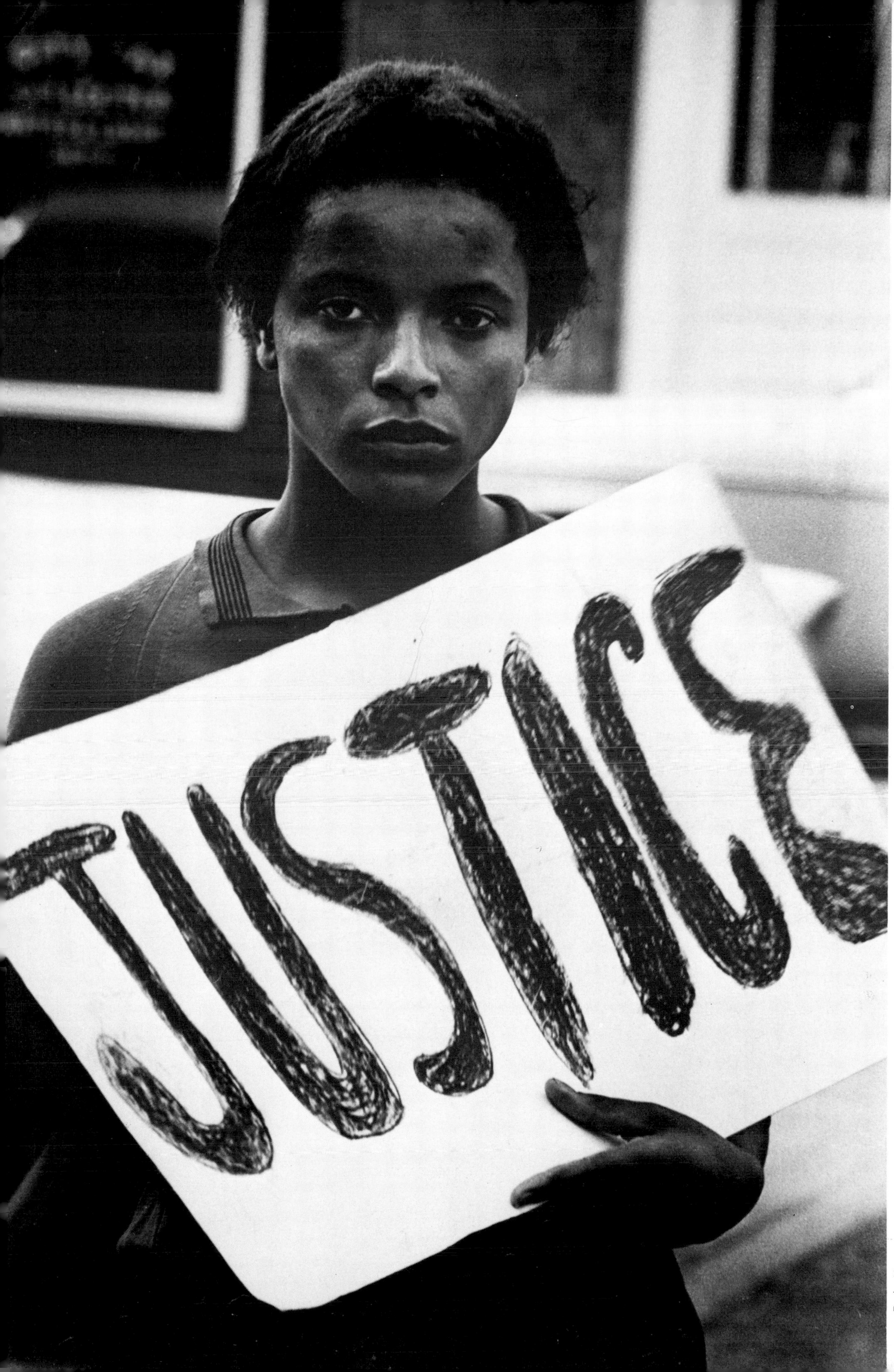
JUSTICE
Declan Haun

Introduction by Coretta Scott King

He was a man who had hoped to be an inspiring preacher in a quiet, small community. Instead, by the time of his death he had led tens of millions of people into shattering the system of Southern segregation, splintering it beyond any possibility of restoration; he had fashioned a mass black electorate which eliminated overt racism from political campaigns and accumulated political power for blacks beyond any they had ever possessed in their history in the United States. Above all, with these and other accomplishments, he brought a new and higher dimension of human dignity to the Black Experience.

Nevertheless, at the time of his death some voices were rising against him. These relatively few but raucous critics (most of whom, ironically, were indebted to him for their freedom to speak out to condemn him) challenged nonviolent social change, interracial coalitions; they called instead for violence and a negatively oriented nationalism which emphasized hate, not pride, and eventuated in a disguised black racism. It is fair to say that in the eight years which have passed since my husband's death, confusion and discord have replaced the clear goals and unity he advocated.

This is a useful time not only to appraise the achievements of the decade, 1955–1965, but also to ascertain what has happened in the period since Martin Luther King's death.

What is immediately apparent is that black nationalism and the experimentation with violence have ended in a disastrous disorganization and retrogression for the movement. Though economic changes caused by recession are primarily responsible for setbacks, the battering experienced by black communities has been made worse by inflating boasts about violence. That violence unleashed a vastly superior force which seized the opportunity to intimidate or destroy organizations and individuals. The tragic sacrifice of misguided lives was bad enough in itself, but far worse was the effect the experience had on all blacks.

Rather than inspiring confidence, instilling dignity and courage as had the earlier Movement, the threats of black violence culminated in crushing defeats followed inevitably by despondency, apathy, and discouragement with all forms of social action. My husband had foreseen this and warned there was no greater folly than for a minority ill-prepared for warfare to seek it out against an adversary greater in number and vastly larger in fire power.

Martin Luther King argued insistently that a minority should use moral force not only because it is right in itself but because with it the minority becomes superior to the majority. This was proved many times in the decade of 1955–1965. Many in recent years have forgotten this lesson and the lives of individuals and organizations were snuffed out in tragically wrong contests.

Yet in these past eight years since my husband's death not everything was negative. The roots of nonviolent protest had penetrated deeply. When the days of marching, sitting-in, and boycotting had passed, a decisive section of the Movement transformed itself. A new emphasis was given to electoral politics and coalition. Blacks moved into elective posts as mayors of major cities, as state and national legislators and as city councilmen. In May of 1975 there were 3,503 blacks holding elective office. In 1955 there were less than 100. More striking, the black electorate became a force so that black concerns were felt in every discussion of legislation.

New economic opportunities opened, especially during more prosperous periods. Blacks, who only yesterday were predominantly workers of the soil, laborers, or house workers are now found in almost every field of gainful employment. In some areas some jobs are tokens, but in the past even tokens were denied. The years of struggle have yielded visible progress in the past eight years, and the martyrdom of Martin Luther King has inspired steps toward a richer life for blacks.

Yet the experience, positive in so many respects, is nevertheless partial and tentative, illustrating once more that the road to freedom is long and winding. An economic recession or depression wipes out far more black than white gains. The economic reserves of a black family or community are far less and the suffering is consequently more intense for blacks.

However, even with the half-fulfilled promise, blacks have achieved a victory of the spirit that had for long eluded them. With the emergence of Martin Luther King and the mass movement he inspired they learned that they could attain unity and hold it until they had won a victory. Beyond this they learned that even after mistakes, lost ground can be recaptured. These are lessons which suggest the future will have fewer defeats and more successes.

If Martin Luther King had lived on, the fight ahead would be easier; but because he did live the fight will take place informed by experience. Ultimately, nonviolence, equality, and justice must prevail in a land whose own fight for independence was guided by these principles.

Chronology

1929   January 15. Martin Luther King, Jr., is born to Reverend and Mrs. Martin Luther King, Sr. (the former Alberta Christine Williams), in Atlanta, Georgia.

1935–1944. King attends David T. Howard Elementary School, Atlanta University Laboratory School, and Booker T. Washington High School. He passes the entrance examination to Morehouse College (Atlanta) without graduating from high school.

1947. King is licensed to preach and becomes assistant to his father, who is pastor of the Ebenezer Baptist Church, Atlanta.

1948   February 25. King is ordained to the Baptist ministry.

June. King graduates from Morehouse College with a B.A. degree in sociology.

September. King enters Crozer Theological Seminary, Chester, Pennsylvania. After hearing Dr. A. J. Muste and Dr. Mordecai W. Johnson preach on the life and teachings of Mahatma Gandhi, he begins to study Gandhi seriously.

1951   June. King graduates from Crozer with a B.D. degree.

1953   June 18. King marries Coretta Scott in Marion, Alabama.

1954   May 17. The Supreme Court of the United States rules unanimously in *Brown* vs. *Board of Education* that racial segregation in public schools is unconstitutional.

1954   October 31. King is installed by Reverend Martin Luther King, Sr., as the twentieth pastor of the Dexter Avenue Church, Montgomery.

1955   June 5. King receives a Ph.D. degree in Systematic Theology from Boston University.

November 17. The Kings' first child, Yolanda Denise, is born in Montgomery.

December 1. Mrs. Rosa Parks, a forty-two-year-old Montgomery seamstress, refuses to relinquish her bus seat to a white man, and is arrested.

December 5. The first day of the bus boycott. The trial of Mrs. Parks. A meeting of movement leaders is held. Dr. King is unanimously elected president of an organization named the Montgomery Improvement Association, a name proposed by Reverend Ralph Abernathy.

December 10. The Montgomery Bus Company suspends service in black neighborhoods.

1956   January 26. Dr. King is arrested on a charge of traveling thirty miles an hour in a twenty-five-mile-an-hour zone in Montgomery. He is released on his own recognizance.

January 30. A bomb is thrown onto the porch of Dr. King's Montgomery home. Mrs. King and Mrs. Roscoe Williams, wife of a church member, are in the house with baby Yolanda Denise; no one is injured.

February 2. A suit is filed in federal district court asking that Montgomery's travel segregation laws be declared unconstitutional.

February 21. Dr. King is indicted with other figures in the Montgomery bus boycott on the charge of being party to a conspiracy to hinder and prevent the operation of business without "just or legal cause."

June 4. A United States district court rules that racial segregation on city bus lines is unconstitutional.

June 27. Dr. King is the guest speaker at the annual NAACP convention in San Francisco.

August 10. Dr. King is a speaker before the platform committee of the Democratic Party in Chicago.

October 30. Mayor Gayle of Montgomery instructs the city's legal department "to file such proceedings as it may deem proper to stop the operation of car pools and transportation systems growing out of the boycott."

November 13. The United States Supreme Court affirms the decision of the three-judge district court in declaring unconstitutional Alabama's state and local laws requiring segregation on buses.

December 20. Federal injunctions prohibiting segregation on buses are served on city and bus company officials in Montgomery. Injunctions are also served on state officials.

December 21. Montgomery buses are integrated.

1957   January 27. An unexploded bomb is discovered on Dr. and Mrs. King's front porch.

January 10–11. The Southern Christian Leadership Conference (SCLC) is formed at the Ebenezer Baptist Church, Atlanta. Dr. King is elected its president.

February 18. *Time* magazine puts Dr. King on its cover.

May 17. Dr. King delivers a speech for the Prayer Pilgrimage For Freedom celebrating the third anniversary of the Supreme Court's desegregation decision. The speech, entitled "Give Us the Ballot," is given at the Lincoln Memorial, Washington, D.C.

June 13. Dr. King has a conference with the vice president of the United States, Richard M. Nixon.

September 2. Dr. King addresses a Labor Day seminar on the twenty-fifth anniversary of the Highlander Folk School, Monteagle, Tennessee.

September. President Dwight D. Eisenhower federalizes the Arkansas National Guard to escort nine Negro students to an all-white high school in Little Rock, Arkansas.

September 9. The first civil rights act since Reconstruction is passed by Congress, creating the Civil Rights Commission and the Civil Rights Division of the Department of Justice.

October 23. A second child, Martin Luther III, is born to Dr. and Mrs. King.

1958   February 8. Dr. King is a guest speaker at a legislative conference of the American Jewish Congress in New York.

June 23. Dr. King, along with Roy Wilkins of the NAACP, A. Philip Randolph, and Lester Granger, meets with President Dwight D. Eisenhower.

September 3. Dr. King is arrested on a charge of loitering (later changed to "failure to obey an officer") in the vicinity of the Montgomery Recorder's Court. He is released on one hundred dollars bond.

September 4. Dr. King is convicted after pleading "not guilty" on the charge of failure to obey an officer. The fine is paid almost immediately, over Dr. King's objection, by Montgomery Police Commissioner Clyde C. Sellers.

September 17. Dr. King's book *Stride Toward Freedom: The Montgomery Story* is published by Harper & Row.

September 20. Dr. King is stabbed in the chest by Mrs. Izola Curry, forty-two, who is subsequently alleged to be mentally deranged. The stabbing occurs in the heart of Harlem while Dr. King is autographing his recently published book. His condition is said to be serious but not critical.

1959   January 30. Dr. King meets with Walter Reuther, president of the United Auto Workers union, in Detroit.

February 2–March 10. Dr. and Mrs. King spend a month in India studying Gandhi's techniques of nonviolence, as guests of Prime Minister Nehru.

August 20. Dr. King delivers a speech to the National Bar Association in Milwaukee.

November 29. Dr. King submits his resignation, effective on the fourth Sunday of January, 1960, as pastor of the Dexter Avenue Baptist Church.

1960   January 24. The King family moves to Atlanta. Dr. King becomes co-pastor, with his father, of the Ebenezer Baptist Church.

February 1. The first lunch counter sit-in to desegregate eating facilities is held by students in Greensboro, North Carolina.

February 17. A warrant is issued for Dr. King's arrest on charges that he did not pay his 1956 and 1958 Alabama state income taxes.

April 15. The Student Non-Violent Coordinating Committee (SNCC) is founded to coordinate student protest at Shaw University, Raleigh, North Carolina, on a temporary basis. (It is to become a permanent organization in October, 1960.) Dr. King and James Lawson are the keynote speakers at the Shaw University founding.

May 28. Dr. King is acquitted of the tax evasion charge by an all-white jury in Montgomery.

June 10. Dr. King and A. Philip Randolph announce plans for picketing both the Republican and Democratic national conventions.

June 24. Dr. King has a conference with John F. Kennedy, candidate for president of the United States, about racial matters.

October 19. Dr. King is arrested at an Atlanta sit-in and is jailed on a charge of violating the state's trespass law.

Oct. 22–27. The Atlanta charges are dropped. All jailed demonstrators are released except for Dr. King, who is ordered held on a charge of violating a probated sentence in a traffic arrest case. He is transferred to the DeKalb County Jail in Decatur, Georgia, and is then transferred to the Reidsville State Prison. He is released from the Reidsville State Prison on a two-thousand-dollar bond.

1961   January 30. A third child, Dexter Scott, is born to Dr. and Mrs. King in Atlanta.

May 4. The first group of Freedom Riders, intent on integrating interstate buses, leaves Washington, D.C., by Greyhound bus. The group, organized by the Congress for Racial Equality (CORE), leaves shortly after the Supreme Court has outlawed segregation in interstate transportation terminals. The bus is burned outside of Anniston, Alabama, on May 14. A mob beats the Riders upon their arrival in Birmingham. The Riders are arrested in Jackson, Mississippi, and spend forty to sixty days in Parchman Penitentiary.

1961   December 15. Dr. King arrives in Albany, Georgia, in response to a call from Dr. W. G. Anderson, the leader of the Albany Movement to desegregate public facilities, which began in January, 1961.

December 16. Dr. King is arrested at an Albany demonstration. He is charged with obstructing the sidewalk and parading without a permit.

1962   February 27. Dr. King is tried and convicted for leading the December march in Albany.

May 2. Dr. King is invited to join the Birmingham protests.

July 27. Dr. King is arrested at an Albany city hall prayer vigil and jailed on charges of failure to obey a police officer, obstructing the sidewalk, and disorderly conduct.

September 20. James Meredith makes his first attempt to enroll at the University of Mississippi. He is actually enrolled by Supreme Court order and is escorted onto the Oxford, Mississippi, campus by U.S. marshals on October 1, 1962.

October 16. Dr. King meets with President John F. Kennedy at the White House for a one-hour conference.

1963   March 28. The Kings' fourth child, Bernice Albertine, is born.

March–April. Sit-in demonstrations are held in Birmingham to protest segregation of eating facilities. Dr. King is arrested during a demonstration.

April 16. Dr. King writes the "Letter from Birmingham Jail" while imprisoned for demonstrating.

May 3,4,5. Eugene ("Bull") Connor, director of public safety of Birmingham, orders the use of police dogs and fire hoses upon the marching protestors (young adults and children.)

May 20. The Supreme Court of the United States rules Birmingham's segregation ordinances unconstitutional.

June 11. Governor George C. Wallace tries to stop the court-ordered integration of the University of Alabama by "standing in the schoolhouse door" and personally refusing entrance to black students and Justice Department officials. President John F. Kennedy then federalizes the Alabama National Guard, and Governor Wallace removes himself from blocking the entrance of the Negro students.

June 12. Medgar Evers, NAACP leader in Jackson, Mississippi, is assassinated in the early-morning darkness by a rifle bullet, at his home. His memorial service is held in Jackson on June 15 and he is buried in Arlington National Cemetery, Washington, D.C., on June 19.

August 28. The March on Washington, the first large integrated protest march, is held in Washington, D.C. Dr. King and other civil rights leaders meet with President John F. Kennedy in the White House, and afterwards Dr. King delivers his "I Have a Dream" speech on the steps of the Lincoln Memorial.

September. Dr. King's book *Strength to Love* is published by Harper & Row.

September 2–10. Governor Wallace orders the Alabama state troopers to stop the court-ordered integration of Alabama's elementary and high schools until he is enjoined by court injunction from doing so. By September 10 specific schools are actually integrated by court order.

November 22. President Kennedy is assassinated in Dallas, Texas.

1964   Summer. COFO (Council of Federated Organizations) initiates the Mississippi Summer Project, a voter-registration drive organized and run by black and white students.

June 21. Three civil rights workers—James Chaney (black) and Andrew Goodman and Michael Schwerner (white)—are reported missing after a short trip to Philadelphia, Mississippi.

May–June. Dr. King joins other SCLC workers in demonstrations for the integration of public accommodations in St. Augustine, Florida. He is jailed.

June. Dr. King's book *Why We Can't Wait* is published by Harper & Row.

July 2. Dr. King attends the signing of the Public Accommodations Bill, part of the Civil Rights Act of 1964, by President Lyndon B. Johnson in the White House.

July 18–23. Riots occur in Harlem. One black man is killed.

August 4. The bodies of civil rights workers James Chaney, Andrew Goodman, and Michael Schwerner are discovered by FBI agents buried near the town of Philadelphia, Mississippi. Neshoba County Sheriff Rainey and his deputy, Cecil Price, are allegedly implicated in the murders.

August. Riots occur in New Jersey, Illinois, and Pennsylvania.

September 18. Dr. King has an audience with Pope Paul VI at the Vatican.

September. Dr. King and Reverend Ralph Abernathy visit West Berlin at the invitation of Mayor Willy Brandt.

December 10. Dr. King receives the Nobel Peace Prize in Oslo, Norway.

February 21. Malcolm X, leader of the Organization of Afro-American Unity and former Black Muslim leader, is murdered by blacks in New York City.

1965   March 7. A group of marching demonstrators (from SNCC and SCLC) led by SCLC's Hosea Williams are beaten when attempting to march across the Edmund Pettus Bridge on their planned march to Montgomery, Alabama, from Selma, Alabama, by state highway patrolmen under the direction of Al Lingo, and sheriff's deputies under the leadership of Jim Clark. An order by Governor Wallace had prohibited the march.

March 9. Unitarian minister James Reeb is beaten by four white segregationists in Selma and dies two days later.

March 15. President Johnson addresses the nation and Congress. He describes the Voting Rights Bill he will submit to Congress in two days and uses the slogan of the civil rights movement, "We Shall Overcome."

March 16. Black and white demonstrators are beaten by sheriff's deputies and police on horseback in Montgomery.

March 21–25. Over three thousand protest marchers leave Selma for a march to Montgomery, protected by federal troops. They are joined along the way by a total of twenty-five thousand marchers. Upon reaching the capitol building they hear an address by Dr. King.

March 25. Mrs. Viola Liuzzo, wife of a Detroit Teamsters Union business agent, is shot and killed while driving a carload of marchers back to Selma.

July. Dr. King visits Chicago. SCLC joins with the Coordinating Council of Community Organizations (CCCO), led by Al Raby, in the Chicago Project.

August–December. In Alabama, SCLC spearheads voter registration campaigns in Greene, Wilcox, and Eutaw counties, and in the cities of Montgomery and Birmingham.

August 6. The 1965 Voting Rights Act is signed by President Johnson.

August 11–16. In Watts, the black ghetto of Los Angeles, riots leave thirty-five dead, of whom twenty-eight are black.

1966   February. Dr. King rents an apartment in the black ghetto of Chicago.

February 23. Dr. King meets with Elijah Muhammad, leader of the Black Muslims, in Chicago.

March 25. The Supreme Court of the United States rules any poll tax unconstitutional.

March. Dr. King takes over a Chicago slum building and is sued by its owner.

Spring. Dr. King makes a tour of Alabama to help elect black candidates.

Spring. The Alabama primary is held, the first time since Reconstruction that blacks have voted in any numbers.

May 16. An antiwar statement by Dr. King is read at a large Washington rally to protest the war in Vietnam. Dr. King agrees to serve as co-chairman of Clergy and Laymen Concerned about Vietnam.

June 6. James Meredith is shot soon after beginning his 220-mile "March Against Fear" from Memphis, Tennessee, to Jackson, Mississippi.

June. Stokely Carmichael and Willie Ricks (SNCC) use the slogan "Black Power" in public for the first time, before reporters in Greenwood, Mississippi.

July 10. Dr. King launches a drive to make Chicago an "open city" in regard to housing.

August 5. Dr. King is stoned in Chicago as he leads a march through crowds of angry whites in the Gage Park section of Chicago's Southwest Side.

September. SCLC launches a project with the aim of integrating schools in Grenada, Mississippi.

Fall. SCLC initiates the Alabama Citizen Education Project in Wilcox County.

1967   January. Dr. King writes his book *Where Do We Go from Here?* while in Jamaica.

March 12. Alabama is ordered to desegregate all public schools.

March 25. Dr. King attacks the government's Vietnam policy in a speech at the Chicago Coliseum.

May 10–11. One black student is killed in rioting on the campus of all-Negro Jackson State College, Jackson, Mississippi.

July 6. The Justice Department reports that more than 50 percent of all eligible black voters are registered in Mississippi, Georgia, Alabama, Louisiana, and South Carolina.

July 12–17. Twenty-three people die, 725 are injured in riots in Newark, New Jersey.

July 23–30. Forty-three die, 324 are injured in the Detroit riots, the worst of the century.

July 26. Black leaders Martin Luther King, Jr., A. Philip Randolph, Roy Wilkins, and Whitney Young appeal for an end to the riots, "which have proved ineffective and damaging to the civil rights cause and the entire nation."

October 30. The Supreme Court upholds the contempt-of-court convictions of Dr. King and seven other black leaders who led 1963 marches in Birmingham. Dr. King and his aides enter jail to serve four-day sentences.

November 27. Dr. King announces the formation by SCLC of a Poor People's Campaign, with the aim of representing the problems of poor blacks and whites.

February 12. Sanitation workers strike in Memphis, Tennessee.

March 28. Dr. King leads six thousand protesters on a march through downtown Memphis in support of striking sanitation workers. Disorders break out during which black youths loot stores. One sixteen-year-old is killed, fifty persons are injured.

April 3. Dr. King's last speech, entitled "I've Been to the Mountaintop," is delivered at the Memphis Masonic Temple.

April 4. Dr. King is assassinated by a sniper as he stands talking on the balcony of his second-floor room at the Lorraine Motel in Memphis. He dies in St. Joseph's Hospital from a gunshot wound in the neck. James Earl Ray is later captured and convicted of the murder.

June 5. Presidential candidate Senator Robert Kennedy is shot in Los Angeles. He dies the next day.

Charles Moore

Chapter One

"There Comes a Time"

The Montgomery Bus Boycott, 1955–1956

"After finishing my schooling, I was called to a little church down in Montgomery, Alabama. I started preaching there, things were going well in that church, it was a marvelous experience.

"But one day a year later a lady by the name of Rosa Parks decided that she wasn't going to take it any longer. She stayed on a bus seat. It was the beginning of a movement where fifty thousand black men and women refused absolutely to ride the city buses, and we walked together 381 days.

"Negroes have to learn to stick together. We sent out the call. No Negroes rode the buses. It was one of the most amazing things I've ever seen in my life. The people of Montgomery asked me to serve as the spokesman, and as the president of the new organization. The Montgomery Improvement Association came into being to lead the boycott. I couldn't say no. And then we started our struggle together."

—Martin Luther King, Jr., 1966

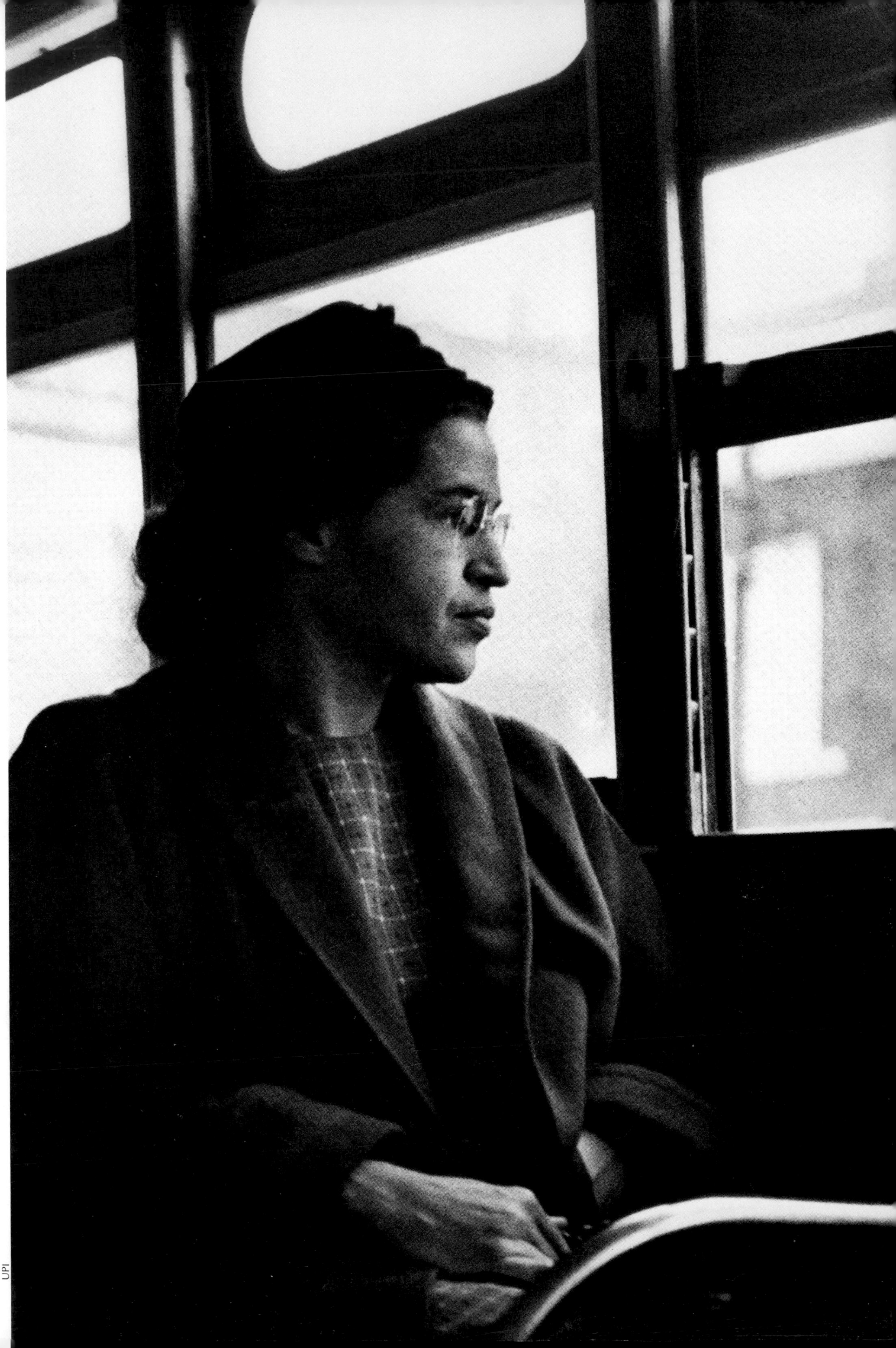
UPI

AN INTERVIEW WITH ROSA PARKS

On December 1, 1955, **Rosa Parks,** *a seamstress and respected citizen of Montgomery's black community, quietly refused to give her bus seat to a white man. She herself describes the episode that triggered the Montgomery bus boycott and signalled the end of segregation in the South.*

"I had been working during the day at the Montgomery Fair Department Store in Montgomery. When I left work that evening and came out of the store I noticed a Cleveland Avenue bus that was quite crowded, and when I got on the bus I wanted to be as comfortable as I could, so I didn't take that bus. I went across the street to the drug store and purchased one or two items, because I had a little pain across my neck and shoulders from using the press at work. As I was coming back across the street to the bus stop, I noticed another bus approaching, and I didn't see anybody standing up in the back. But by the time I did get to the bus door, a number of people had gotten on ahead of me, and when I got on the Negro section in the back was well filled, and all of the seats were taken. But there was one vacant seat in the middle section, that part of the bus we could use as long as no white people wanted the seats. The rule was that if the front section filled up and one white person came to sit in the middle section, we would all have to get up and stand in the back. A man was sitting next to the window, so I took a seat next to him. Across this aisle from us there were two women. I was just thinking of getting home and doing my work.

"Of course, when I got on the bus, I noticed the bus driver and recognized him as one who several years before, oh, I think about 1943, had evicted me from the bus because I had refused to put my fare in the front and go around to the back to get in. That was another rule that they had, and sometimes when you got around to the back door the driver just started the bus and left you behind. On the third stop a few white people boarded the bus, and they took all of the designated white seats, and there was this one white man standing. The driver just turned around and he said he needed those front seats, which meant the ones where we were sitting, in order for this man to take a seat. That was segregation.

"The four of us would have to stand up in order to accommodate this one white passenger. When he first spoke, didn't any of us move; but then he spoke a second time with what I would call a threat, because he said, "You all better make it light on yourselves and let me have those seats." And at that point the man sitting next to me by the window stood up. The two women stood up and moved out into the aisle. I just moved my legs for him to pass and moved over to the window. The driver looked at me and asked me if I was going to stand up. I told him no, I wasn't. He said, "If you don't stand up, I'm going to have you arrested." I told him to go on and have me arrested. He didn't exchange any more words with me. He got off the bus, and when he came back he stood in the well of the front door and didn't say anything, but he was looking towards the back. By this time quite a few people had left the bus, some of them I guess didn't want to be inconvenienced and probably got off to get other buses, but there were still several people on the bus. It was all quiet, and there were no arguments or any type of confrontation. When the policemen got on the bus, the driver pointed me out and said that he needed the seats. He said, "The other ones stood up." So the policemen approached me and asked me if the driver hadn't asked me to stand. I said yes. He asked "Why didn't you stand up?" I said I didn't think I should have to. I asked him, "Why do you push us around?" He said, "I don't know, but the law is the law, and you are under arrest." So the moment he said I was under arrest, I stood up. One picked up my purse, one picked up my shopping bag, and we got off the bus. They escorted me to the car, and I sat down. They had to wait until the driver told them whether he would swear out a warrant or whether he just wanted me off the bus. He wanted to swear out a warrant against me. They took me on to the city hall, where I was booked, and from there to the jail.

"As we were getting in the car, I remember asking them if they would give me back my purse and things, and they handed them to me, and I got in the back seat with them. Of course, when I got down to the jail, my things were taken and held, and I had to go in to the cell. I wasn't happy at all; I don't recall being extremely frightened, but I felt very much annoyed and inconvenienced because I had hoped to go home and get my dinner, and do whatever else I had to do for the evening. But now here I was sitting in jail and couldn't get home."

. Rosa Parks, Montgomery, Alabama

On the surface Montgomery was a peaceful town when Martin Luther King, Jr., arrived in 1954 to assume the pastorate of the Dexter Avenue Baptist Church. **"But the peace,"** King noted, **"was achieved at the cost of human servitude.". .**

"One place where the peace had long been precarious was on the city-wide buses. Here the Negro was daily reminded of the indignities of segregation. There were no Negro drivers, and although some of the white men who drove the buses were courteous, all too many were abusive and vituperative. It was not uncommon to hear them referring to Negro passengers as 'niggers,' 'black cows,' and 'black apes'. .". .

. . . Actually, no one can understand the action of Mrs. Parks unless he realizes that eventually the cup of endurance runs over, and the human personality cries out, 'I can take it no longer.' Mrs. Parks' refusal to move back was her intrepid affirmation that she had had enough. It was an individual expression of a timeless longing for human dignity and freedom. She was not 'planted' there by the NAACP, or any other organization; she was planted there by her personal sense of dignity and self-respect. She was anchored to that seat by the accumulated indignities of days gone by and the boundless aspirations of generations yet unborn. She was a victim of both the forces of history and the forces of destiny. She had been tracked down by the *Zeitgeist*—**the spirit of time.". .**

On the evening of the first day of the bus boycott, King addressed over five thousand people at the Holt Street Bap-

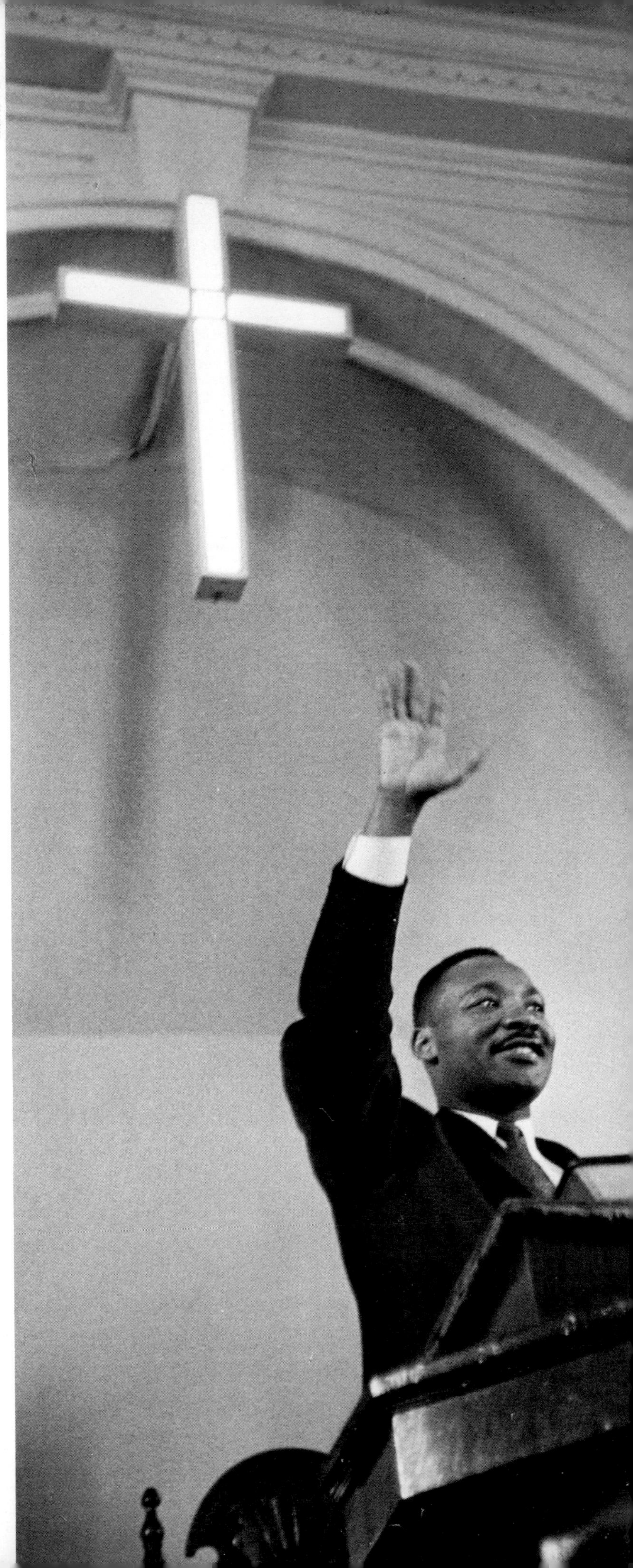

Charles Moore

The Holt Street Baptist Church. In accepting the presidency of the Montgomery Improvement Association on December 5, 1955, King becomes the spokesman for the new organization, which is to guide the boycott for over a year.

Opposite page:
The philosophy of nonviolence is disseminated and constantly reaffirmed through regular mass meetings at the various churches in Montgomery. King's closest friend and associate, Ralph Abernathy, and Rosa Parks attend one such meeting.

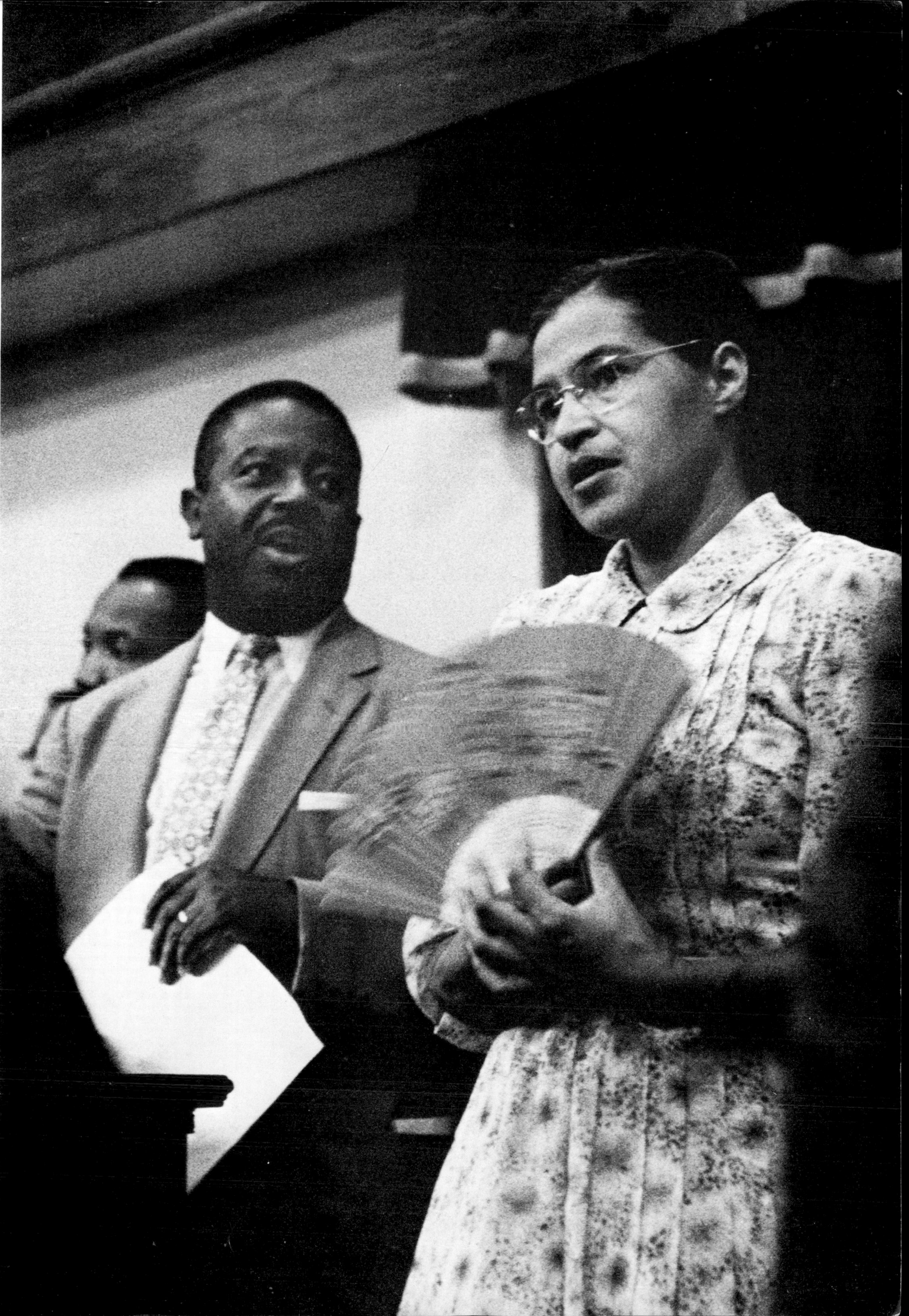

Charles Moore

tist Church, setting the tone for the entire nonviolent movement: **"You know, my friends, there comes a time when people get tired of being trampled over by the iron feet of oppression. There comes a time, my friends, when people get tired of being flung across the abyss of humiliation where they experience the bleakness of nagging despair. There comes a time when people get tired of being pushed out of the glittering sunlight of life's July, and left standing amidst the piercing chill of an Alpine November. We are here this evening because we are tired now. Now let us say that we are not advocating violence. We have overcome that. I want it to be known throughout Montgomery and throughout this nation that we are a Christian people. We believe in the teachings of Jesus. The only weapon we have in our hands this evening is the weapon of protest. . . . My friends, don't let anybody make us feel that we ought to be compared in our actions with the Ku Klux Klan or with the White Citizens Council. There will be no crosses burned at any bus stops in Montgomery. There will be no white persons pulled out of their homes and taken out on some distant road and murdered. There will be nobody among us who will stand up and defy the Constitution of this nation. We only assem-**

For many protestors, the act of walking becomes a symbolic gesture, substituting "tired feet for tired souls."

Wide World

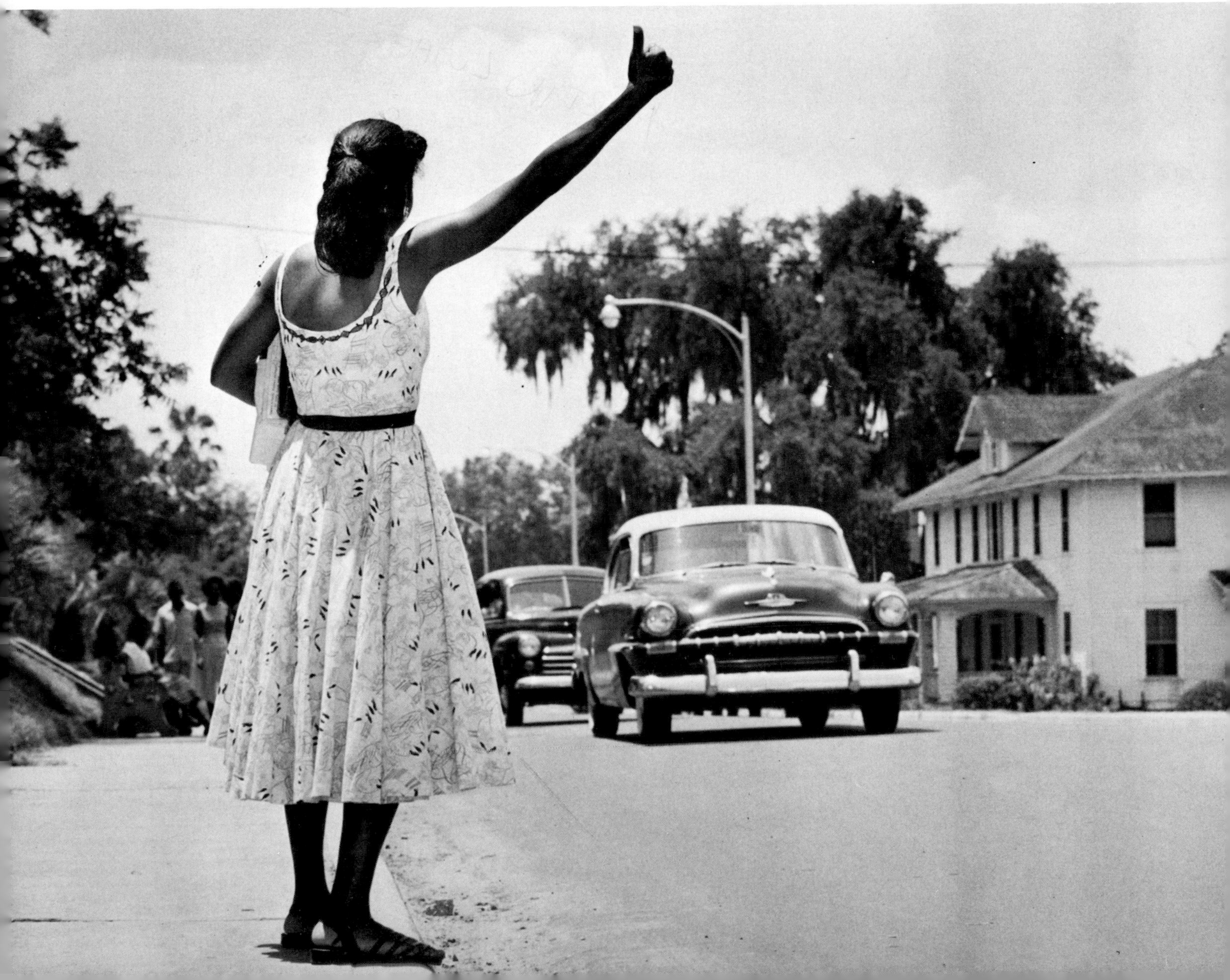

ble here because of our desire to see right exist."

Throughout the days of the Montgomery boycott, King was often forced to rethink and reaffirm his philosophy of nonviolence. **"From the beginning a basic philosophy guided the movement. This guiding principle has since been referred to variously as nonviolent resistance, noncooperation, and passive resistance. But in the first days of the protest none of these expressions was mentioned; the phrase most often heard was 'Christian love.' It was the Sermon on the Mount, rather than a doctrine of passive resistance, that initially inspired the Negroes of Montgomery to dignified social action. It was Jesus of Nazareth that stirred the Negroes to protest with the creative weapon of love. . . .**

"What we were really doing was withdrawing our cooperation from an evil system rather than merely withdrawing our economic support from the bus company. The bus company, being an external expression of the system, would naturally suffer, but the basic aim was to refuse to cooperate with evil.

"At this point I began to think about Thoreau's essay on civil disobedience. . . . I became convinced that what we were preparing to do in Montgomery was related to what Thoreau had expressed. We were simply saying to the white community, 'We can no longer lend our cooperation to an evil system.'

Overleaf:
Street violence in Montgomery
Photo by Charles Moore

"No riders today." Montgomery City Lines reject all attempts to work out a solution to the bus problem.

UPI

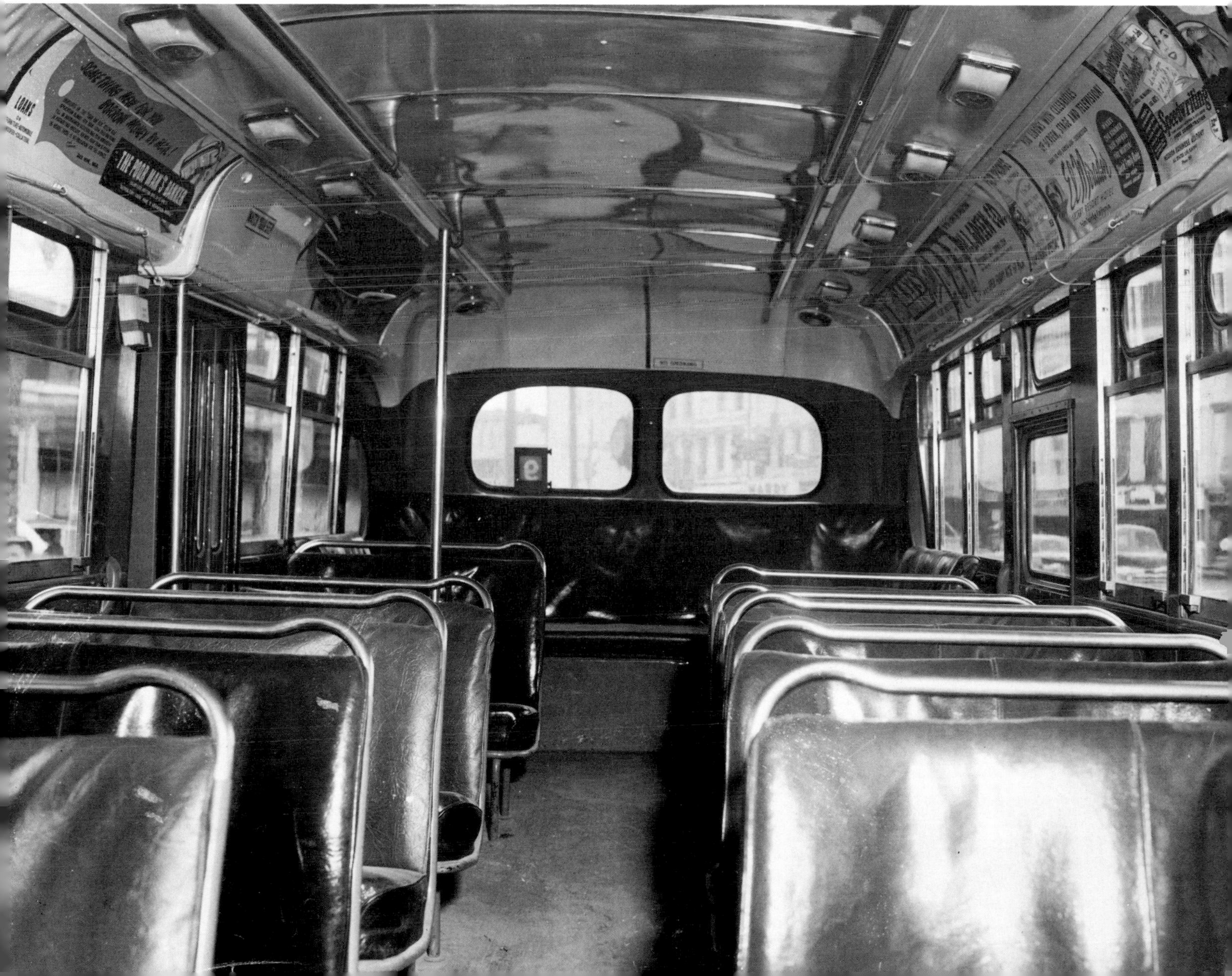
LOANS
THE POOR MAN'S BANKER

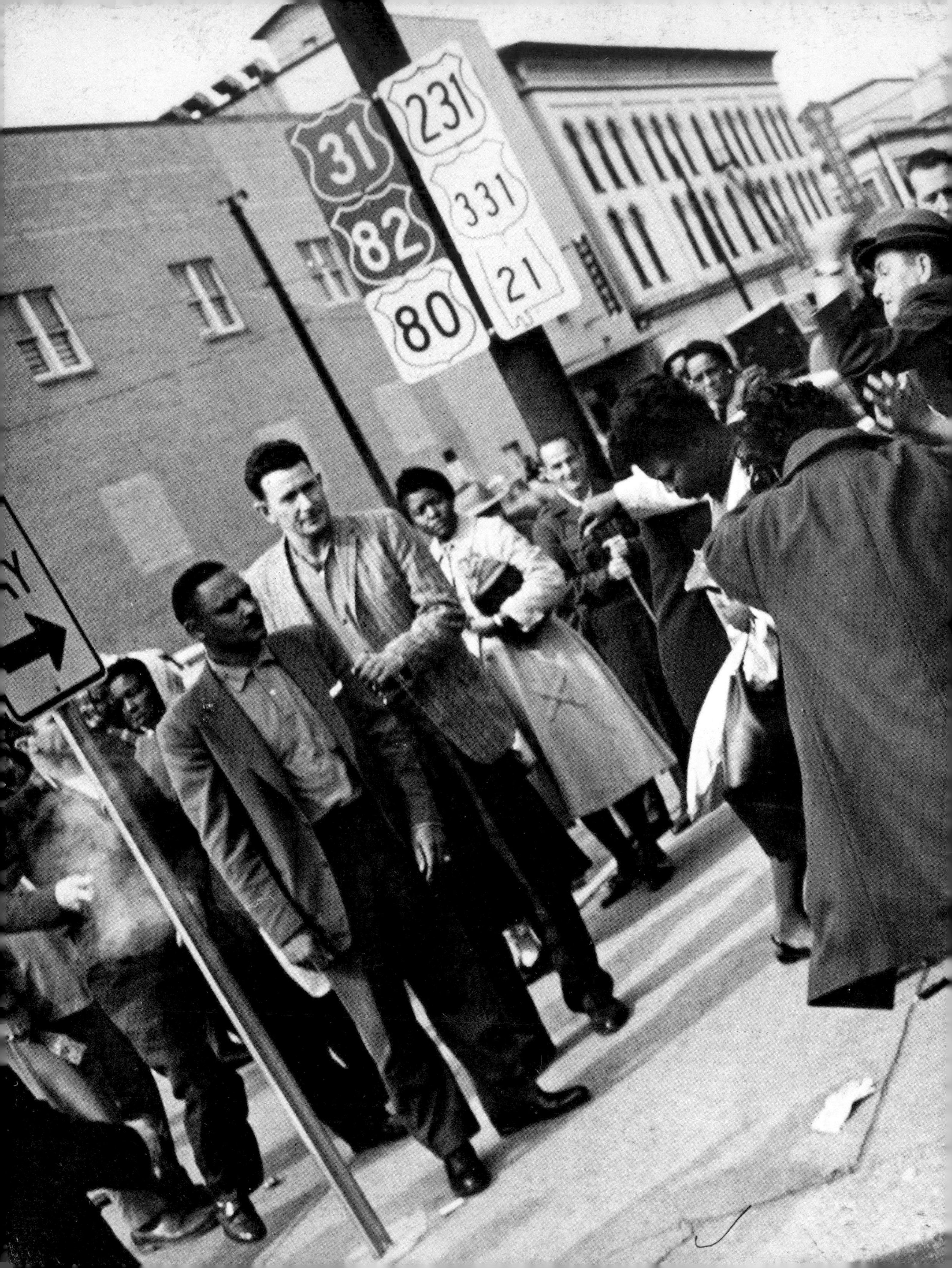
31
82
80
231
331
21

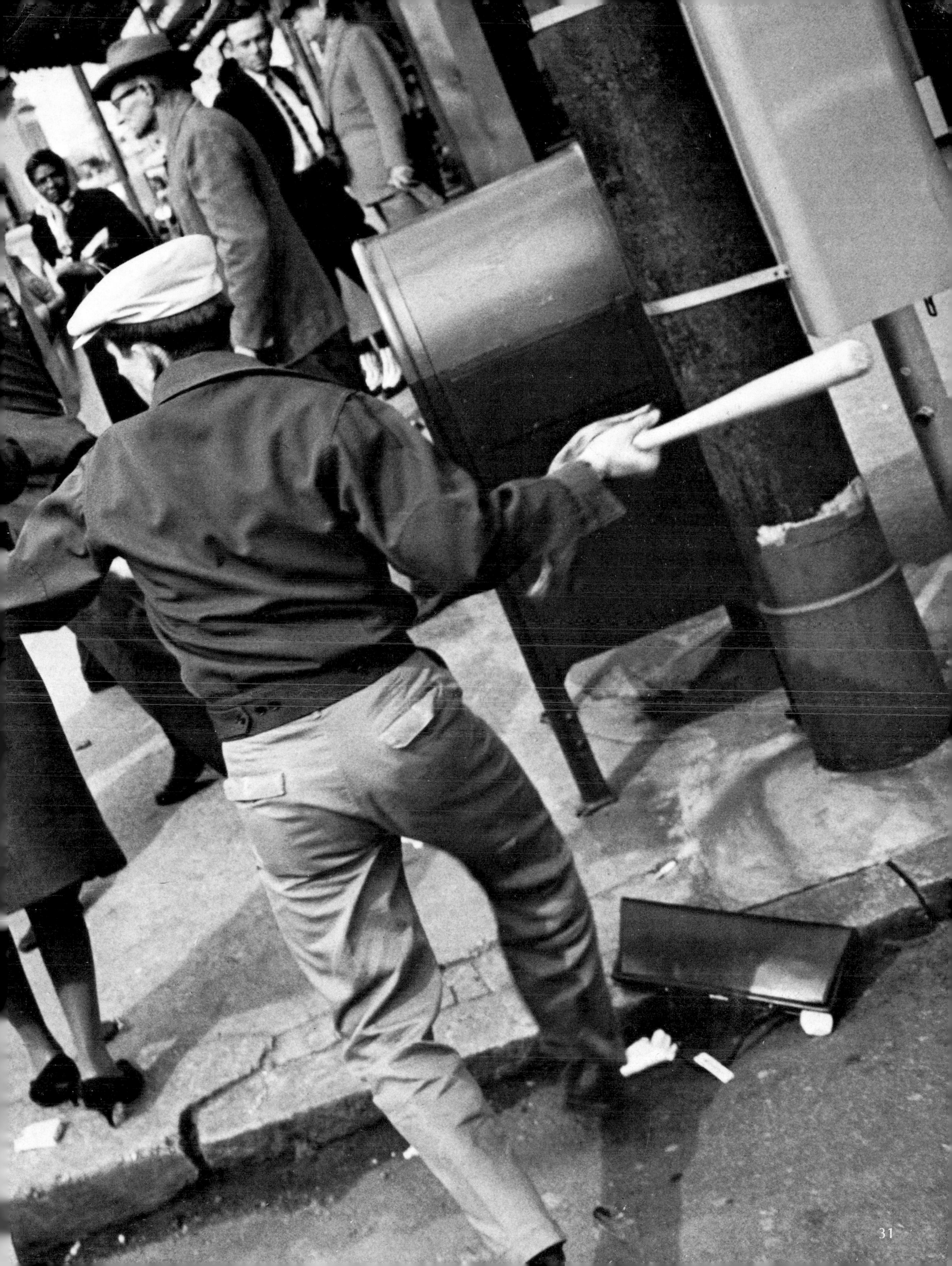

"Something began to say to me, 'He who passively accepts evil is as much involved in it as he who helps to perpetrate it. He who accepts evil without protesting against it is really cooperating with it.' When oppressed people willingly accept their oppression they only serve to give the oppressor a convenient justification for his acts. . . . So in order to be true to one's conscience and true to God, a righteous man has no alternative but to refuse to cooperate with an evil system. This I felt was the nature of our action. From this moment on I conceived of our movement as an act of massive noncooperation. . . .

"Nonviolent resistance emerged as the technique of the movement, while love stood as the regulating ideal. In other words, Christ furnished the spirit and motivation, while Gandhi furnished the method. . . .

"Gandhi was probably the first person in history to lift the love ethic of Jesus above mere interaction between individuals to a powerful and effective social force on a larger scale. For Gandhi love was a potent instrument for social and collective transformation. It was in this Gandhian emphasis on love and nonviolence that I discovered the method for social reform that I had been seeking for so many months. . . .

"Nonviolent resistance is not a method for cowards; it does resist. If one uses this method because he is afraid or merely because he lacks the instrument of violence, he is not truly nonviolent. This is why Gandhi often said that if cowardice is the only alternative to violence, it is better to fight. He made this statement conscious of the fact that there is always another alternative: no individual or group need submit to any wrong nor need they use violence to right that wrong;

photos by Charles Moore

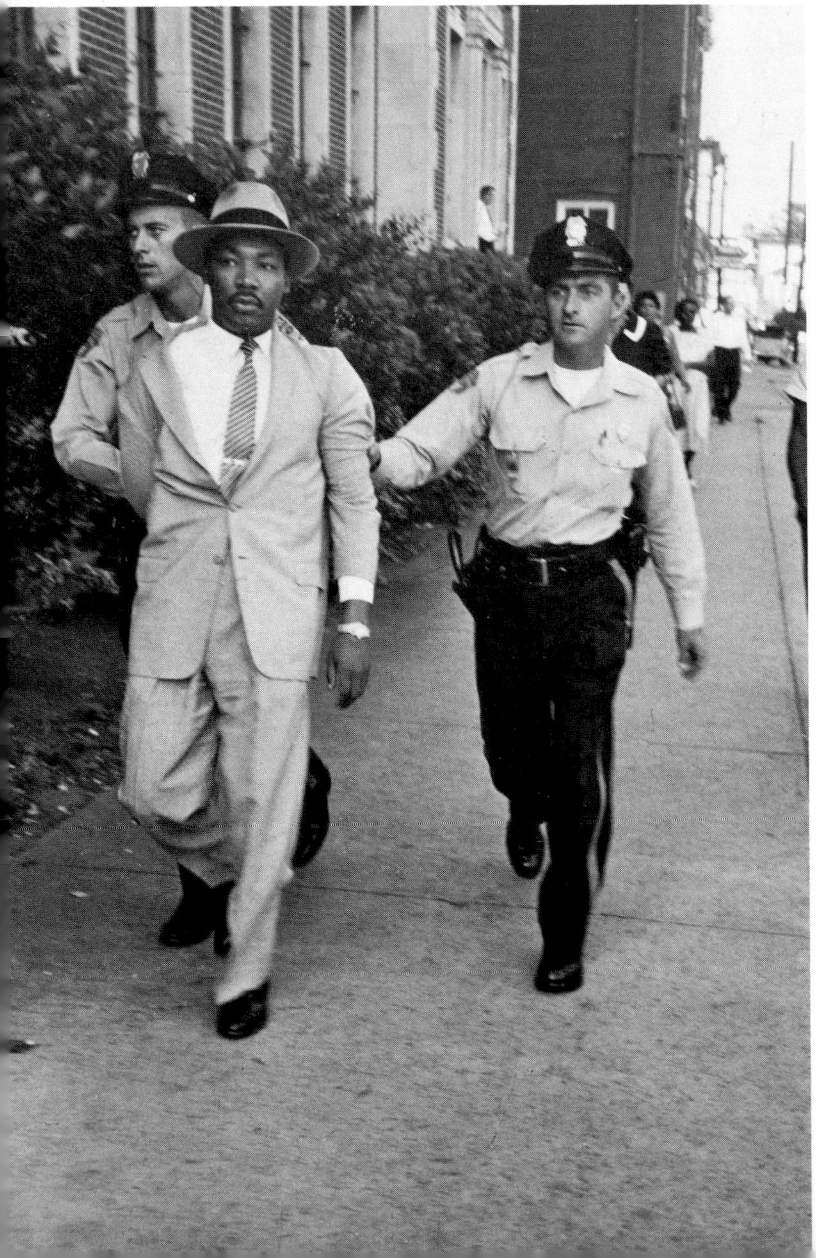

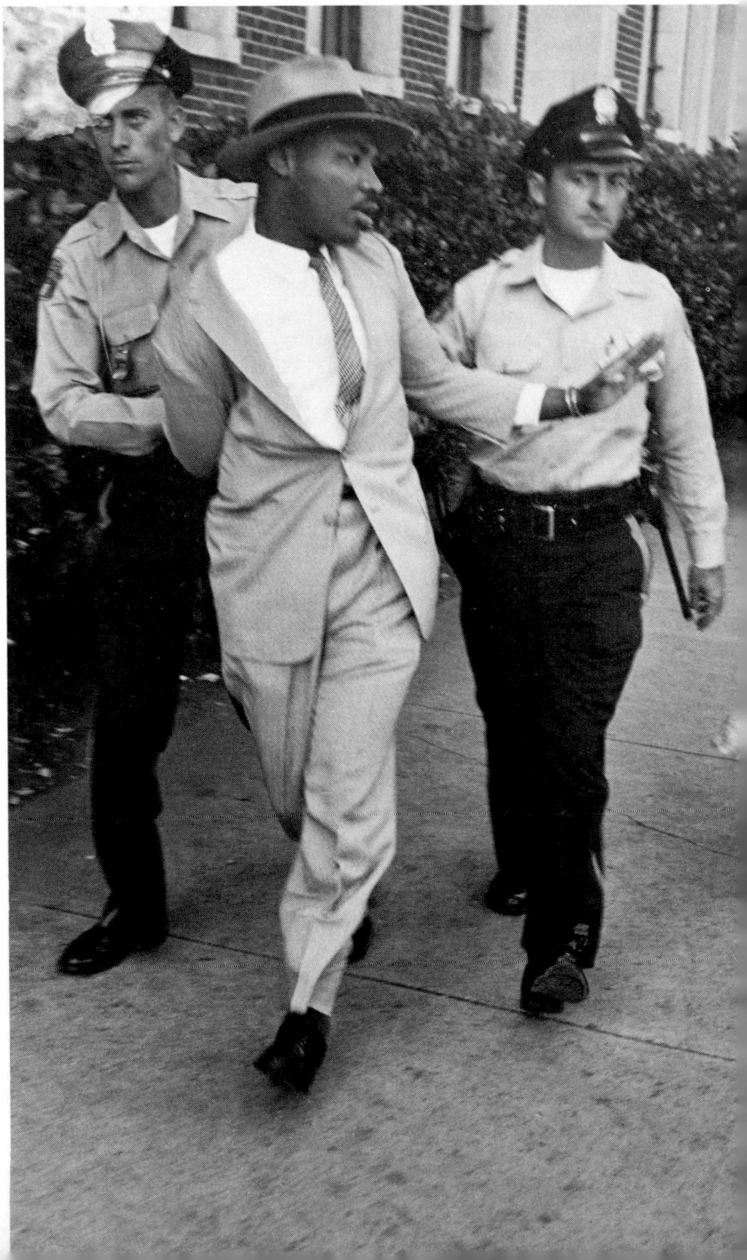

While trying to gain admittance to the trial of his colleague Ralph Abernathy on September 3, 1958, King is arrested for "loitering on the courthouse steps" in Montgomery.

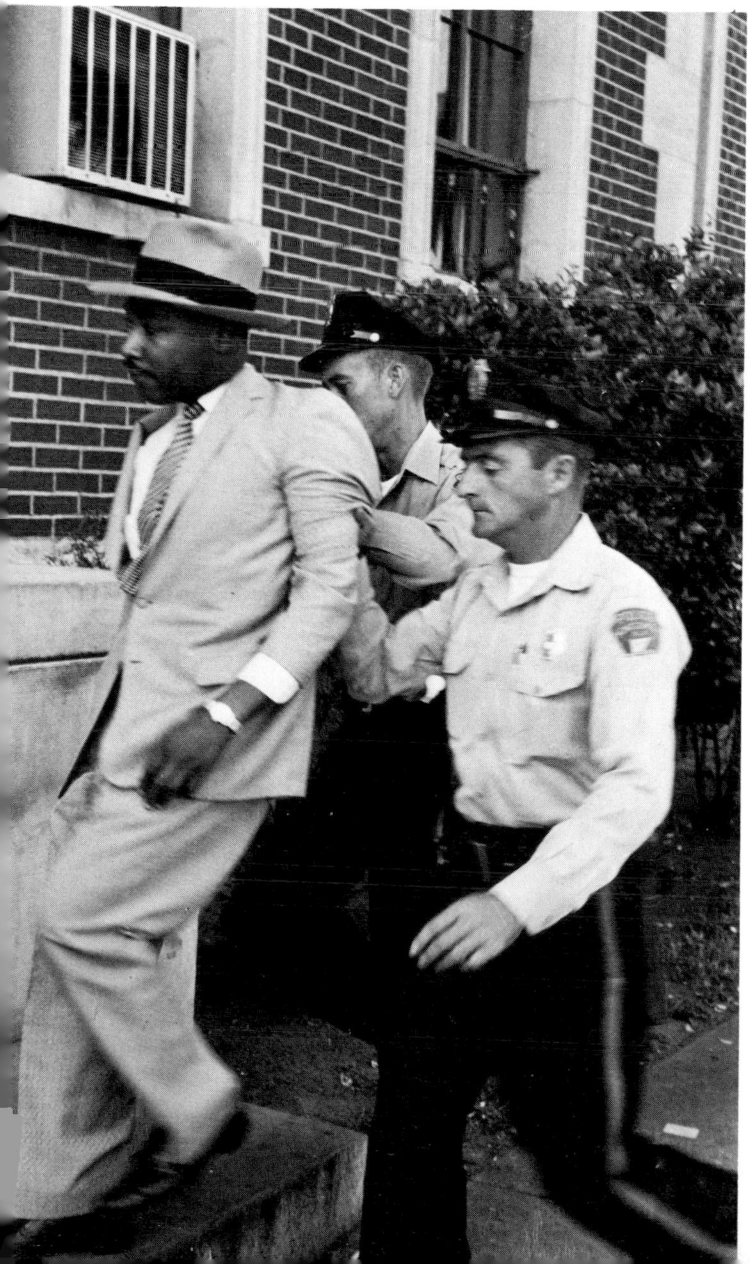

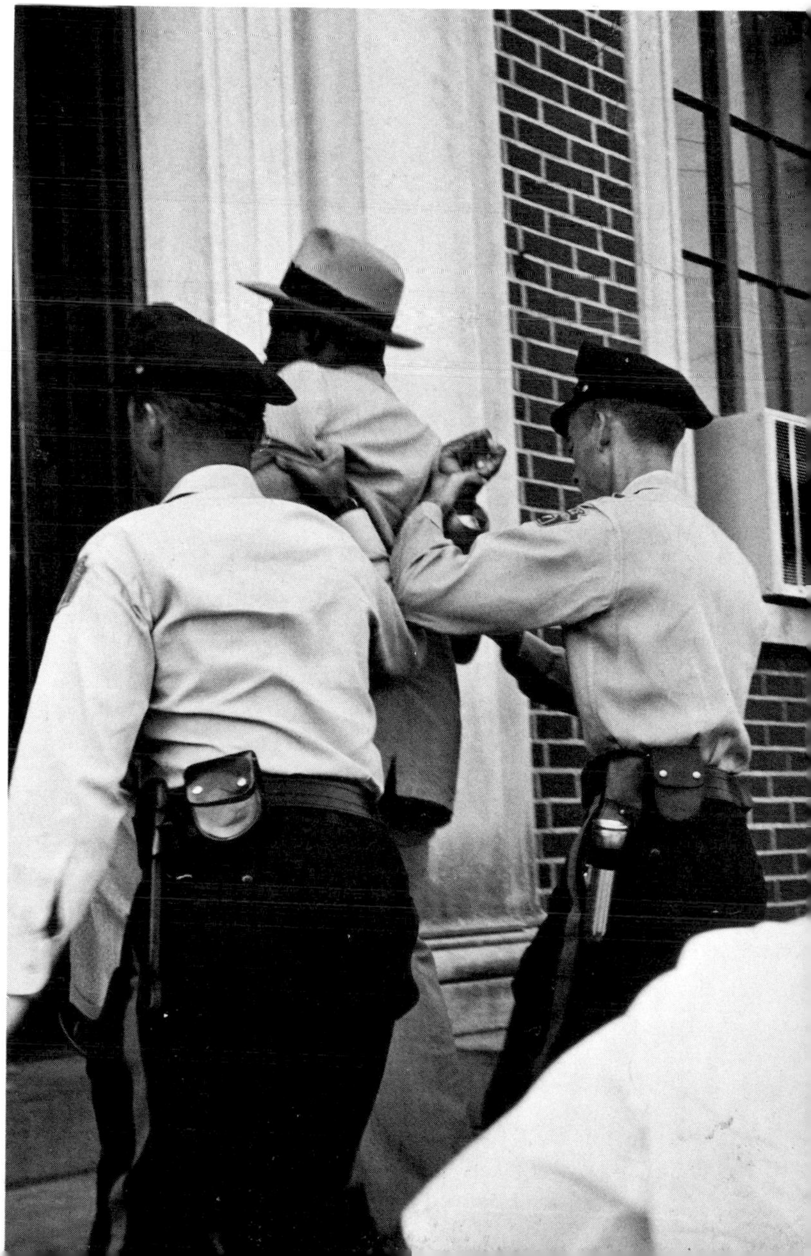

there is always the way of nonviolent resistance. This is ultimately the way of the strong man."

The bus boycott ended thirteen months after it began when the Supreme Court of the United States affirmed the decision of a special three-judge U.S. District Court declaring unconstitutional Alabama's state and local laws requiring segregation on buses. The marriage between the protest movement and the legal system was thus consummated. That marriage was to effect significant changes throughout the civil rights movement.

King admonished blacks to accept their victory in Montgomery with dignity and restraint. His own people heeded the plea for nonviolence, but the white power structure refused to accept the blacks' newly-won equality without a fight. A reign of terror followed the Supreme Court mandate. City buses were fired upon throughout the city. A teenage girl was beaten by four or five white men as she alighted from a bus. A pregnant black woman was shot in the leg. Black homes and churches were bombed. The Ku Klux Klan rode.

When seven white men were arrested and tried for the bombings, the terrorism abated, even though they were not convicted. And Montgomery made a grudging peace with its black citizens.

Montgomery was a victory for the black man, but it had taken its toll. And King was forced to prophesy, **"It is becoming clear that the Negro is in for a season of suffering."**

Charles Moore

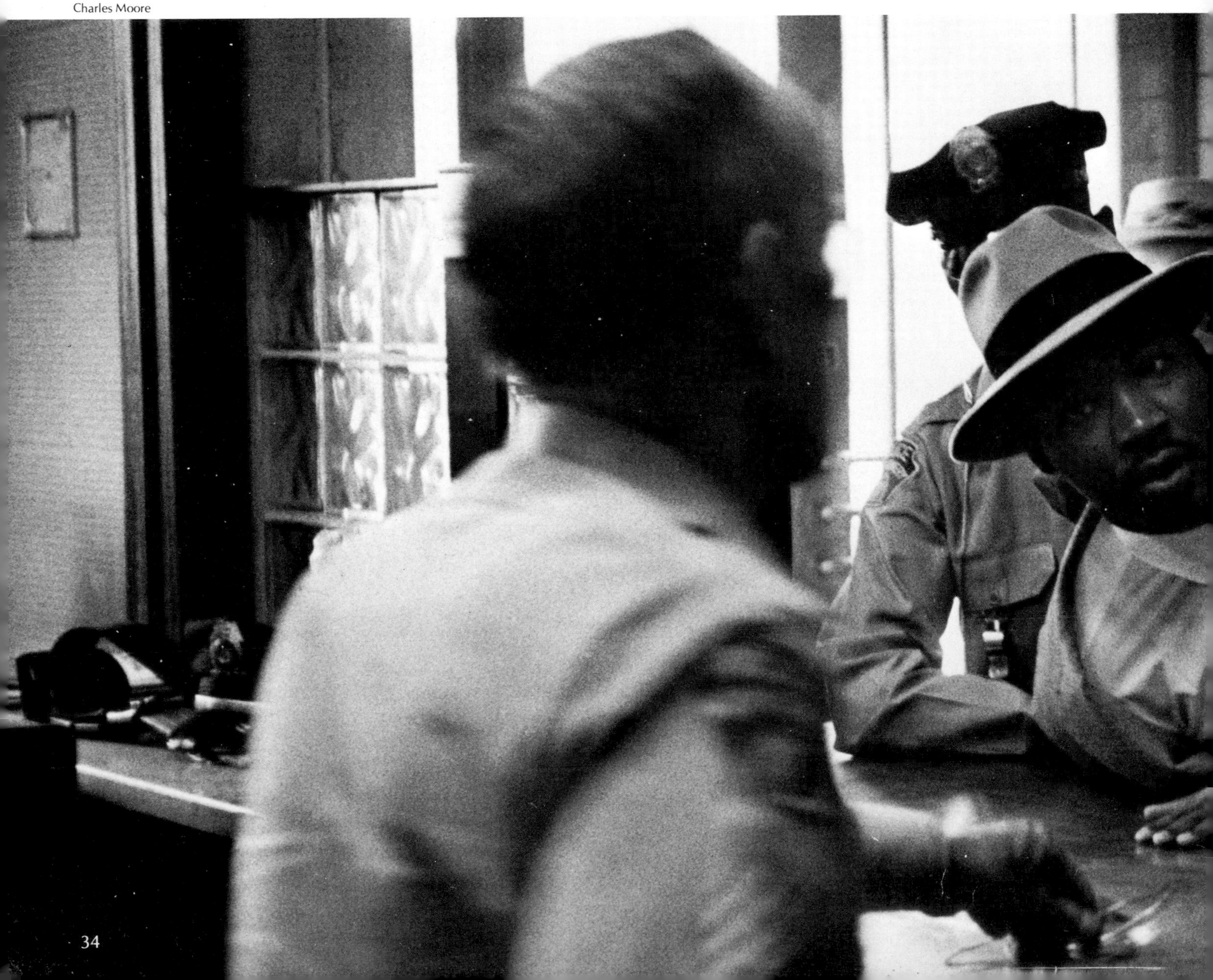

At the Montgomery city jail King's wife Coretta remains by his side. After he decides to serve fourteen days in prison, King's fine is mysteriously paid by a city commissioner to prevent him from using the jail "for his own selfish purposes."

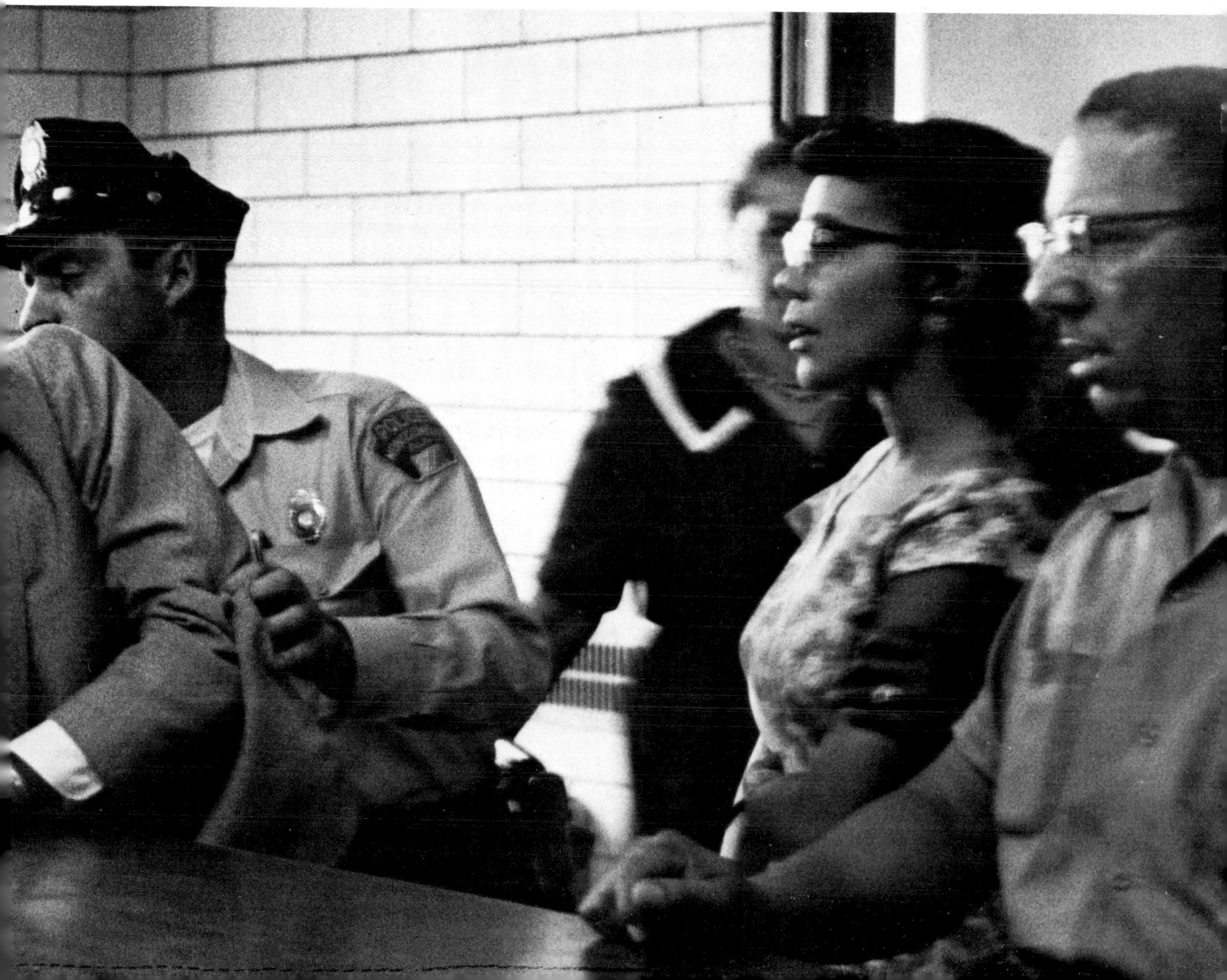

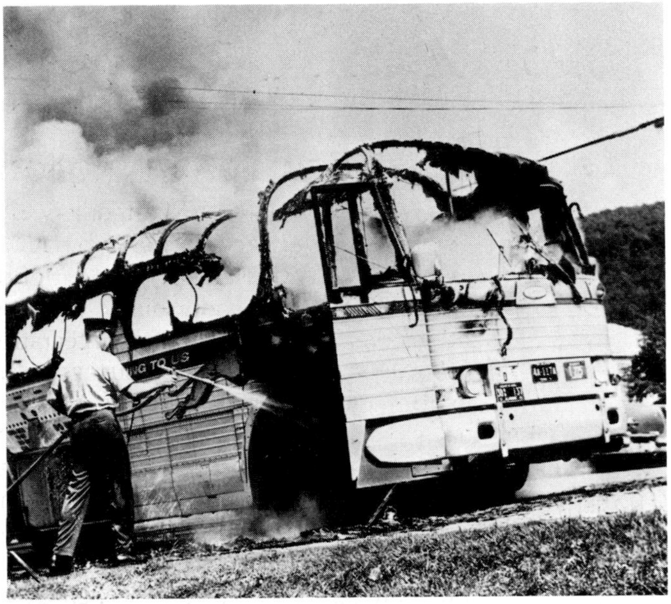
UPI

Chapter Two

"Season of Suffering"

Sit-ins, Freedom Rides, Demonstrations,

1960–1962 King emerged from the Montgomery Boycott a national leader with popular backing and international recognition. In January, 1957, he was elected president of the newly-formed Southern Christian Leadership Conference (SCLC), an organization committed to nonviolent integration.

In the months following the Montgomery success, King made a pilgrimage to India, the homeland of Mahatma Gandhi, the spiritual source of the nonviolent movement. Shortly after his return, the next major phase of the protest movement began; Montgomery had been only the beginning. In early 1960, black students in Greensboro, North Carolina, spontaneously took seats at a segregated Woolworth's lunch counter. Their action ignited a student revolt throughout the state, and the sit-in movement began. In the spring of 1961, the Congress of Racial Equality (CORE), backed by the SCLC and the newly-formed Student Nonviolent Coordinating Committee (SNCC), decided to mobilize the sit-ins. Thus began the Freedom Rides. Students and civil rights workers joined in a nonviolent invasion of the south designed to desegregate all public facilities. Unfortunately, their peaceful tactics were met by angry violence and lawlessness which precipitated the next phase of protest—mass demonstrations.

LUNCH COUNTER SIT-INS

Joseph McNeill, a student at the all-black North Carolina Agricultural and Technical College, tried on January 31, 1960, to get something to eat at the Greensboro bus terminal's lunch counter. He was refused with a curt, "We don't serve Negroes." McNeill and his roommate, Ezell Blair, Jr., decided to undertake their own nonviolent protest. The next day, two other students joined them as they took seats at the Woolworth lunch counter. Refused service, they continued this action every day. Within two weeks, students throughout North Carolina were demanding integrated service in department stores and bus terminals.

By the end of March, the nonviolent sit-ins had spread to more than fifty southern cities. During the first months the students acted spontaneously, with little or no effective organization, but in April the Student Nonviolent Coordinating Committee (SNCC) was born. Though the students introduced a more urgent, perhaps more radical note to the civil rights movement, they accepted

Sit-in demonstrators and hostile whites.

Wide World

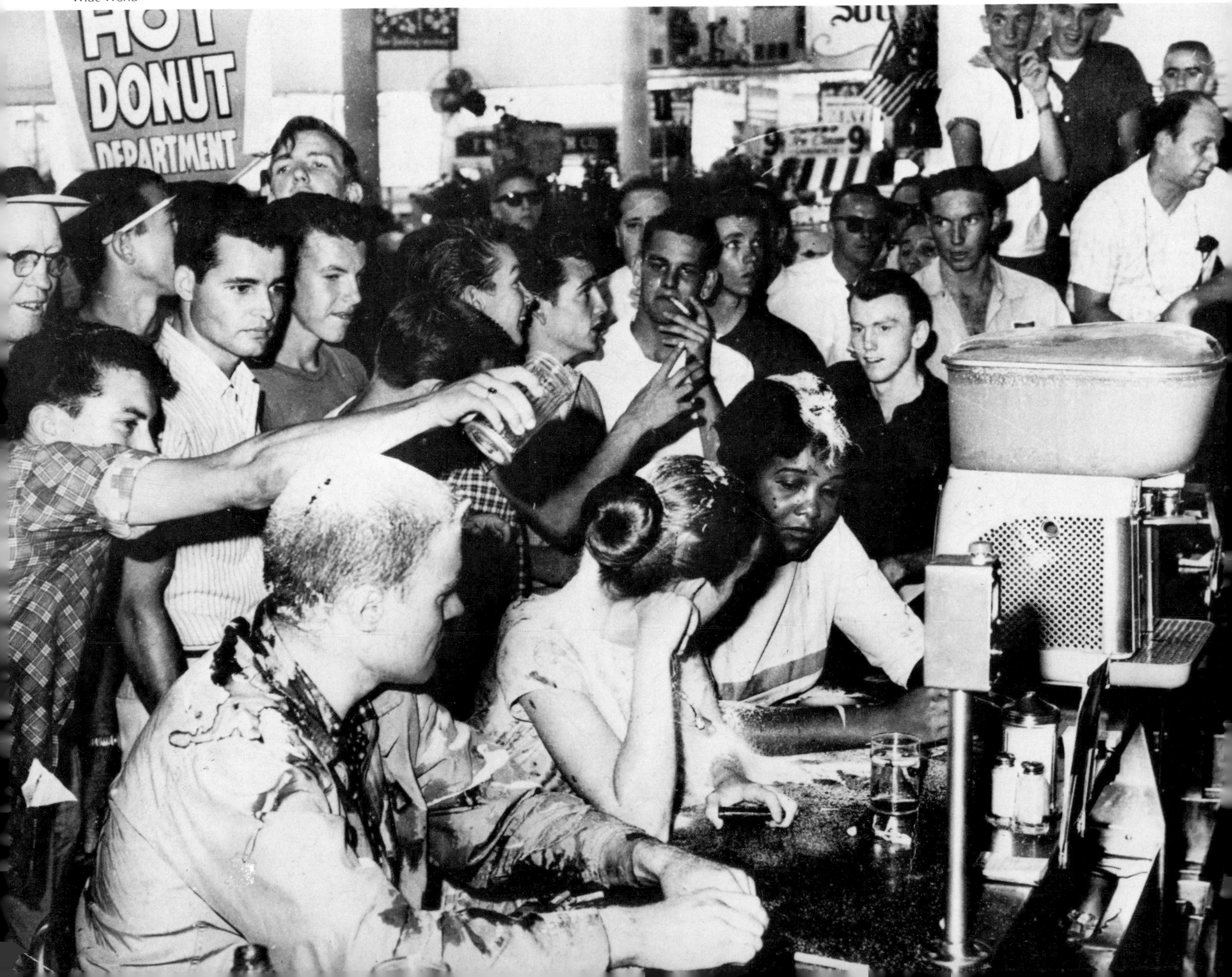
HOT
DONUT
DEPARTMENT

King as their symbolic leader and strove toward his philosophy of nonviolence.

Many demonstrators carried a printed reminder with them: "Remember the teachings of Jesus Christ, Mahatma Gandhi, and Martin Luther King. Remember love and nonviolence." Nevertheless, the sit-ins provoked arrests and outbreaks of violence in some southern cities.

Like King, the students were willing to **"fill the jails"** rather than pay fines or bail. In mid-October, after addressing the embryonic SNCC, King and thirty-six others were arrested for trespassing because of their attempts to be served at the lunch counter of Rich's Department Store in Atlanta. When they refused to post bond, they were jailed. King announced that he would **"stay in jail a year or ten years"** if it took that long to integrate Rich's. Mayor William Hartsfield intervened, proposing a two-month truce during which the protestors' demands could be reviewed.

Martin Luther King's brother, A. D. King, participates in a lunch counter sit-in. Seated next to him is Reverend C. T. Vivian. Reverend Wyatt Tee Walker stands behind them.

Lee Lockwood

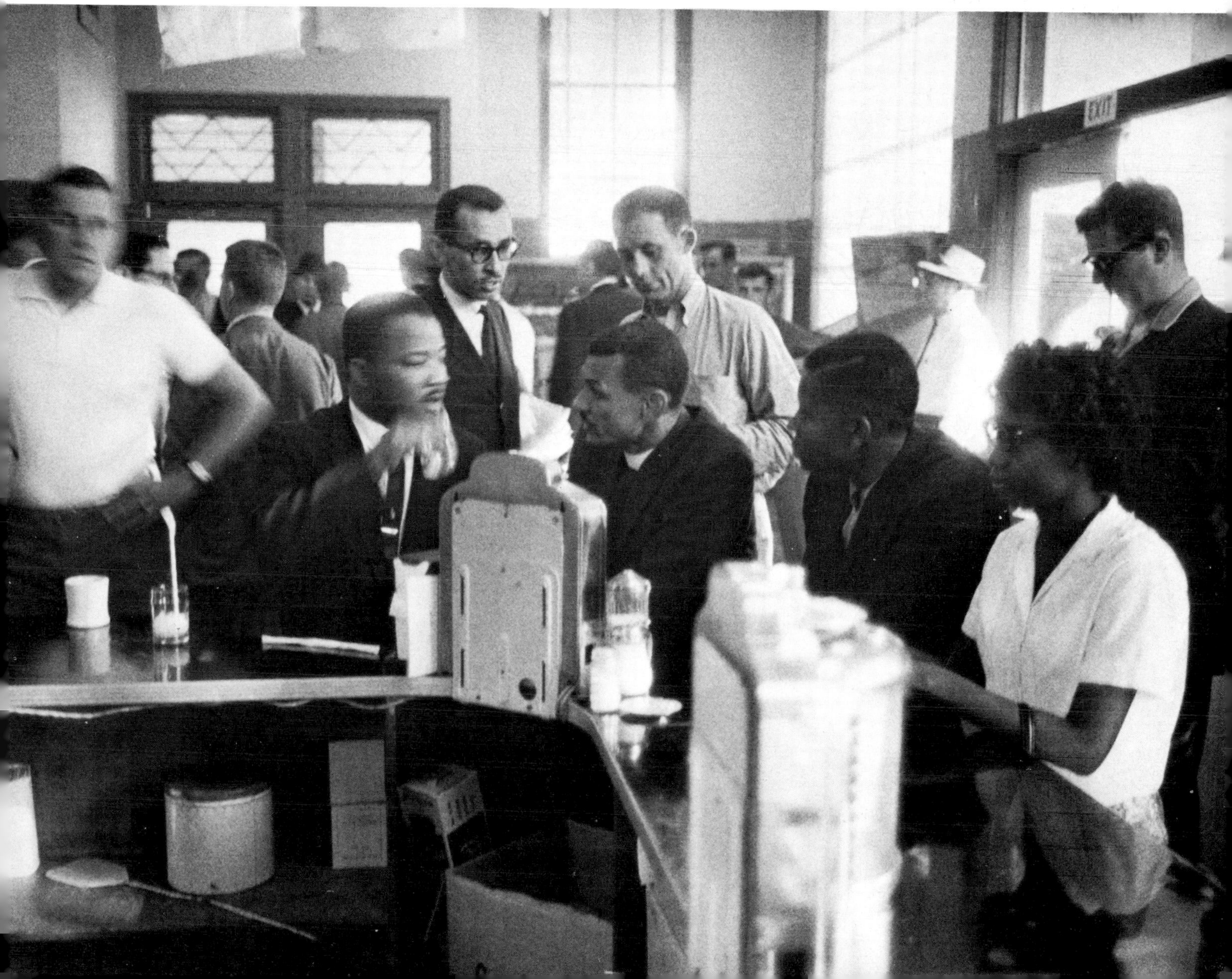

EXIT

FREEDOM RIDES

The sit-ins continued. In March, 1961, CORE announced a new campaign—"to put the sit-ins on the road." The project was a major test of strength which involved the whole movement, and a challenge to the Kennedy administration, which had responded equivocally to black demands.

In early May, six pairs of volunteers, black and white, joined by a CORE observer, boarded Greyhound and Trailways interstate buses in Washington, D.C., to travel through Virginia, the Carolinas, Georgia, Alabama, and Mississippi. The plan was to test the public facilities at each stop, sitting in segregated waiting rooms and seeking service at segregated lunch counters.

Freedom Riders were arrested in North and South Carolina, but in one case the charges were dropped and in the other the Rider was acquitted by a local judge on the basis of a Supreme Court decision in December, 1960, which declared segregation in interstate bus terminals illegal.

In Alabama the reception became ugly. When the Greyhound bus arrived in Anniston, it was greeted by an angry white mob. Armed with iron bars, they smashed windows, punctured tires, and hurled a bomb that set the bus on fire. Some of the Freedom Riders were attacked and beaten as they emerged from the burning bus. Although nine white men were later arrested for their part in the violence, none were punished.

The second bus reached Birmingham, where the police stood by while angry whites savagely assaulted the Freedom Riders. Throughout these brutal beatings, the protestors adhered to their principles of nonviolence.

When the bus companies refused to take the group on to Montgomery, a second group of Freedom Riders left Nashville to continue the journey. When they reached Montgomery on May 20, the new Freedom Riders were met by three hundred antagonistic

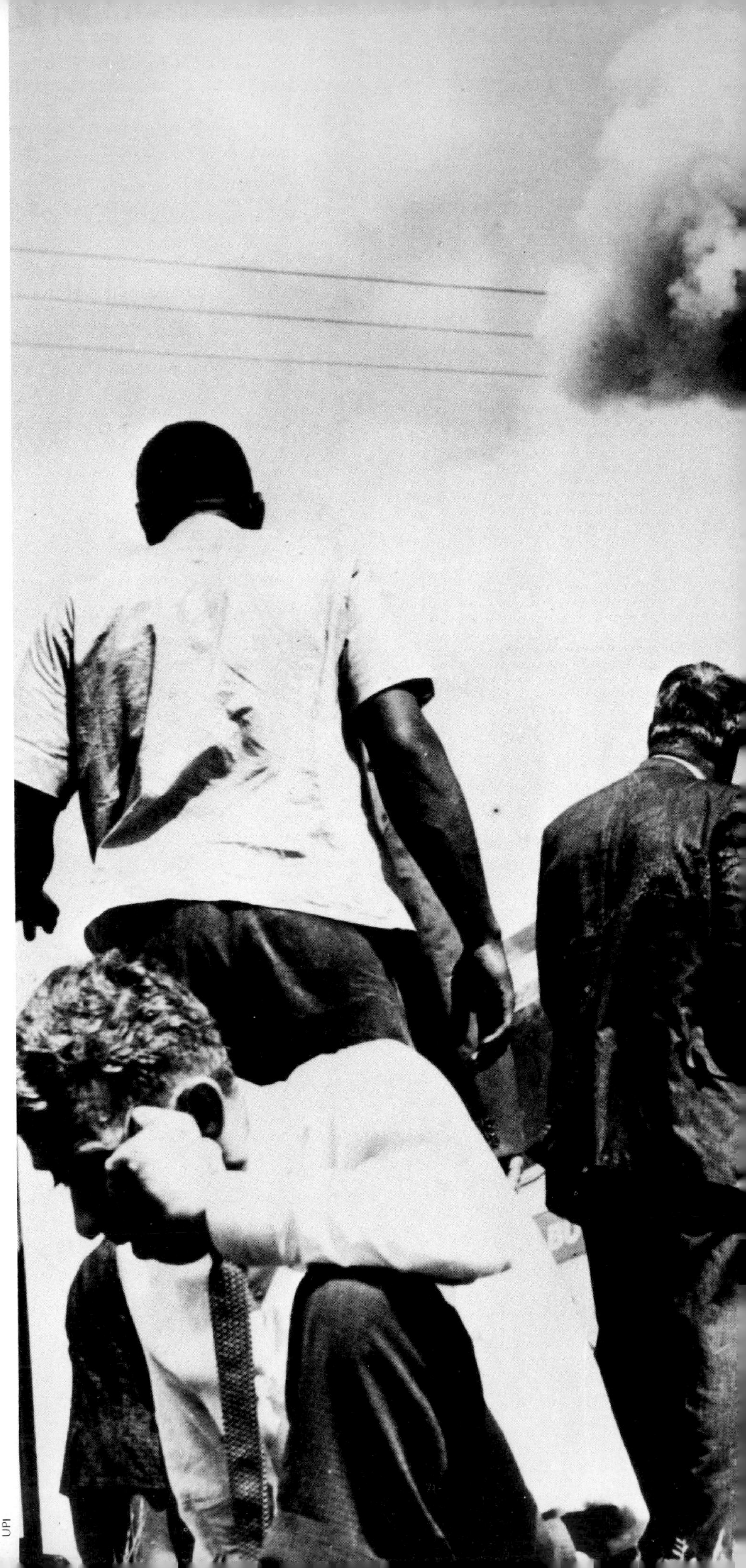

Anniston, Alabama, May 15, 1962. The first Freedom Riders are met with incendiary bombs.

UPI

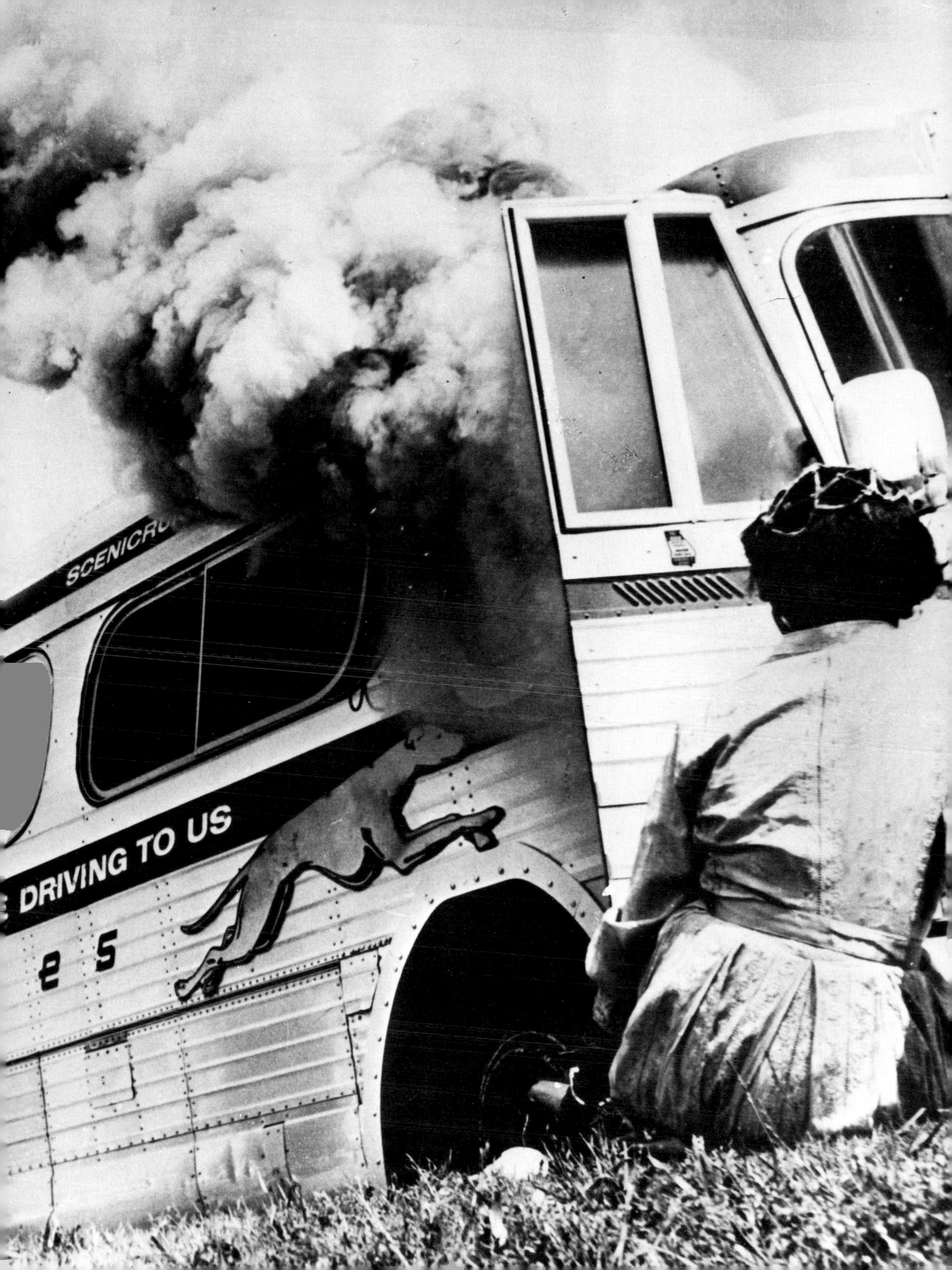
SCENICRU
DRIVING TO US
es

whites, many of whom were Ku Klux Klansmen. The Freedom Riders were fiercely mauled as they left the bus. The police were conspicuously absent. Often the white Freedom Riders, labeled "nigger lovers," were the victims of the most savage attaks.

Several days before, Alabama Governor John Patterson had condoned the mob action by saying, "The people of Alabama are so enraged that I cannot guarantee protection for this bunch of rabble rousers."

The mob raged for twenty minutes before the police appeared, and only when the numbers approached a thousand did the police clear the area with tear gas. The violence continued throughout the day until Attorney General Robert Kennedy sent nearly seven hundred U.S. marshals. Even then Governor Patterson insisted the marshals were unnecessary and threatened to arrest them.

The next evening King addressed more than twelve hundred blacks at a mass meeting at Ralph Abernathy's First Baptist Church in Montgomery. His anger was barely concealed as he exclaimed:

"The ultimate responsibility for the hideous action in Alabama last week must be placed at the doorstep of the governor of the state. We hear the familiar cry that morals cannot be legislated. This may be true, but behavior can be regulated. The law may not be able to make a man love me, but it can keep him from lynching me."

As the Freedom Riders leave Montgomery for Jackson, Mississippi, on May 21, they are accompanied by six armed soldiers and escorted by twenty-two highway patrol cars, two battalions of National Guardsmen, three U.S. Army reconnaissance planes, and two helicopters.

Lee Lockwood

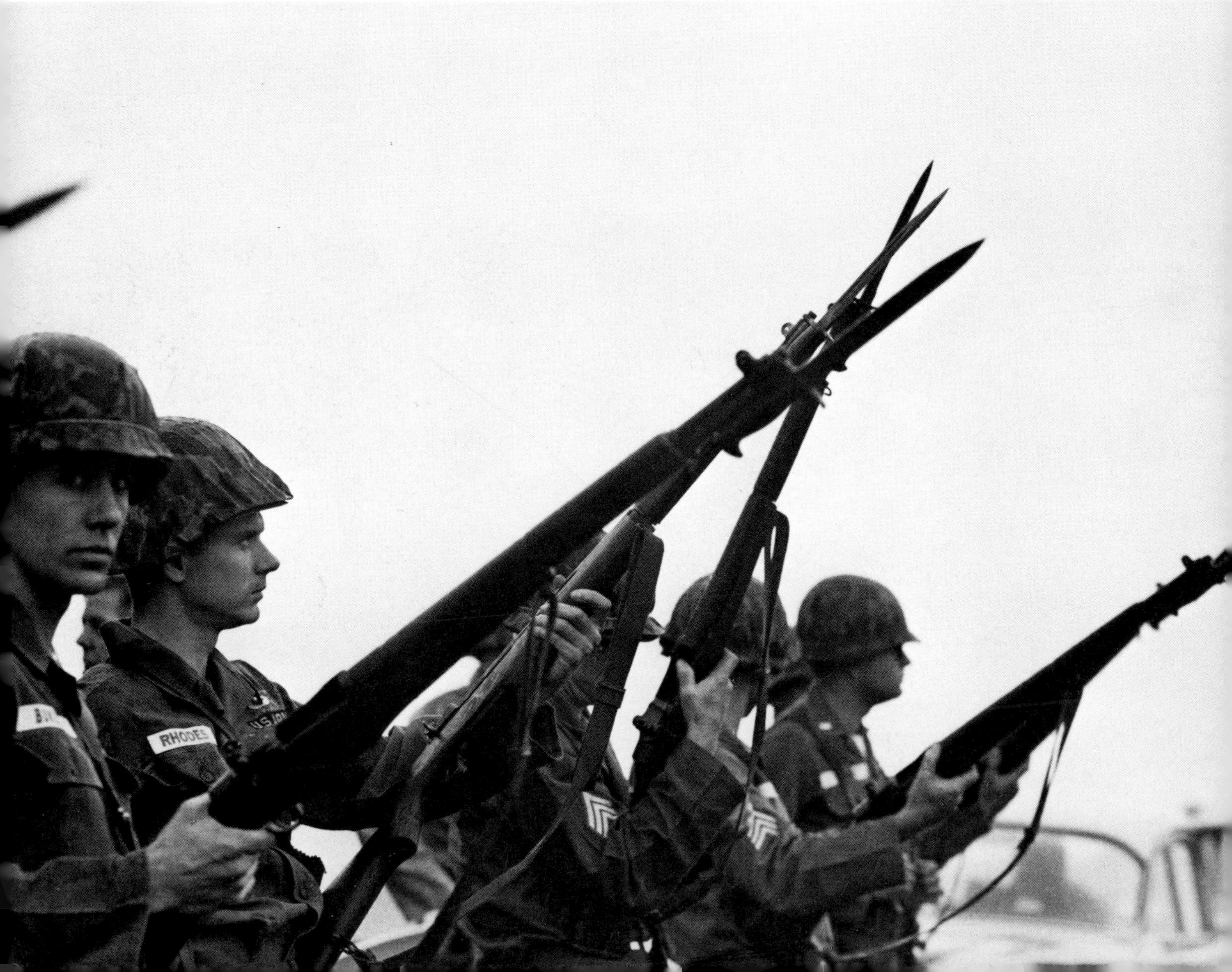

RHODES

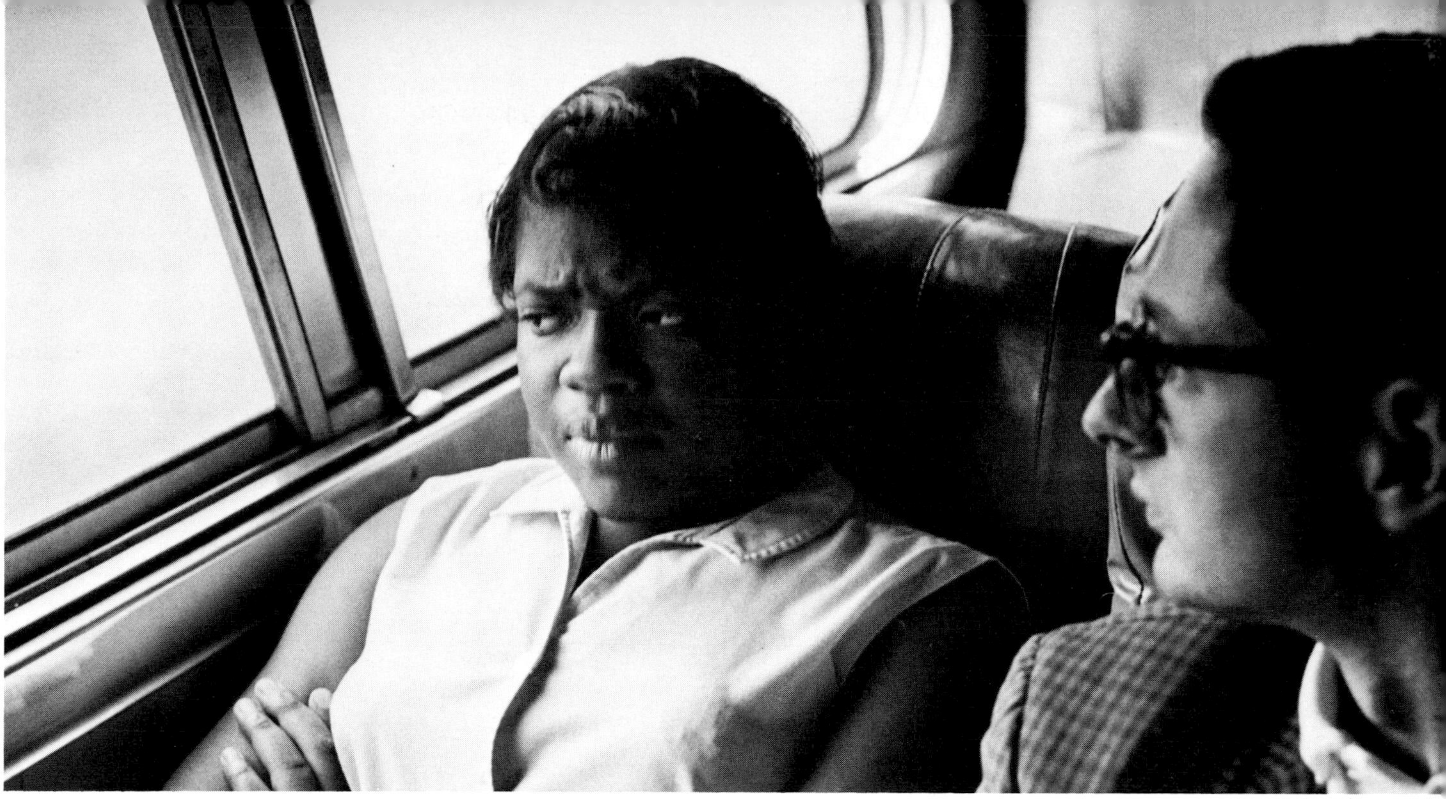

Lee Lockwood

Lee Lockwood

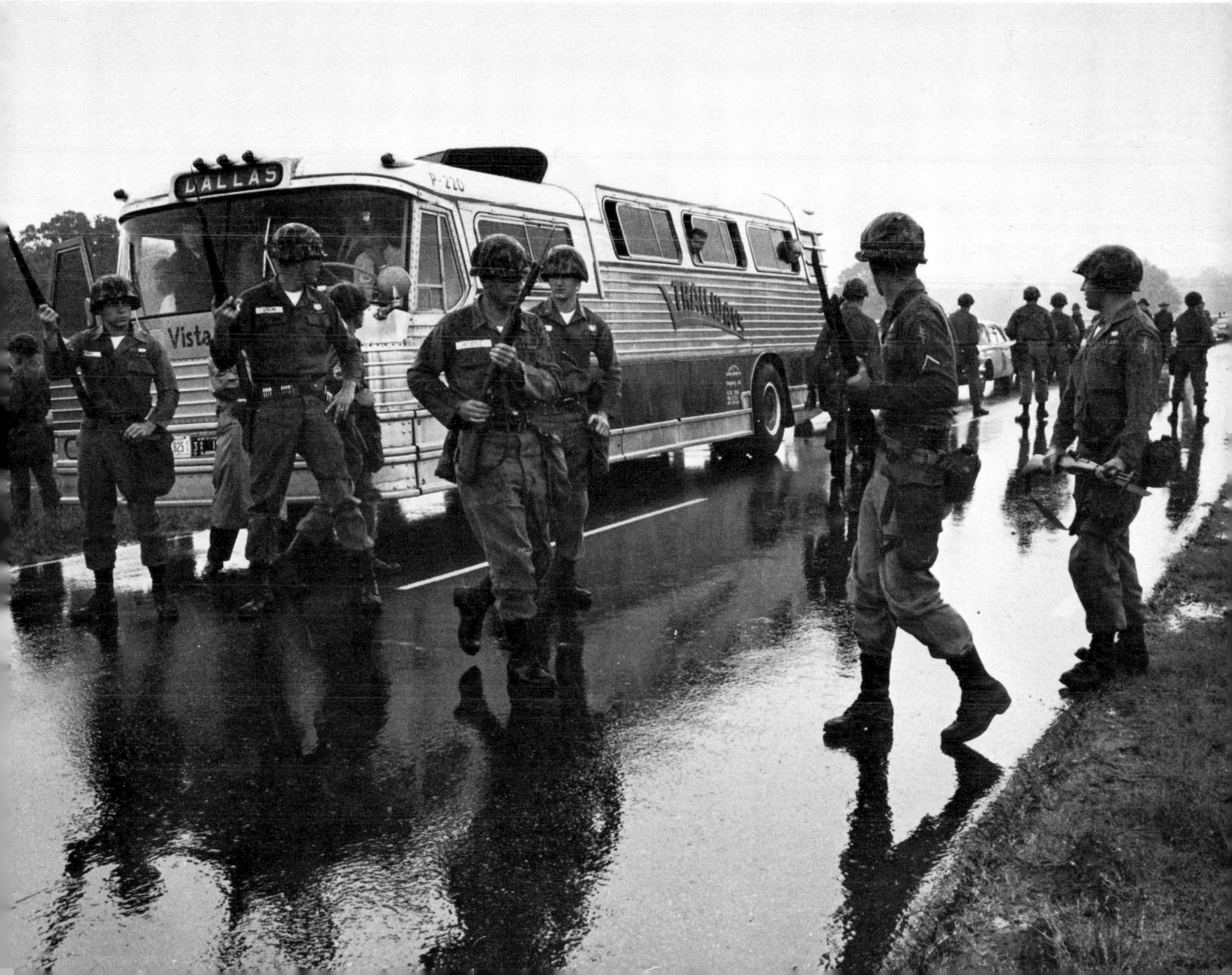
DALLAS
P-220
Vista

The crowd fervently sang "We Shall Overcome" while the white mob which had gathered outside barraged the church with bottles and stones. The segregationists fought the U.S. marshals in the streets of the capital of the old Confederacy. Finally, under pressure from Washington, Governor Patterson deployed the National Guard.

King agreed to serve as the chairman and spokesman for the Freedom Rider Coordinating Committee, and to prepare for the continuation of the campaign the committee held nonviolent training sessions. At the last of these sessions, King reiterated the purposes of the rides: **"to test the use of transportation facilities, according to federal law; to encourage others to demand use of the facilities; to direct the spotlight of public attention to areas which still segregate."** He concluded: **"Freedom Riders must develop the quiet courage of dying for a cause. We would not like to see anyone die. We all love life and there are no martyrs here—but we are well aware that we may have some casualties."**

The Freedom Rides continued throughout the summer. Many protestors went to jail, but by November there were indications of change. The Interstate Commerce Commission effected an order banning segregation in buses, trains, and supportive facilities. And King interpreted the Freedom Rides as **"the psychological turning point in our legal struggle."**

Right:
James Zwerg, a student from the University of Wisconsin, was beaten mercilessly when his Greyhound bus arrived in Montgomery on May 20. He made no attempt to strike back. As no white ambulances would service the Freedom Riders, he waits stoically for a black ambulance.

King at a planning session after his election as spokesman of the Freedom Rider Coordinating Committee.

Lee Lockwood

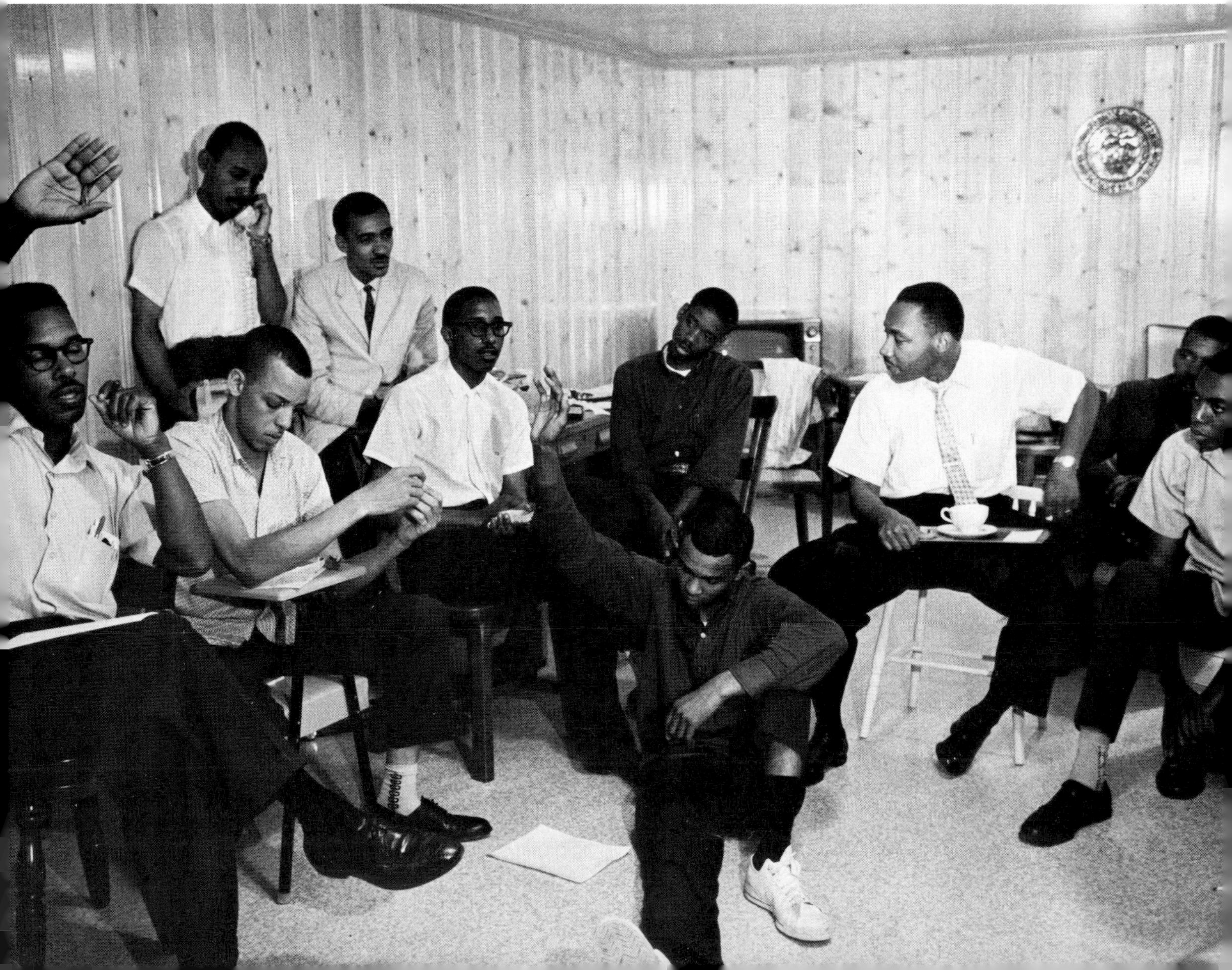

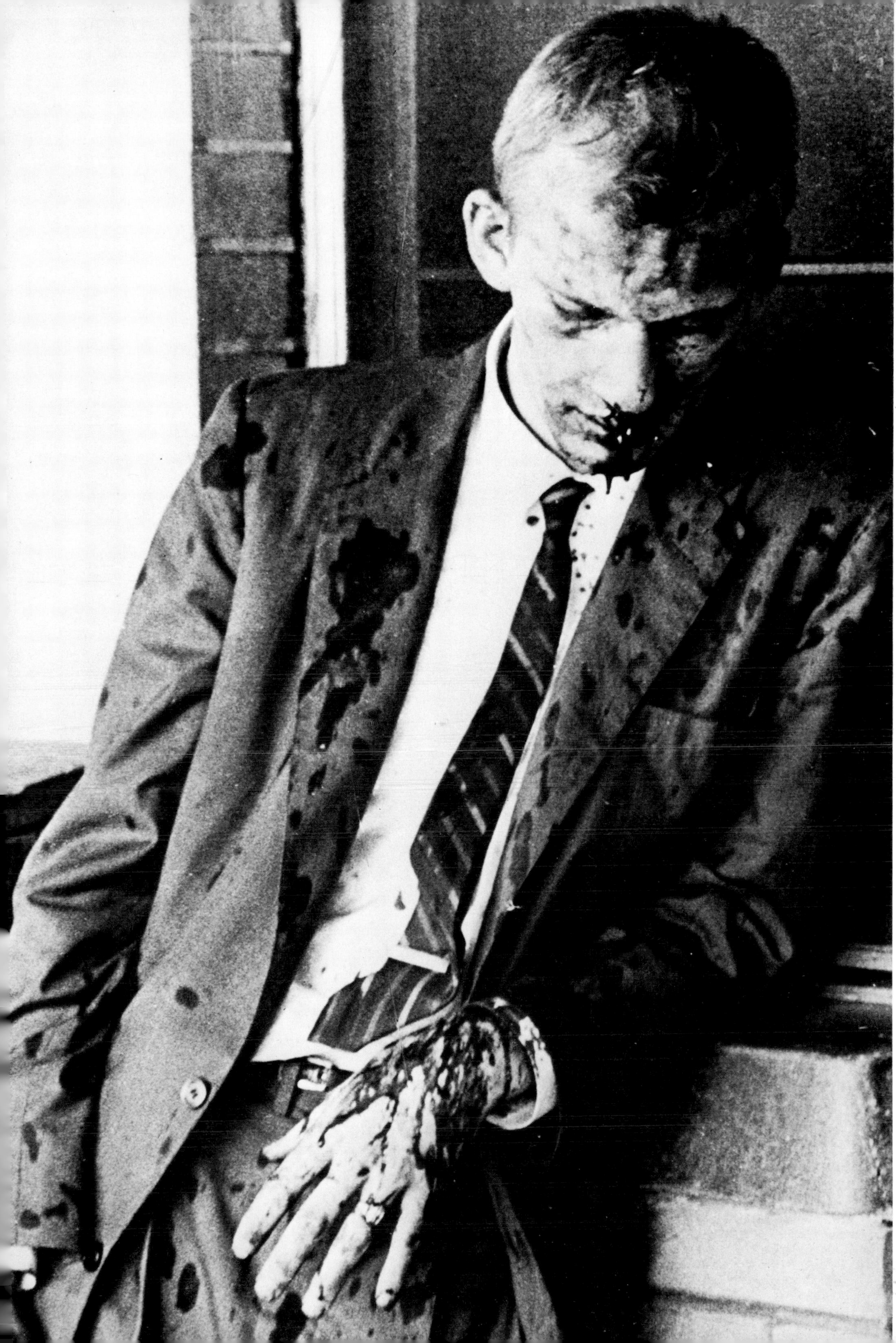
UPI

DEMONSTRATIONS

Although King had been the symbolic leader of the Freedom Riders, he had not originally organized the movement, nor was he ever able to give his unreserved support to the more radical student movement that saw nonviolence as a tactic, not as a way of life.

By the beginning of 1962, he felt the need to put his words into actions by spearheading his first major campaign since Montgomery.

Although he did not choose the battleground, the situation in Albany, Georgia, seemed to provide the opportunity. Local black citizens and SNCC field workers had already established the embryo of a movement in Albany, modelled after the Montgomery Improvement Association. The Albany Movement grew out of a Freedom Ride into Albany in December, 1961. When ten Freedom Riders were jailed, the Movement quickly mobilized a protest march. In all, 560 black marchers were arrested and 300 of them chose to remain in jail. On the invitation of the local leaders, King and his associates arrived in Albany in December with no planned strategy.

With the words, **"Get on your walkin' shoes; walk together, children, and don'tcha get weary,"** King organized the Freedom Movement's first mass confrontation. He stated, **"We will wear them down by our capacity to suffer."**

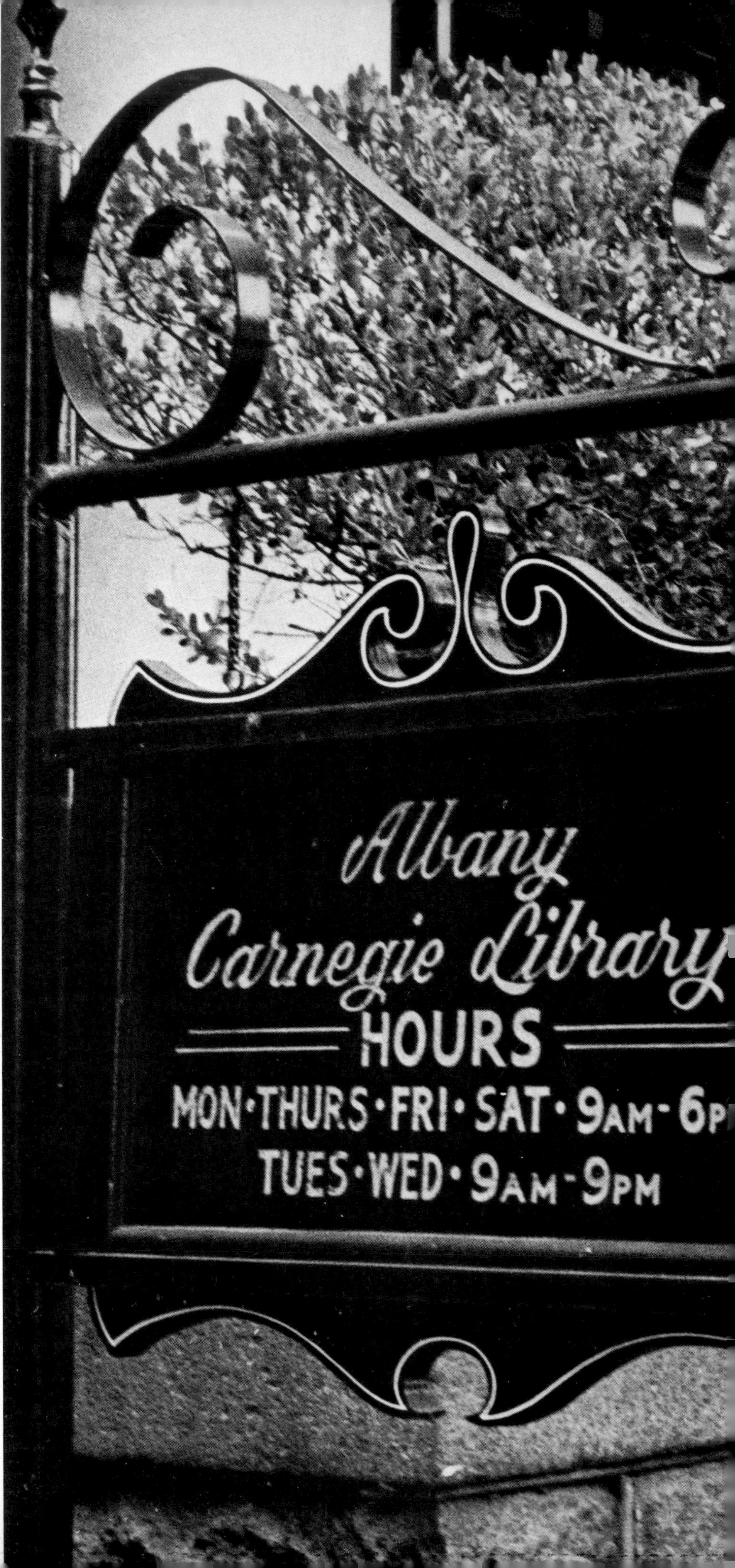

Albany
Carnegie Library
HOURS
MON·THURS·FRI·SAT·9AM-6P
TUES·WED·9AM-9PM

When demonstrations in Albany, Georgia, are met with increasing violence, King calls a halt and declares "A Day of Penitence," limiting direct action to small prayer vigils. Nevertheless, on July 31, 1962, police arrest the group of teenagers gathered at the front of the Albany Carnegie Library to pray and sing.

UPI

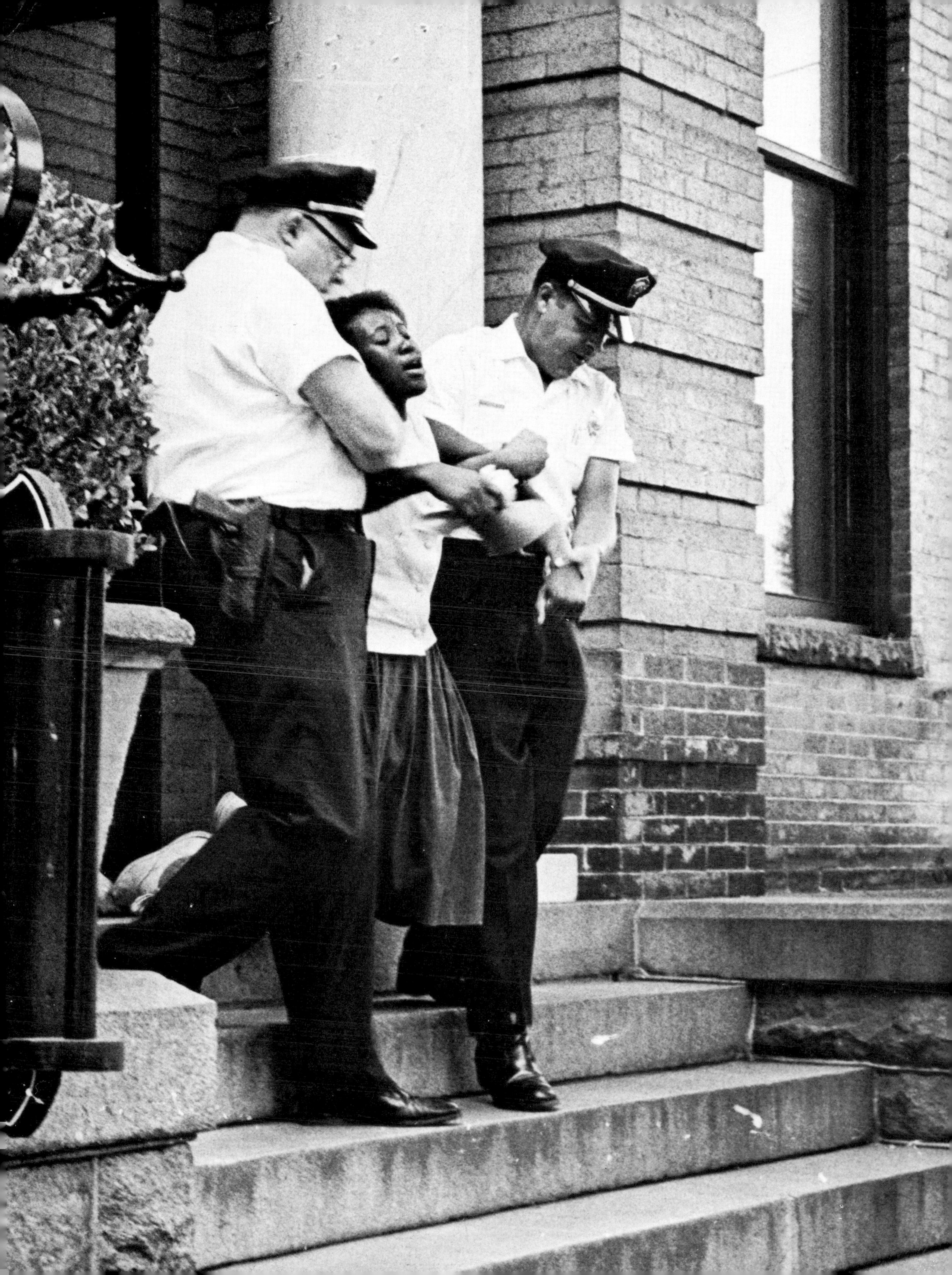

Following mass meetings and nonviolence workshops, the black community of Albany embarked on a series of marches on city hall, sit-ins at libraries and recreational facilities, and prayer vigils. They initiated selective buying campaigns in an effort to force merchants to hire black sales clerks, open lunch counters, and pressure city hall. But the black population of Albany was not large enough to exert effective economic pressure.

As in Montgomery, a boycott was launched against the city's bus line. Although the bus company agreed to desegregate and hire at least one black driver, the protestors decided to wait for a written promise from the city commissioners before they resumed riding the buses. No such promise was forthcoming, and the bus line went out of business.

Albany Police Chief Laurie Pritchett arrested demonstrators at every turn for loitering, parading without a permit, and disturbing the peace. No clubs, dogs, or hoses were used in Albany. The brutality that did exist occurred "off-camera" in barns and pastures that served as temporary prisons. At no time did the federal government intervene in Albany—even to enforce the law. King was arrested on three separate occasions during the Albany demonstrations.

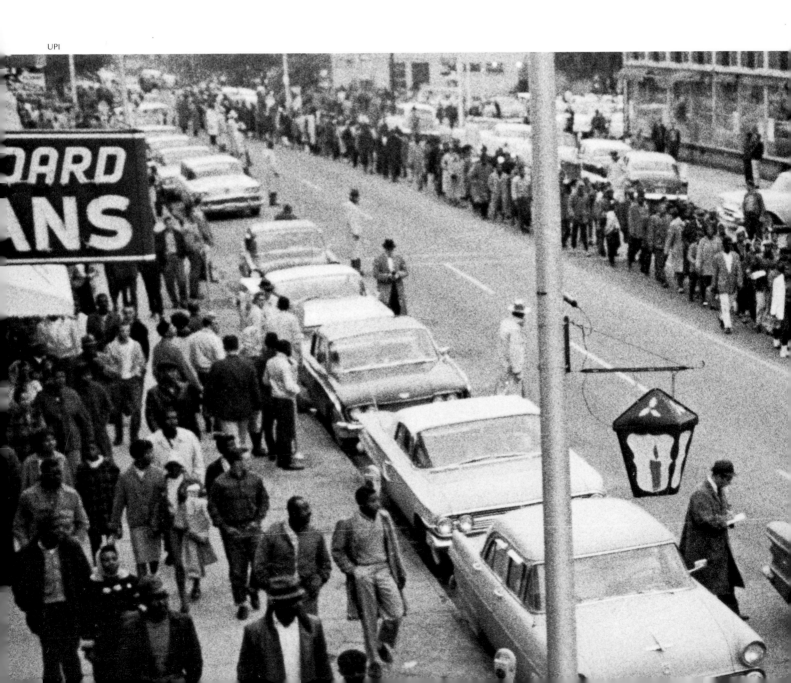

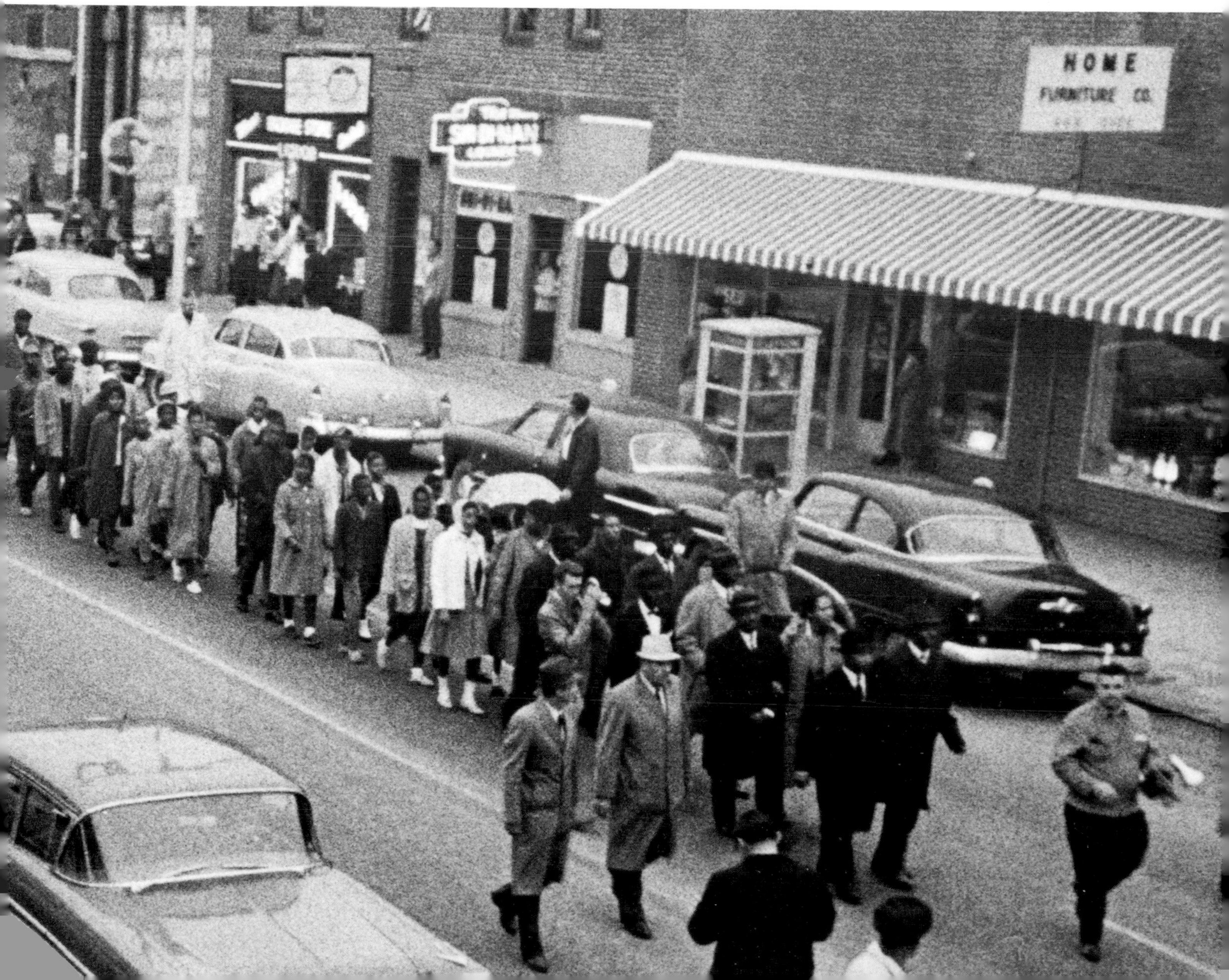
HOME
FURNITURE CO.

A new protest technique is introduced in Albany—mass demonstrations.

From his jail cell he wrote: "**Albany has become a symbol of segregation's last stand almost by chance. The ferment of a hundred years' frustration has now come to the fore . . . the major significance of what is being done in Albany is not so much the reconciliation that it will bring between Negro and white people through our democratic process in this one instance, but more especially Albany will serve as a guidepost for other communities to grapple with the dilemma of accelerating the painfully slow process of desegregation which has blocked the capacities of so many lives and scarred so many souls."**

King was never able to count Albany among his victories because he did not succeed in his avowed goal of opening up public facilities to all people regardless of race. But the Albany campaign did have significant effects. An entire community was mobilized; parks, libraries, and bus lines were closed even to whites; the attention of the world was attracted; and a new form of protest was introduced—the mass demonstration. Many have conducted post-mortems to determine what went wrong at Albany. Their judgments include factionalism among the leaders, the absence of an organized strategy, and an unfamiliarity with the specific situation in Albany.

King himself, saddened by the defeat, noted still that "**Albany in fact has proved how extraordinary was the Negro response to the appeal of non-violence. Approximately five percent of the total Negro population went willingly to jail. Were that percentage duplicated in New York City, some fifty thousand Negroes would overflow its prisons. If a people can produce from its ranks five percent who will go voluntarily to jail for a just cause, surely nothing can thwart its ultimate triumph."**

After being arrested for "parading without a permit," King waits in the office of Police Chief Laurie Pritchett. Over two thousand blacks went to jail during the spring and summer of 1962.

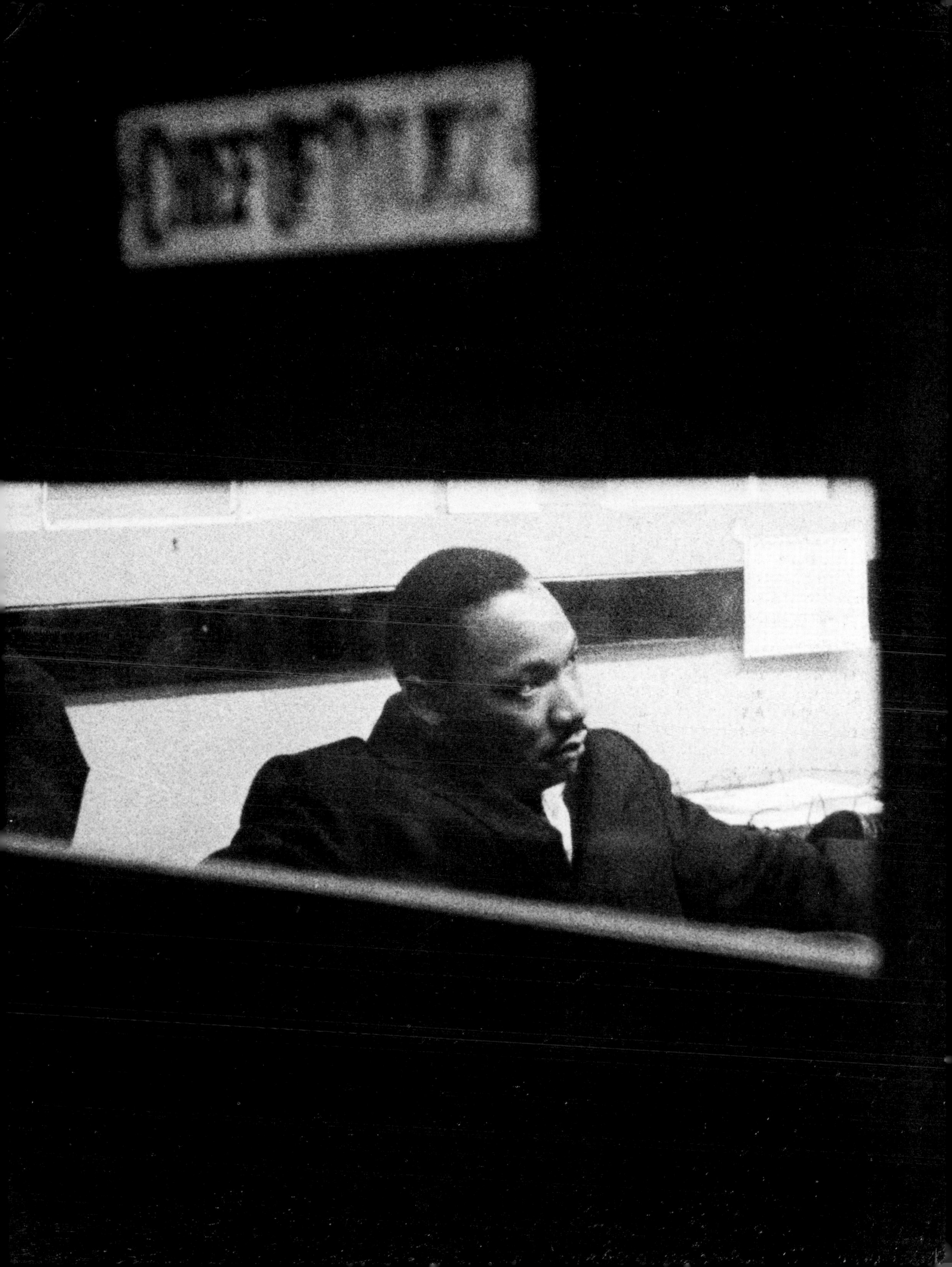

Fred Ward

Chapter Three

"Sheep in the Midst of Wolves"

Meredith Enters the University of Mississippi, 1962

In September, 1962, when King was planning the strategy that would make Birmingham the success that Albany was not, James Howard Meredith became the first black student to enter the University of Mississippi. Ole Miss was a bastion of segregation, and the state itself had already become the symbol of defiance of the desegregation mandates.

Meredith's fight was long and bloody. His lifelong desire to attend this university, and in the process shatter the segregation barriers of his native state, ultimately brought federal and state governments into the most brutal conflict since the civil war. Two died in the combat.

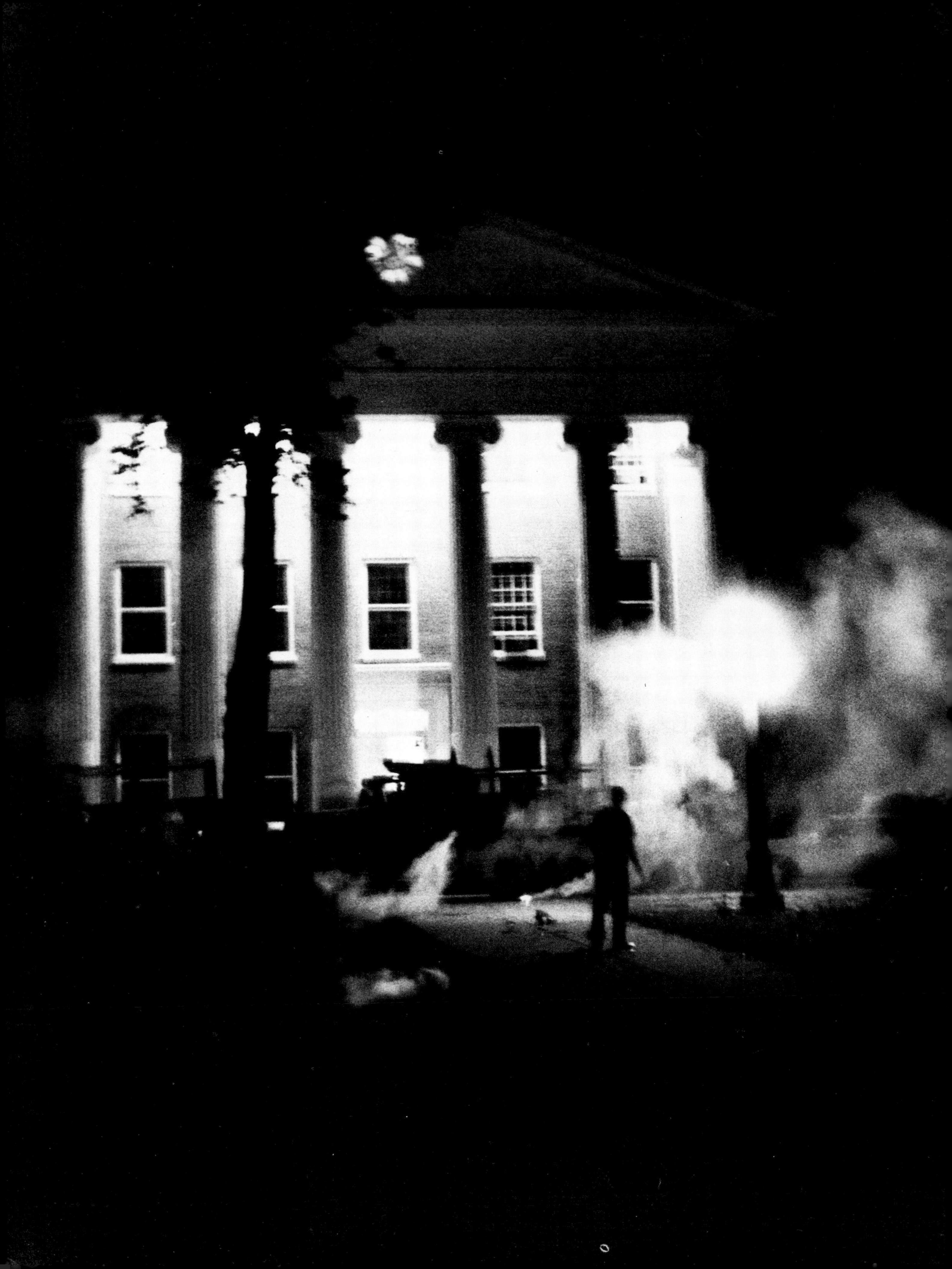

May 25, 1961. The fight begins. James Meredith's application for admission to the University of Mississippi is rejected.

May 31, 1961. NAACP attorney Constance Baker Motley files suit on Meredith's behalf, charging that Meredith was refused admission "solely because of his race." She demands an injunction barring Ole Miss from refusing to admit Meredith on racial grounds.

December 12, 1961. U.S. District Judge Sidney C. Mize rejects Meredith's request for a preliminary injunction.

June 25, 1962. After a full trial and another defeat, the case is appealed to the Fifth Circuit Court of Appeals in New Orleans. In a 2-1 decision, the court issues an injunction forcing Ole Miss to admit Meredith.

September, 1962. The Supreme Court upholds the decision to admit Meredith.

September 13, 1962. The skirmish becomes a battle. Mississippi Governor Ross Barnett, later to be called the South's most militant segregationist governor, appears on television, directing state officials to go to jail rather than obey such court orders. "We will not drink from the cup of genocide," he says. "There is no case in history where the Caucasian race has survived social integration." The scene is set for violence.

September 20, 1962. Meredith's attorneys announce he will attempt to enroll at Ole Miss that same day. Police forces have already begun to build up on campus. The university trustees designate Governor Barnett acting registrar. When Meredith, accompanied by four U.S. marshals and a contingent of Justice Department lawyers, arrives at the university auditorium, Barnett tells Meredith his application has been rejected.

Right:
Meredith, accompanied by Chief U.S. Marshal James J. P. McShane (center) and Justice Department attorney John Doar (rear), is refused entrance to the campus by Lieutenant Governor Paul Johnson.

Governor Ross Barnett on the campus of the University of Mississippi at Oxford.

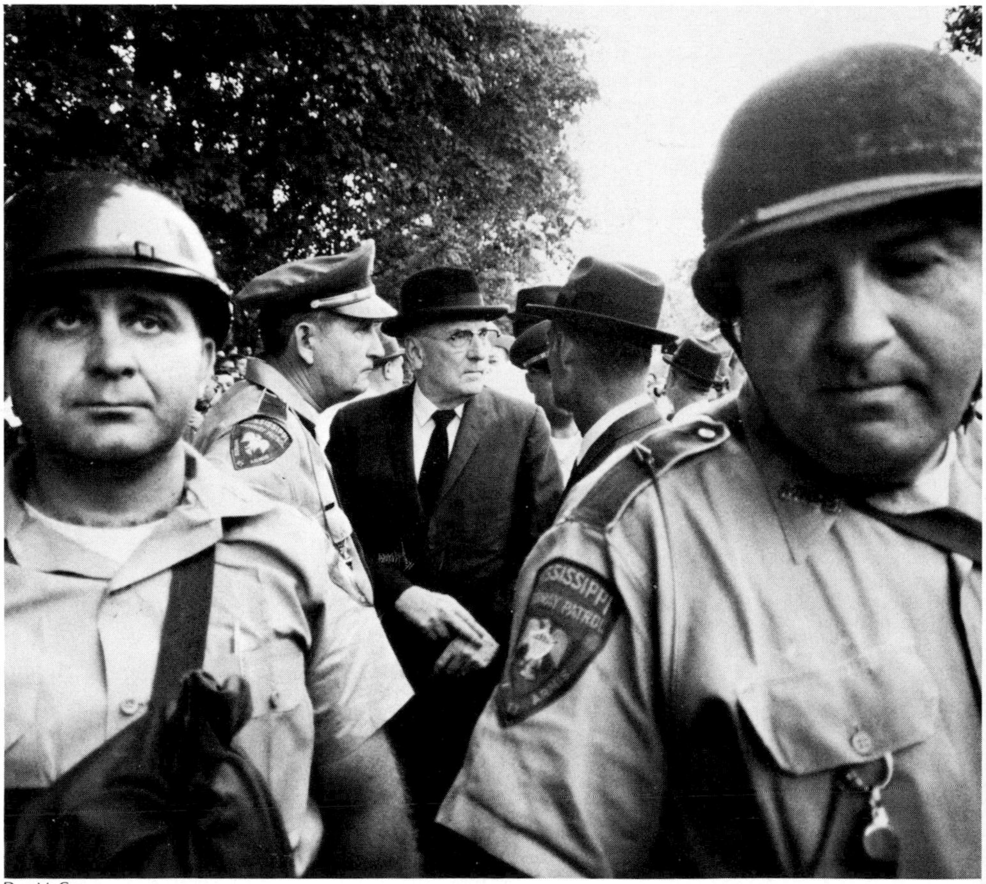

MISSISSIPPI

Dan McCoy

Overleaf:
A tear gas cannister explodes on the Ole Miss campus as U.S. marshals battle rioters, September 30, 1962.
photo by Flip Schulke

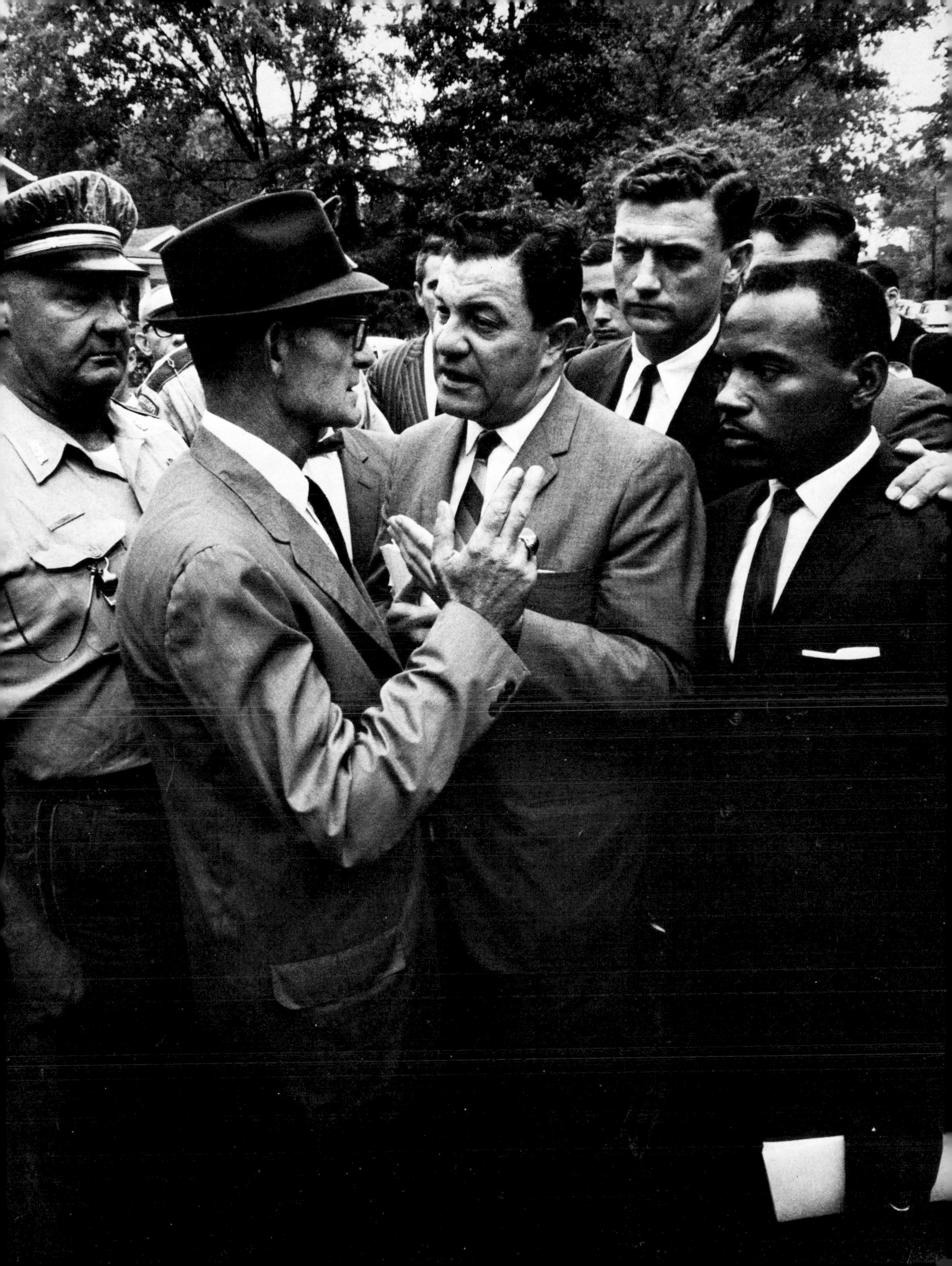

September 21, 1962. Judge Mize refuses to cite university officials for contempt of court.

September 24, 1962. It becomes known that Governor Barnett has issued an executive order directing state police to arrest anyone who tries to arrest or fine a state official in connection with the Meredith case. However, the Fifth Circuit Court of Appeals in New Orleans makes it clear that their authority supersedes that of the governor and that they are perfectly willing to cite Barnett for contempt. University trustees agree to enroll Meredith.

September 25, 1962. Despite the agreement of the university trustees, the governor again refuses Meredith admission, saying that he is acting "to prevent violence and a breach of the peace, in order to preserve the peace, dignity, and tranquility of the state of Mississippi."

September 26, 1962. The campus swarms with police from all over the state when Meredith arrives to make a new attempt to enter. This time Lieutenant Governor Paul Johnson turns him away.

September 27, 1962. State and federal governments clash. Under continuing pressure from the president and Attorney General Robert Kennedy, Governor Barnett makes a face-saving deal to surrender to the pretense of federal force. However, fearing that he will not be able to keep the immense crowd of students and agitators under control, he postpones his submission. Meanwhile, additional U.S. marshals and army troops begin to converge on the college town of Oxford, Mississippi.

September 29, 1962. President Kennedy federalizes the Mississippi National Guard. Hundreds of additional military police and U.S. marshals move toward Oxford. Simultaneously, segregationists from all over the South are gathering on campus.

6:15 P.M. Meredith, accompanied by John Doar of the Justice Department and Deputy Marshal Cecil Miller, arrives in Oxford.

Right:
Segregationist agitators work Ole Miss students into a frenzy.

A U.S. marshal shot by angry rioters lies injured in the administration building, September 30, 1962. It was hours before an ambulance could push through the mob to help the injured.

Charles Moore

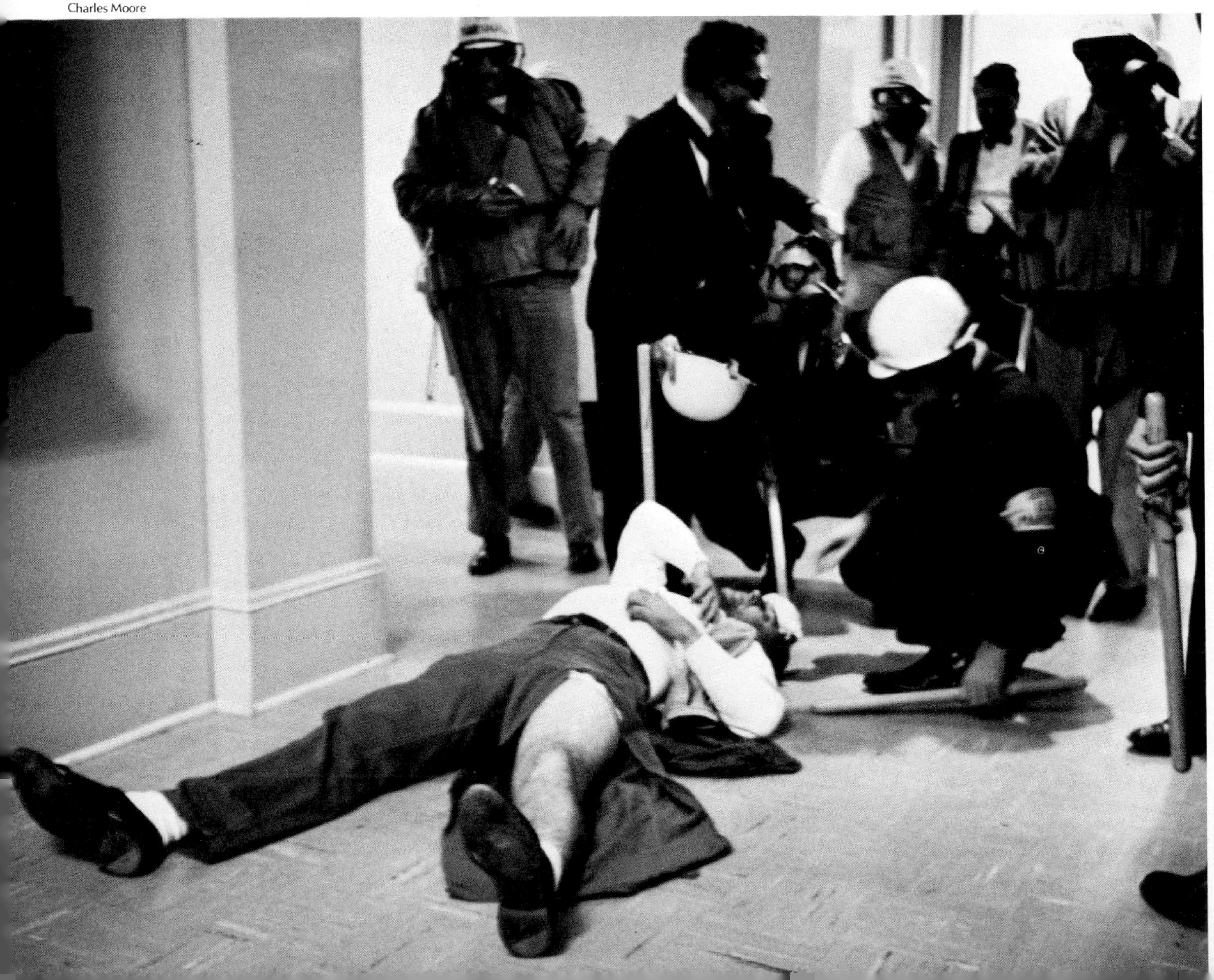

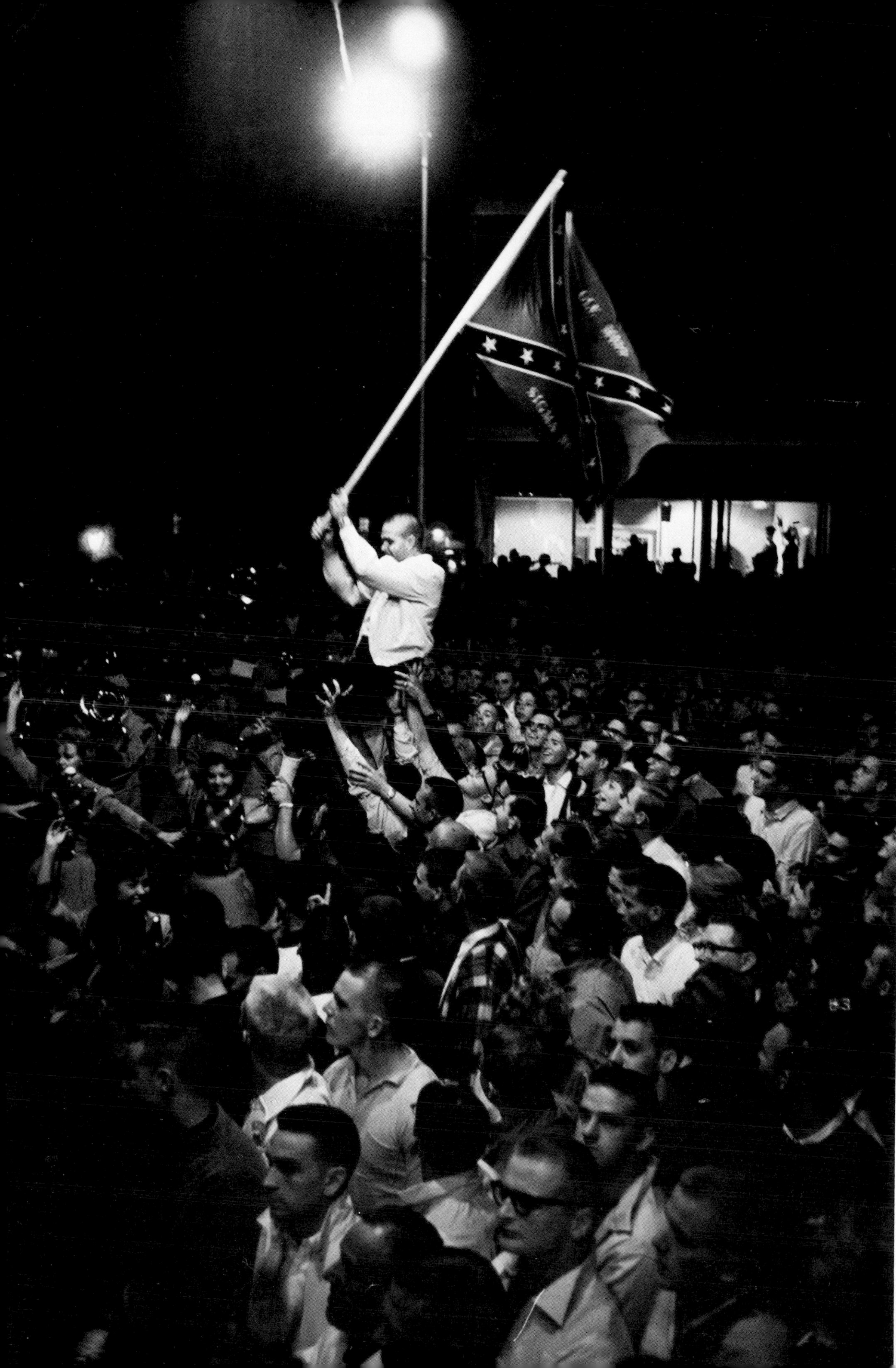

Flip Schulke

September 30, 1962. Anticipating trouble the next day, Barnett agrees to enroll Meredith even though it is Sunday.

7:00 P.M. The crowd on campus has grown to nearly two thousand. It is quickly becoming a mob. Reporter Gordon Yoder of Dallas, Texas, is viciously attacked by students when they see his TV camera. Governor Barnett gives his reluctant surrender statement: "My heart says 'never,' but my calm judgment abhors the bloodshed that would follow."

7:25 P.M. The Mississippi highway patrol withdraws from campus, leaving only the marshals and campus police to quell rioters. The mob grows.

7:50 P.M. Chief Federal Marshal McShane orders his men to fire tear gas in response to the onslaught of rocks, bricks, and Molotov cocktails from the rioters.

8:00 P.M. President Kennedy addresses the nation, saying, "Americans are free, in short, to disagree with the law, but not to disobey it . . . no man, however prominent and powerful, and no mob, however unruly or boisterous, is entitled to defy a court of law."

9:00 P.M. Retired Major General Edwin Walker stirs rioters to a frenzy. "I want to compliment you all on the protest you make tonight . . . don't let up now."

9:15 P.M. Paul Guillard, a French journalist slain by an unknown killer, becomes the first fatality.

9:25 P.M. The marshals are out of gas. They are fighting with billy clubs against guns, rocks, bricks, Molotov cocktails. Carloads of armed segregationists continue to arrive.

9:30 P.M. Assistant Attorney General Ramsey Clark orders Major General Walker's arrest.

9:50 P.M. A National Guard unit is called in. The crowd is pushing toward the administration building to get Meredith. Meredith is actually sleeping in a dormitory.

10:53 P.M. Agitators try to crash the administration building with a bulldozer. Army troops called earlier still haven't left Memphis.

11:00 P.M. Barnett makes a radio address, telling Mississippians that his ear-

Flip Schulke

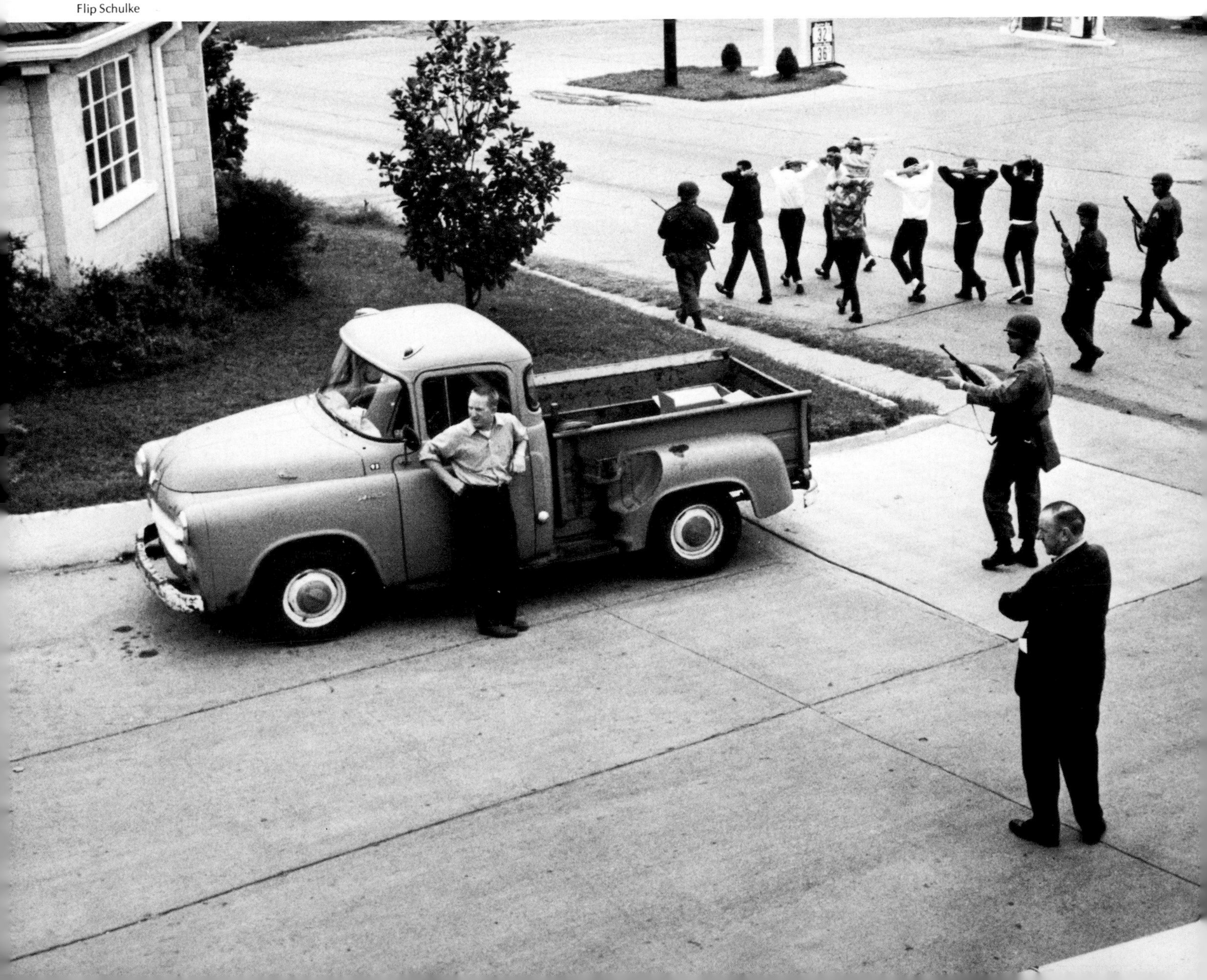

lier statement should not be interpreted as surrender. The crowd surges.

11:45 P.M. Two are dead: bystander Ray Gunter is shot and killed by a sniper.

October 1, 1962

12:10 A.M. Additional military police begin to arrive. Most of the troops still haven't moved.

2:00 A.M. The troops finally roll.

2:45 A.M. Eight hundred and forty more MP's are on their way. The marshals are taking prisoners.

5:00 A.M. The mob begins to retreat. The marshals have ninety-three prisoners.

7:30 A.M. Meredith is quietly registered by Registrar Robert Ellis after a sixteen-month battle.

9:00 A.M. A slightly-built, reserved black man takes a seat in his first class at Ole Miss: Colonial American History.

Through all of the indignities that followed Meredith's original application to Ole Miss, he retained *his* dignity. Later King was to say of him: **"One day the South will recognize its real heroes. They will be the James Merediths, with the noble sense of purpose that enables them to face jeering and hostile mobs, and with the agonizing loneliness that characterizes the life of the pioneer."**

National Guardsmen, federalized by President Kennedy, round up rioters on the morning after the bloody battle.

After a night of bloodshed, Meredith is enrolled as an Ole Miss student. The subsequent days were lonely ones, as white students refused to recognize his presence.

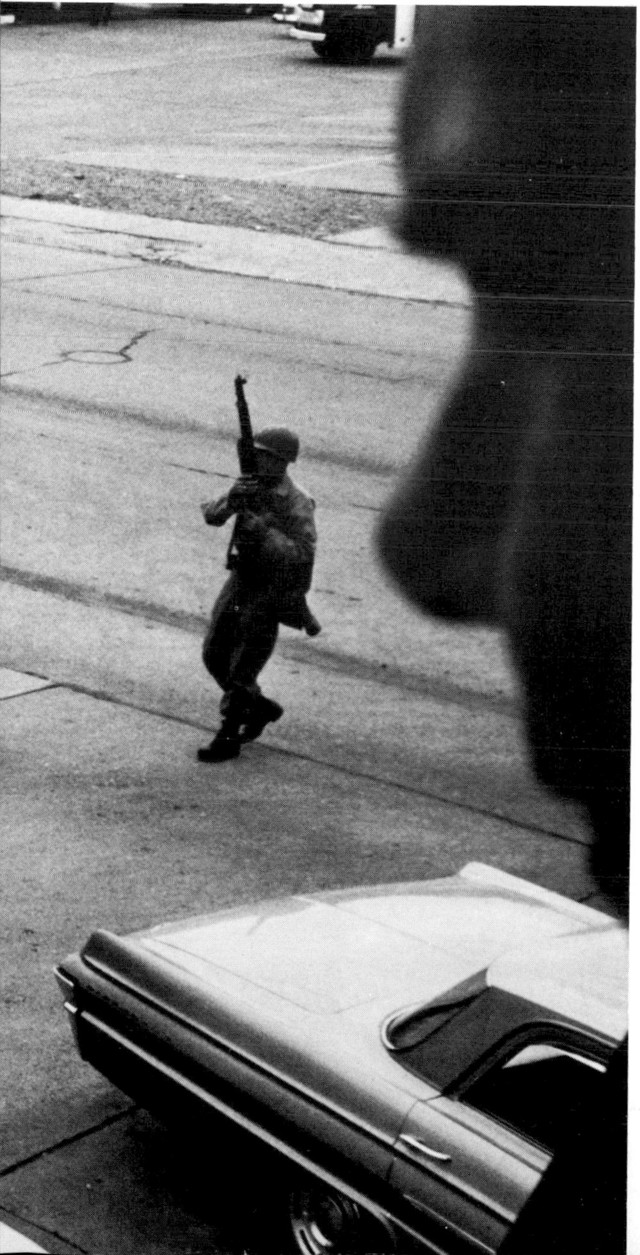

Flip Schulke

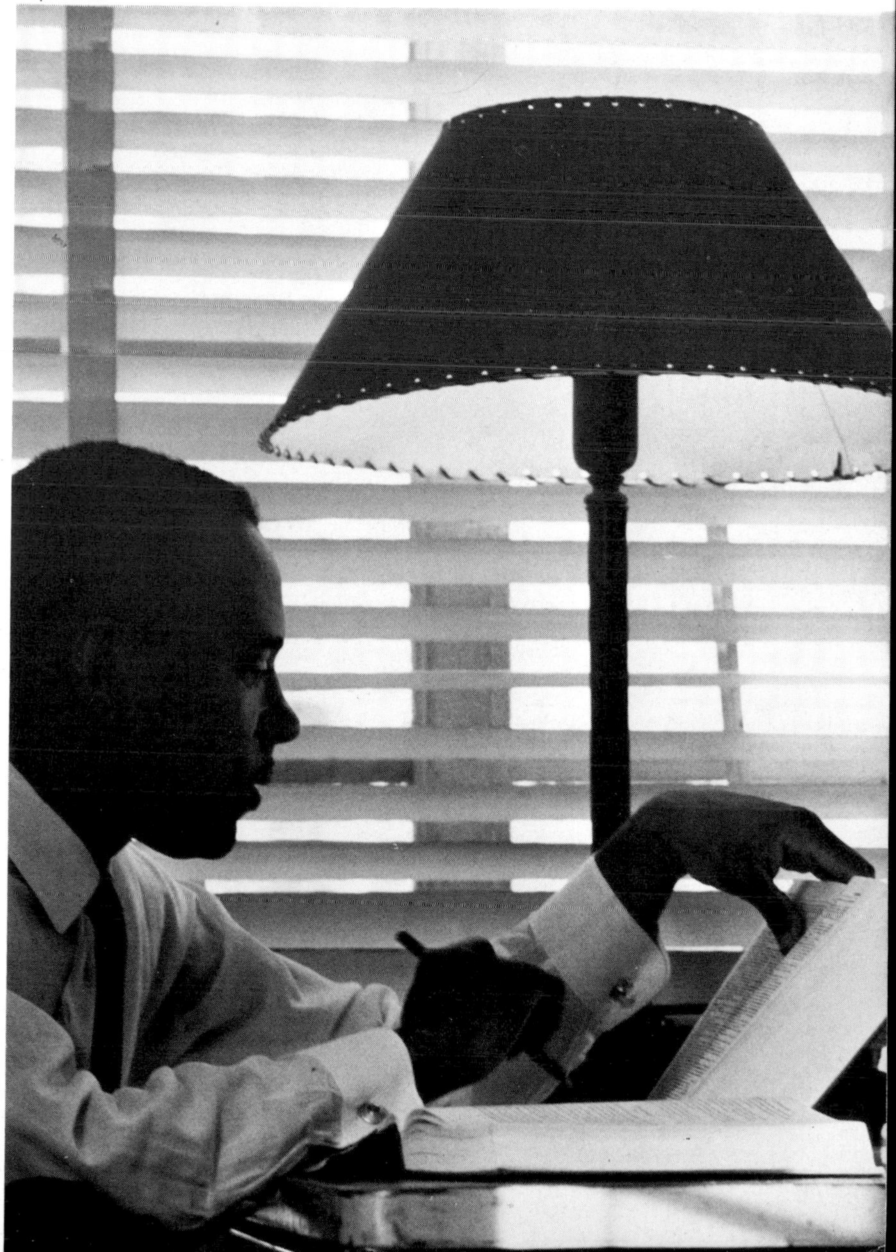

Charles Moore

Chapter Four

"Freedom Must Be Demanded"

Birmingham, 1963 When the *Birmingham News* appeared on the stands on Wednesday, April 3, 1963, celebrating Albert Boutwell's mayoral victory over Eugene T. ("Bull") Connor, the front-page headline blared: "New Day Dawns for Birmingham." The irony was not yet apparent. Birmingham's white citizens could not have known that King and his colleagues were ready to initiate Project "C" that very day in their city. Nor did they know that the "C" stood for confrontation.

LETTER FROM BIRMINGHAM JAIL

On April 12, 1963, King, Abernathy, and a group of demonstrators were arrested for violating a Birmingham court injunction against demonstrations. While in jail, King composed a letter responding to eight fellow clergymen who had called his activities in Birmingham "unwise and unjust." The complete text of the letter, from which the following excerpts are taken, begins on page 214.

. . . Nonviolent direct action seeks to create such a crisis and foster such a tension that a community which has constantly refused to negotiate is forced to confront the issue. It seeks so to dramatize the issue that it can no longer be ignored. . . . We know through painful experience that freedom is never voluntarily given by the oppressor; it must be demanded by the oppressed. . . . For years now I have heard the word "Wait!" It rings in the ear of every Negro with piercing familiarity. This "Wait" has almost always meant "Never." . . .

. . . Perhaps it is easy for those who have never felt the stinging darts of segregation to say, "Wait." But when you have seen vicious mobs lynch your mothers and fathers at will and drown your sisters and brothers at whim; when you have seen hate-filled policemen curse, kick, and even kill your black brothers and sisters; when you see the vast majority of your twenty million Negro brothers smothering in an airtight cage of poverty in the midst of an affluent society; . . . when you are forever fighting a degenerating sense of "nobodiness"—then you will understand why we find it difficult to wait. There comes a time when the cup of endurance runs over, and men are no longer willing to be plunged into the abyss of despair. . . .

. . . I have been arrested on a charge of parading without a permit. Now, there is nothing wrong in having an ordinance which requires a permit for a parade. But such an ordinance becomes unjust when it is used to maintain segregation and to deny citizens the First-Amendment privilege of peaceful assembly and protest.

I hope you are able to see the distinction I am trying to point out. In no sense do I advocate evading or defying the law, as would the rabid segregationist. That would lead to anarchy. One who breaks an unjust law must do so openly, lovingly, and with a willingness to accept the penalty. I submit that an individual who breaks a law that conscience tells him is unjust, and who willingly accepts the penalty of imprisonment in order to arouse the conscience of the community over its injustice, is in reality expressing the highest respect for law.

. . . though I was initially disappointed at being categorized as an extremist, as I continued to think about the matter I gradually gained a measure of satisfaction from the label. Was not Jesus an extremist for love: "Love your enemies, bless them that curse you, do good to them that hate you, and pray for them which despitefully use you, and persecute you." . . . Was not Martin Luther an extremist: "Here I stand; I cannot do otherwise, so help me God." . . . And Thomas Jefferson: "We hold these truths to be self-evident, that all men are created equal. . . ." So the question is not whether we will be extremists, but what kind of extremists we will be. . . .

. . . I have no fear about the outcome of our struggle in Birmingham, even if our motives are at present misunderstood. We will reach the goal of freedom in Birmingham and all over the nation, because the goal of America is freedom. Abused and scorned though we may be, our destiny is tied up with America's destiny. . . . If the inexpressible cruelties of slavery could not stop us, the opposition we now face will surely fail. We will win our freedom because the sacred heritage of our nation and the eternal will of God are embodied in our echoing demands.

King in the Birmingham ja[il]

Birmingham police arresting King on Good Friday, April 12, 1963. This was the first time the protestors had defied a court order.

Charles Moore

64

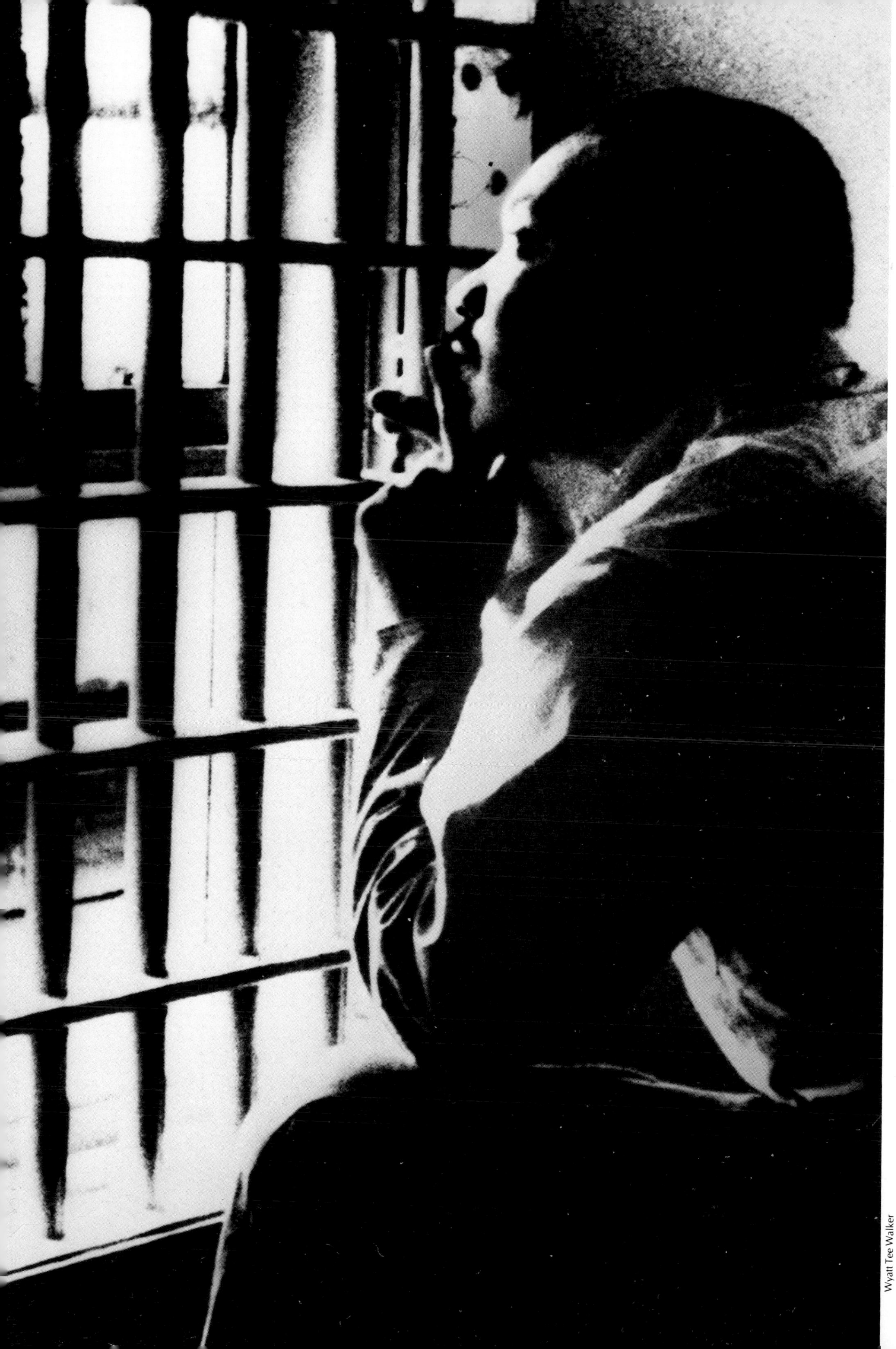

Wyatt Tee Walker

AN INTERVIEW WITH CONGRESSMAN ANDREW J. YOUNG

Andrew J. Young, *member of the United States House of Representatives from the state of Georgia. Formerly executive vice president of SCLC. He joined the organization in 1961 and was director from 1964 to 1967. Young is an ordained minister of the United Church of Christ.*

"I started working with Martin basically in 1961 out of Atlanta, but the first major confrontation operation I was involved in was in Birmingham in 1963....

"Martin kept very much in touch. . . . He concentrated largely on the morale of the people who would become his troops. He worked a lot with the students. He spent his time, say, in the morning with black business leaders, helping them understand the process of a nonviolent movement. In the evenings after school, he would meet with the students from the high schools or colleges and encourage them to support the movement.

"When the students began to get involved in demonstrations, everybody was ready and the whole school system unloaded. We had better than five thousand people in jail within a week. But it was because months of preparation had gone before that.

"Everybody looks at the Birmingham demonstration and thinks that there was some sort of miracle performed, but it was a lot of hard work. Birmingham was not a nonviolent city. Birmingham was probably the most violent city in America, and every black family had an arsenal. To talk in terms of nonviolence to the blacks in Birmingham was really . . . folks would look at you like you were crazy because they had been bombing black homes. They had been beating up black people and the blacks thought that there was no alternative for them but to kill or be killed.

"They were trained to understand that Bull Connor wanted them to fight back, and that it was not really brave to throw a rock at somebody who had a machine gun. That was stupid. They understood that the Wallace forces and the Connor forces could deal with violence, because if violence broke out they had an excuse to machine-gun a large number of black people. They didn't have that excuse if there was nonviolence.

"Birmingham really pulled together this coalition of conscience which ran this nation from 1963 until the time of Vietnam, in say, sixty-six. That's three years. That coalition of conscience and good will passed the Civil Rights Act of 1964, which not only desegregated public accommodations but gave new statutes in terms of school desegregation and desegregated jobs; it paved the way for the popular programs and all sorts of people-oriented legislation that came out of the sixties. It gave birth to the great society, and it was a coalition of labor, civil rights, young white college students, and church people. Whether you agree with it philosophically or not, practically the only thing that would have worked in the south was a nonviolent approach to social change."

Andrew You

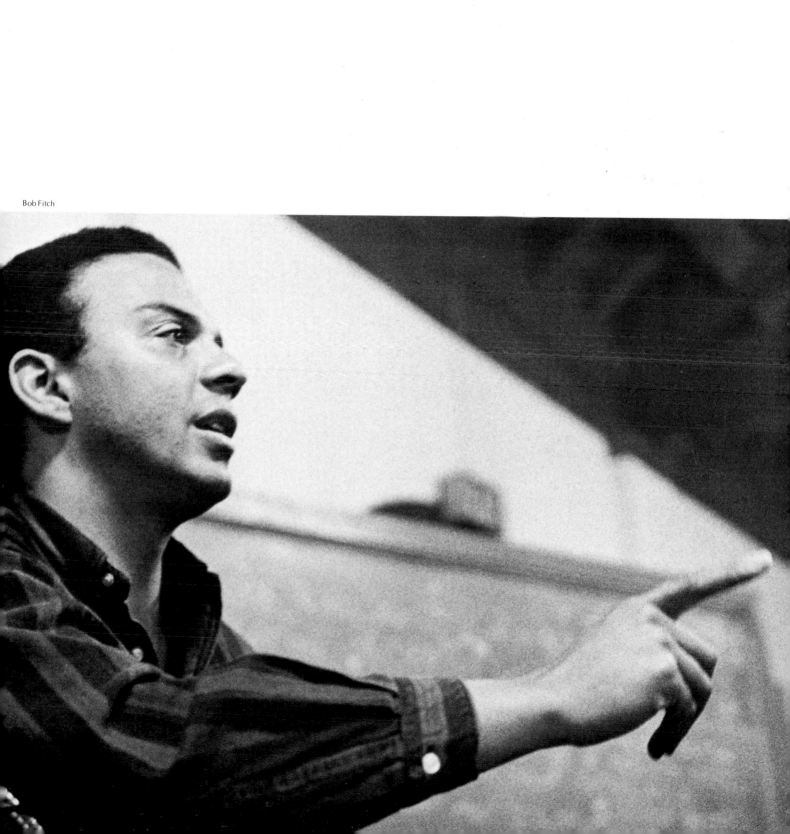

Bob Fitch

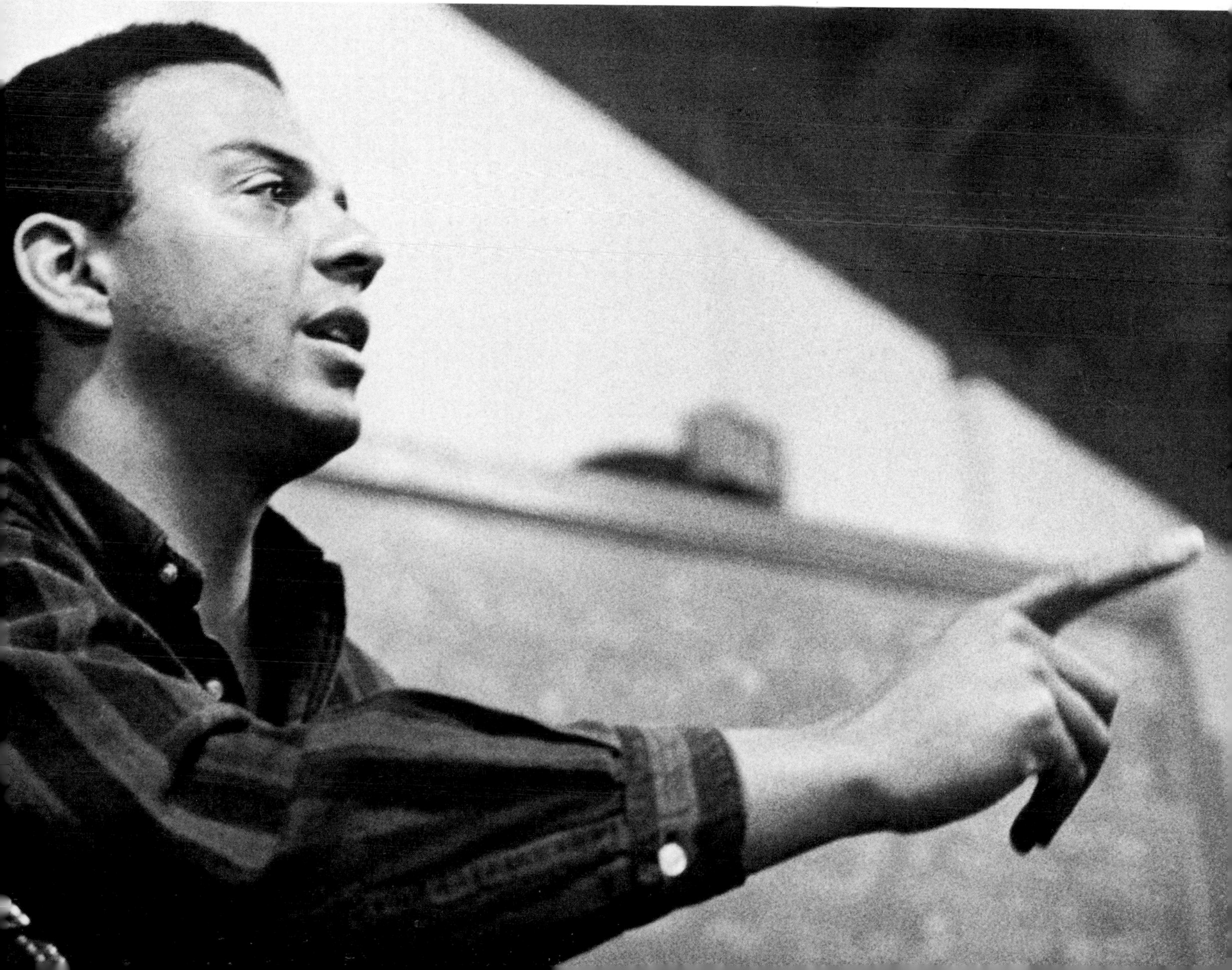

Birmingham's racist position had long been personified by Bull Connor, the city's commissioner of public safety. When King and the SCLC agreed to work with Reverend Fred Shuttlesworth, a respected Birmingham civil rights leader, the city was governed by three commissioners. However, in the spring of 1963, Birmingham was to change over to a government by a mayor and city council, and Connor was the leading mayoral candidate. Although both of his opponents were admitted segregationists, they were more moderate than he.

King postponed the Birmingham demonstrations for six months, fearing that a direct action by blacks would antagonize the white population enough to help Connor win the election.

But even after his defeat, Connor was to be King's principal antagonist in Birmingham. Despite the results of the runoff election, the three city commissioners had taken the position that they could not legally be removed from office until 1965, when their terms expired. So, for the duration of the Birmingham movement, the city was effectually operating under two governments.

King opened the Birmingham campaign the day after the election, promising to lead demonstrations until **"Pharaoh lets God's people go."** The activities of the first few days were limited to sit-ins. Having learned a lesson in Albany, King knew the importance of starting cautiously, devising a long-term strategy, and consolidating forces. He spent the early days attempting to rally the support of Birmingham's black community and its leaders. He was surprised to find that many blacks echoed the opinion of Attorney General Robert Kennedy that the protest was ill-timed. Give the new mayor a chance, they said. Without Bull Connor, the situation is certain to improve.

But King had already delayed Project "C" twice, and he agreed with his associate Fred Shuttlesworth that Boutwell was "just a dignified Bull Connor."

King and his co-workers established four goals for the Birmingham protest.

The beginning of nonviolent demonstrations in Birmingham's commercial district, April, 1963.

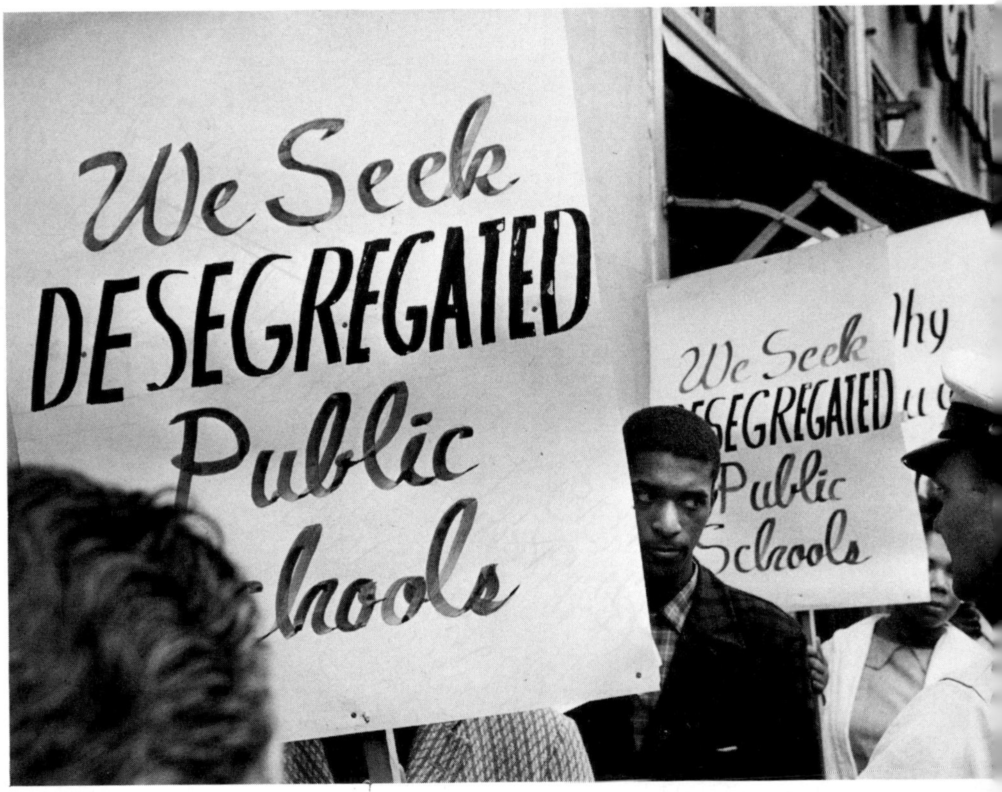
We Seek
DESEGREGATED
Public
chools
We Seek
ESEGREGATED
Public
Schools

Flip Schulke

The desegregation of lunchcounters, fitting rooms, rest rooms, and drinking fountains in department stores; the upgrading and hiring of blacks throughout the industrial and commercial community; amnesty for the demonstrators; and the creation of a biracial committee to work out a timetable for desegregation elsewhere in the city.

The Birmingham confrontation went into full swing on April 6 when a group of carefully selected demonstrators marched on City Hall. As they approached the government center, the police ordered the marchers to disperse. When they refused, the protestors were quietly escorted into paddy wagons. Connor, too, had learned a lesson from Albany. He remembered Laurie Pritchett's success in combatting nonviolence with nonviolence.

Each day the demonstrations grew stronger. So, too, did the Easter boycott of downtown stores. King had purposely chosen the busy Easter shopping season for his boycott, and, in contrast to their fellows in Albany, Birmingham's black population wielded enough economic clout to make their nonsupport felt.

Meanwhile, Connor decided to move from the streets into the courts. He was convinced he had effectively stopped the movement when a court injunction

Demonstrators pour out of Birmingham's Sixteenth Street Baptist Church, which became the gathering place for the Birmingham movement.

Charles Moore

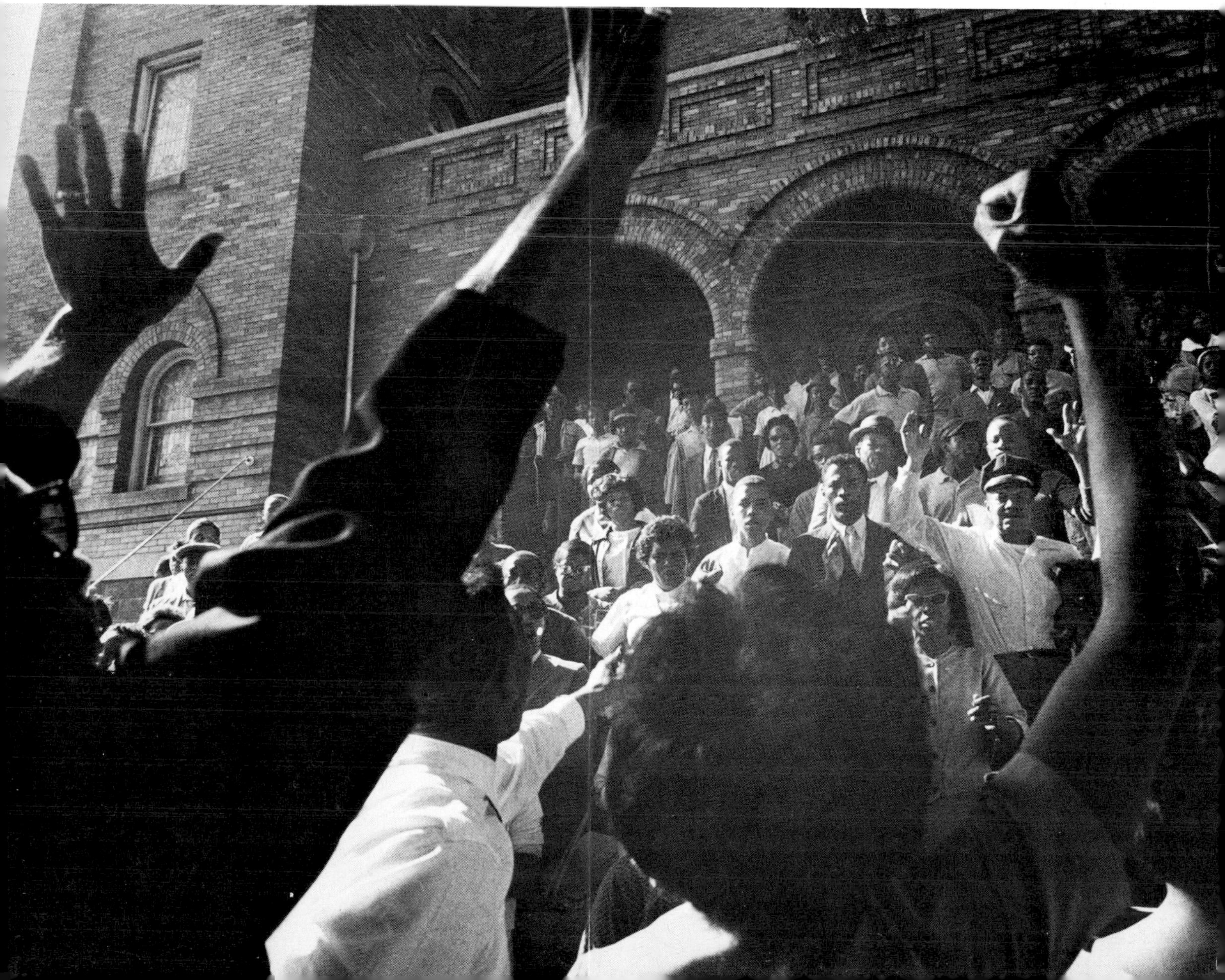

ordered the demonstrations to halt. King had never before violated a court order. But the civil rights leader and his staff had already chosen their course of action in the event of such an order. King told his people, in the words of St. Augustine, that **"an unjust law is no law at all."** Men, he said, were required to obey only just laws. And he defined a just law as one that **"squares with the moral law, or the law of God."** As he was to write several days later from his jail cell: **"Any law that uplifts human personality is just. Any law that degrades human personality is unjust. All segregation statutes are unjust because segregation distorts the soul and damages the personality."**

And so, for the first time, civil disobedience and the nonviolent movement merged.

King announced that he and Ralph Abernathy would go to jail on Good Friday, even though he knew there might be no money with which to post bond. **"It's better to go to jail with dignity,"** he said, **"than accept segregation in humility."**

His nemesis, Bull Connor, responded, "You can rest assured that I will fill the jail if they [the Negroes] violate the laws as long as I am in City Hall."

On April 12, almost one thousand black people lined the streets and sang "We Shall Overcome" when King and Abernathy led their group toward downtown Birmingham. They had marched only eight blocks when Connor ordered his men to arrest the fifty-three demonstrators and their leaders.

Police dogs are turned onto the demonstrators by order of Eugene "Bull" Connor, commissioner of public safety.

Charles Moore

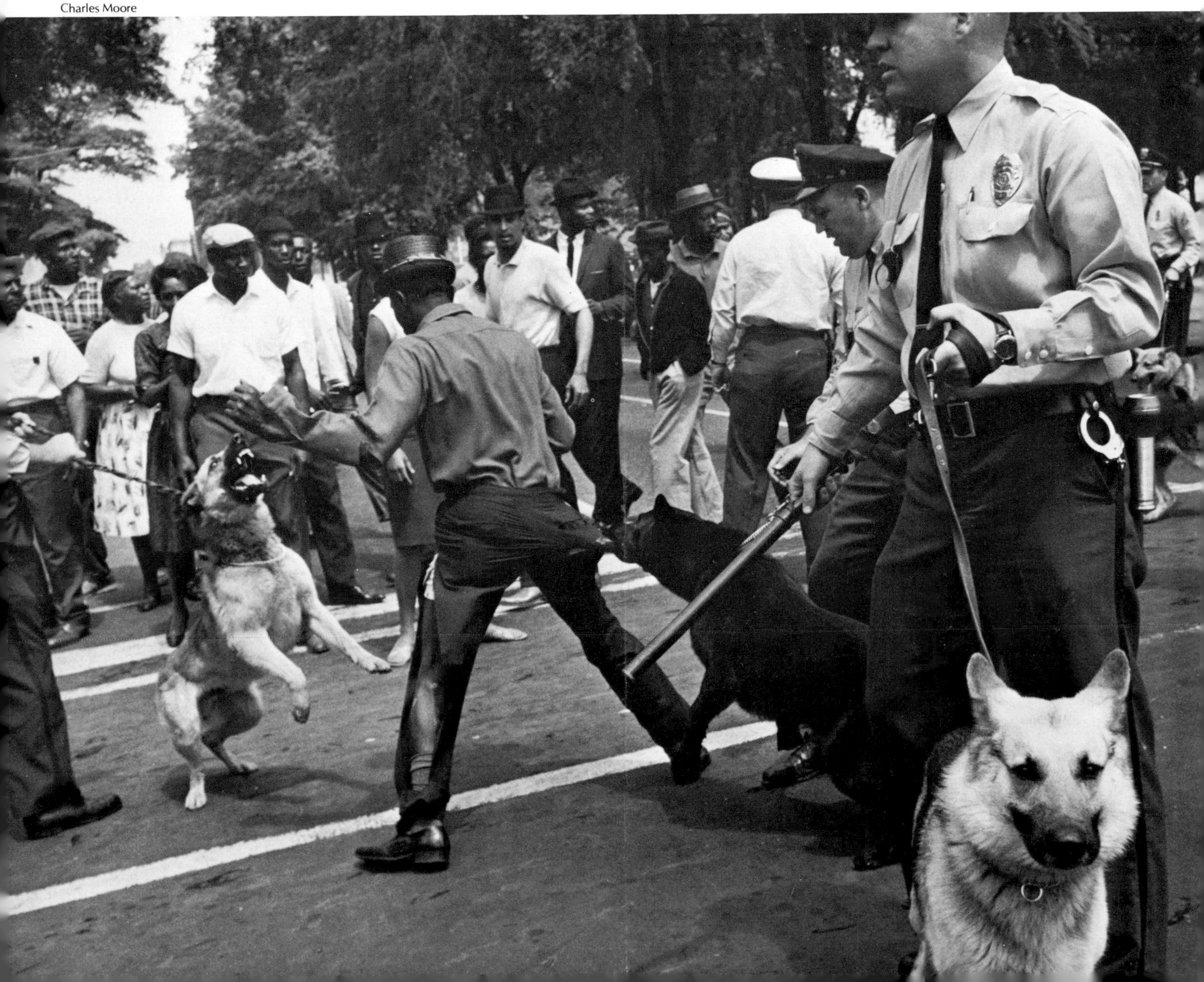

King was placed in solitary confinement and was not allowed to make any phone calls—even to his wife, who had just given birth to their fourth child two weeks before. Coretta King attempted to call President Kennedy; failing to reach him, she spoke to his brother, the attorney general. The next day, the president telephoned Mrs. King and assured her that the FBI had been to see her husband, that he was fine and would be home shortly. A few minutes later, King called home. Only then did he learn of the president's intervention.

On Easter Sunday, while King remained in jail, several small groups of blacks sought admittance to six white churches. Several, including King's lieutenant Andrew Young, were welcomed cordially by white clergymen. Others were turned away rudely.

King was released from jail when his friend Harry Belafonte raised fifty thousand dollars to use toward bail. The singer promised to raise whatever King and his demonstrators needed.

It was at this point that the Birmingham Movement became a children's crusade. King was criticized sharply for risking the lives of children in the protests. But that move was to influence significantly the course of the entire civil rights movement.

Birmingham's black students were proselytized and trained in nonviolence. On May 2 they were ready to lend their support to the struggle. Over one thousand young people were arrested that day as they set out from the Sixteenth Street Baptist Church. They sang freedom songs as they were carted off to jail.

Even more students marched the following day, chanting "We Want Freedom" as they went. When they were ordered to stop, they continued marching and chanting. Livid, Connor ordered fire engines to turn their high-powered hoses on the demonstrators. Knocked to the sidewalks by crushing streams of water, the young people remembered their lessons in nonviolence.

Bull Connor. "The civil rights movement owes Bull Connor as much as it owes Abraham Lincoln," said President Kennedy.

Charles Moore

But across the street in Kelly Ingram Park, the fifteen hundred spectators were not part of King's disciplined, nonviolent army. Angry at the treatment of these children, they began shouting threats. They threw rocks, bottles and bricks at policemen.

This was all the excuse Bull Connor needed to abandon his nonviolent tactics. The mood changed in Birmingham when he unleashed his police dogs. The next day newspapers throughout the world carried photographs of dogs biting black children.

"Look at 'em run," Bull Connor was heard to say, "look at those niggers run." But in fact, most of them did not run. They stood their ground and turned their cheek. When Reverend Shuttlesworth was blasted by high-pressure hoses and injured, Connor told a newsman, "I waited to see Shuttlesworth get hit with a hose. I'm sorry I missed it. I wish they'd carried him away in a hearse."

The violence continued, Alabama Governor George Wallace promised to "take whatever action I am called upon to take" to preserve law and order. The laws he intended to preserve were Alabama's segregation laws.

With the mounting pressure of world opinion, the Kennedy administration was finally forced to intervene to seek a truce in Birmingham. Assistant Attorney General Burke Marshall was sent to represent the president in negotiations. But

Charles Moore

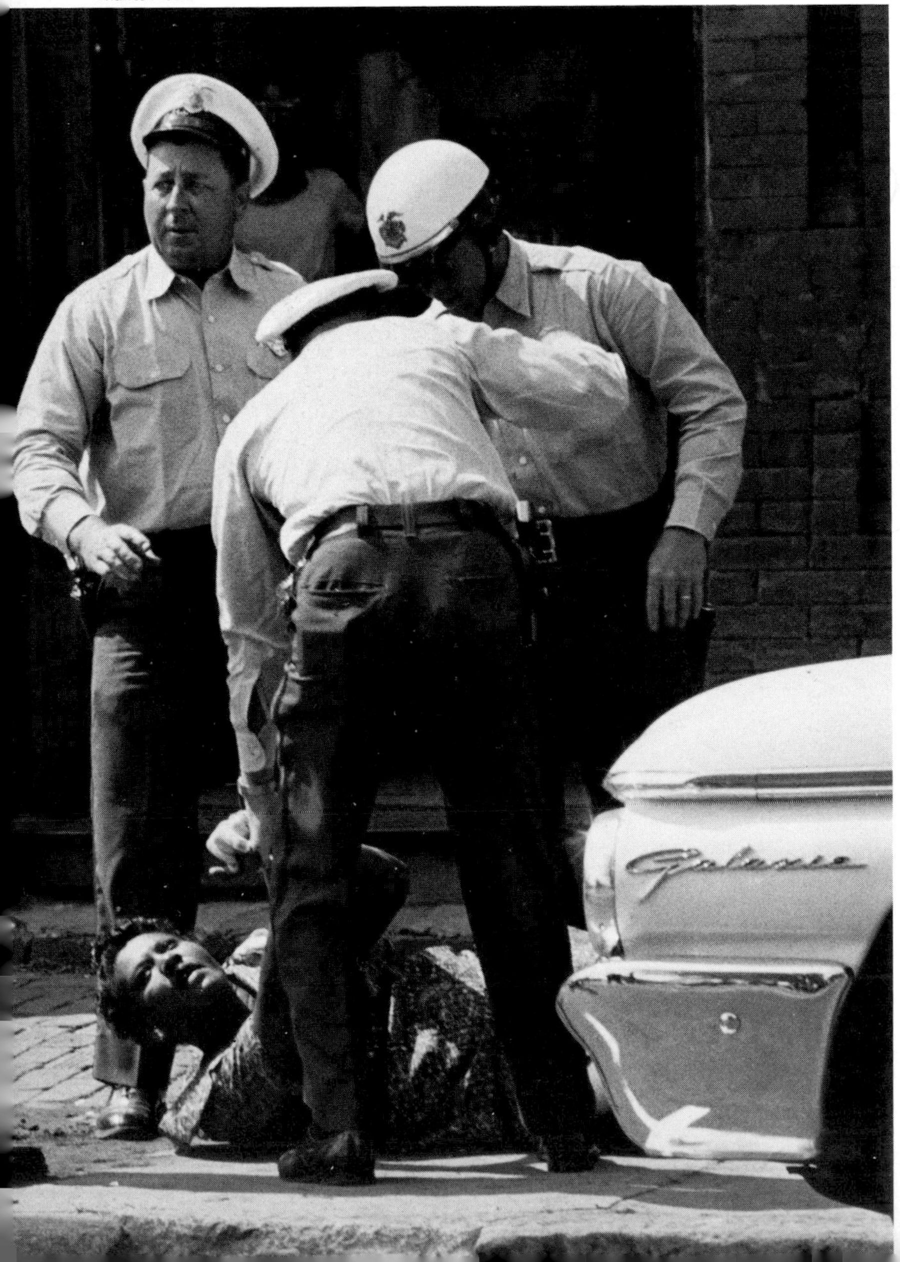
Galaxie

Charles Moore

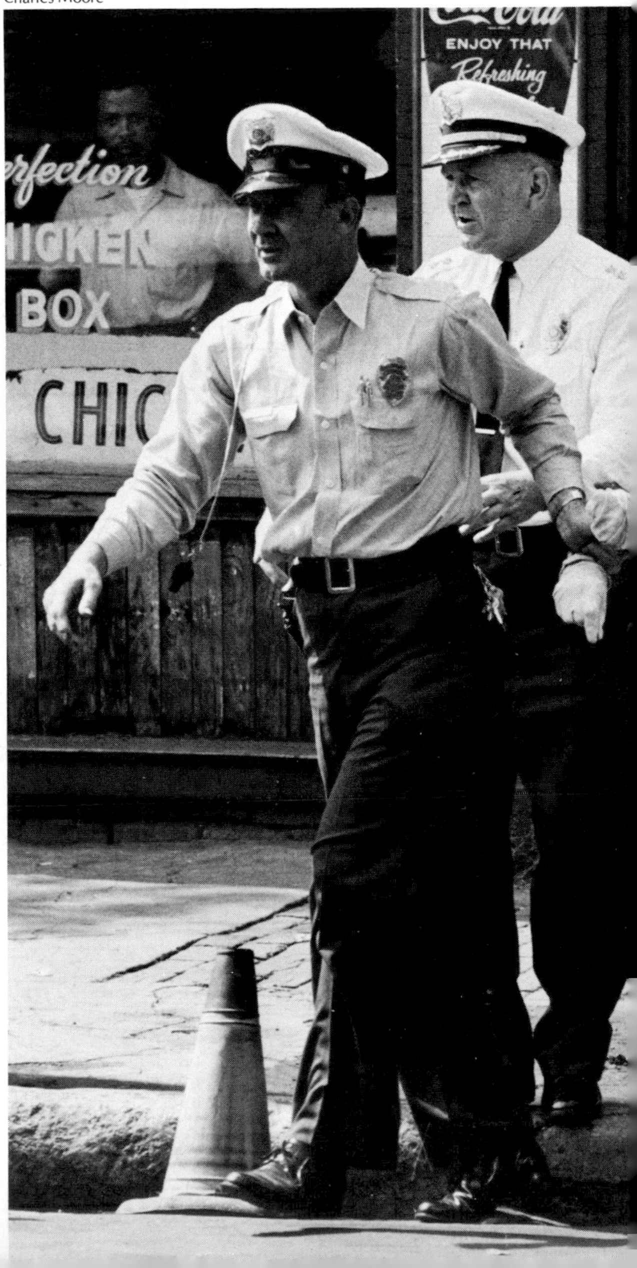
ENJOY THAT
Refreshing
BOX
CHIC

King had no intention of easing the pressure until the black peoples' demands were met. **"If the white power structure of this city will meet some of our minimum demands, we will consider calling off the demonstrations,"** he said. **"But we want promises, plus action."**

The demonstrations and violence continued while negotiations were taking place. At the height of the campaign, there were over twenty-five hundred protestors in jail.

"Activities which have taken place in Birmingham over the last few days, to my mind, mark the nonviolent movement's coming of age," said King. **"This is the first time in the history of our struggle that we have been able, literally, to fill the jails."** The same day, May 8, his chief antagonist, Bull Connor, said: "We have just started to fight, if that's what they want. We were trying to be nice to them, but they won't let us be nice."

The Birmingham black and white citizens finally reached an agreement on May 10. But the city's troubles were far from over. The next night, following a meeting of the Ku Klux Klan, a bomb wracked the house of King's brother, Reverend A. D. King. A second explosion blasted King's headquarters in Room 30 of the Gaston Motel.

The truce was forgotten. Thousands of angry blacks poured into the streets. Fighting ensued. People who had never been part of the nonviolent movement took the bombings as their cue. Despite

Overleaf:
photo by Charles Moore

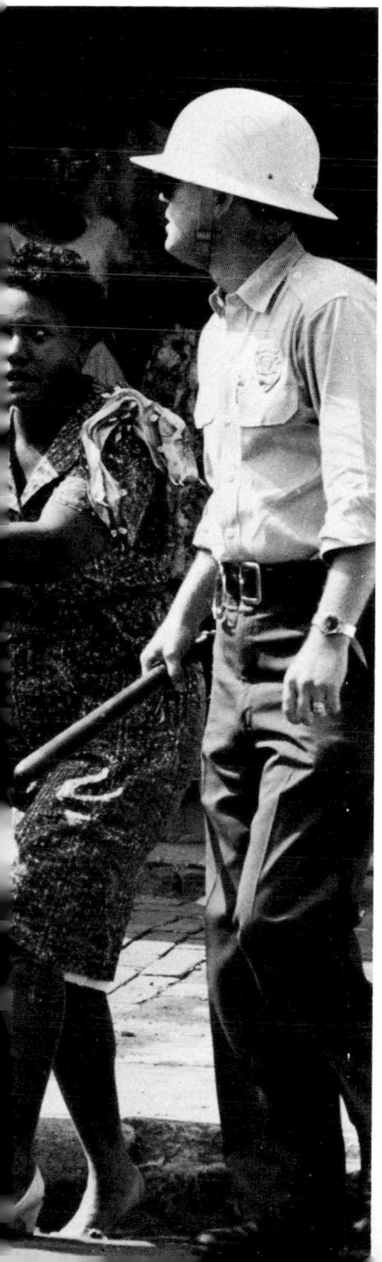

Charles Moore

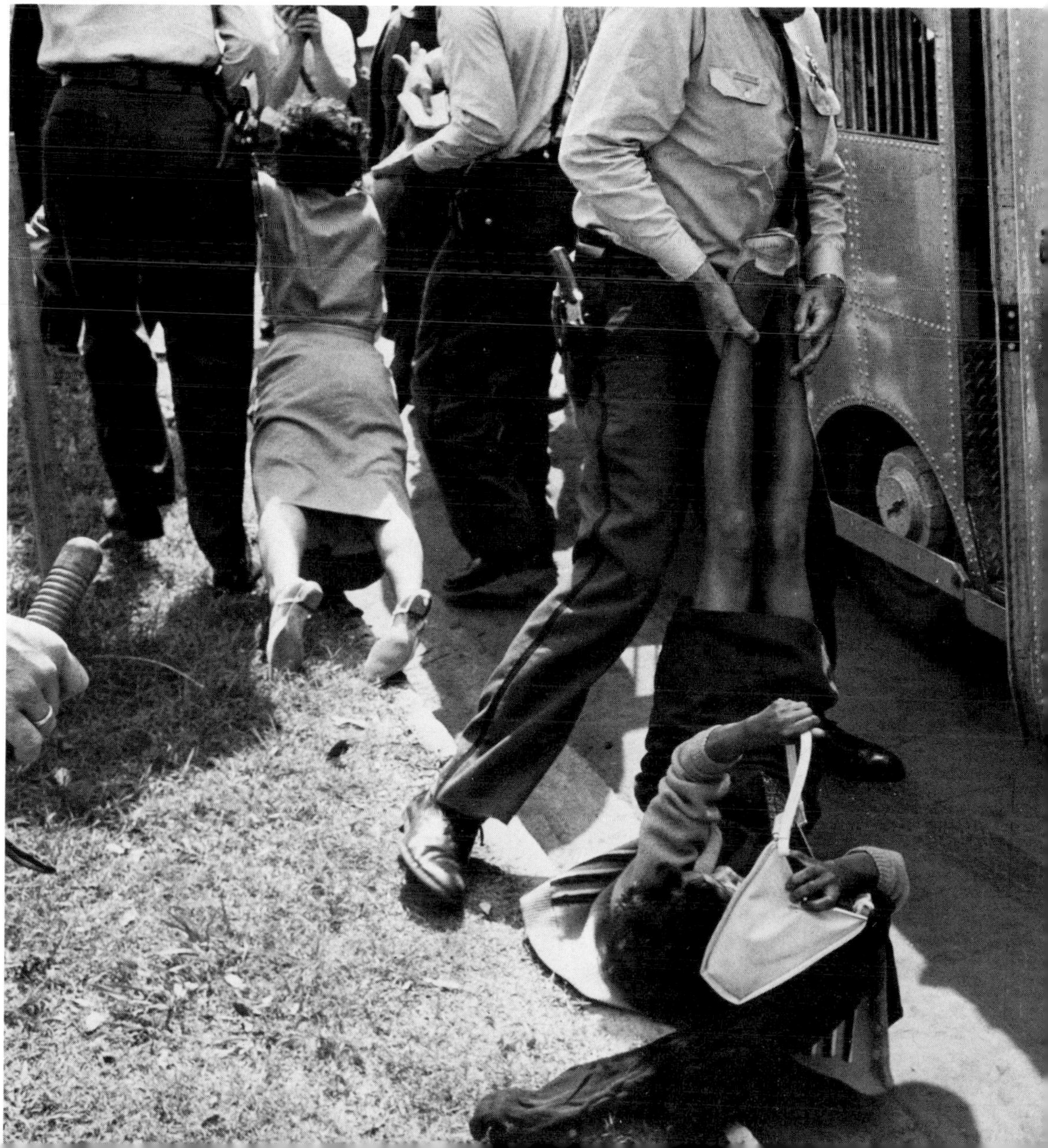

The police become more violent in their response to the demonstrations.

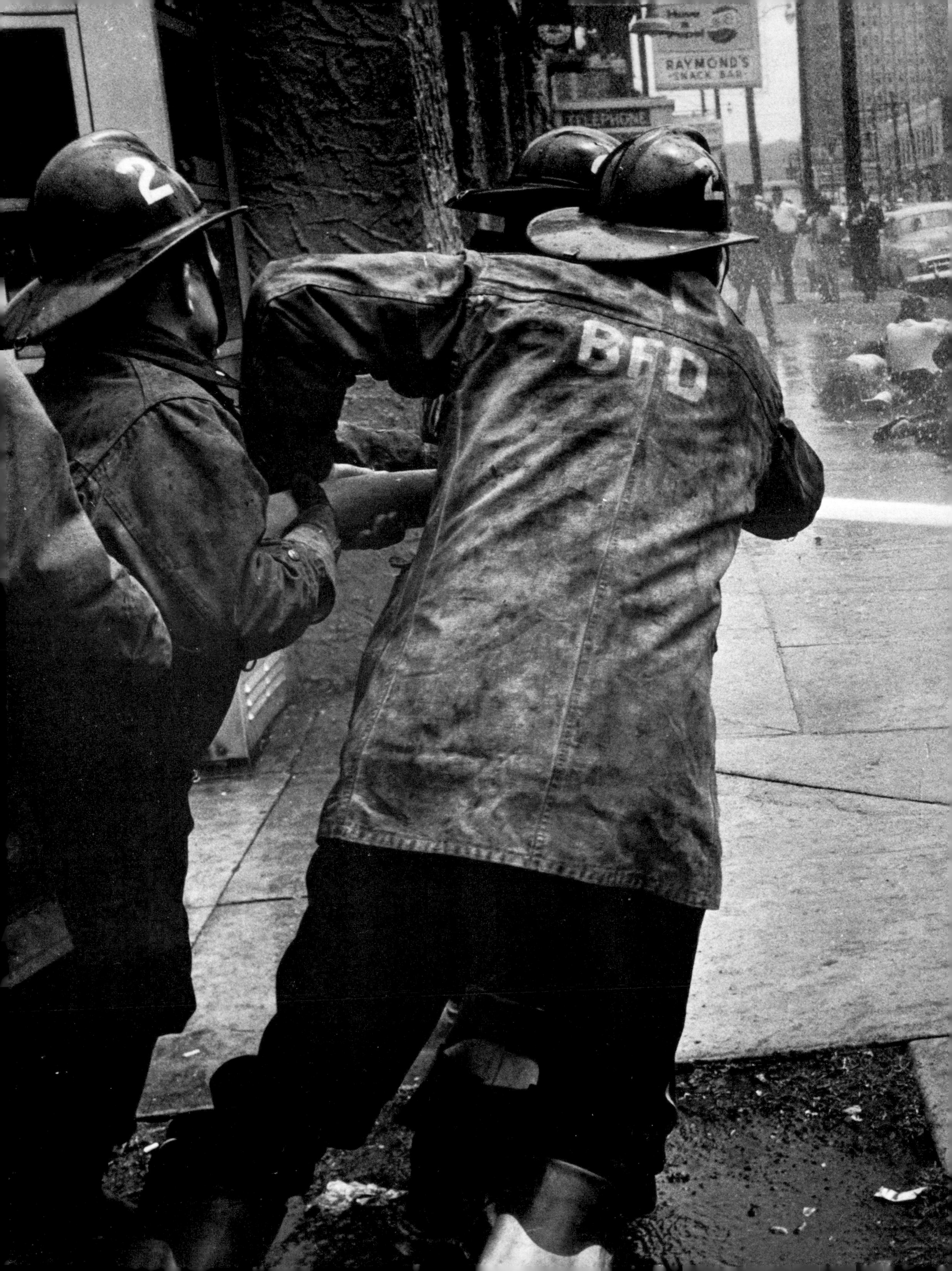
RAYMOND'S
SNACK BAR
2
BFD

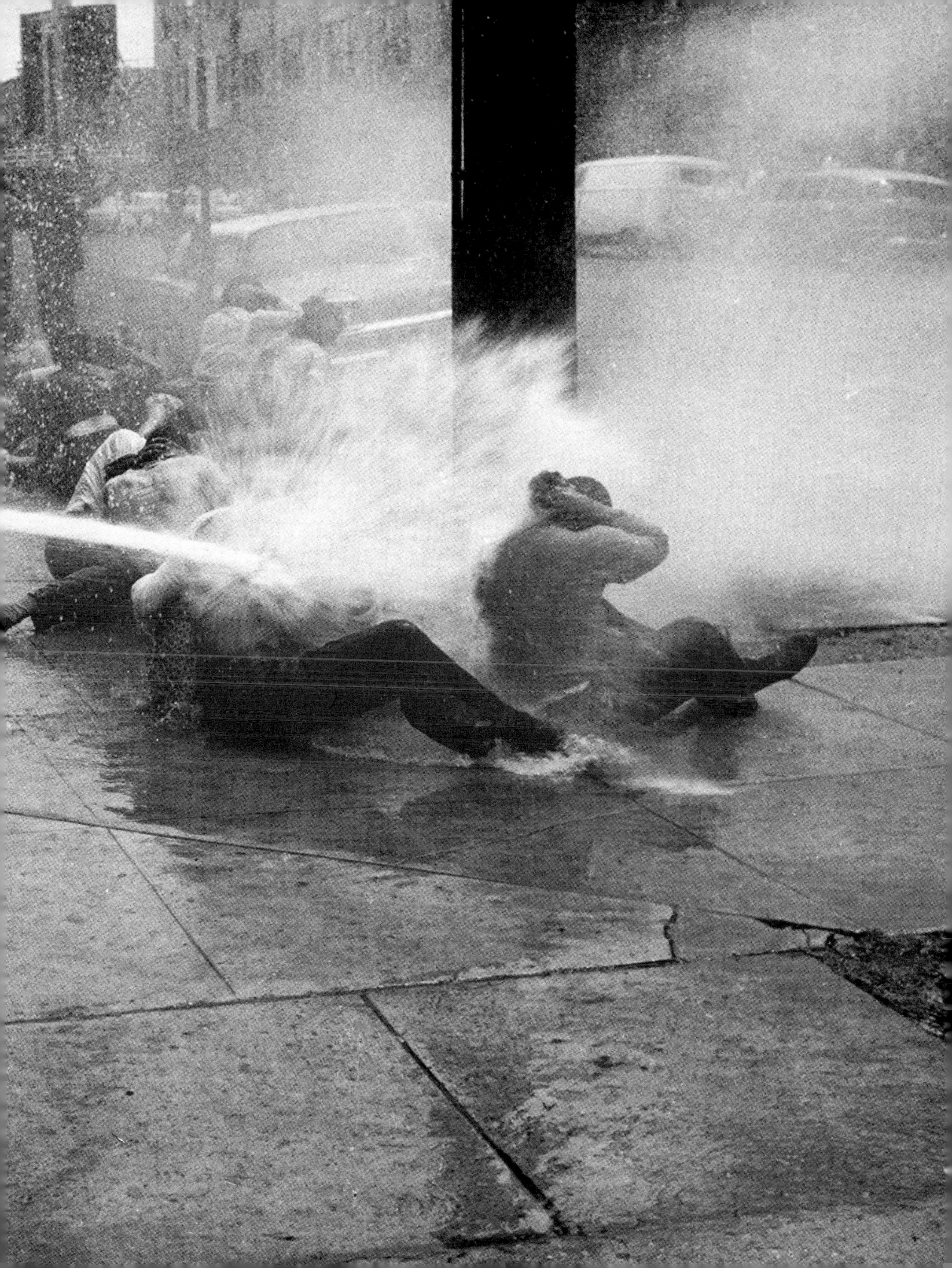

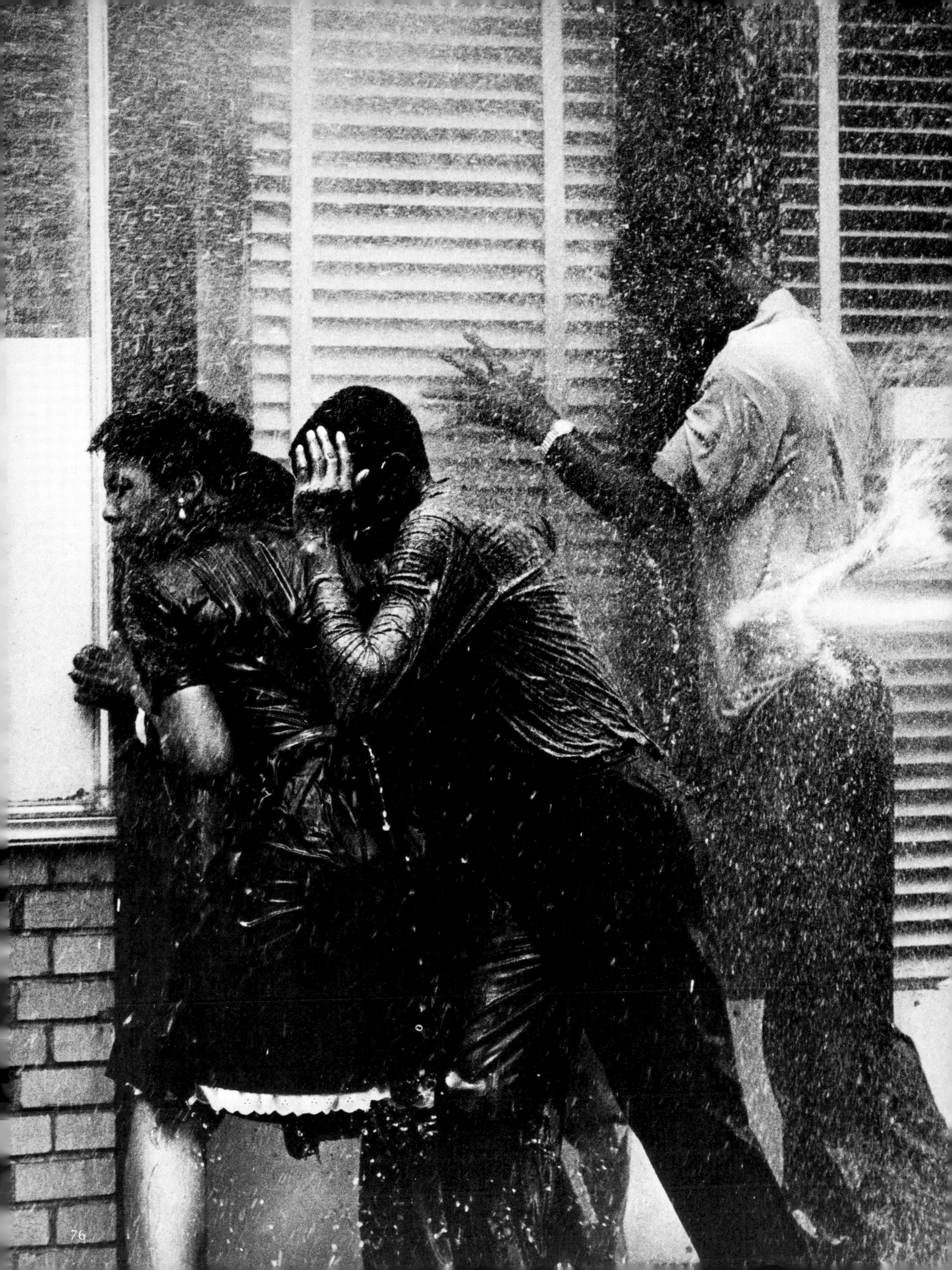

the urging of men like Wyatt Tee Walker and A. D. King, the enraged blacks burned and looted white establishments.

By the next day, Mother's Day, 250 state troopers had been called into the riot-torn city. President Kennedy told the nation that the federal government intended to protect the agreement, and he ordered three thousand federal troops to military bases near Birmingham to stand by.

King, feeling that the bombings had been intended to create just this kind of violent reaction, set out on his "poolroom pilgrimage." He and Abernathy walked into bars and pool halls to plead with young black men not to walk into the trap of violence that was being set for them.

Tensions eased over the next few weeks, and, simultaneously, the Alabama Supreme Court ruled that Connor and the two other city commissioners had no right to remain in office. Connor no longer held power in Birmingham.

That summer the civil rights movement spread from the South to the rest of the nation. In Chicago, Los Angeles, and Detroit black people were demanding "Freedom Now." In June, 1963, President Kennedy asked Congress to pass the most far-reaching civil rights bill ever proposed by a president.

Four months later, the deaths of four children in Birmingham would prove that the battle was not yet over, but, as King pointed out to his followers, victory was **"close at hand."**

Overleaf:
Jubilant black youths sing freedom songs in downtown Birmingham, and a settlement is successfully negotiated on May 10, 1963.
photo by Charles Moore

A shaft of water pins three demonstrators against the front of a building.

Charles Moore

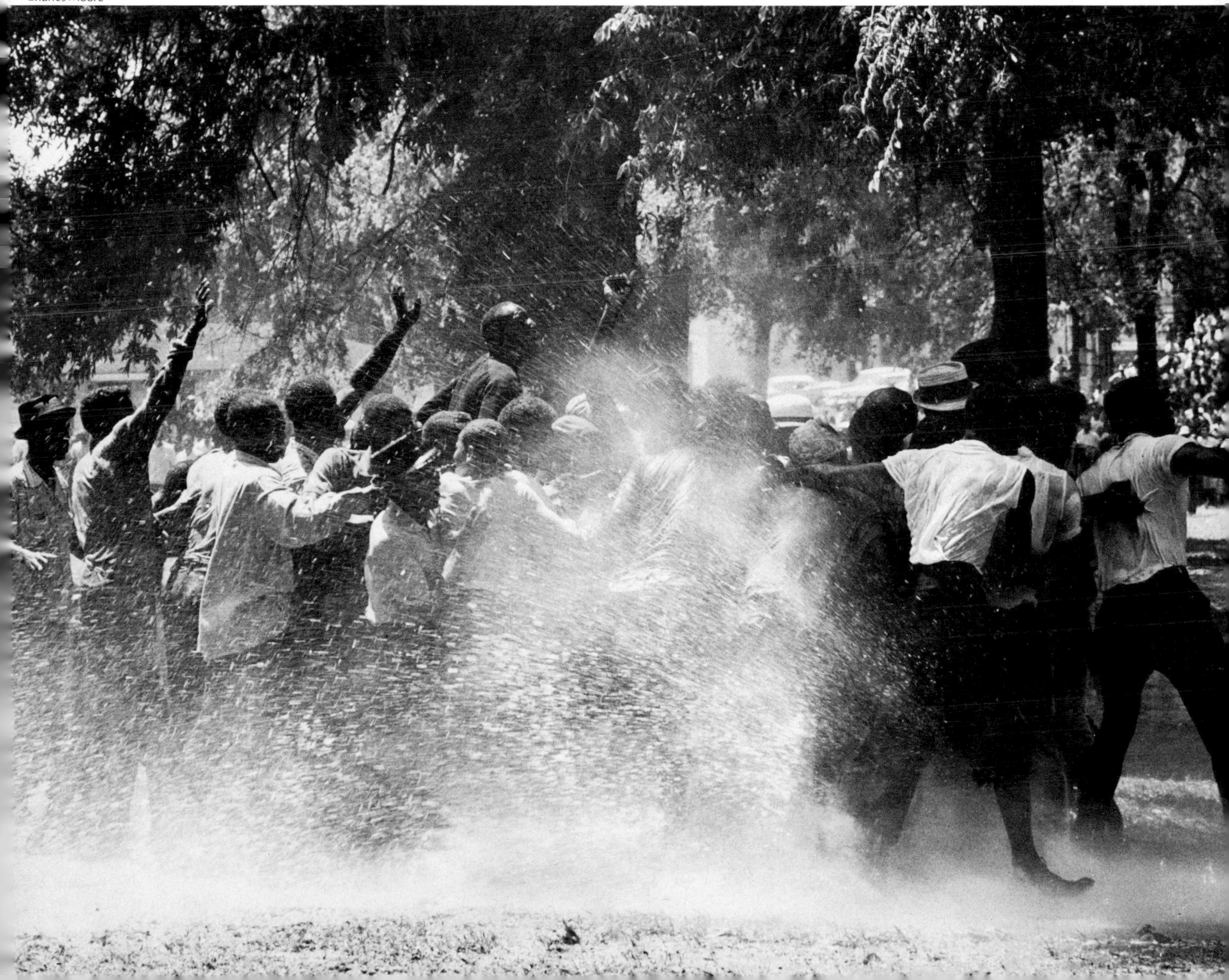

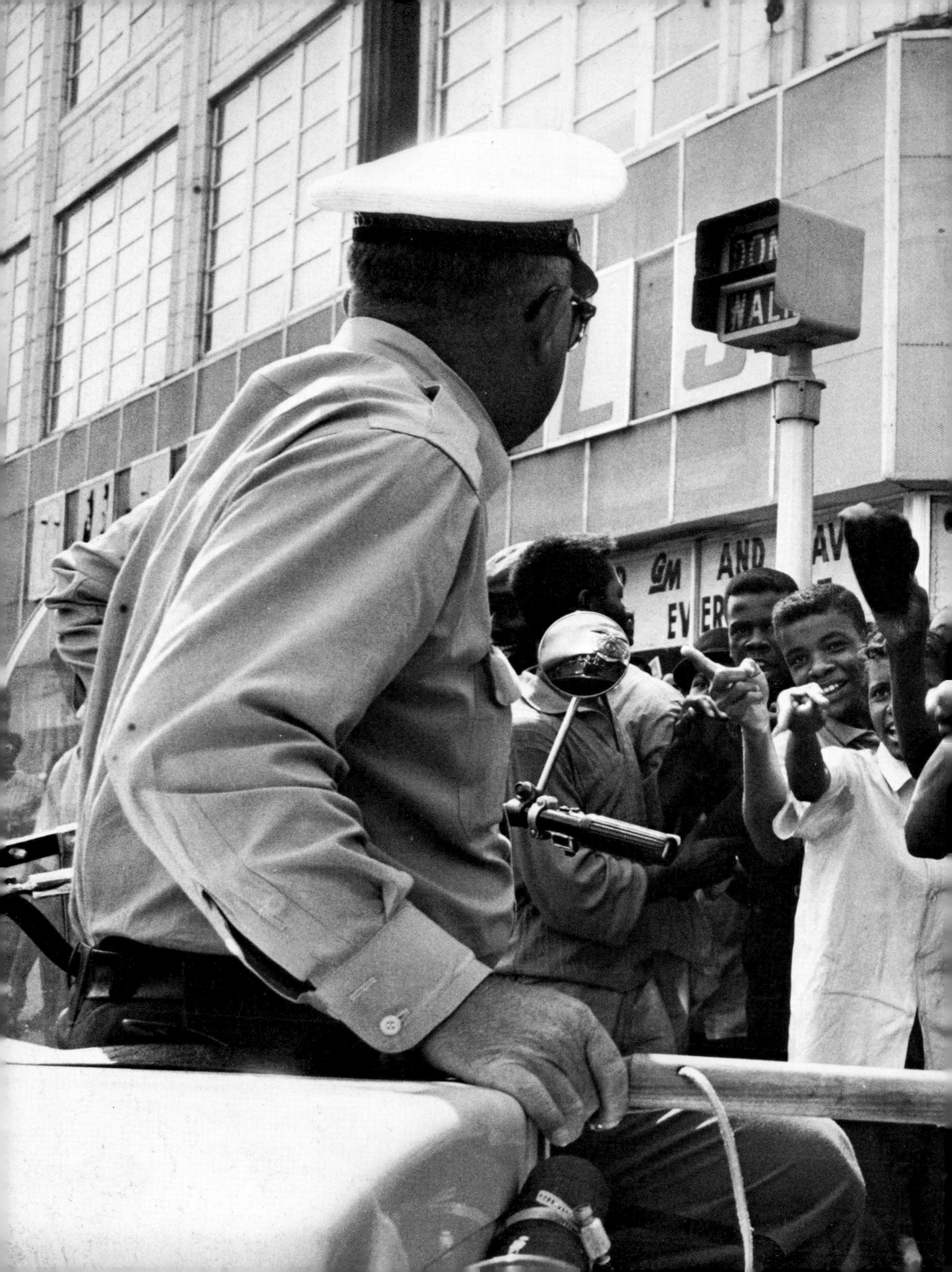
GM
AND

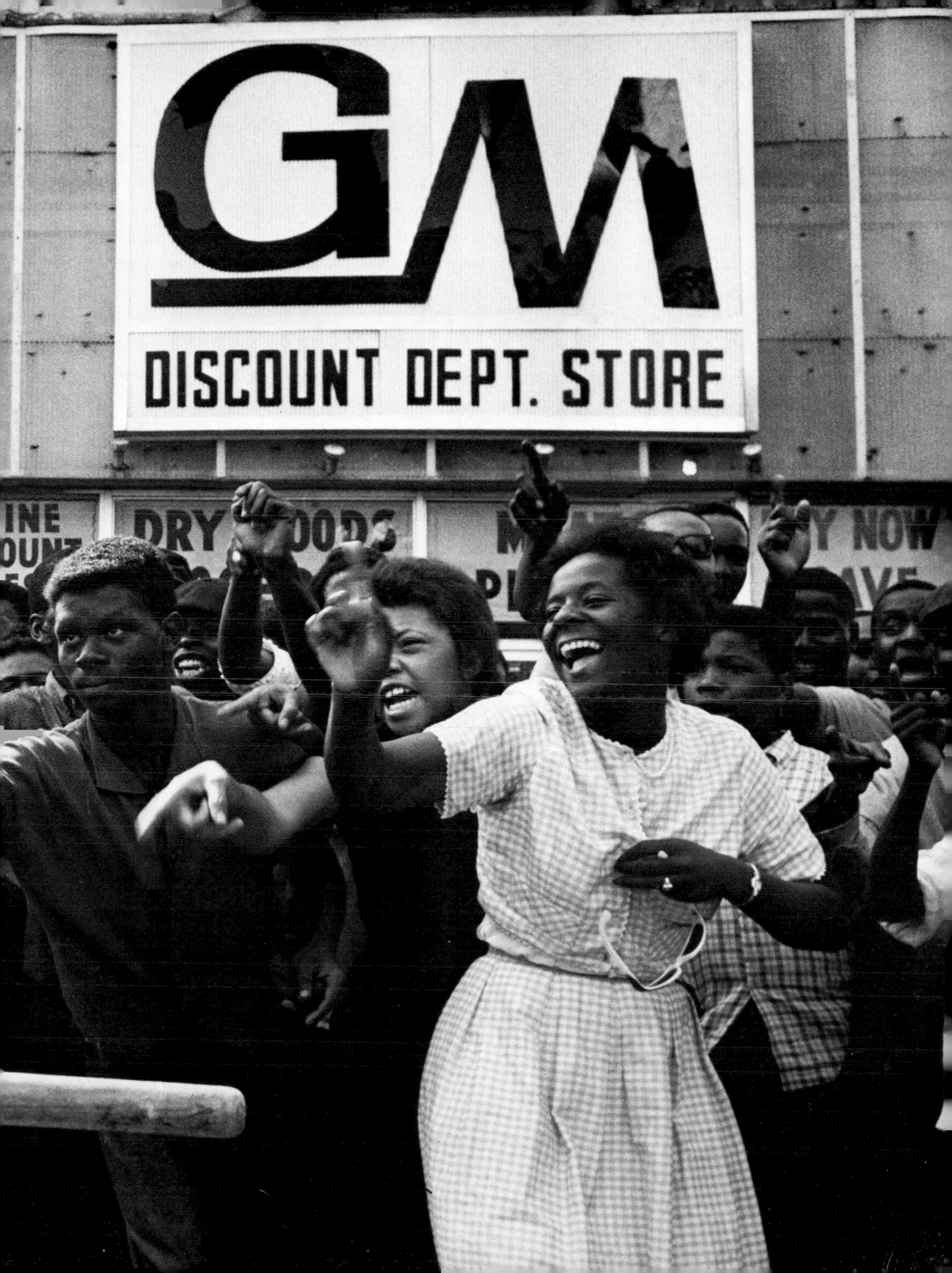
GM
DISCOUNT DEPT. STORE

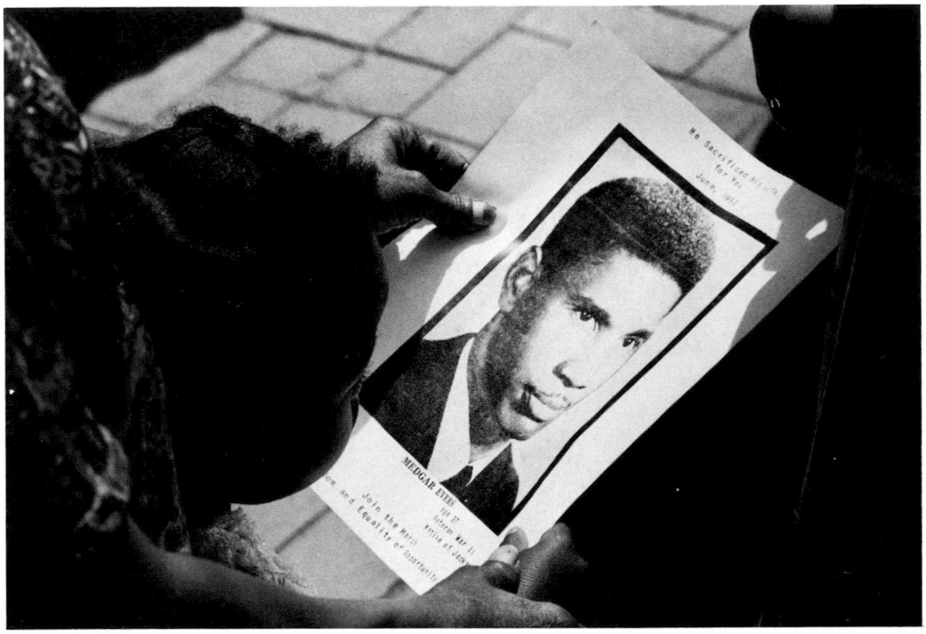
He Sacrificed
for You
MEDGAR EVERS
Join the March
and Equality of Opportunity

Flip Schulke

Chapter Five

"You Can't Kill an Idea"

The Assassination of Medgar Evers, June, 1963 King's labors in Georgia and Alabama were in many ways paralleled in Mississippi by the work of Medgar Evers, state field secretary of the NAACP. Although often denounced as an outside agitator, Evers was a native son of Mississippi. In 1954, eight years before James Meredith entered the University of Mississippi, Evers had unsuccessfully attempted to enroll at the university's law school. By 1963, he had spent nearly a decade actively fighting segregation in his home state.

A wave of protests and mass demonstrations throughout the south mirrored the events in Birmingham. Jackson, the capital of Mississippi, was the national headquarters of the White Citizens Council, and even the governor of the state, Ross Barnett, was a member of this organization devoted to white supremacy. Jackson's white citizens were not only prepared but determined to fight integration actively.

In early May, 1963, the Mississippi NAACP organization met in Jackson and drew up a set of demands calling for integration of rest rooms, lunch counters, libraries, schools, parks, and other public facilities. Other demands listed were equal opportunity in hiring, elimination of discriminatory business practices, and establishment of a biracial committee to achieve these goals.

Local officials refused to negotiate, and demonstrations began. The protestors in Jackson, unlike those who peopled King's campaigns, had not been trained in passive resistance. Experience and necessity had taught them the lesson of violence. Crowds frequently responded to white attacks by heaving bricks and bottles. Early in the conflict, a Molotov cocktail was hurled at the Evers' home. Fortunately, it landed on the carport and did only minor damage.

That episode, along with frequent threats, caused Evers to become obsessed with the idea of his own death. He talked about it constantly with his wife, Myrlie. He prepared for it. He

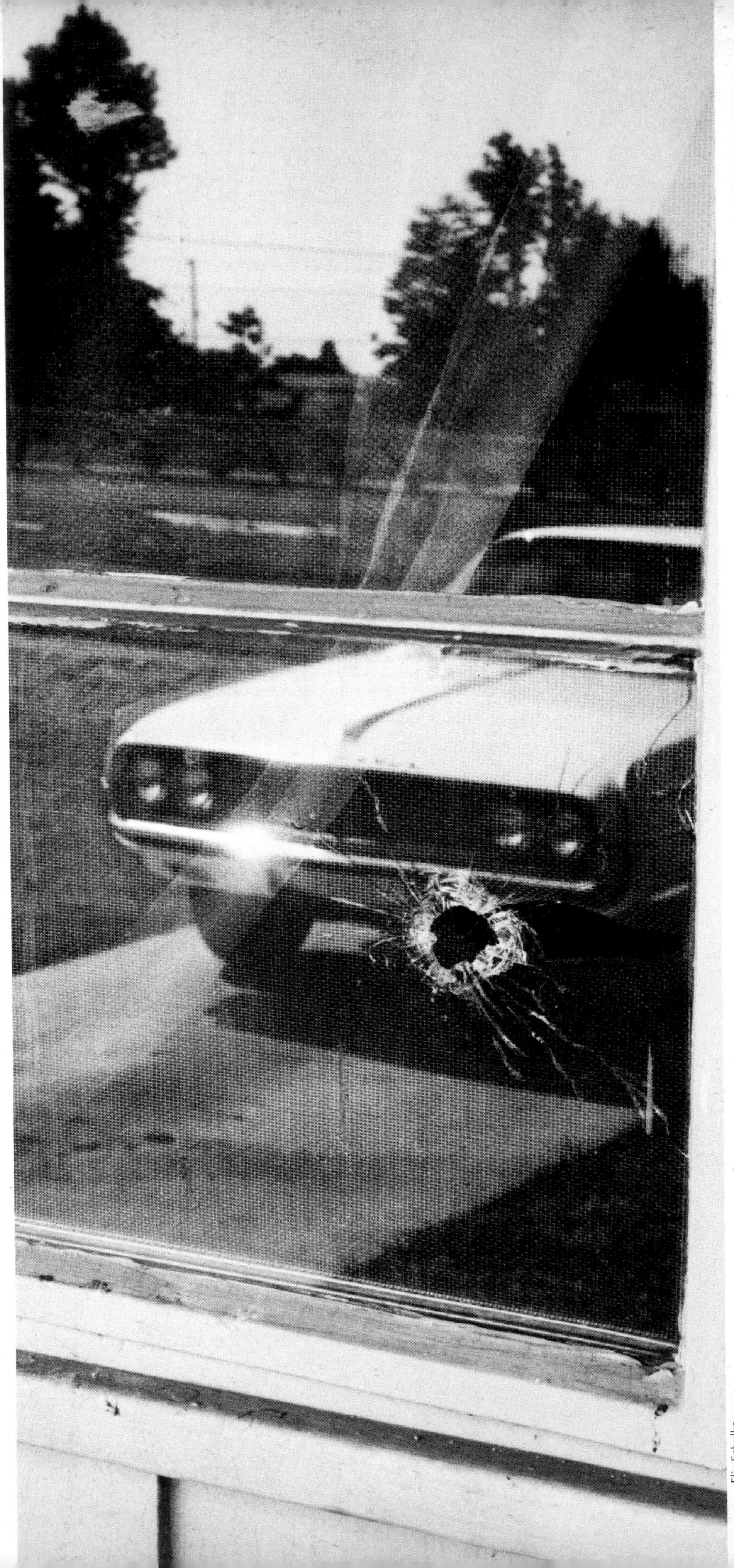

The bullet that hit Medgar Evans in the back and killed him tore a hole in the living room screen and window, entered the house, smashed through the living room wall to the kitchen, where it broke a tile and dented the refrigerator. Evers' murderer might have been convicted but for the fact that the bullet was too badly damaged to be positively identified.

Right:
For Myrlie Evers, Medgar's wife of twelve years, and his youngest son, Van, the days of loneliness begin.

Flip Schulke

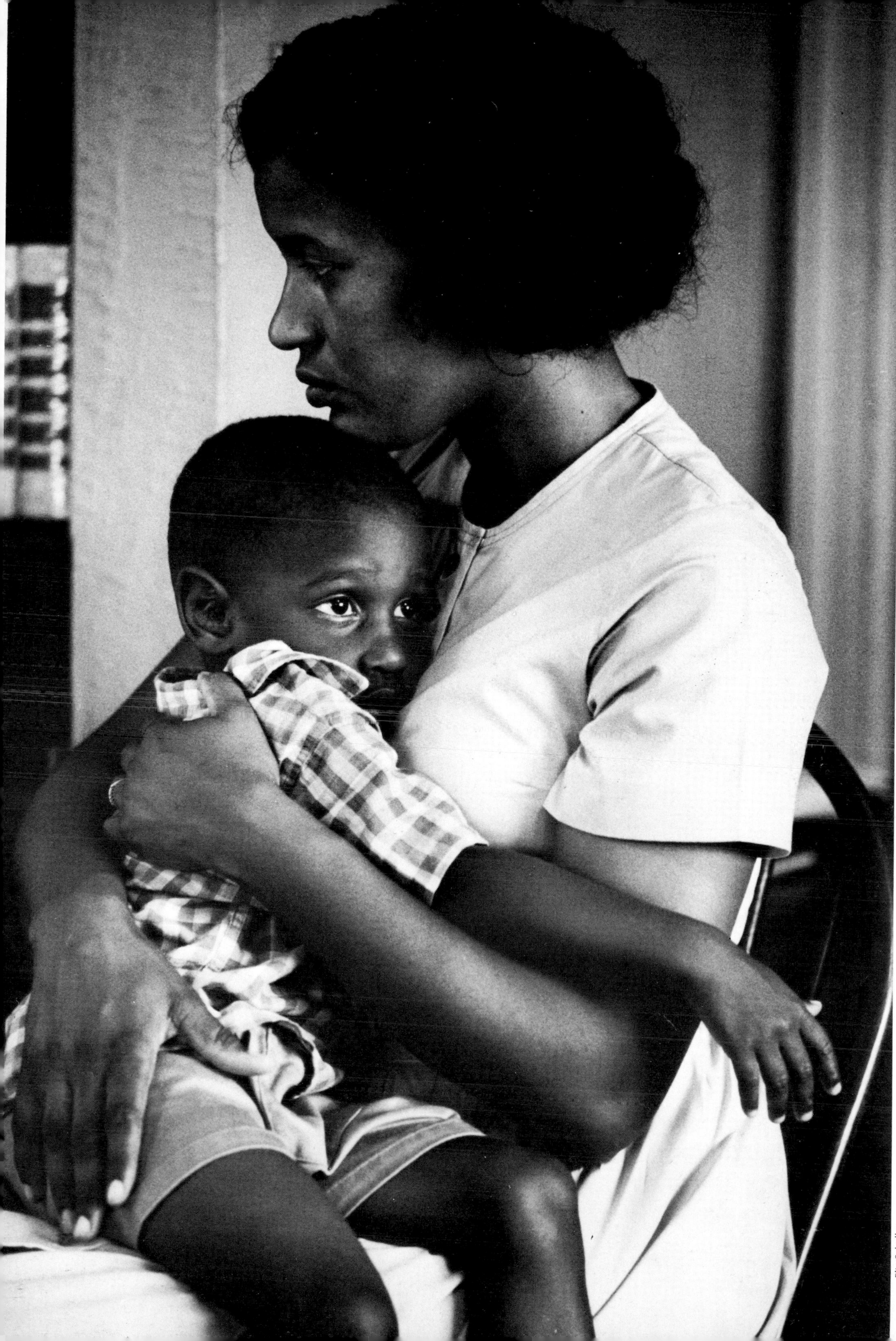

Flip Schulke

taught his wife and children to stay away from lighted windows and to drop to the floor whenever they heard a strange sound.

He told followers at a mass meeting during the demonstrations: "It's not enough just to sit here tonight and voice your approval and clap your hands and shed your tears and sing and then go out and do nothing about this struggle. Freedom has never been free. . . . "I love my children and I love my wife with all my heart. And I would die, and die gladly, if that would make a better life for them."

No day in the history of the civil rights movement can boast as many significant events as June 11, 1963. It was the morning of the "schoolhouse door" confrontation in which Deputy U. S. Attorney General Nicholas Katzenbach bested Alabama Governor George Wallace. After Wallace's surrender, Vivian Malone and James Hood became the first black students to enter the University of Alabama since Autherine Lucy, who had been enrolled and promptly expelled in 1956.

That evening President Kennedy went on national television with a strongly worded appeal for equal rights. After congratulating the students at the University of Alabama for their peaceful behavior, he said: "One hundred years of delay have passed since President Lincoln freed the slaves; yet their heirs, their grandsons, are not fully free. They are not yet fully freed from the bonds of injustice. They are not yet freed from social and economic oppression, and this nation, for all its hopes and all its boasts, will not be fully free until all its citizens are free." Kennedy closed with a plea to Congress to pass effective civil rights legislation as quickly as possible.

Hours after the president's address, Medgar Evers was shot. As he returned to his home shortly after midnight, the assassin lurked in a thicket across the street. As Evers walked toward his door, the blast rang out. By the time his wife and children reached him, Evers was sprawled face down at the door, his keys grasped tightly in his hand.

Evers was rushed to the hospital by friends, but he died almost immedi-

Flip Schulke

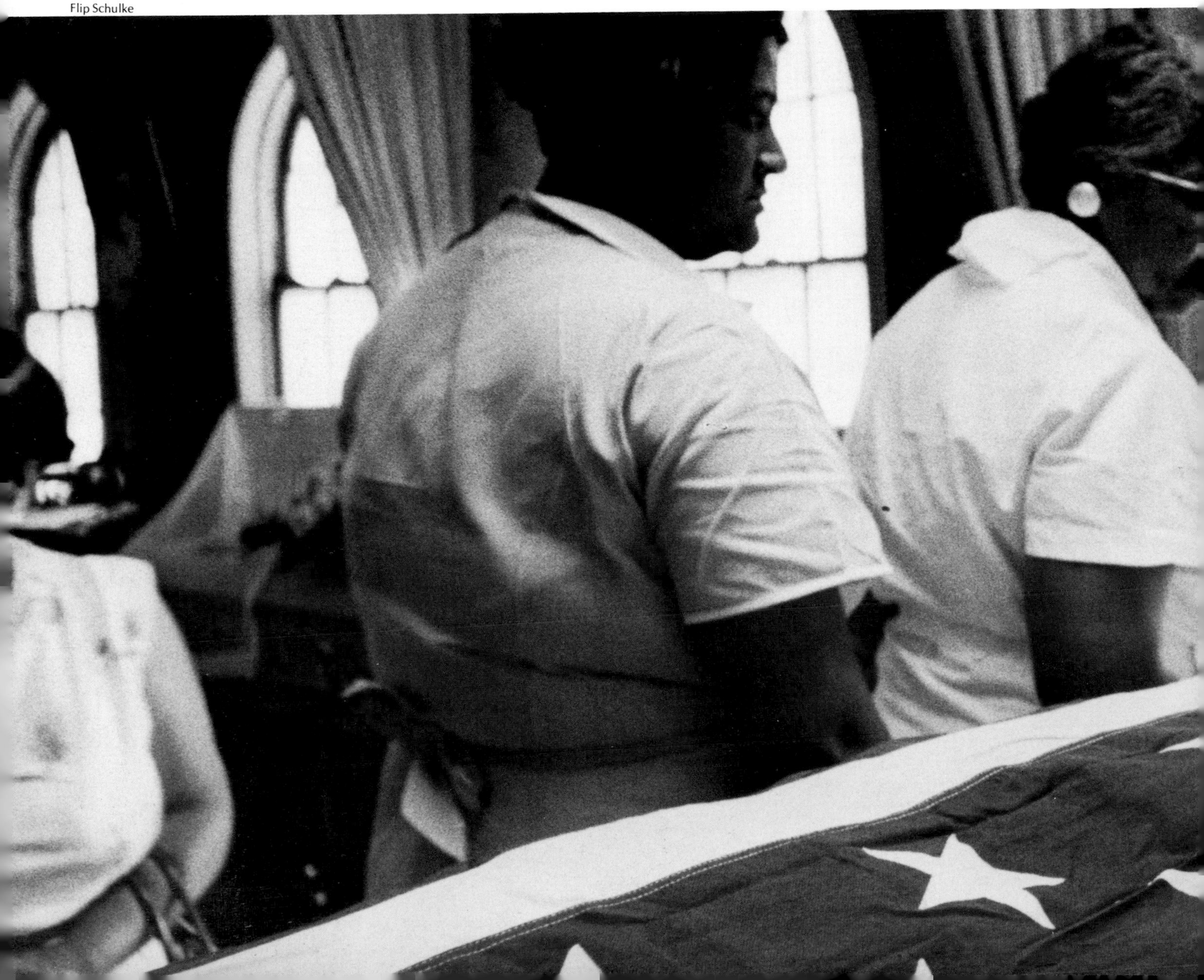

ately—the first civil rights leader to be assassinated.

The evening of Evers' death, tears streamed down the face of his widow as she told nine hundred people, "Nothing can bring Medgar back, but the cause can live on."

Upon hearing of the tragedy, King said: **"This tragic occurrence should cause all persons of good will to be aroused and . . . to be more determined than ever before to break down all of the barriers of racial segregation and discrimination, and I'm sure that the movement in the South will go on and that the movement in Mississippi will go on—even in a more determined manner as a result of this dastardly act on the part of those who are against democracy."**

Almost four thousand people, including prominent civil rights leaders from all over the country attended Evers' funeral at the Masonic temple which had been his NAACP headquarters. Roy Wilkins, director of the NAACP, delivered the eulogy. He accused southern politicians of being as responsible for Evers' murder as the man who actually pulled the trigger. "Medgar was more than just an opponent," he said. "In life, he was a constant threat to the system,

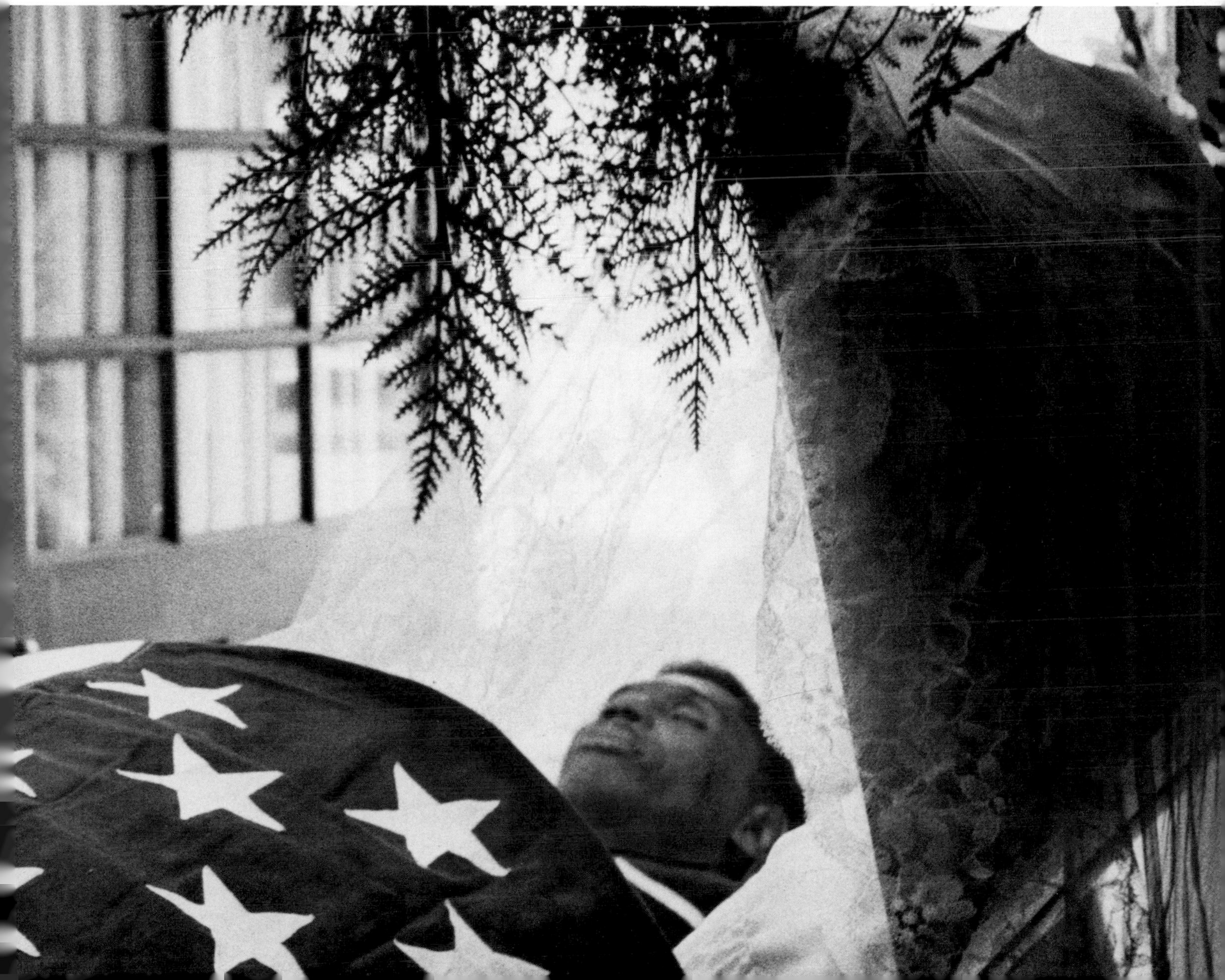

The mourners file past Evers' bier.

the system that murdered him. . . . In the manner of his death, he was the victor over that system. The bullet that tore away his life four days ago tore away at the system and helped to signal its end.''

Evers was buried at Arlington National Cemetery in Washington, D.C.

Ironically, many of the battles which Evers fought in life were won with his death. Three days after his funeral, the mayor of Jackson and black leaders worked out a preliminary agreement. The city would begin hiring blacks as policemen and school-crossing guards. Within two days, the first black policeman was actually sworn onto the force. Within a year the Jackson schools began a grade-by-grade desegregation plan, and in the following year Congress passed the Civil Rights Act of 1964.

Evers' assassination could not be ignored, even in Mississippi, and an intensive manhunt was launched. This was not to be an example of the ''Mississippi justice'' to which blacks had grown accustomed. Within days a suspect was identified. Fingerprints on the murder weapon and the rifle itself were traced to Byron de la Beckwith, an ardent segregationist. Beckwith was indicted and prosecuted vigorously. The jury of twelve white men were hopelessly deadlocked after eleven hours of deliberation and twenty ballots. The judge declared a mistrial and set a date for a new trial. The second jury was also unable to reach a verdict. But to blacks in Mississippi even a hung jury represented a kind of triumph.

Forced by the rest of the world, Mississippi was beginning to change. And many would learn the lesson that Medgar Evers had expressed years before: ''No people were ever given their freedom without a struggle. And a struggle means sacrifices.''

Right:
Myrlie Evers at the memorial service.

King and Abernathy mourn the death of their friend and colleague at the memorial service in Jackson, Mississippi, June 15, 1963.

Flip Schulke

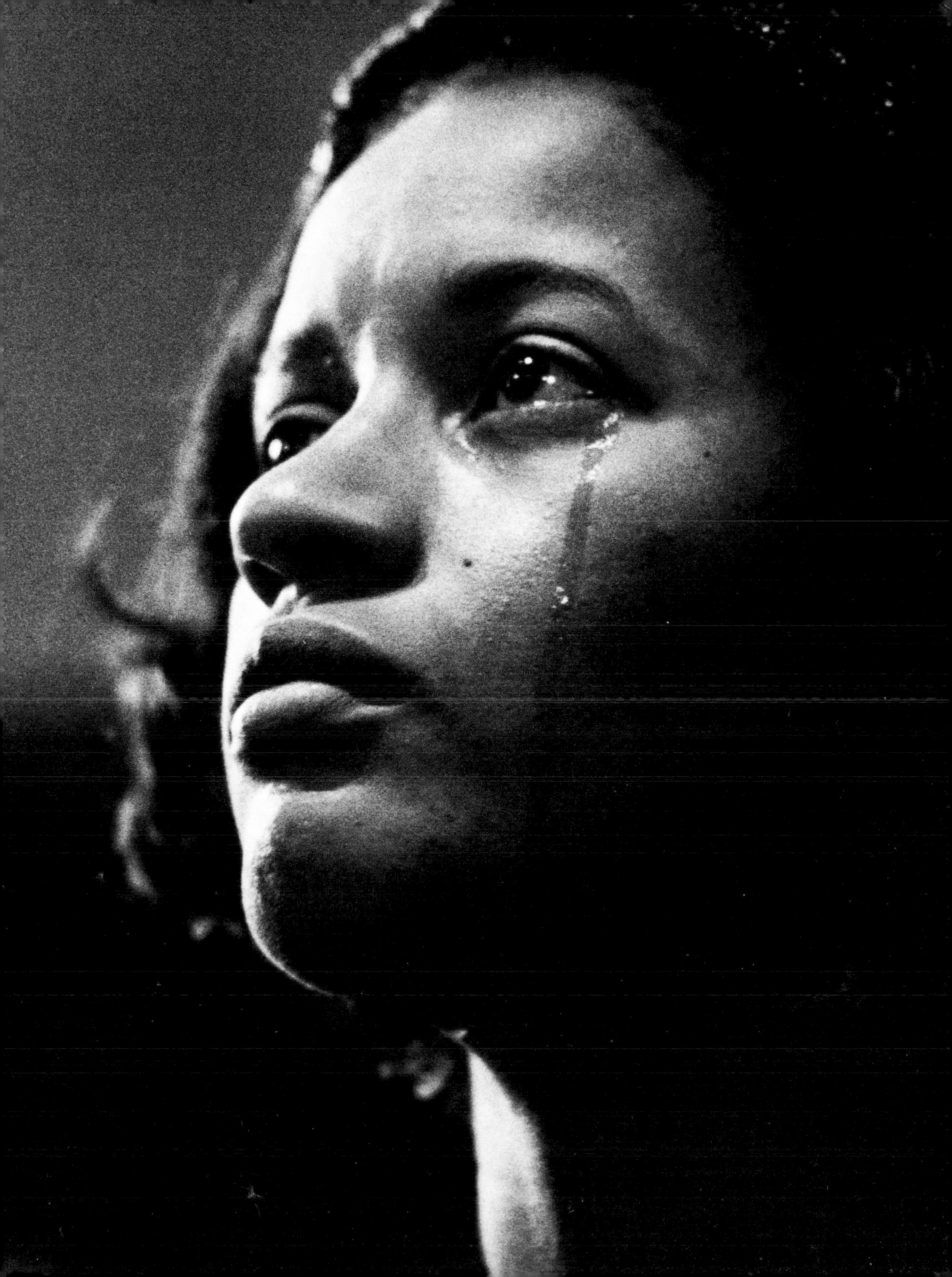

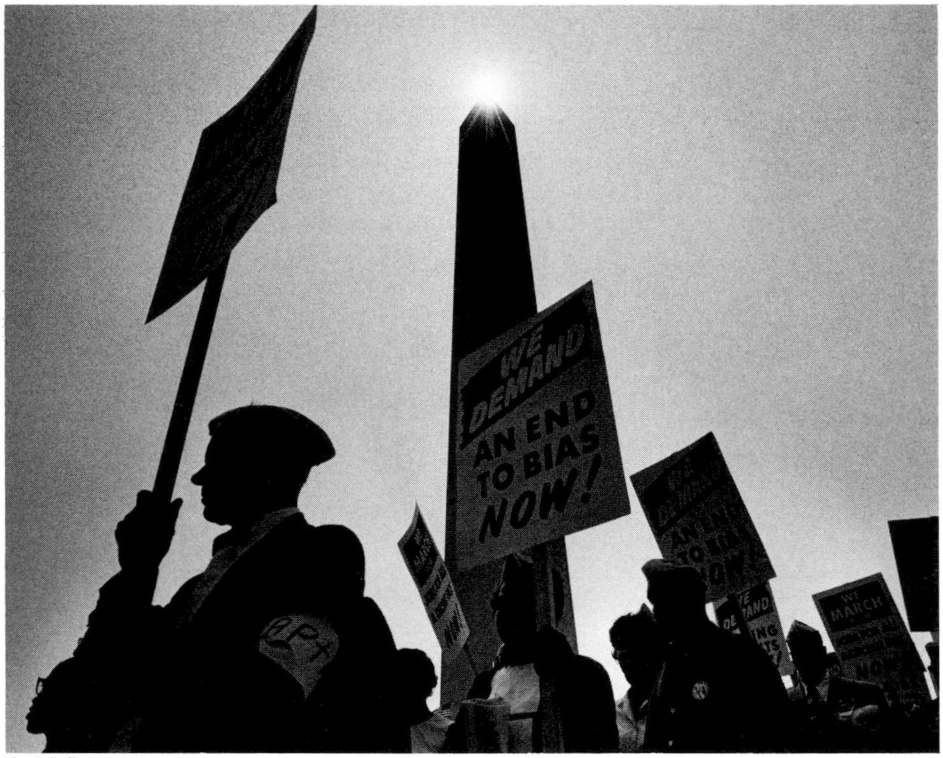
WE DEMAND
AN END TO BIAS NOW!
WE MARCH

Flip Schulke

Chapter Six

"I Have a Dream"

The March on Washington, August 28, 1963 The summer of protests and demonstrations throughout the nation, tempered by Evers' death, was both disturbing and exhilarating to civil rights leaders. To capitalize on the momentum, they joined forces with white labor leaders and clergymen to plan a massive "March on Washington for Jobs and Freedom."

From today's perspective, the significance of the March on Washington is manifold. It united black leaders regardless of the often divergent goals of their organizations. It was the first large-scale participation of whites in the black movement—and the first determined effort by white clergymen. It catapulted King to international prominence. And, of no little importance, it uplifted spirits and morale and encouraged blacks to accelerate their fight for freedom.

The heads of SCLC, CORE, SNCC, the NAACP, and the Urban League met with A. Philip Randolph, the elder statesman of the civil rights movement and the only black on the executive council of the AFL-CIO, and Walter Reuther, the president of the United Auto Workers, to lay the groundwork for the climactic march. The committee appointed Bayard Rustin national coordinator for the march. Hoping for 100,000 participants, the planners urged black and white clergymen to support the project and to involve their congregations.

Planes, trains, buses, and cars began bringing protestors from all over America to the capital on the eve of the March. By mid-morning of August 28, the crowd at the base of the Washington Monument had reached ninety thousand. Here the exuberant demonstrators listened to scores of entertainers as they waited for the march to begin. Burt Lancaster, Harry Belafonte, Paul Newman, Charlton Heston, and Sidney Poitier were but a few of the actors who came to lend their support. Folksingers Joan Baez, Peter, Paul, and Mary, and Bob Dylan led the crowd in freedom songs.

Meanwhile, the black leaders met with President Kennedy, Vice President Johnson, Secretary of Labor Willard Wirtz, and Burke Marshall, head of the Justice Department's civil rights division. The march organizers spoke with the president about the urgency of strong civil rights legislation and the prospects for passage of the bill which Kennedy had proposed. Many felt with John Lewis, chairman of SNCC, that the president's bill was both too weak and

Demonstrators arrive at Washington's Union Station, August 28, 1963. Man travelled all night by train, by bus, or foot to participate in the march.

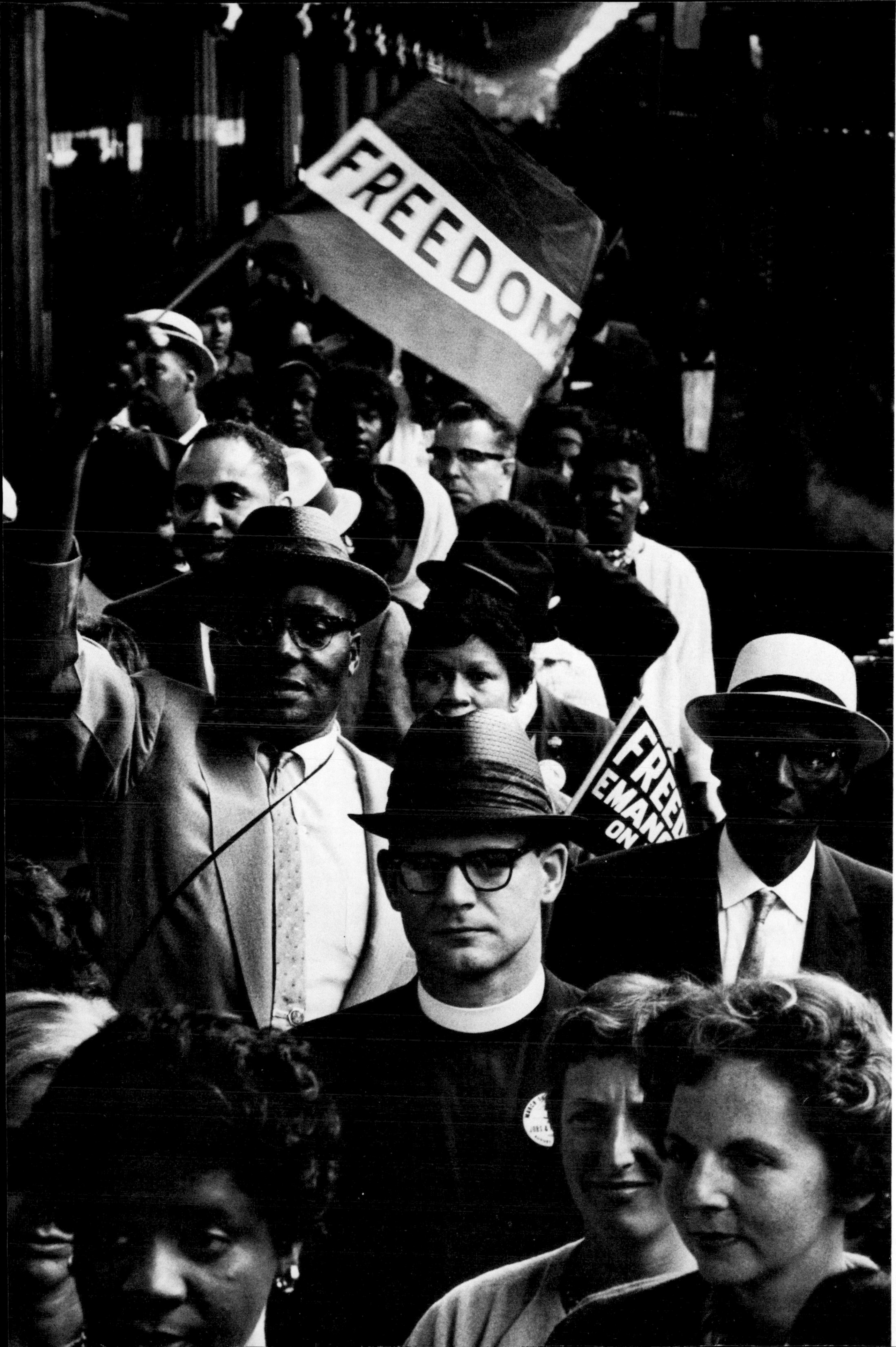
FREEDOM

Flip Schulke

too late. But the meeting was cordial, and Kennedy said afterwards: "One cannot help but be impressed with the quiet dignity that characterizes the thousands who have gathered in the nation's capital from across the country to demonstrate their faith and confidence in our democratic form of government."

The march route covered nearly a mile along the banks of the reflecting pool from the Washington Monument to the Lincoln Memorial. Wave after wave of marchers chanted "We want freedom" as they made their way to the Memorial. By 1:00 P.M., when singer Camilla Williams opened the program with the "Star Spangled Banner," 250,000 people were assembled. Millions more were watching on television.

The spirit was that of a mammoth, friendly picnic. Many carried picket signs; even more carried sandwiches. It was in an atmosphere of amiable chaos that King's associate from Birmingham, Reverend Fred Shuttlesworth, gave the invocation. One by one the civil rights leaders spoke to the crowd and to the nation. Randolph presided, introducing each of the speakers, and the rostrum included Whitney Young, director of the Urban League, Ralph Abernathy, and Roy Wilkins. Dick Gregory commented wryly, "The last time I saw so many of us together, Bull Connor was doing all the talking."

The audience was particularly moved by the aggressive words of John Lewis. Although he had tempered his doubts about President Kennedy at the insistence of Patrick A. O'Boyle, Catholic archbishop of Washington, Lewis still delivered an emotionally charged speech: "We are tired!" he bellowed. "We are tired of being beaten by policemen. We are tired of seeing our people locked up in jail over and over again! And then you holler 'Be patient.'

Flip Schulke

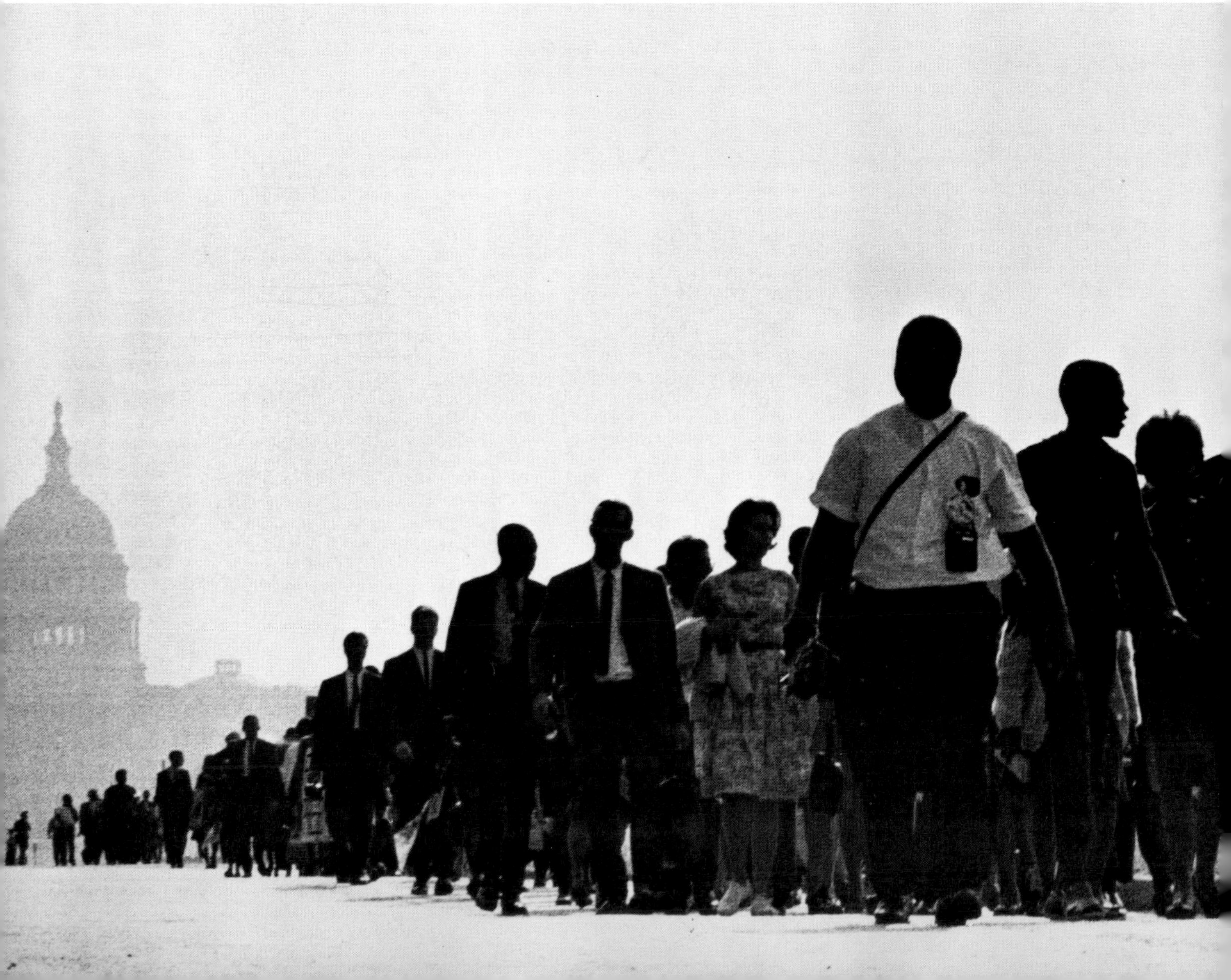

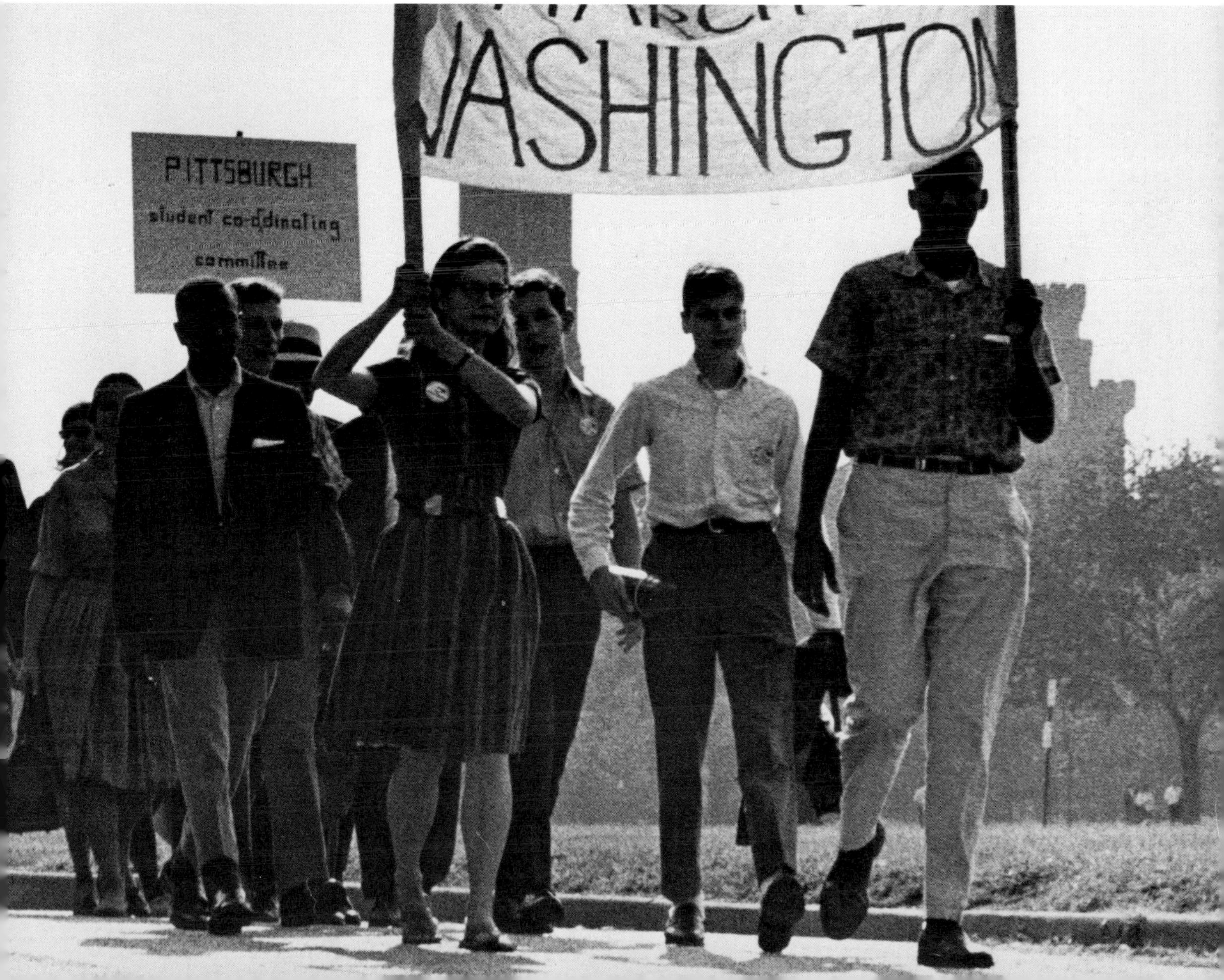
WASHINGTON
PITTSBURGH
student co-ordinating
committee

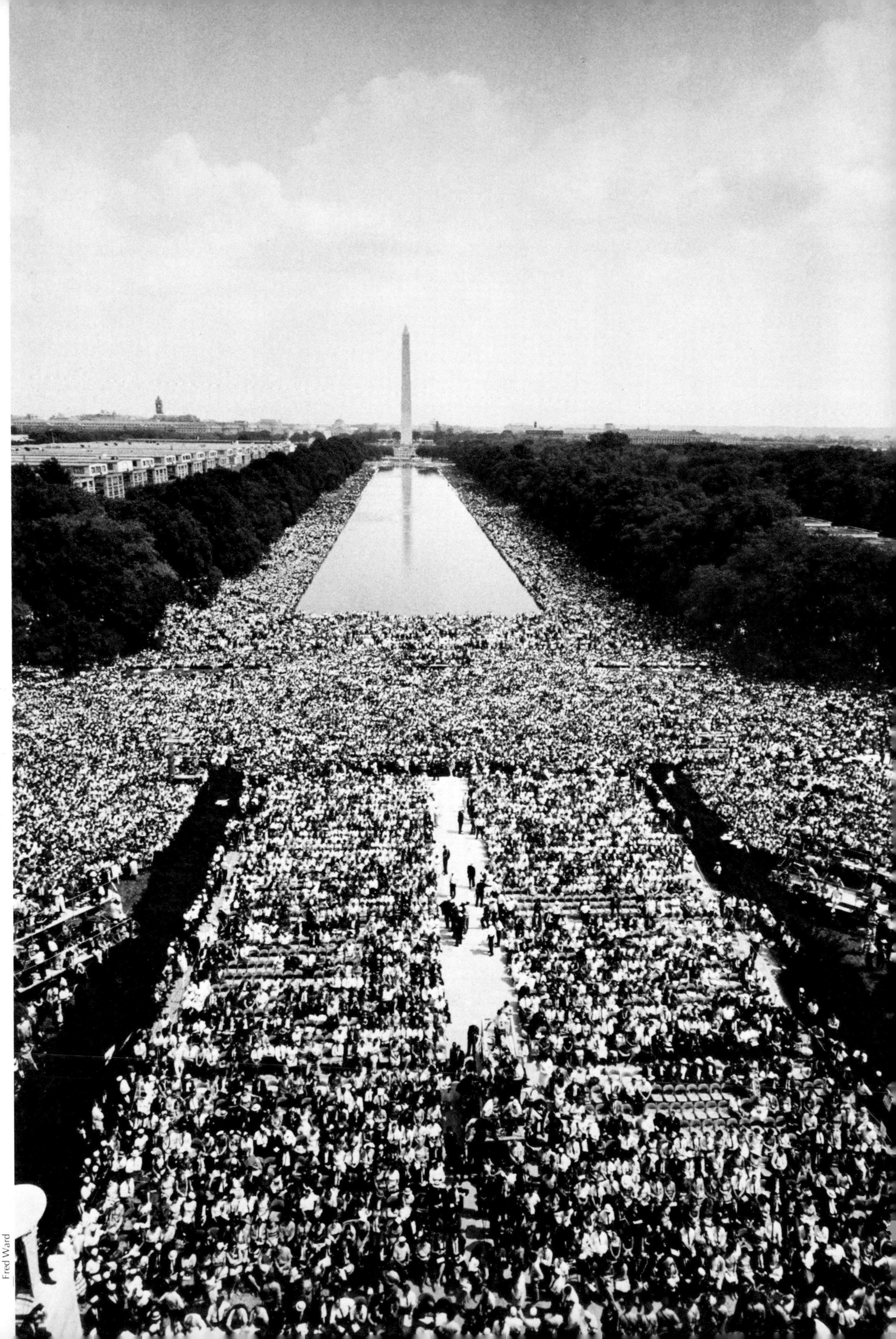
Fred Ward

How long can we be patient? We want our freedom and we want it now! We do not want to go to jail, but we will go to jail if this is the price we must pay for love, brotherhood and true peace. I appeal to all of you to get in this great revolution which is sweeping this nation—get in and stay in the streets of every city . . . until the revolution of 1776 is completed."

James Farmer of CORE was in a Louisiana jail on the day of the March but sent a message which was read by Floyd McKissick. "We will not stop," he wrote, "until the dogs stop biting us in the South and the rats stop biting us in the North." The program also included sympathetic white speakers, such as Walter Reuther and various clergymen.

Left:
Hundreds of thousands of protestors join together in the largest demonstration in the history of the civil rights movement.

During the march black leaders meet with President John F. Kennedy and members of his staff. King is flanked by Whitney Young (left) and John Lewis. Kennedy chats with A. Philip Randolph; to his left are Vice President Lyndon B. Johnson, Walter Reuther, and Roy Wilkins.

Fred Ward

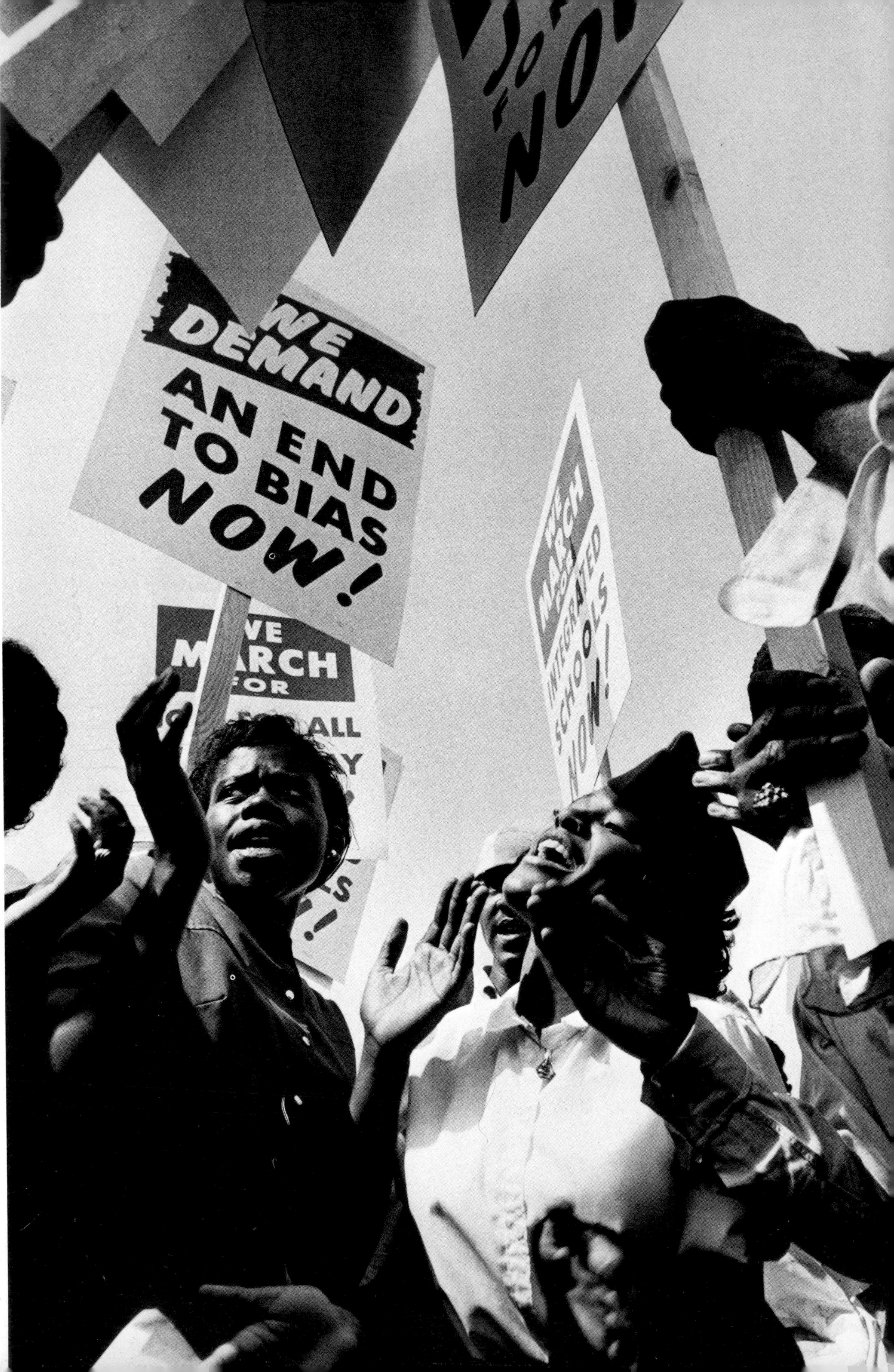
WE DEMAND
AN END TO BIAS NOW!
WE MARCH FOR INTEGRATED SCHOOLS NOW!

Flip Schulke

The crowd was beginning to thin by late afternoon when Mahalia Jackson's rendition of "I Been 'Buked and I Been Scorned" brought tears to the eyes of the remaining rallyers. Those who departed before King spoke missed the high point of the demonstration.

Thousands applauded when Randolph introduced King as "the moral leader of the nation." King's voice hushed the crowd: **"Fivescore years ago, a great American in whose symbolic shadow we stand today signed the Emancipation Proclamation. . . . But one hundred years later, the Negro is still not free."** His voice seemed to invite the crowd not only to listen but to participate.

Many marchers marked an "equality sign" on the forehead to symbolize their commitment.

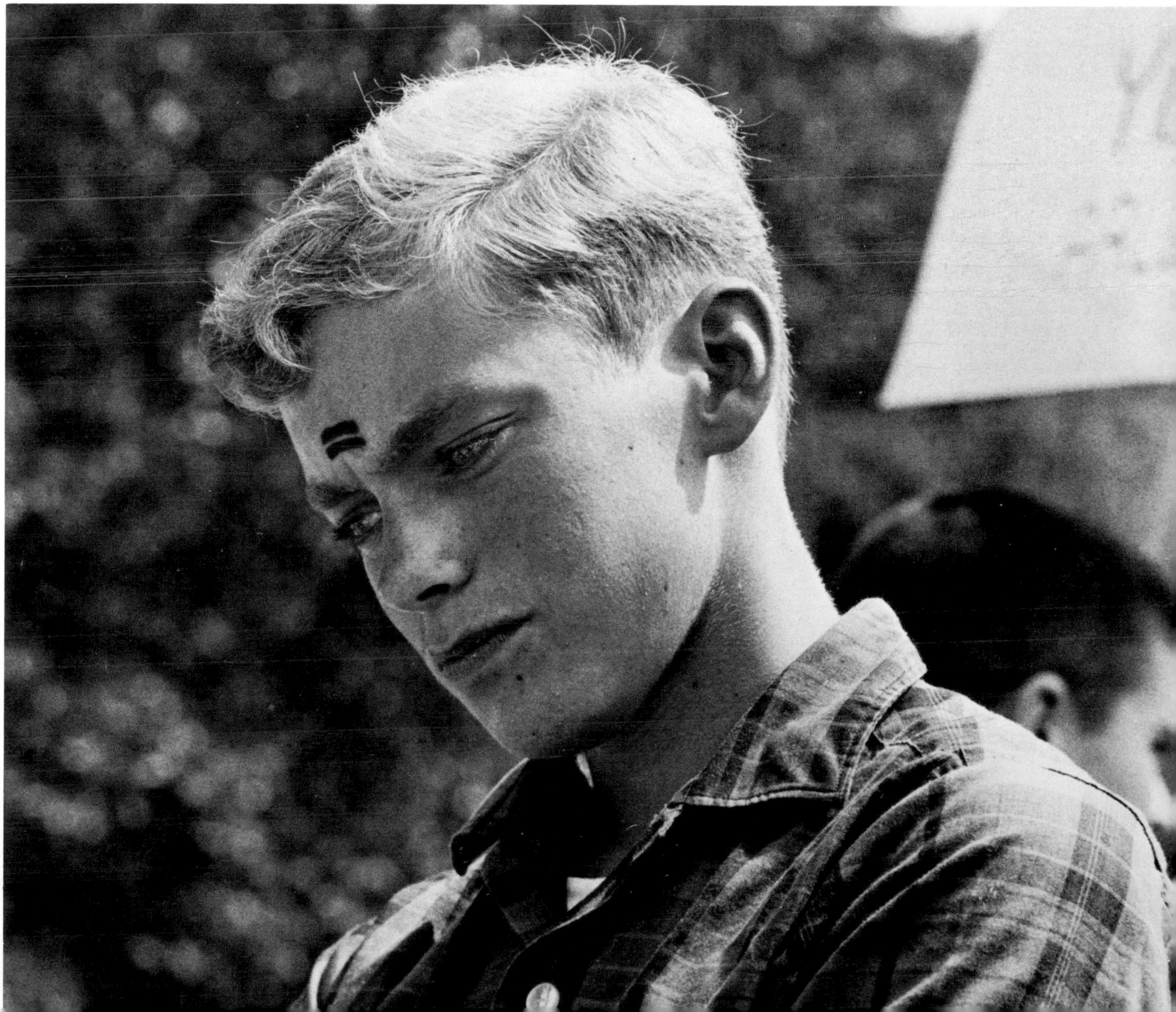

Flip Schulke

"I have a dream," he cried.

"Tell us, tell us," the crowd pleaded.

"I have a dream that one day on the red hills of Georgia, the sons of former slaves and the sons of former slave owners will be able to sit down together at the table of brotherhood."

"Yes! Yes! I see it!" responded the listeners.

In the tradition of the southern Baptist preacher, King combined eloquence with spontaneous energy. He spoke to the massive audience as to a congregation, his rhythmic cadence and repetitive phrases building towards the climax.

"I have a dream that little children will one day live in a nation where they will be judged not by the color of their skins but by the content of their character. I have a dream today. I have a dream that one day down in Alabama, with its racists, with its governor having his lips dripping with the words of interposition and nullification, one day right there in Alabama, little black boys and black girls will be able to join hands with little white boys and white girls as sisters and brothers."

His speech was not a logical legal brief on the specifics of the civil rights bill, nor an intellectual treatise on the plight of black people. It was a fervent, emotional sermon, forged out of the language and spirit of democracy. King's mastery of the spoken word, his magnetism, and his sincerity raised familiar platitudes from cliché to commandment.

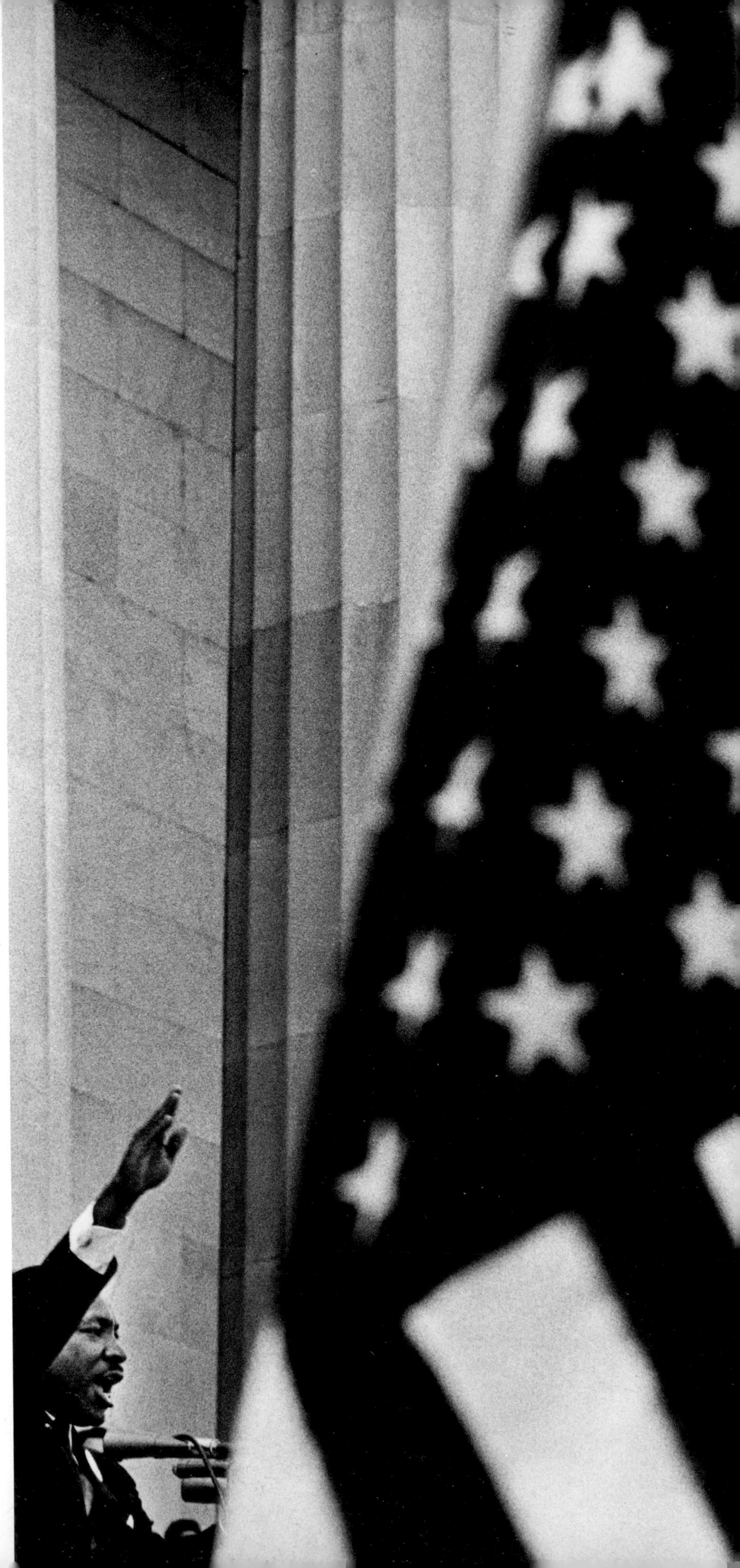

King shares his dream of a future free from discrimination.

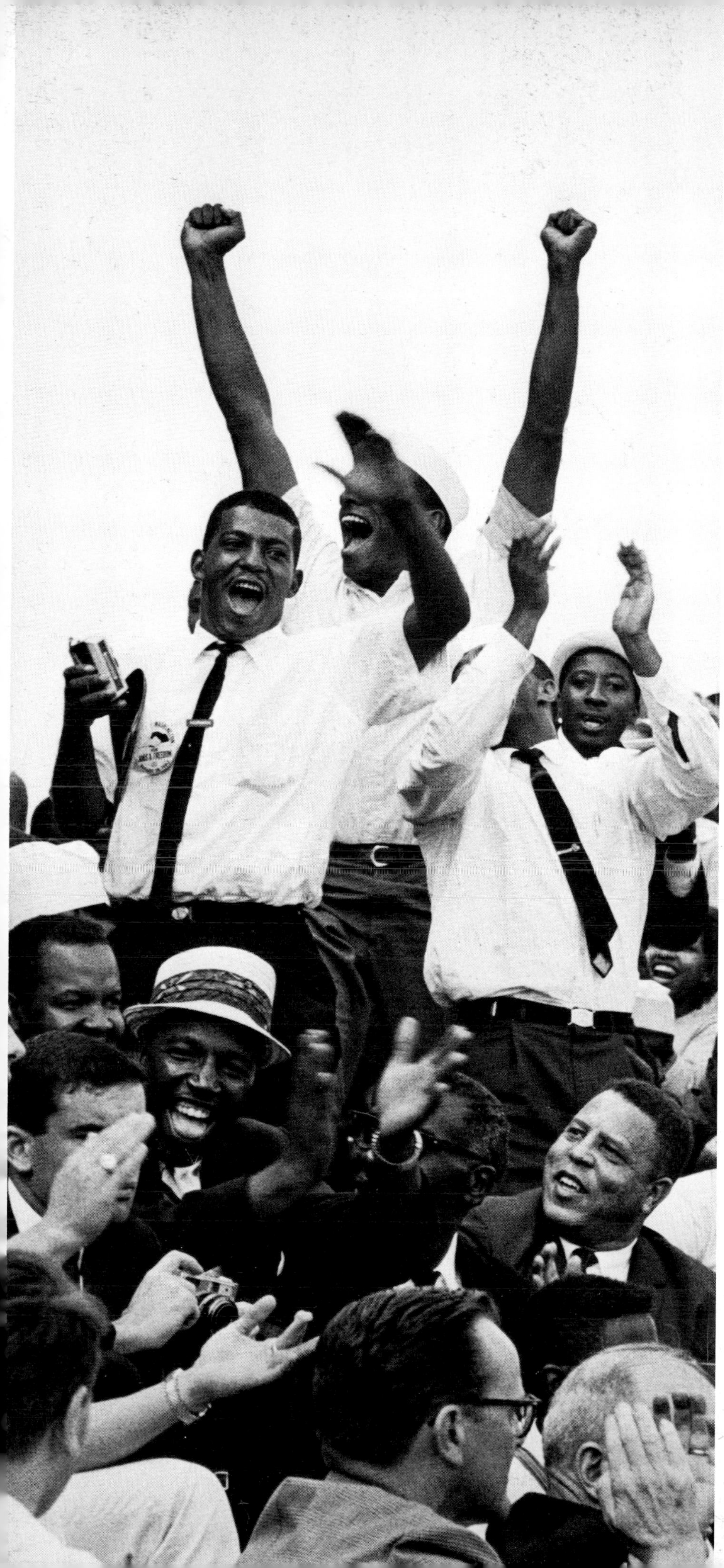

"Let freedom ring," he enjoined. **"And when this happens, when we allow freedom to ring, when we let it ring from every village and hamlet, from every state and every city, we will be able to speed up that day when all of God's children, black men and white men, Jews and Gentiles, Protestants and Catholics will be able to join hands and sing in the words of the old Negro spiritual: 'Free at last, free at last, thank God Almighty, we're free at last.' "**

The day was a personal victory for King. The orderly conduct of the massive March was an active tribute to his philosophy of nonviolence. Equally significant, his speech made his voice familiar to the world and lives today as one of the most moving orations of our day. **"I have a dream,"** he said. And countless millions accepted his dream as their own. **"I have a dream,"** he repeated. And people of all sorts and conditions recognized the dreamer as the conscience of an entire nation.

"Free at last, free at last, thank God Almighty, we're free at last."

Flip Schulke

Chapter Seven

"The Doors of Opportunity"

School Desegregation, September, 1963
The battle for equal rights was waged on many fronts, from lunch counters to buses to voting booths. But each September, since the Supreme Court of the United States had ordered schools to desegregate with "all deliberate speed," the battle line shifted to the schoolhouse door.

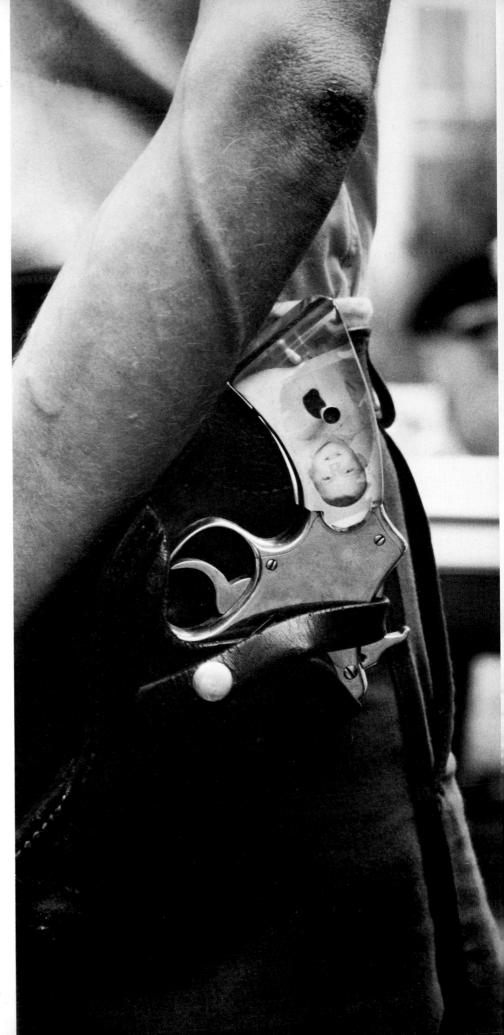

In many parts of the Deep South, schools were integrating for the first time in the fall term of 1963. In most places, including Tennessee, South Carolina, Texas, Florida, Maryland, and Georgia, integration occurred in an atmosphere of tranquility, without even token hostility. Alabama was the major exception.

Under federal court order, Birmingham, Huntsville, Macon County (Tuskegee), and Mobile planned to register a token number of blacks in previously all-white schools. Because no one was certain whether the governor would interfere, tension mounted as the cities prepared to admit the black students. Governor Wallace had won election by promising to stand in the "schoolhouse door" if necessary to prevent integration. Several months earlier he had done exactly that by physically barring Vivian Malone and James Hood from the University of Alabama. He had given in only when confronted by the federalized National Guard.

On September 2, when Tuskegee High School was due to admit thirteen black pupils, Governor Wallace ordered it to postpone its opening for a week. Although there had been no indication of trouble, Wallace said the school's opening was being delayed to "preserve the peace." One hundred and eight state troopers sealed off the high school to enforce the governor's order.

The Board of Education of Tuskegee issued a statement reaffirming its intention to desegregate. But their rejection of

A policeman stands guard, preventing the integration of a Birmingham high school, September, 1963.

Right:
Governor George Wallace of Alabama.

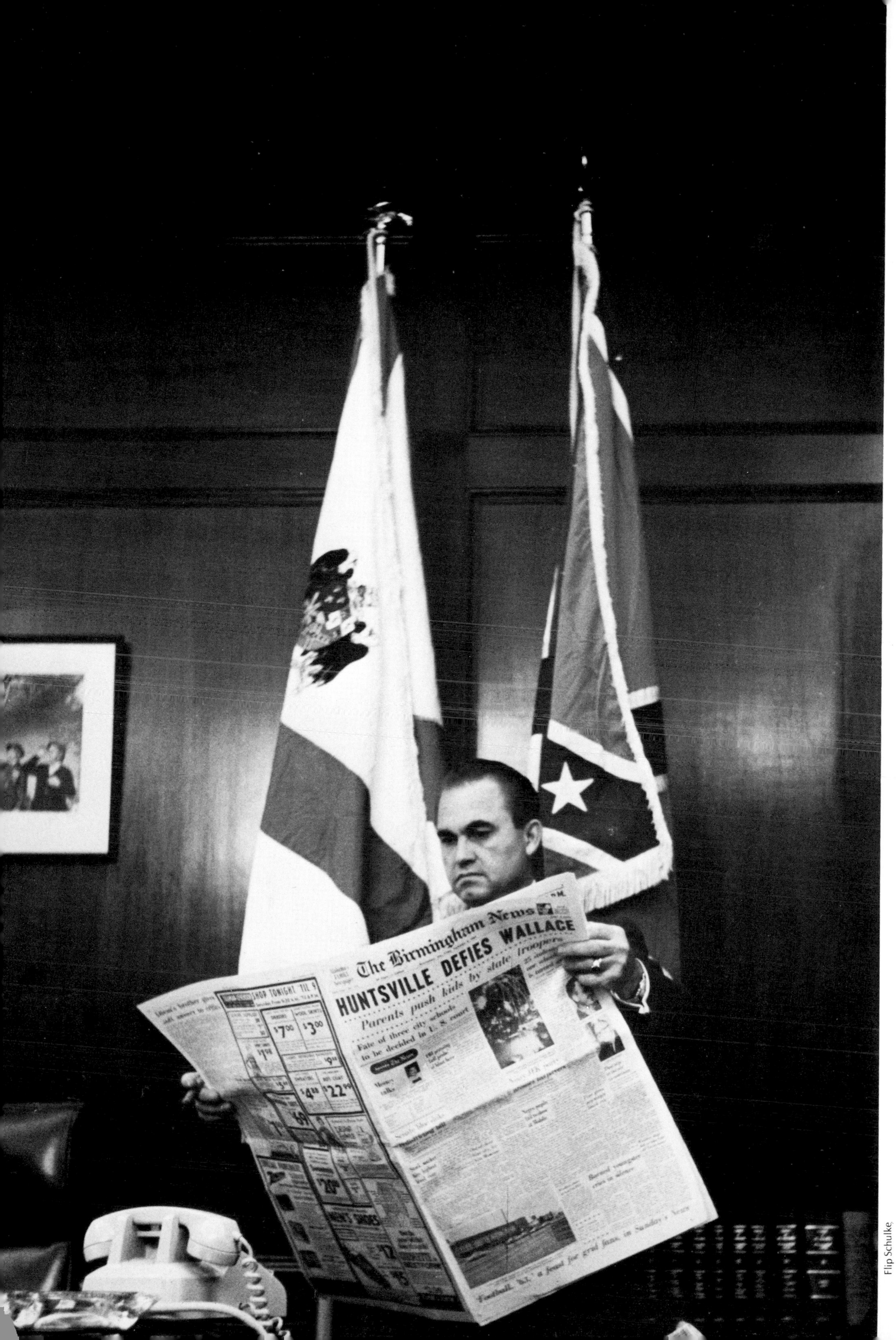
The Birmingham News
HUNTSVILLE DEFIES WALLACE
Parents push kids by state troopers
Fate of three city schools to be decided in U.S. court
SHOP TONIGHT 'TIL 9

Flip Schulke

Wallace's order served as little more than symbolic defiance; the school remained ringed by troopers.

The governor's action caused strong resentment, even among white segregationists. Many felt the court-ordered integration was inevitable and wanted to avoid a racial incident. Blacks outnumbered whites by better than 75 percent in Macon County, and Tuskegee was just beginning to recover from a three-year boycott of white merchants.

Wallace's strategy seemed clear. He would force President Kennedy to send in federal troops to uphold the court orders. Confronted, he would back down, but he would still be able to claim that he had tried with all his power to fulfill his election pledge: "Segregation today, segregation tomorrow, segregation forever."

The opening of schools in Huntsville and Mobile was also deferred for several days in compliance with Wallace's request. This tactic seemed designed to create a showdown in Birmingham, where the fear of serious trouble was greatest and where Wallace commanded his strongest support.

At the urging of his advisors, the governor did not send his troopers to block registration at the three Birmingham

White students in Birmingham demonstrate against integration of their high school.

Flip Schulke

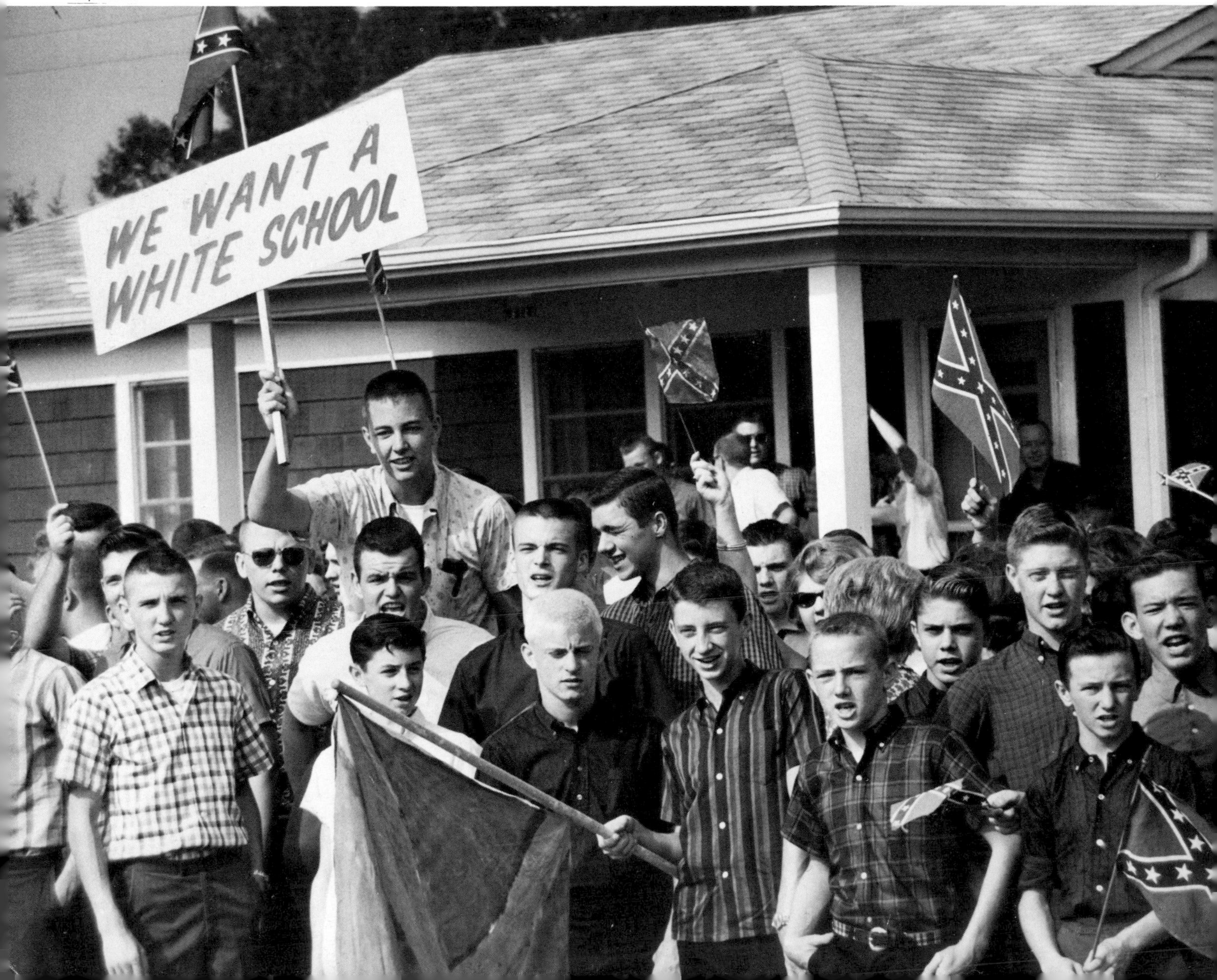
WE WANT A
WHITE SCHOOL

schools scheduled to integrate on September 4. But, as predicted, rioting broke out, led by the National States Rights Party, a vocal segregationist and anti-Semitic group.

That evening a bomb exploded at the home of Arthur Shores, the black attorney who had won the school desegregation case. The rioting that followed gave Wallace the excuse he needed to close the schools in Birmingham.

Meanwhile, the governor moved his troops to Huntsville, where four black students were to enter four different schools. The Huntsville Board of Education sought to defy the governor and open the schools. "We want the governor and his troops to stay out of here," said one member of the board. Challenging the order, twenty-five white mothers escorted their children past the state troopers and into the empty school.

The schools were allowed to open on September 9, but police prevented black students from entering except in Huntsville, where the City Council had passed a resolution condemning the governor's action. Later that day all five of Alabama's federal district judges signed an injunction prohibiting Wallace and the police from obstructing the integration orders. Wallace responded

The National States' Rights party encourages resistance to school integration.

Flip Schulke

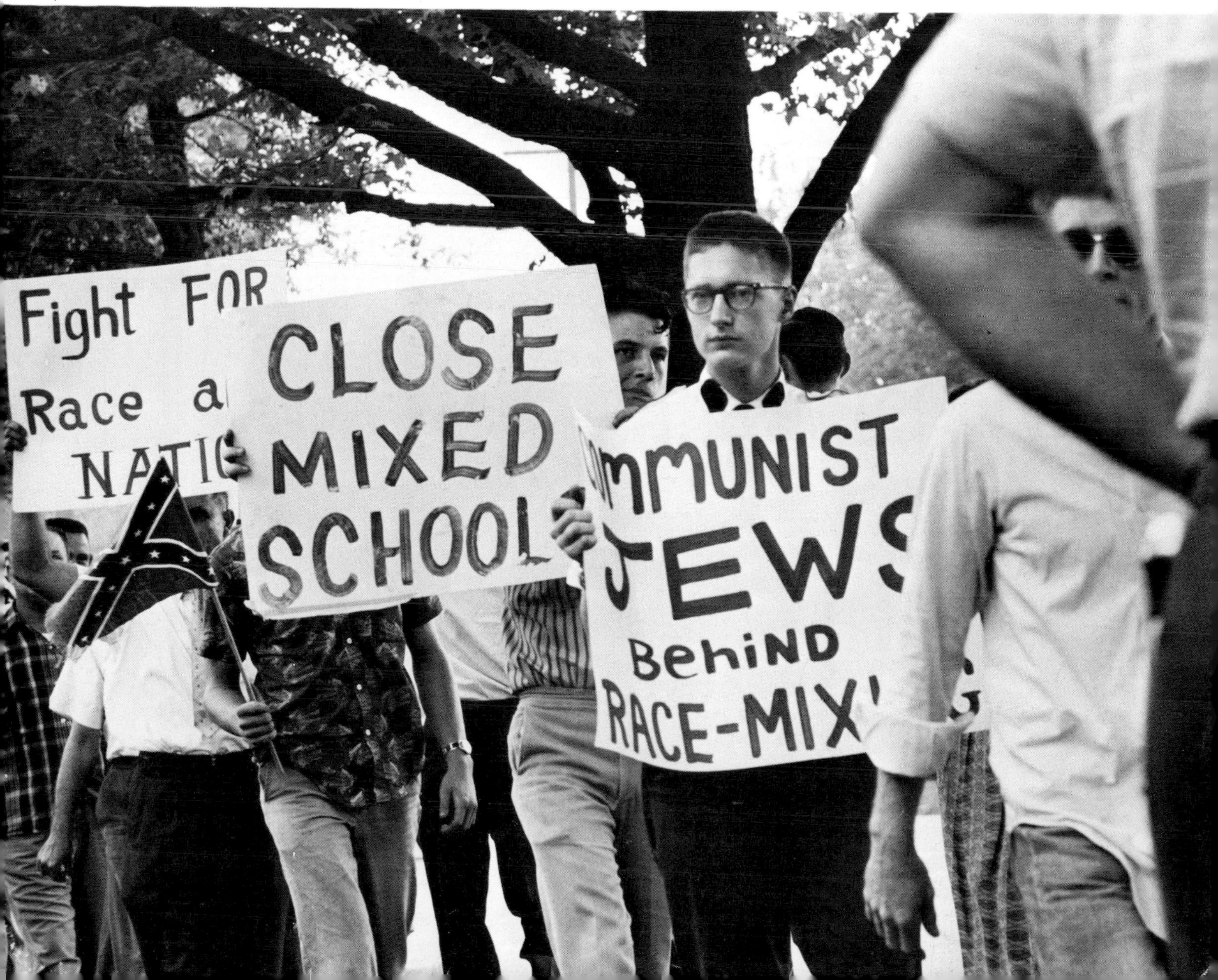
Fight FOR
Race a
NATI
CLOSE
MIXED
SCHOOL
JEWS
BehiND
RACE-MIX

by replacing the state police with National Guardsmen. The next day, President Kennedy federalized the National Guard and ordered them to withdraw from the schools. Twenty black children peacefully entered all-white schools.

But for every success in the black movement, a tragedy seemed to follow close behind. On September 15, five days after school integration began, a bomb exploded in the Sixteenth Street Baptist Church in Birmingham. Sunday school was in session, and four little girls were killed. Twenty other youngsters were injured in the blast.

Birmingham erupted in violence again. Fights between blacks and whites broke out in the streets. Crowds became hysterical. Two innocent black teenagers were shot and killed. Many, both black and white, blamed Governor Wallace for the incident.

King could not conceal his anger. **"Certainly,"** he said, **"the governor of Alabama has to take a great deal of the responsibility for this evil act, for his defiant, irresponsible words and actions have created the atmosphere for violence and terror all over the state. . . . The murders of yesterday stand as blood on the hands of Governor Wallace."**

At the memorial service for the martyred children, novelist John Killens said the tragic bombing marked the demise of nonviolence in the freedom movement. "Negroes must be prepared to protect themselves with guns," he insisted. Christopher McNair, the father of one of the murdered children, disagreed, "What good would Denise have done with a machine gun in her hand?"

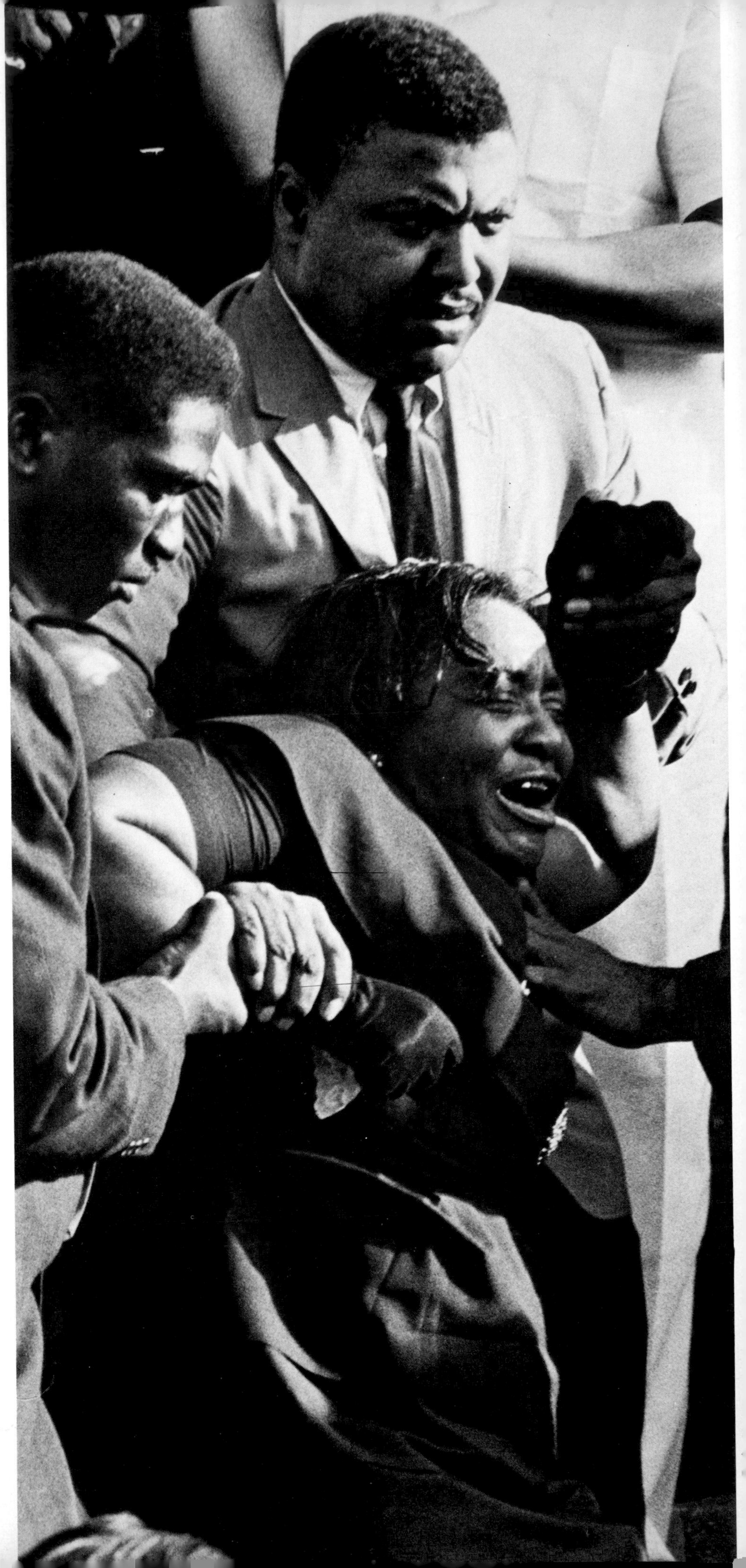

On September 15, 1963, a bomb explodes in Birmingham's Sixteenth Street Baptist Church, killing four little girls and injuring dozens of worshippers. Here a woman collapses in grief.

Right:
Interior of the shattered church.

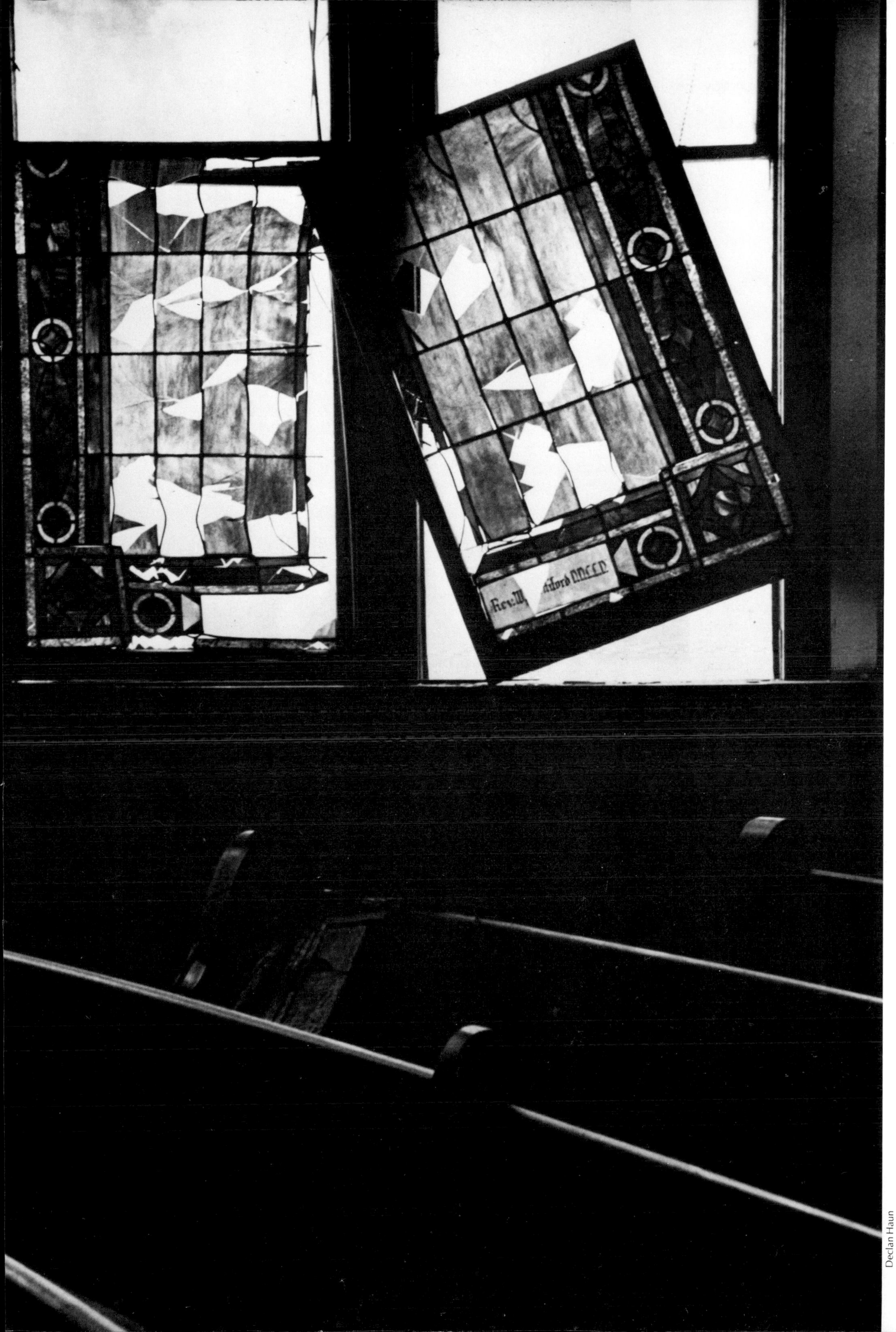

Declan Haun

King delivered the eulogy, his hope dominating his anger: **"They did not die in vain. God still has a way of wringing good out of evil."**

But the murders of 1963 did not end in Birmingham. In November, President Kennedy was assassinated in Dallas. King wrote: **"Our late president was assassinated by a morally inclement climate. . . . It is a climate where men cannot disagree without being disagreeable and where they express their disagreement through violence and murder."** King was moved to prophesy to his wife, **"That's the way I'm going to go."**

As 1963 came to a close, Kennedy's death had created uncertainty among civil rights leaders. It was not to last long. One week after he became president, Lyndon Baines Johnson urged Congress to end the legislative deadlock immediately and submit a strong civil rights package for his approval. King's confidence in the new president continued to grow. By the end of his tenure, Johnson had been instrumental in the passage of three civil rights bills. The first was signed into law on July 2, 1964.

Overleaf:
Civil rights leaders and members of Congress witness the signing of the Civil Rights Act of 1964 (Public Accommodations Bill) by President Lyndon B. Johnson.

Cecil Stoughton
Courtesy of Lyndon Baines Johnson Library

Attending the funeral services for the four girls killed in the bombing, family members comfort a younger relative.

Vernon Merritt

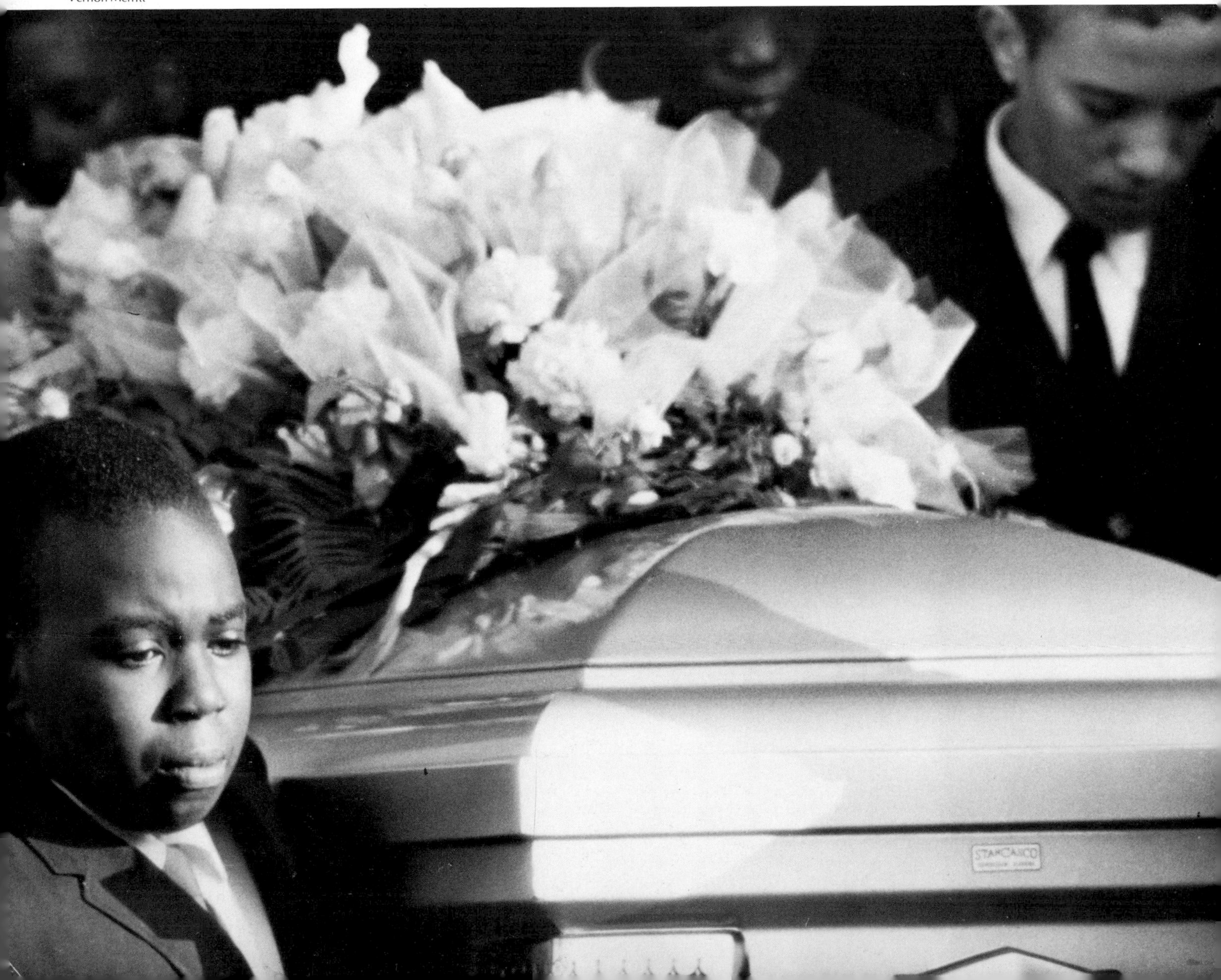

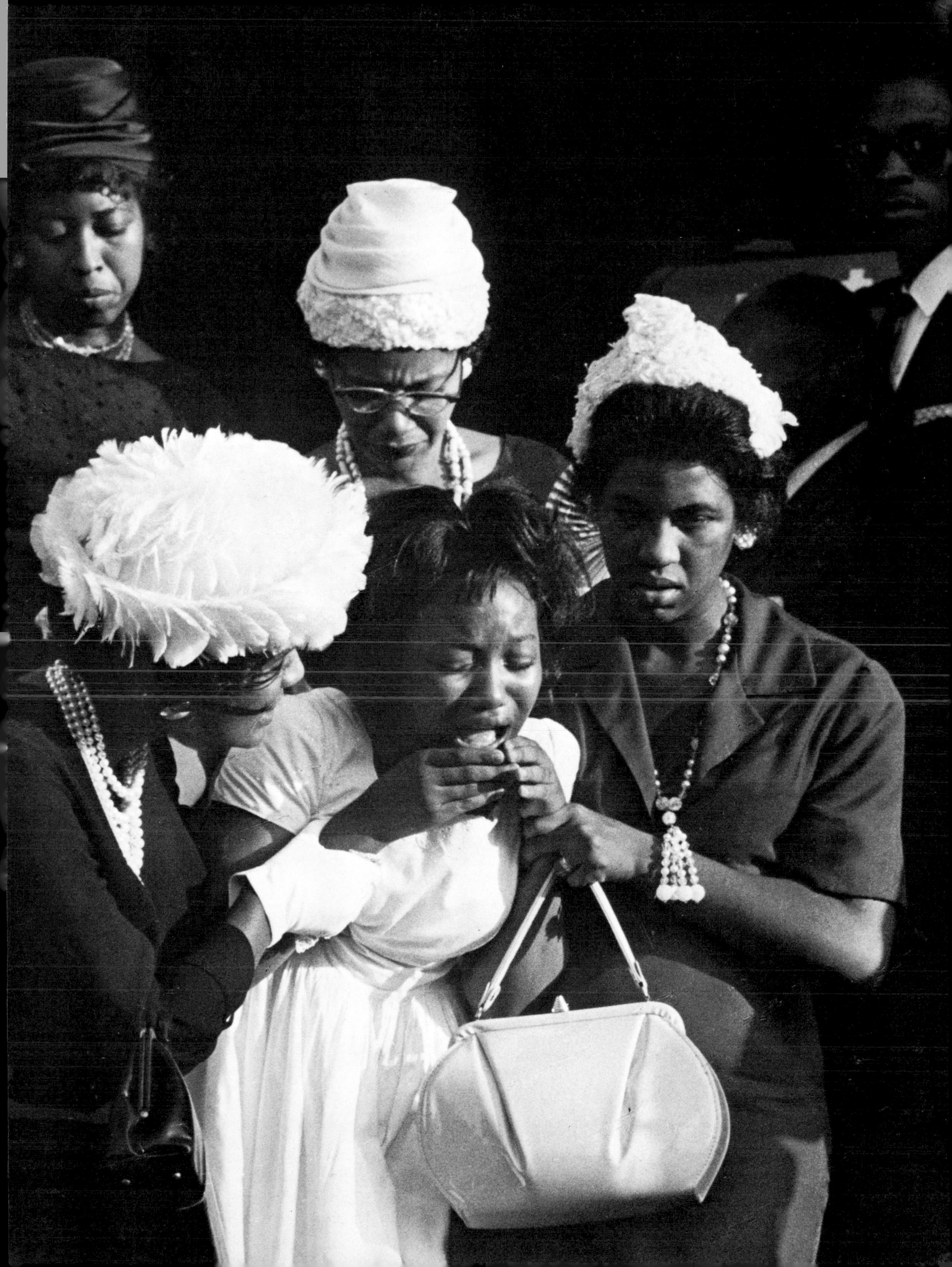

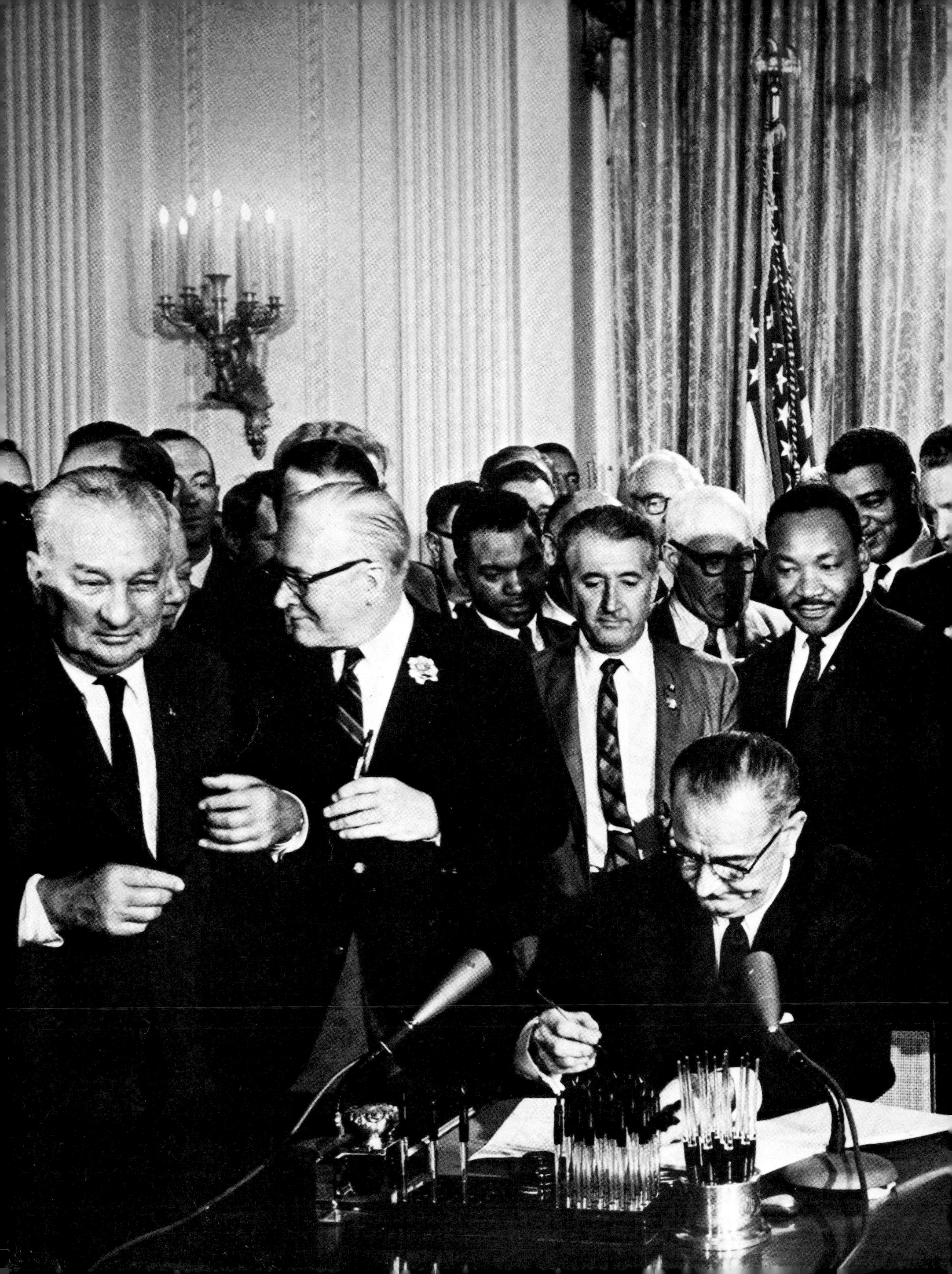

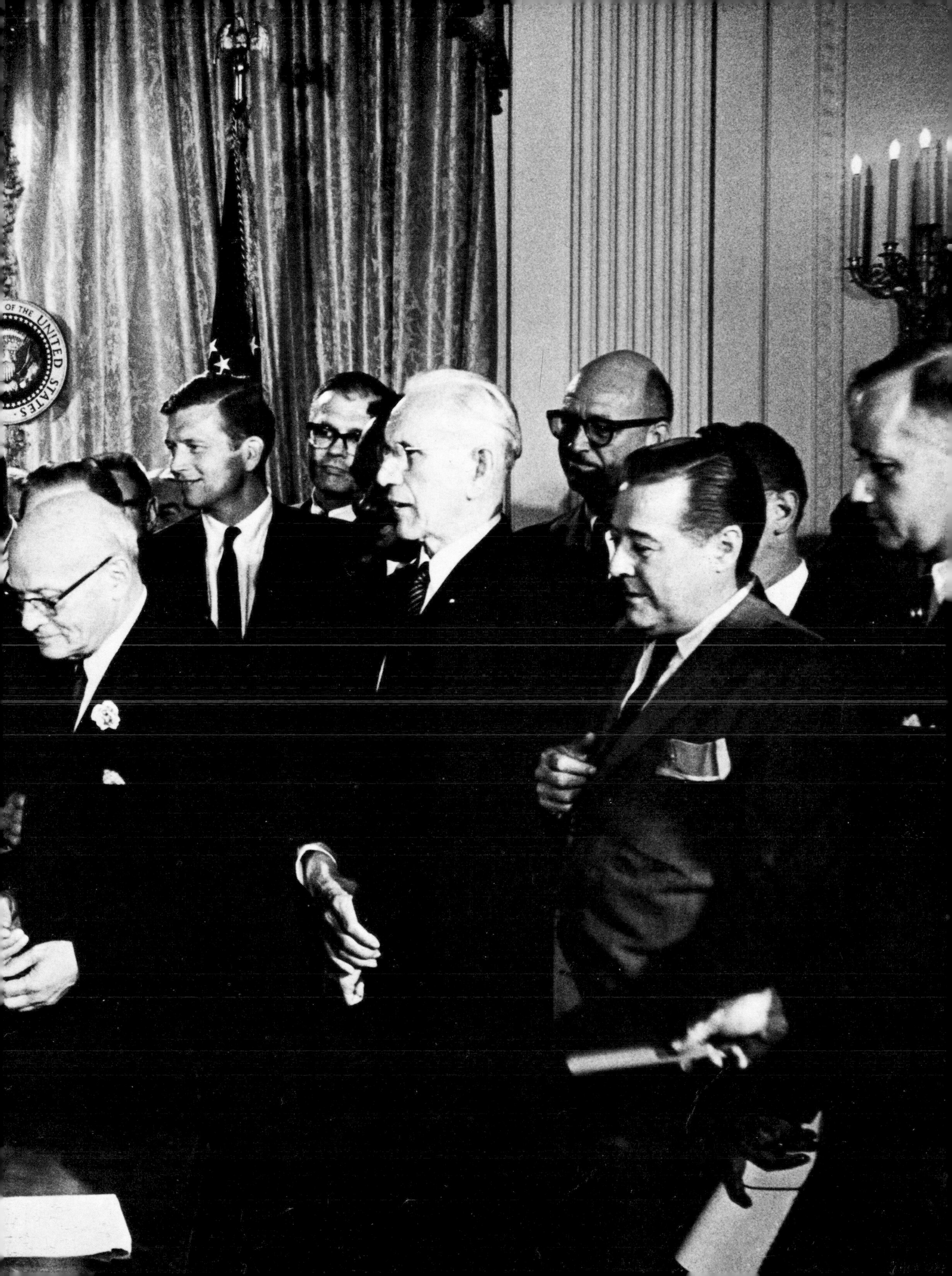
OF THE UNITED STATES

Flip Schulke

Chapter Eight

"Man Is a Child of God"

King—the Minister and the Man   "Dr. King felt very strongly, as I do, that our civil rights involvement was merely an extension of our Christian ministry.... Any Christian minister must be involved in the human rights struggle. We cannot preach the gospel in the four walls of the church and let it stop there. We must take it into the streets and let Jesus live in the hearts and minds and souls and bodies of all individuals."

—Reverend Ralph Abernathy, president of SCLC, 1975

As a minister and as a human being, King had a profound impact on those whose lives were touched by his. His father, Martin Luther King, Sr., recalls the earliest seeds of commitment in his son: "He was always a very sensitive child and always above his age in his thinking and in his carriage. I wouldn't say he was a peculiar child, but he was a little different in that he always made friends with good books from the time he was a small child." Of his son's passion for equality, King, Sr., recollects: "One day he told his mother, 'Daddy got in arguing with a white man, and he told the white man he didn't have enough nerve to pull the trigger.' " Seeing his mother upset, the young boy promised, "You know, when I get to be a man, I'm gonna hit this thing, and I'm gonna hit it hard. . . .Mother, there is no such thing as one people being better than another. The lord made all of us equal, and I'm gonna see to that."

His father also remembers King's first inclination to join the ministry. "We thought he was going to be a lawyer. . . . We let him go to a tobacco farm up in Connecticut during the summer when he was in college. They appointed him to lead the devotions for all the students that were there for the summer. So, he

Martin Luther King, Sr., preaches at the Ebenezer Baptist Church in Atlanta, Georgia, where, in 1960, his son joined him as co-pastor.

Flip Schulke

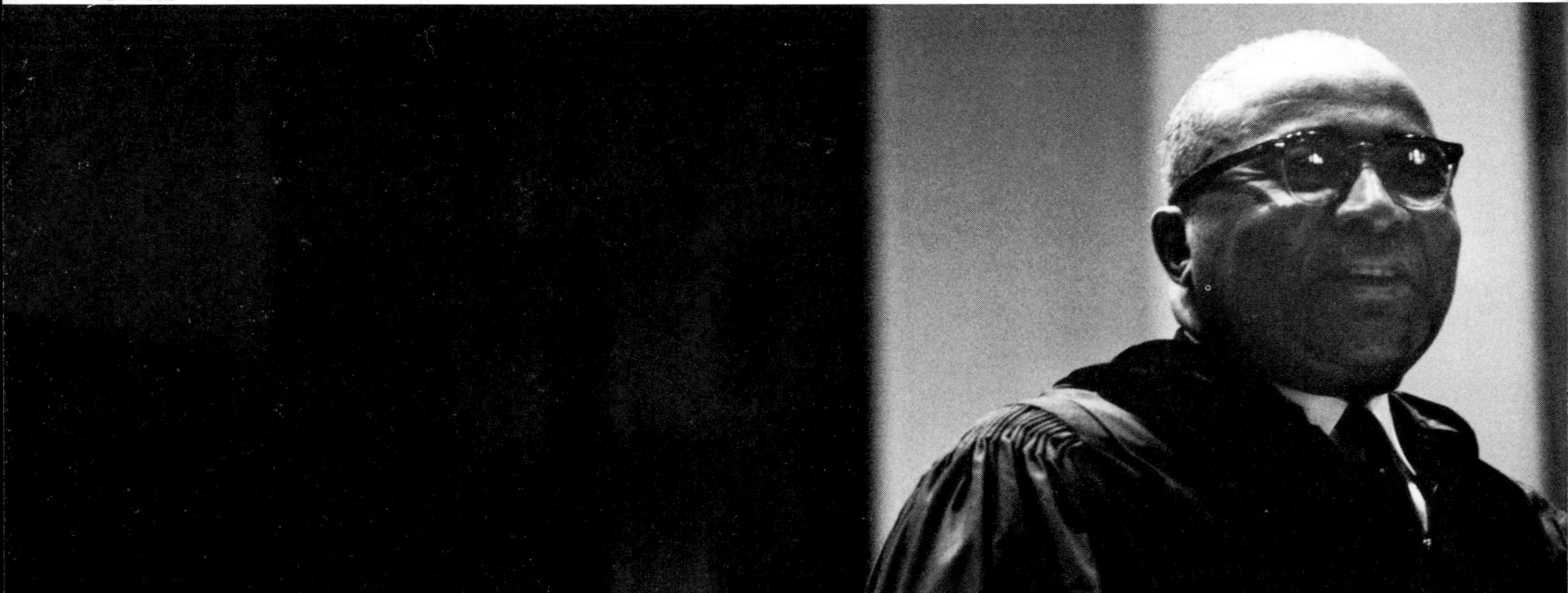

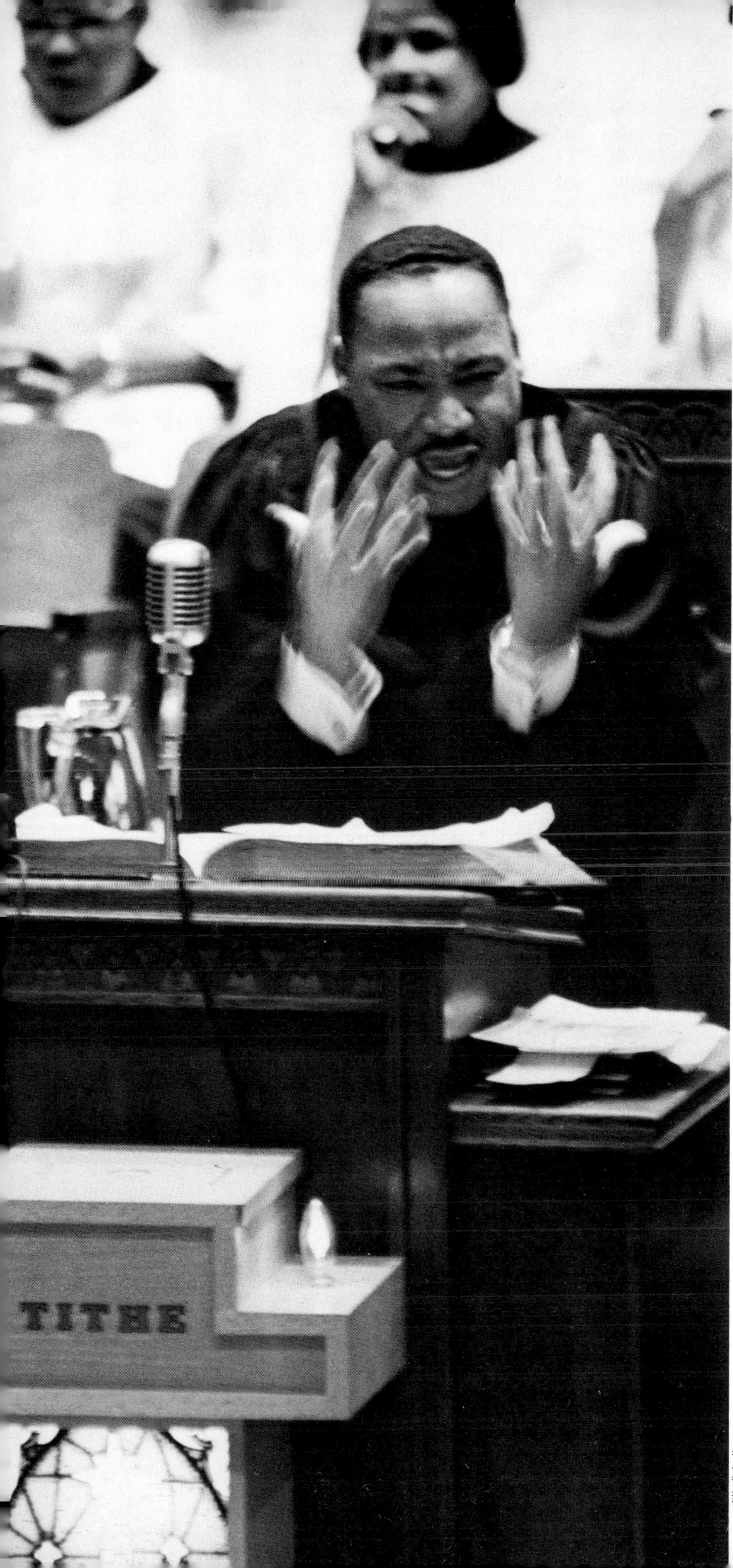
TITHE

Flip Schulke

started reading the scripture and commenting on it, and he just held his colleagues and classmates spellbound when he talked." After that experience, King decided he wanted to attend the best white seminary he could, according to his father, "to convince white folks that all black folks are not dumb."

King chose Crozer Theological Seminary in Chester, Pennsylvania, where he became president of the student body and was graduated at the head of his class.

Those with whom King worked in his day by day struggle against injustice have tried to analyze and understand the man who inspired and led them. "We throw the word 'genius' around lightly, but he was a genius," insists Jesse Jackson, head of the SCLC in Chicago. "Just in terms of his understanding of systematic theology and its application. He was a 'doctor' of theology in the best sense of the word. Beyond that, he was one of the most profound and one of the most powerful preachers to ever live, because he closed the gap between what he talked about and what he did. 'So in him the word became flesh and dwelt among men.' He didn't just talk brotherhood; he was a brother. He didn't just talk friendship; he was a friend. . . . He didn't wish for change; he changed things."

ON DIGNITY

"I think the greatest victory of this period was . . . something internal. The real victory was what this period did to the psyche of the black man. The greatness of this period was that we armed ourselves with dignity and self-respect. The greatness of this period was that we straightened our backs up. And a man can't ride your back unless it's bent."

ON CIVIL DISOBEDIENCE

"There comes a time when a moral man can't obey a law which his conscience tells him is unjust. And the important thing is that when he does that, he willingly accepts the penalty—because if he refuses to accept the penalty, then he becomes reckless, and he becomes an anarchist . . . there were those individuals in every age and generation who were willing to say, 'I will be obedient to a higher law.' . . . It is important to see that there are times when a man-made law is out of harmony with the moral law of the universe."

ON POVERTY

"Now we are a poor people. Don't let anybody fool you, we're poor. A vast majority of black people in the United States are smothering in an airtight cage of poverty in the midst of an affluent society. . . . Most of the poor people in this country are working every day, but earning so little that they cannot begin to function in the mainstream of economic life of our nation. They're working on full time jobs for part-time pay. We've got to do something about joblessness, and we are going to Washington to demand an economic bill of rights."

Flip Schulke

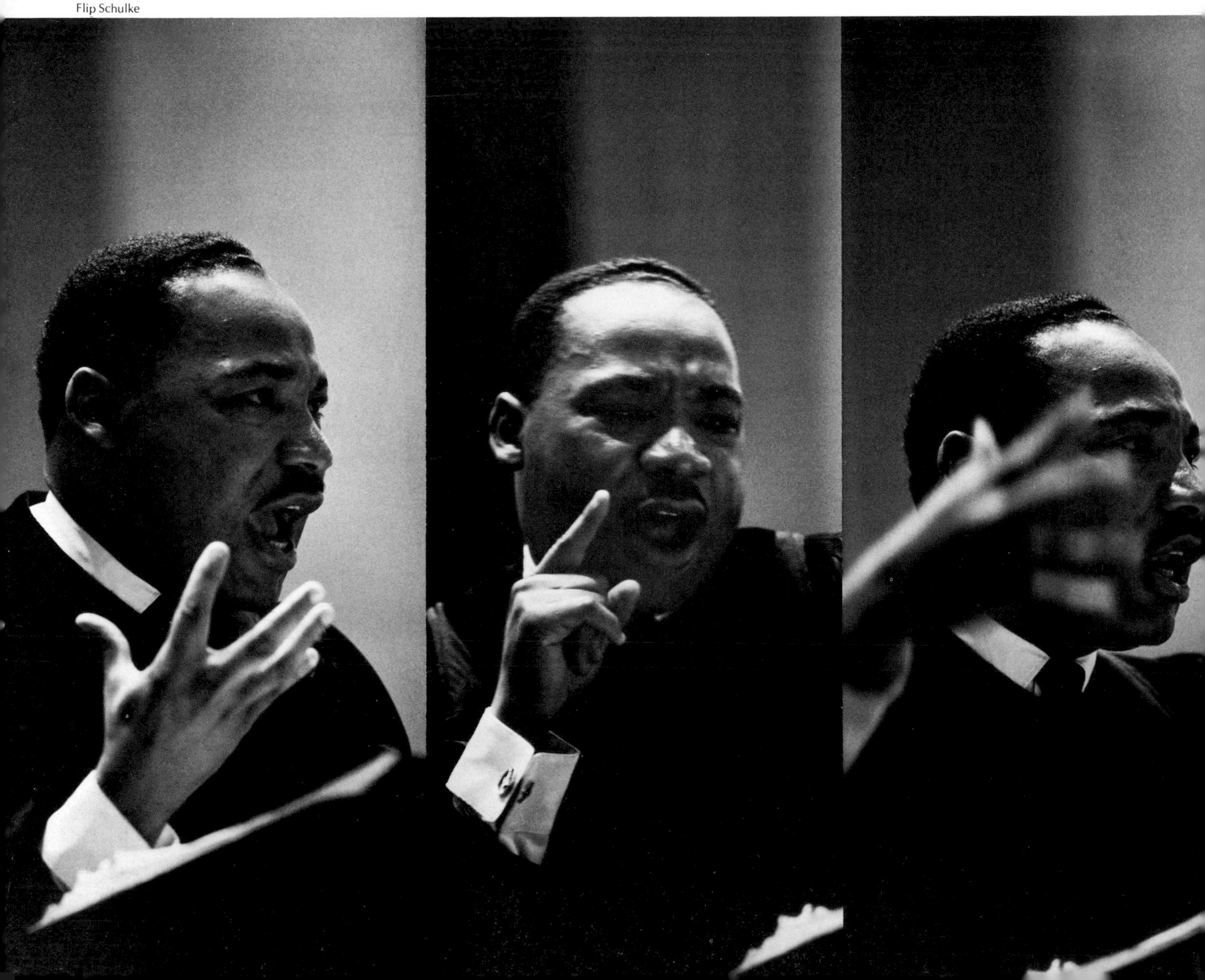

ON NONVIOLENCE

"We have a power, power that can't be found in Molotov cocktails, but we do have a power. Power that cannot be found in bullets and in guns, but we have a power. It is a power as old as the insights of Jesus of Nazareth and as modern as the techniques of Mahatma Gandhi."

ON VIETNAM

"Somehow this madness must cease. We must stop now. I speak as a child of God and a brother to the suffering poor of Vietnam. . . . I speak for the poor of America who are paying the double price of smashed hopes at home and death and corruption in Vietnam. I speak as a citizen of the world, for the world as it stands aghast at the path we have taken. I speak as an American to the leaders of my own nation. The great initiative in this war is ours. The initiative to stop it must be ours."

ON INTEGRATION

"Our cultural patterns are an amalgam of black and white. Our destinies are tied together; none of us can make it alone . . . There is no separate black path to power and fulfillment that does not have to intersect with white roots. Somewhere along the way the two must join together, black and white together, we shall overcome, and I still believe it."

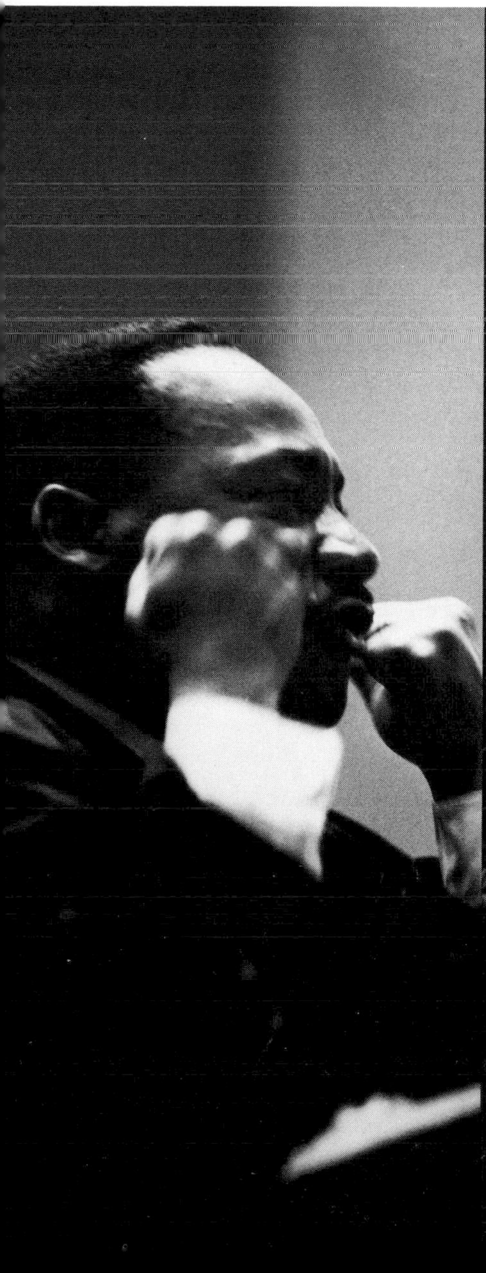

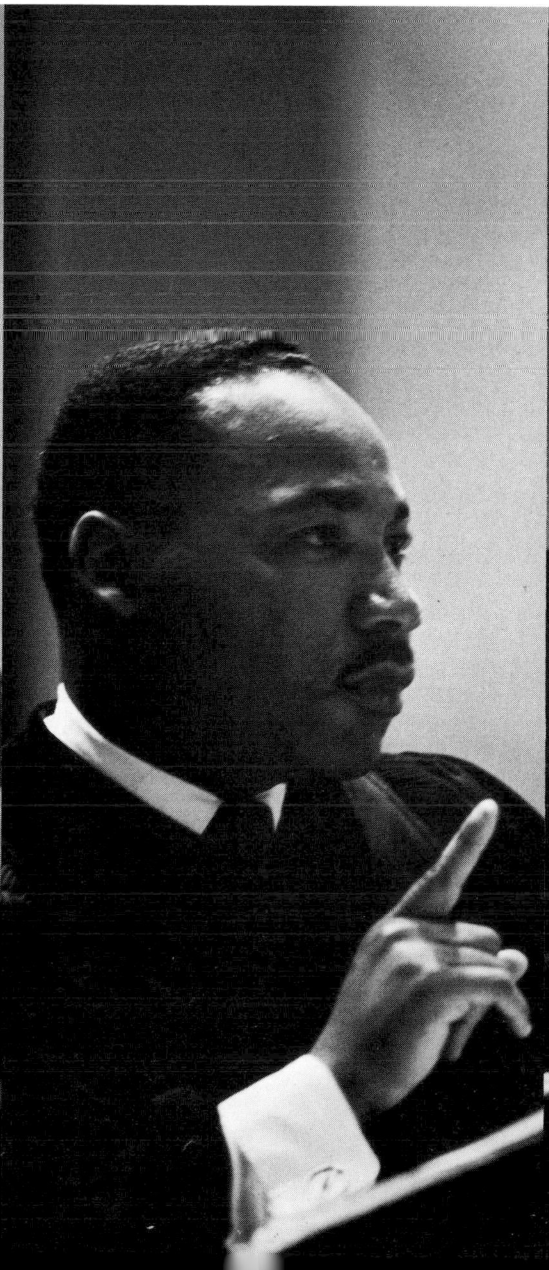

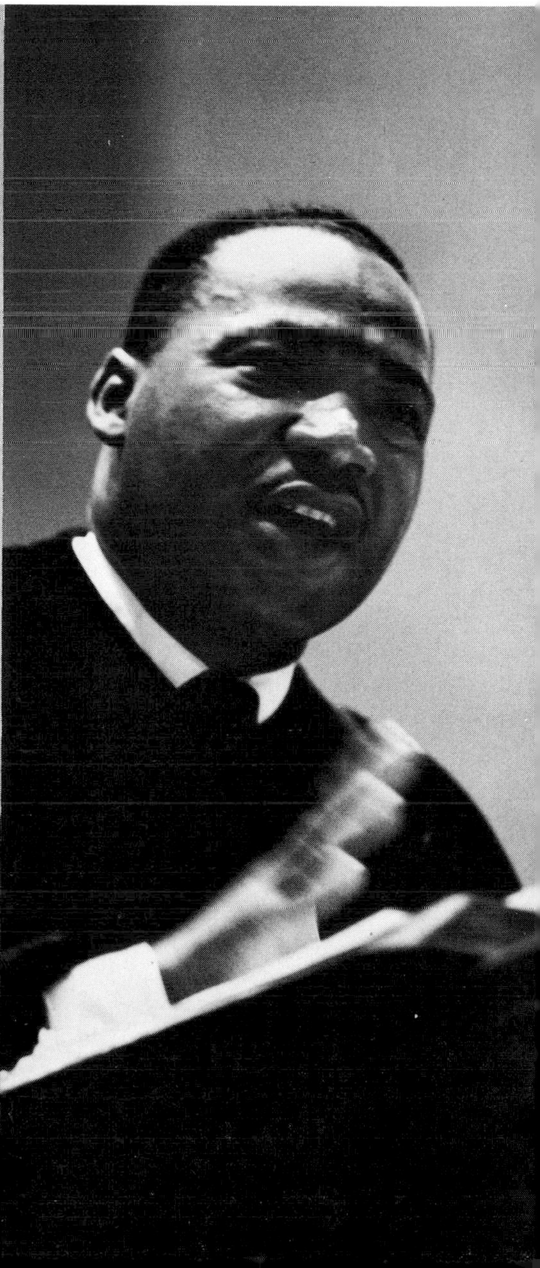

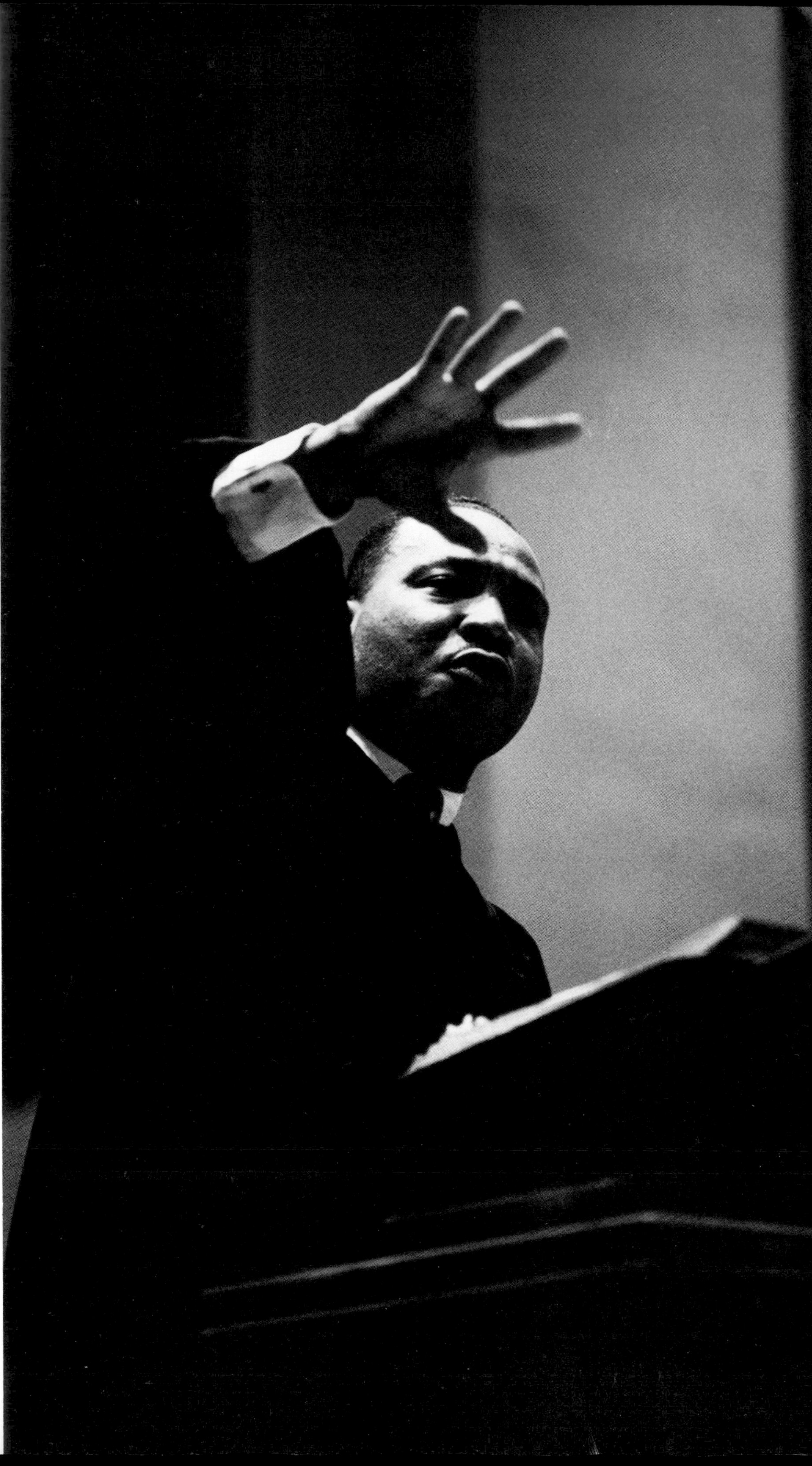

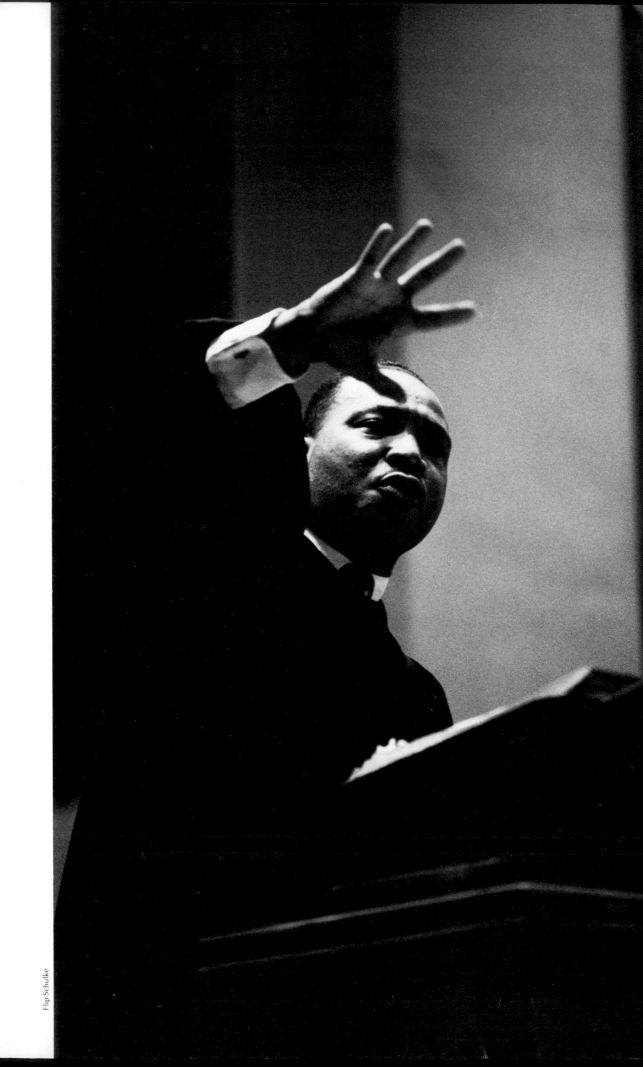

Flip Schulke

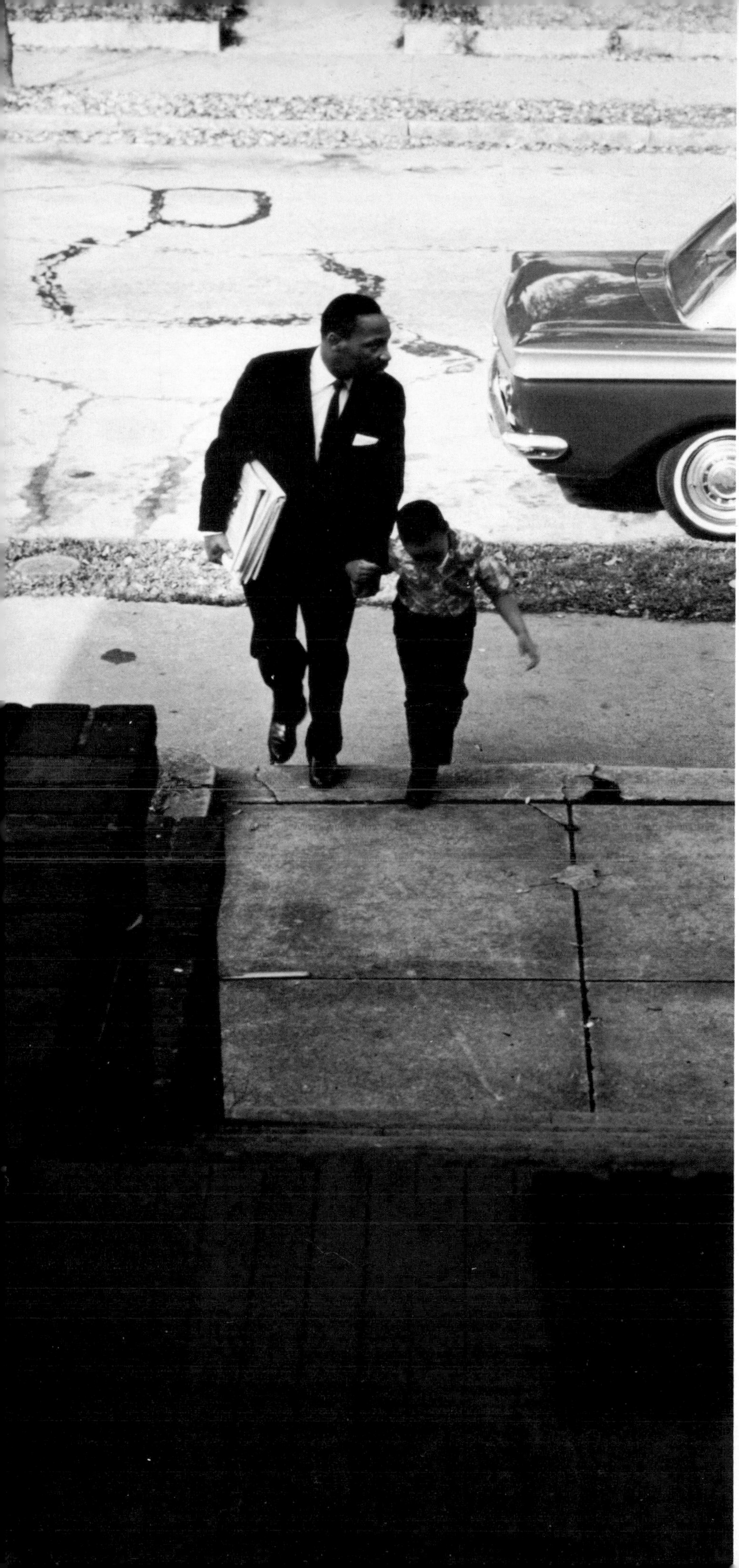

Perhaps no one knew the strength of King's character as well as his wife, Coretta: "He was good—such a very good man. His conscience was a formidable thing that kept him on the path he thought was right. If he ever did something a little wrong, or committed a selfish act, his conscience fairly devoured him. He would, throughout his life, really suffer if he felt there was some possibility that he had wronged anyone or acted thoughtlessly. . . . He felt that having been born into what was a middle-class Negro family was a privilege he had not earned, just as he felt the many honors heaped on him in the later years were not his alone. He would constantly examine himself to determine if he were becoming corrupted, if he were accepting honors too easily. . . . He was a truly humble man and never felt he was adequate to his positions. That is why he worried so much, worked so hard, studied constantly, long after he had become a world figure."

For King, the pinnacle of public recognition and personal achievement came in 1964, when he received the Nobel Peace Prize, which is given annually to the individual who has contributed the most to the "furtherance of

King enjoys an afternoon with his oldest son, Martin Luther III.

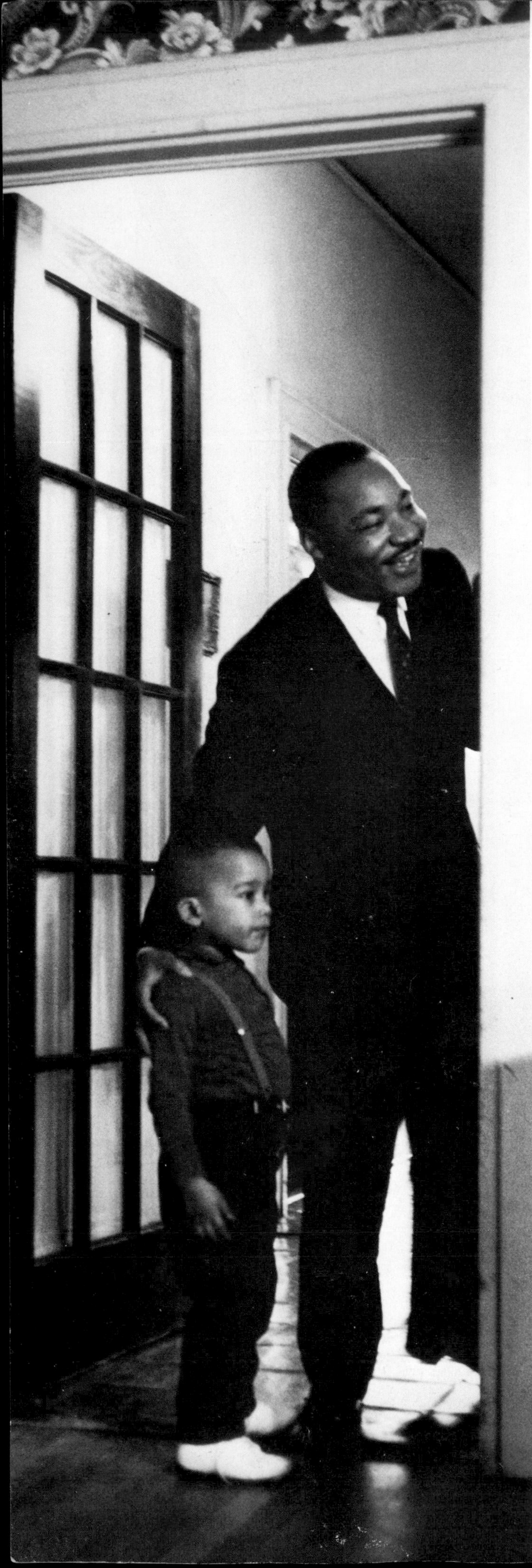

Right:
Mrs. Coretta King assists the Kings' youngest daughter, Bernice Albertine, at a Sunday family dinner.

In the weeks preceding his trip to Norway, King has an opportunity to recuperate from his exhausting schedule and to enjoy his children, Dexter Scott (left) and Yolanda Denise (below).

Flip Schulke

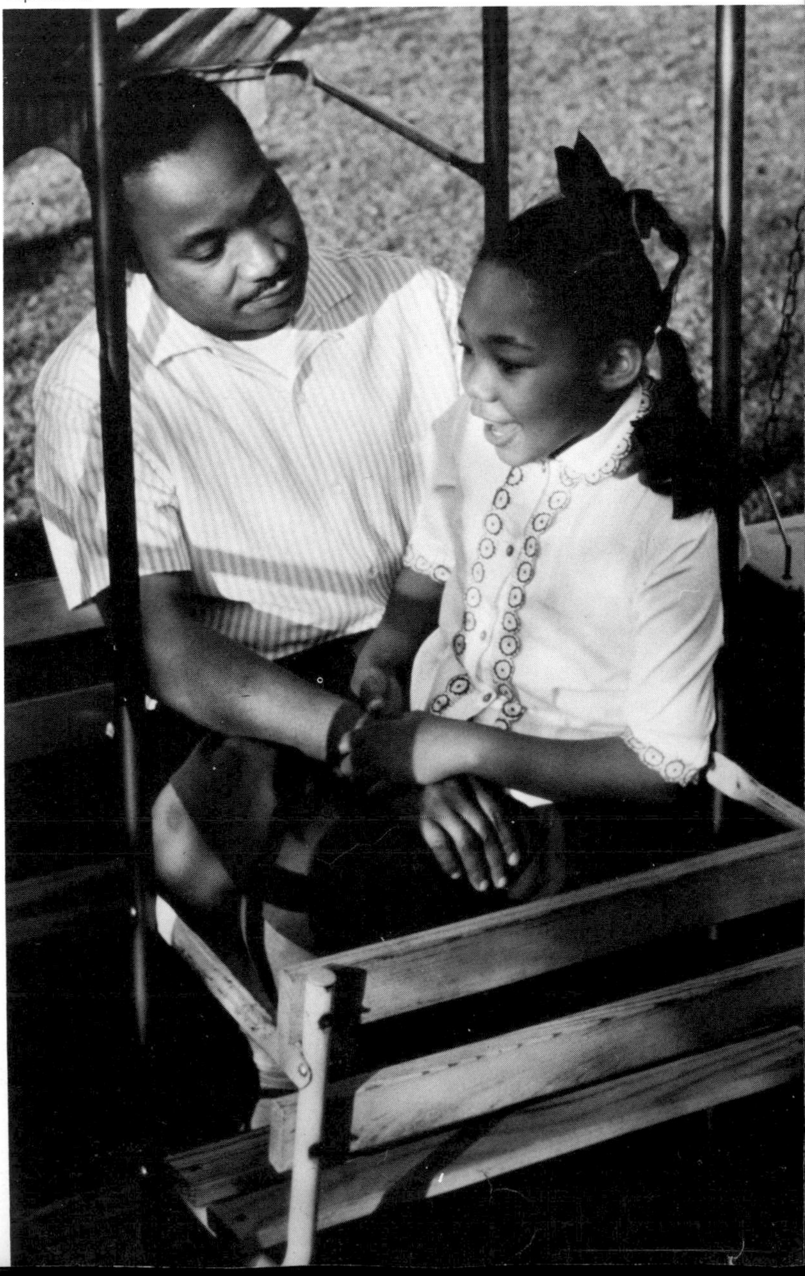

Flip Schulke

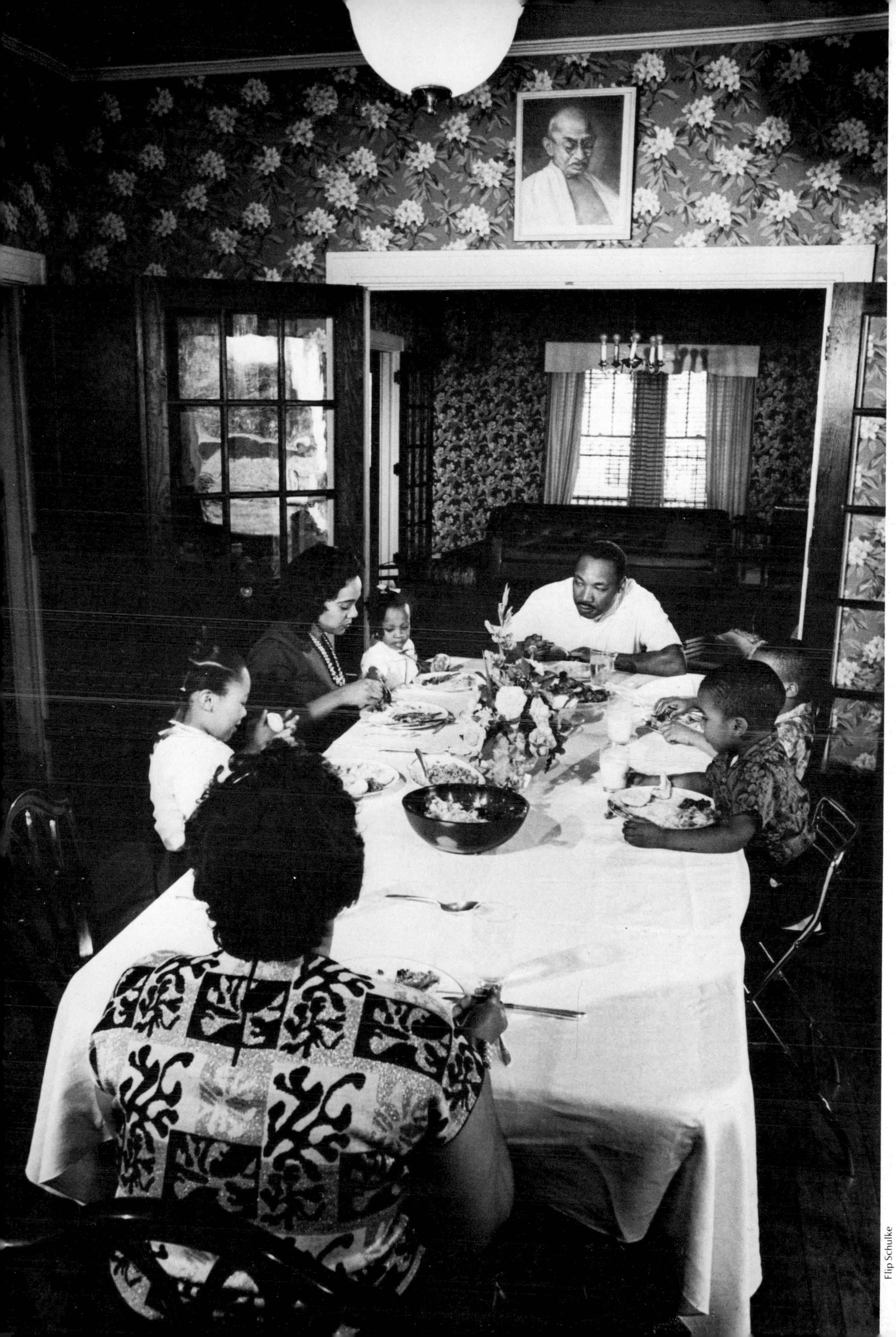

Flip Schulke

peace among men." Only one other American black, Ralph Bunche of the United Nations, had won the prize; and King was the youngest man ever to have won it.

King's family, closest friends, and associates accompanied him to Oslo, Norway, for the presentation. Before leaving the United States, he had insisted that the entire $54,000 prize be donated to the black movement—to all of those whom he believed deserved equal recognition.

King received the award with humility. **"I am mindful that only yesterday in Birmingham, Alabama, our children, crying out for brotherhood, were answered with fire hoses, snarling dogs, and even death,"** he said.**"I am mindful that only yesterday in Philadelphia, Mississippi, young people seeking to secure the right to vote were brutalized and murdered. Therefore I must ask why this prize is awarded to a Movement which is beleaguered and committed to unrelenting struggle; to a Movement which has not won the very peace and brotherhood which is the essence of the Nobel Prize. After contemplation I conclude that this award, which I receive on behalf of the Movement, is a profound recognition that nonviolence is the answer to the crucial political and racial questions of our time—the need for man to overcome oppression without resorting to violence."**

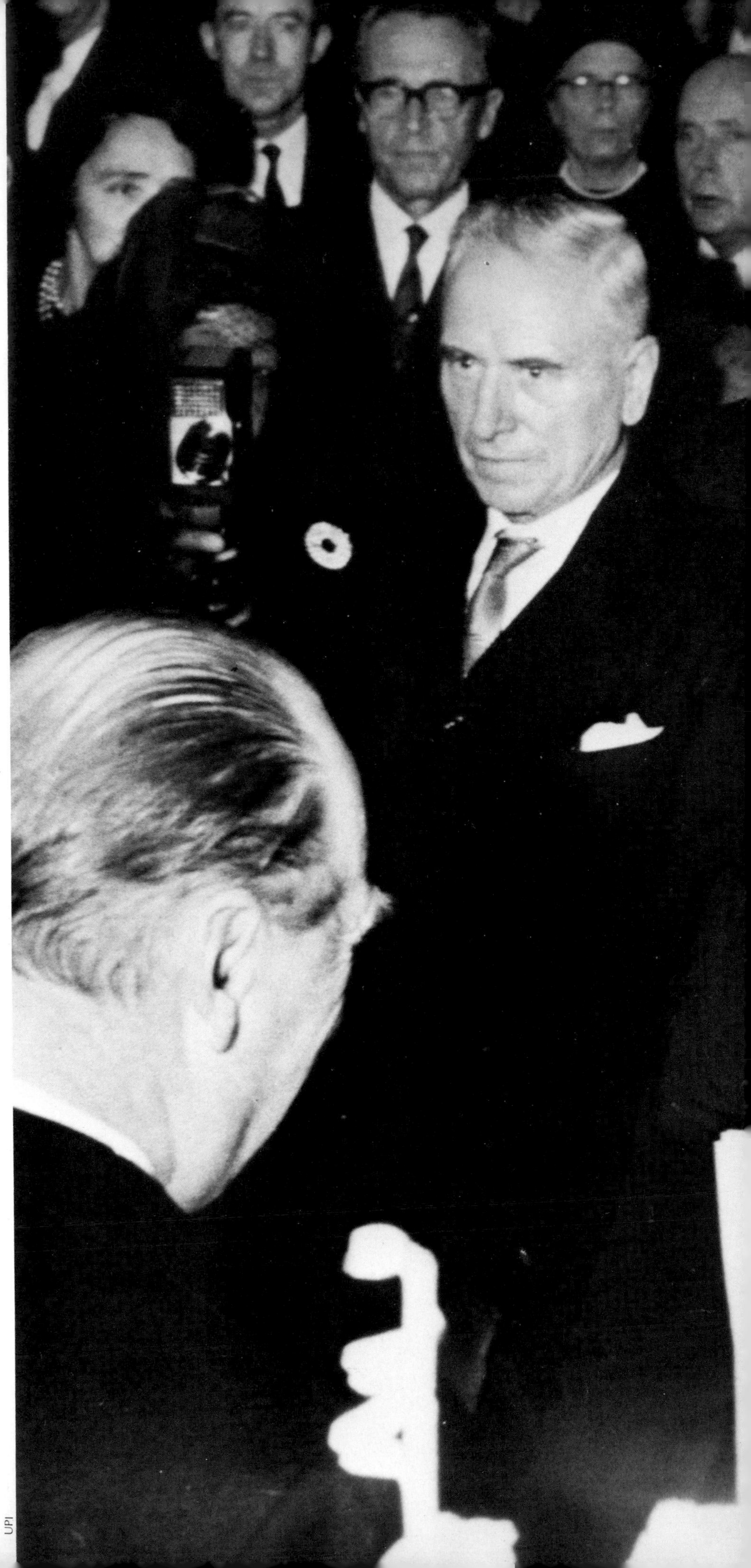

December 10, 1964. King becomes the youngest man ever to win the Nobel Peace Prize. King Olav V of Norway congratulates him after the ceremony in Oslo, Norway.

UPI

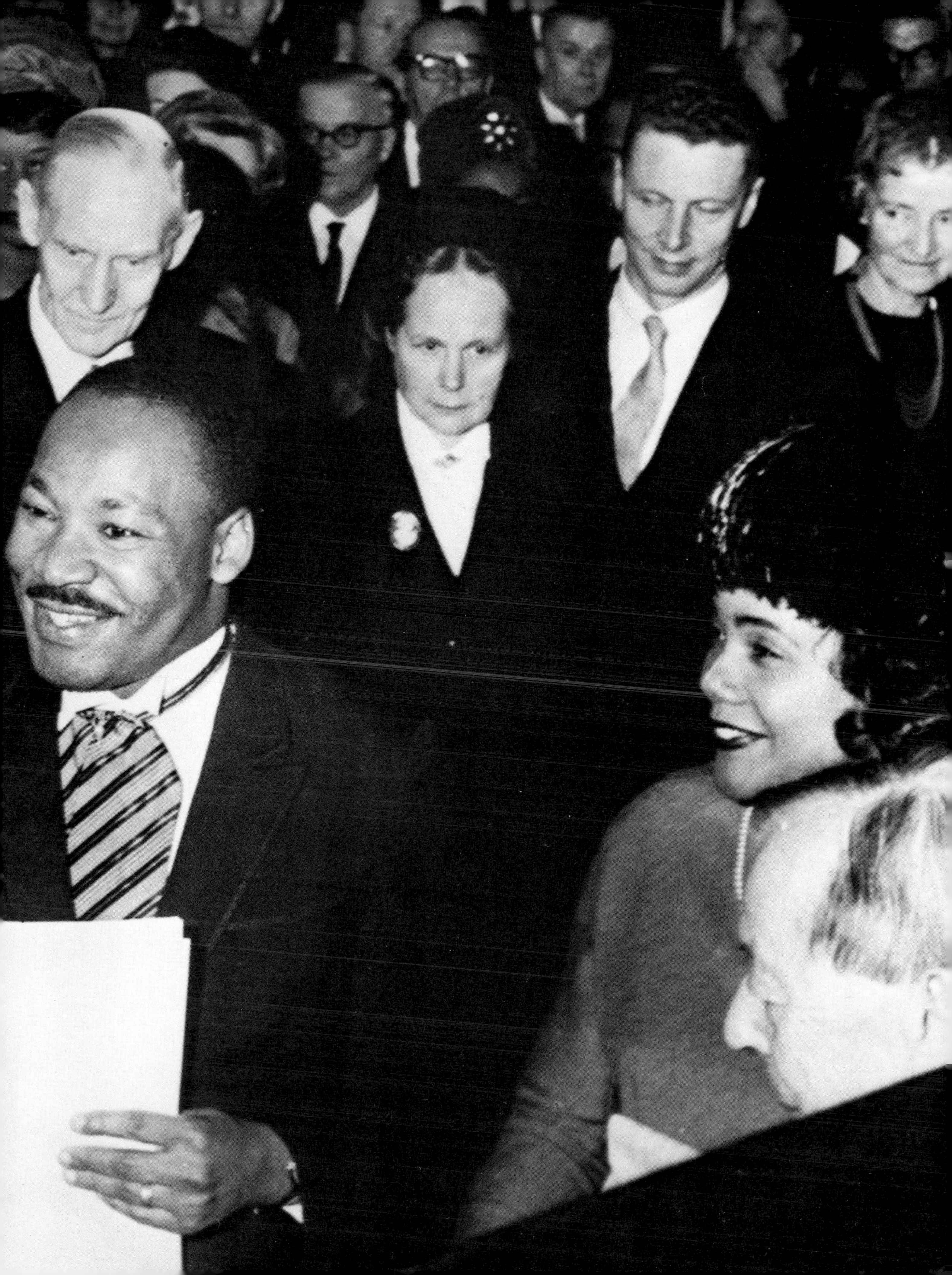

Mike Mauney

Chapter Nine

"We Shall Overcome"

Voter Registration and Selma, Alabama, 1964–1965 King knew that if the Nobel Prize was to mean anything, he must commit himself more than ever to attaining the goals of the black movement through peace. **"I have been on a mountaintop,"** he said shortly after becoming Nobel laureate. **"I really wish I could just stay on the mountain; but I must go back to the valley. I must go back, because my brothers and sisters down in Mississippi and Alabama are sweltering under the heat of injustice. There are people starving in the valley, and people who don't have jobs, and people who can't vote."**

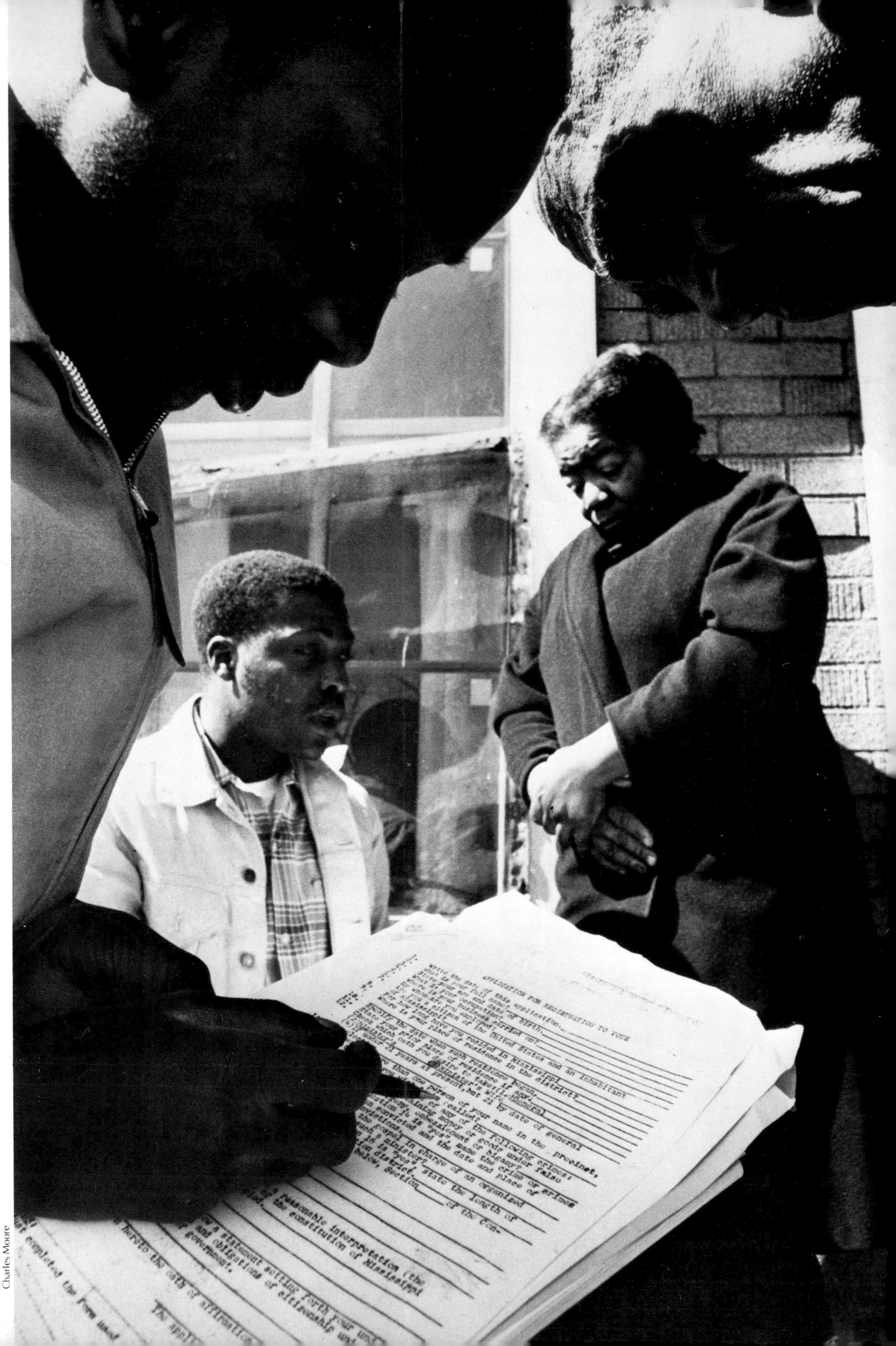
APPLICATION FOR REGISTRATION TO VOTE

Charles Moore

PROLOGUE

The campaign to register voters in Selma ushered in the new year, 1965. The previous year had witnessed the heights of the Nobel Peace Prize and the civil rights bill and the depths of riots in northern ghettos, failure in St. Augustine, and the tragic murder of three civil rights workers in Mississippi.

St. Augustine, Florida, had been the target for demonstrations in the previous spring because the nation and the press were focusing on the four hundredth birthday celebration of America's oldest city. The protests to desegregate public accommodations received unexpected publicity when one arrested picketer turned out to be Mrs. Malcolm Peabody, mother of the governor of Massachusetts.

Left:
In the spring of 1964, the civil rights movement begins a major drive to register black voters in the South.

The old slave market in the town square of St. Augustine is the focal point of the Ku Klux Klan demonstrations in May and June, 1964.

Steve Shapiro

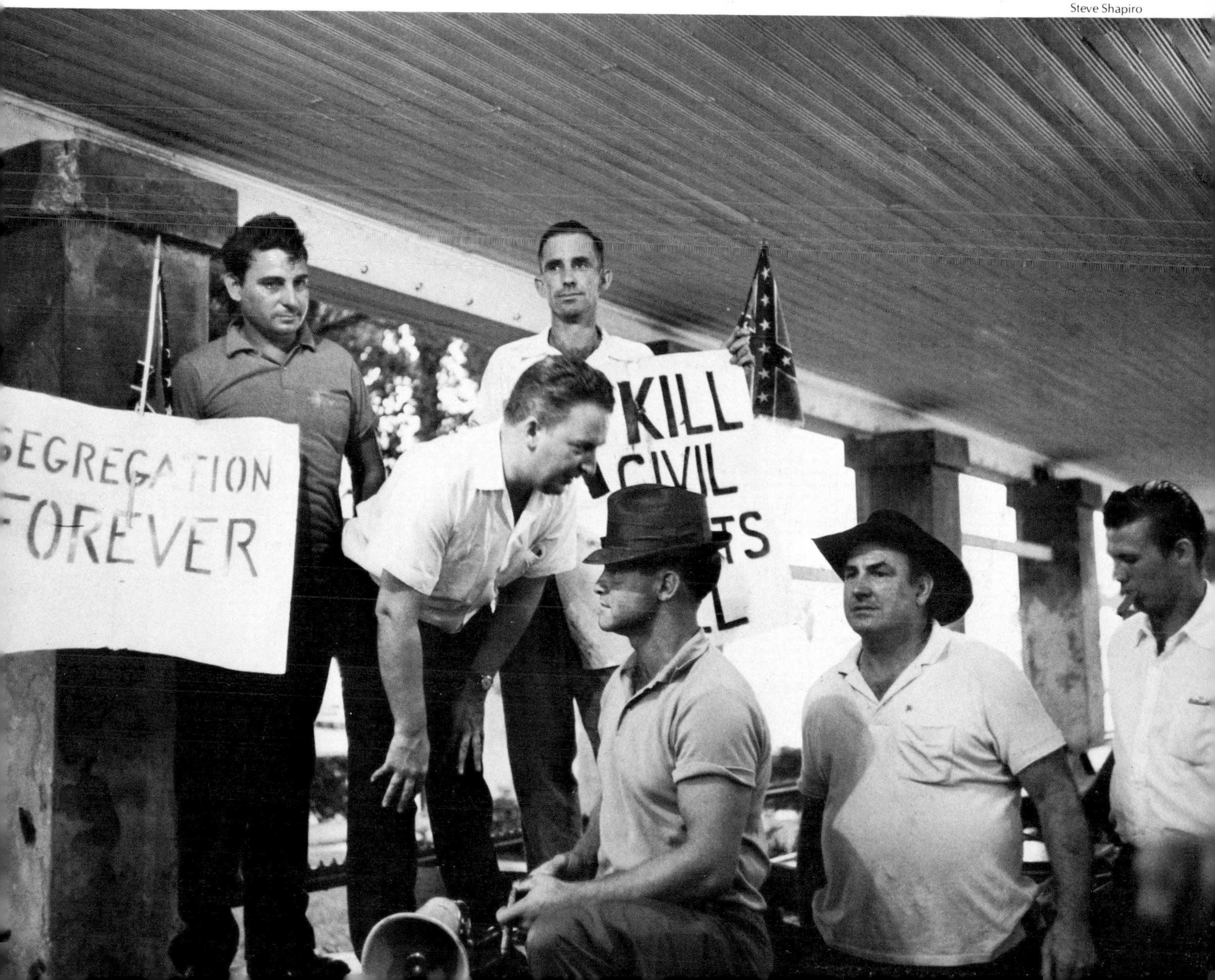

EGREGATION
FOREVER
KILL
CIVIL

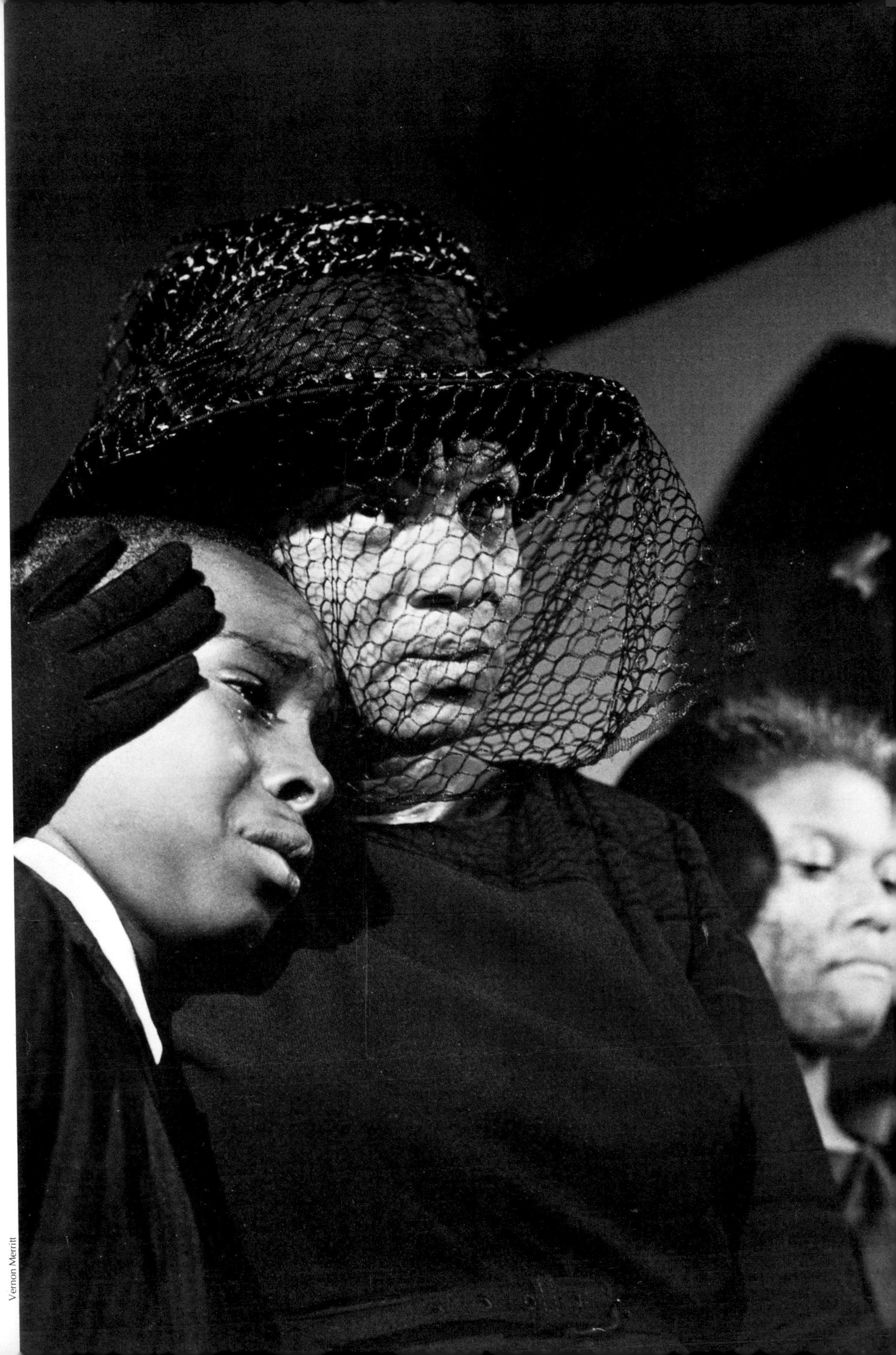
Vernon Merritt

Philadelphia, Mississippi, August, 1964. Friends mourn the deaths of civil rights workers Chaney, Goodman, and Schwerner.

Below:
Deputy Sheriff Cecil Price of Philadelphia, Mississippi, is convicted of conspiracy in the murders. The trial is the first in which a Mississippi jury returns a verdict of guilty in a civil rights murder.

Vernon Merritt

King and the protest organizers faced different problems in St. Augustine than they had experienced in other cities. Although the police were not actively hostile, they stood by passively while white segregationists viciously attacked demonstrators. Violence continued unchecked until Governor Farris Bryant sent state troopers to quiet the disruption. King, Abernathy, and sixteen other protestors were arrested and jailed as "unwanted guests" for attempting to be served at a white restaurant. But in the end, the St. Augustine crusade petered out and ended inconclusively.

On the heels of disillusionment in St. Augustine came despair. In August, 1964, the bodies of civil rights workers James Chaney, Michael Schwerner, and Andrew Goodman were found buried in a dam near Philadelphia, Mississippi. The three young men had been working on the Mississippi Project, trying to register black voters before the upcoming election. On June 21, they were reportedly arrested for speeding in Mississippi. They were not seen again. Local authorities claimed they had been released from prison shortly after the arrest. President Johnson ordered the FBI to make a full inquiry. Sheriff Lawrence Rainey, his deputy, Cecil Price, and sixteen others, including the Imperial Wizard of the Ku Klux Klan, were indicted by a Federal grand jury for conspiring to deprive the murdered men of their constitutional rights to life and liberty. The accused men could not be indicted for murder, a state offense, because the state courts had taken no action. Price and six other conspirators were found guilty, the first time a Mississippi jury had returned a "guilty" verdict in a civil rights murder case. Rainey was acquitted.

When the nation learned of the killings, hundreds of civil rights workers rushed to Mississippi and neighboring states to pursue the mission of the three martyred young men. And thus the scene was set for Selma.

AN INTERVIEW WITH HOSEA WILLIAMS

Hosea Williams, *vice president of SCLC, and president of the Atlanta, Georgia, chapter is a veteran of many of Dr. Martin Luther King's civil rights campaigns. Currently a member of the Georgia House of Representatives, he began his career as a chemist with the U.S. Department of Agriculture before joining SCLC. Skilled in "grass roots' organizing, he has been jailed more than fifty times during rights campaigns in the South.*

"I read about Martin Luther King, Jr., in Montgomery, Alabama. Here was a guy who stood at the head of the line; he didn't tell us how to get free, but showed us how to get free. I began to say this is my leader. The other thing was, I was fascinated with King's ability to hold the Montgomery bus boycott together, because this was unheard of in modern history. That an organizer could organize this many people and keep them together for this long, so many different groups, keep them together until they won that victory, this was unheard of.

"All right, I was violent by nature, reared up with no father; I'm a bastard child—my mother was never married to my father—reared up on a white man's plantation. I had been exposed to all the ingredients that make one violent. But I began to read about this man, how he dealt with the Montgomery bus boycott through nonviolence, and how he drew world-wide sympathy and how he crystallized public opinion on all the important issues of the black struggle.

"Martin was a genius at surrounding himself with talents that could become truly experts in their different areas. He wanted me for a field general. I became SCLC's Castro. I became the tough guy, the nervy guy. But I saw Martin do things that truly made my flesh shake on my bones, so to speak. That's how I really got with him.

"Now we had dealt in Montgomery with transportation, dealt in Birmingham and St. Augustine with public accommodations, so we decided after a

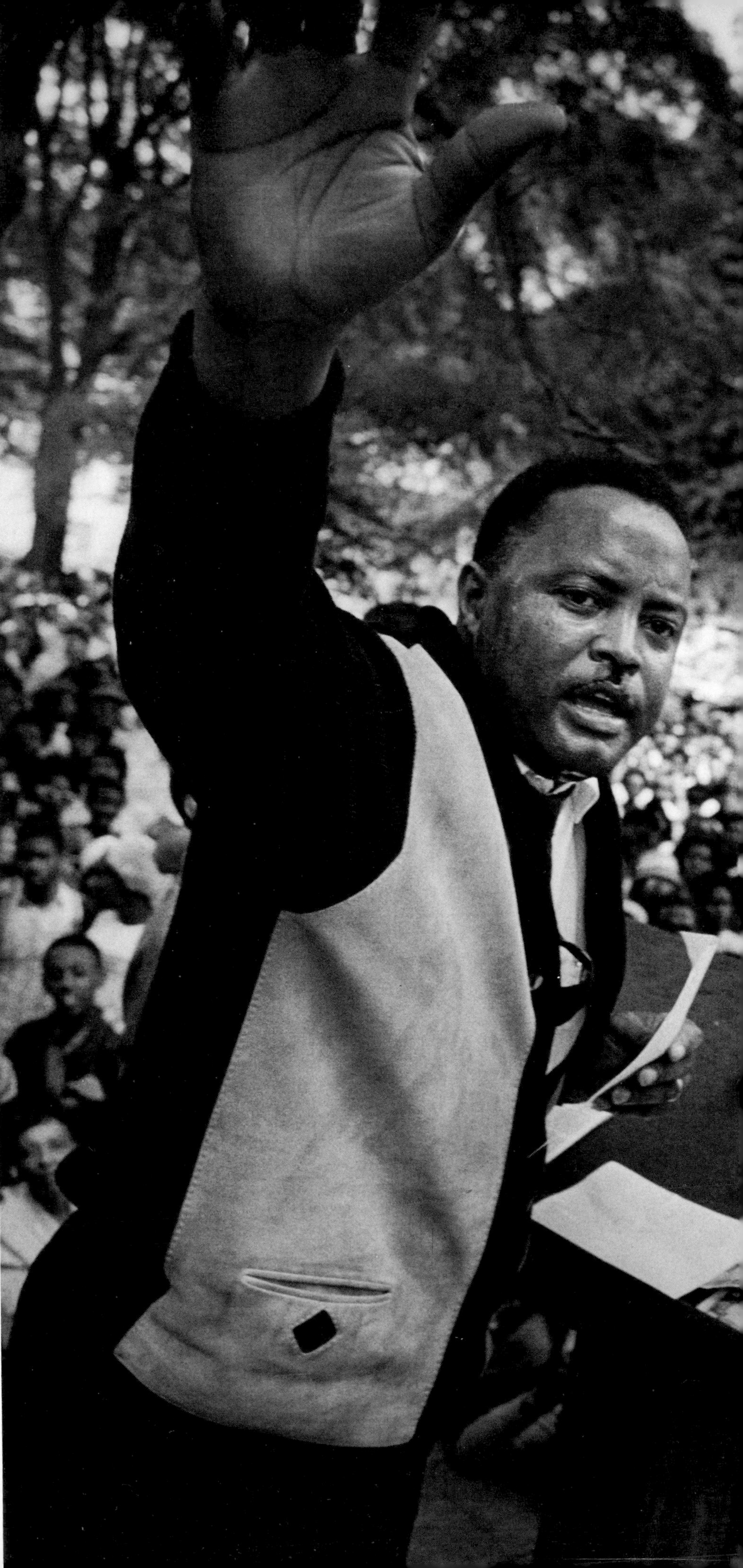

Bob Fitch

long three- or four-day session that the next move was the franchise, voter registration. It was the political arena. It came out that the man in Selma, Alabama, Jim Clark [County Sheriff], didn't even allow black folks to meet. Any time four or more people got together, they were arrested. Jim Clark even sent deputies into churches, where people would be having worship service, to see whether they were serving God or whether they were talking civil rights in there. So Dr. King sent James Bevel to Selma and said: 'Go tell the people down there that I will be there on the first of January, and we are going to have a mass rally. We're going to have a march. We're going to launch a voter registration campaign.' He went and challenged Jim Clark.

"The most fearful day of my life was that day in Selma when we were supposed to march to take all these folks from Brown's Chapel to the courthouse to register. The FBI claimed there were supposed to be three places where they planned to assassinate Dr. King. They [the FBI] had found two of them, but they couldn't find the third place.

"Andy Young kept holding up the march, waiting to give the FBI a chance to find this other place; and I don't believe the FBI ever found any place. Finally, Dr. King said, we got all these people here, and I have to go. As we were going for that courthouse, honest to God, everywhere I looked, I saw a man standing behind a rock; I'd duck and I'd look and see and didn't see anybody. But my imagination, fear had really taken control of my whole body. So we marched on down to the jailhouse. That's one day they spit on him, and they cursed him and abused him all along that march, cussing him and spitting on him. He was smiling and still walking.

"Now we had had quite a bit of experience with Jim Clark by then, Jim Clark, who was an egomaniac and a publicity hound; and when we got to the courthouse I noticed something. I'm very observant. We had about a thousand people in line, but when the people would go into the courthouse they wouldn't let them register. They'd give them a number and send them out to the back of the courthouse. Supposedly, they were going to call them back down later on to register. But I could just feel something was wrong. Of course, I was scared to death, that was one thing. But Jim Clark came, and you know he is big and handsome and dressed immaculately, he came to the front of that door. All the cameras and everybody switched around and people started snickering, 'That's Jim Clark.' He stood up there, let them take all the pictures, and then he walked right down the steps, walked right by Dr. King and got in a car and drove away. I just knew something was wrong then. Jim Clark drives away and leaves Martin King there. Well, about that time a boy went into the courthouse and came back to me and said, 'Hosea, they must have five hundred white men in that courthouse, and they got axe handles, they got pitchforks, they got everything. All up the stairsteps, all the rooms filled.' And I began to figure that damn thing out.

"I was convinced then, what they were trying to do was force Dr. King to get arrested. If he got arrested, then the news would follow him, the news media, and the white men were going to come out of that courthouse, and they were going to slay us! Next thing, Dr. King became very disturbed and he told me: 'Look here, get me twelve people to go into that courthouse with me. It's not right. People come down here, take off from their job, and they won't let these folks register, just give them a number and send them back home. So, I'm going in the courthouse.' I wouldn't tell him that the man was in the courthouse because I knew that if I told him, he was going in that courthouse. So I didn't tell him. I started pleading with him and arguing with him. I said, let's leave the courthouse, you're supposed to see Jimmie Lee Jackson in the hospital, leave there and go to integrate Holiday Inn; and we're supposed to go from there down to Gee's Bend. There was not one black person registered down there; it was a bad town. Dr. King said, 'Well, I'm going in. If you don't get me twelve men, I'm going to get them myself.' At about that time Andy Young drove up in a car. I went to Andy and told him. 'Andy,' I said, 'please get him away from here.' Across the street from the courthouse then, there was a mob of about three hundred to five hundred people, white, cursing and raving and chewing at the bits. They really were going after him. Andy said, 'Get in the car.' He [Dr. King] said, 'No, I'm going to walk.' You know, that man turned around to leave, and he went dead toward that mob. He got about three or four feet away, and you could hear them breathing. They got just as quiet as a mouse. And Dr. King smiled and said, 'Excuse me, please.' And the line just opened up. He walked right on up through them and got on the sidewalk. The line just opened up as he went along and closed behind. And not one of them touched him. They got so quiet, it was like they were all spellbound, I guess, that the man who they were all raving about would come and submit his body to them. They didn't touch him.

"That's why I say, and often say this to young people at these colleges and universities, Dr. King was the most militant black man that lived during my time. He would never go into a place and make a firebrand speech and catch the next plane out when the riots broke out. The difference in Stokely, Rap Brown, and Dr. King was the fact that Dr. King would go into a black haven like Harlem or a black church and he would say virtually the things they would say other than, 'Kill! Kill! Violence to the violent!' But when he would finish his speech in Harlem or South Chicago or a black church, then he went back to George Wallace, and he went back to Bull Connor. He went back where the true enemy was, and said, 'I have come to try you.' None of those other guys ever did anything like that. They were militant from a rhetoric standpoint, but Dr. King was militant as a way of life."

ea Williams, vice president of
C, in charge of direct action
ests at Selma.

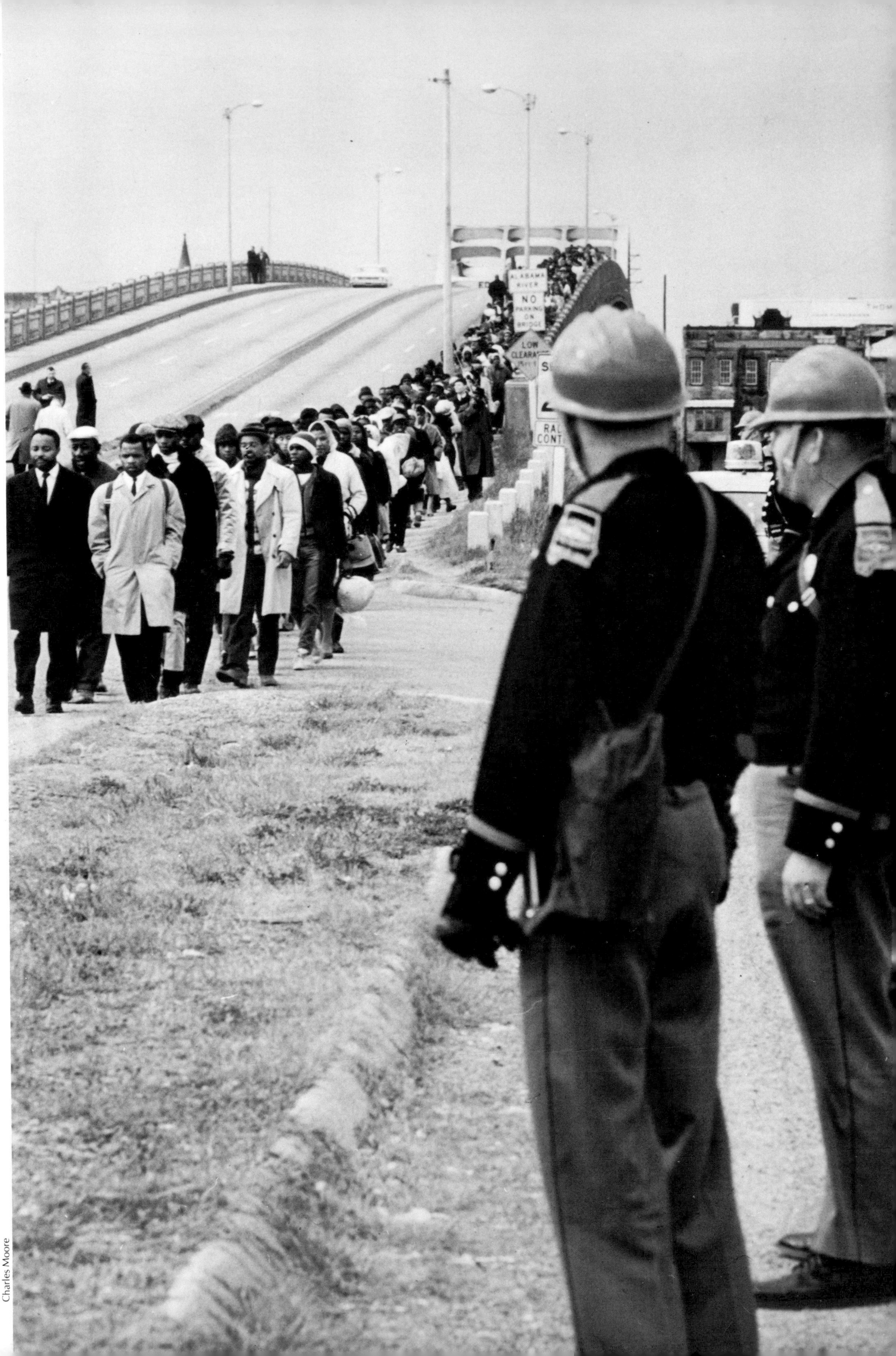
ALABAMA RIVER
NO PARKING ON BRIDGE
LOW

Charles Moore

CONFRONTATION

January 2, 1965. Addressing seven hundred blacks at Brown's Chapel Methodist Church in Selma, King initiates the campaign. **"We are going to start a march on the ballot boxes by the thousands. We must be willing to go to jail by the thousands. We are not asking, we are demanding the ballot."** Selma's white population, with the support of Commissioner of Public Safety Captain J. Wilson Baker, plans to ignore the action. Captain Baker and the city's white residents have learned from Montgomery and Birmingham that brutality only induces sympathy for the protestors.

January 18, 1965. Captain Baker watches silently as King becomes the

State troopers sent by Governor Wallace command the marchers to halt and disperse at the Edmund Pettus Bridge on the outskirts of Selma.

And when they refuse . . .

Charles Moore

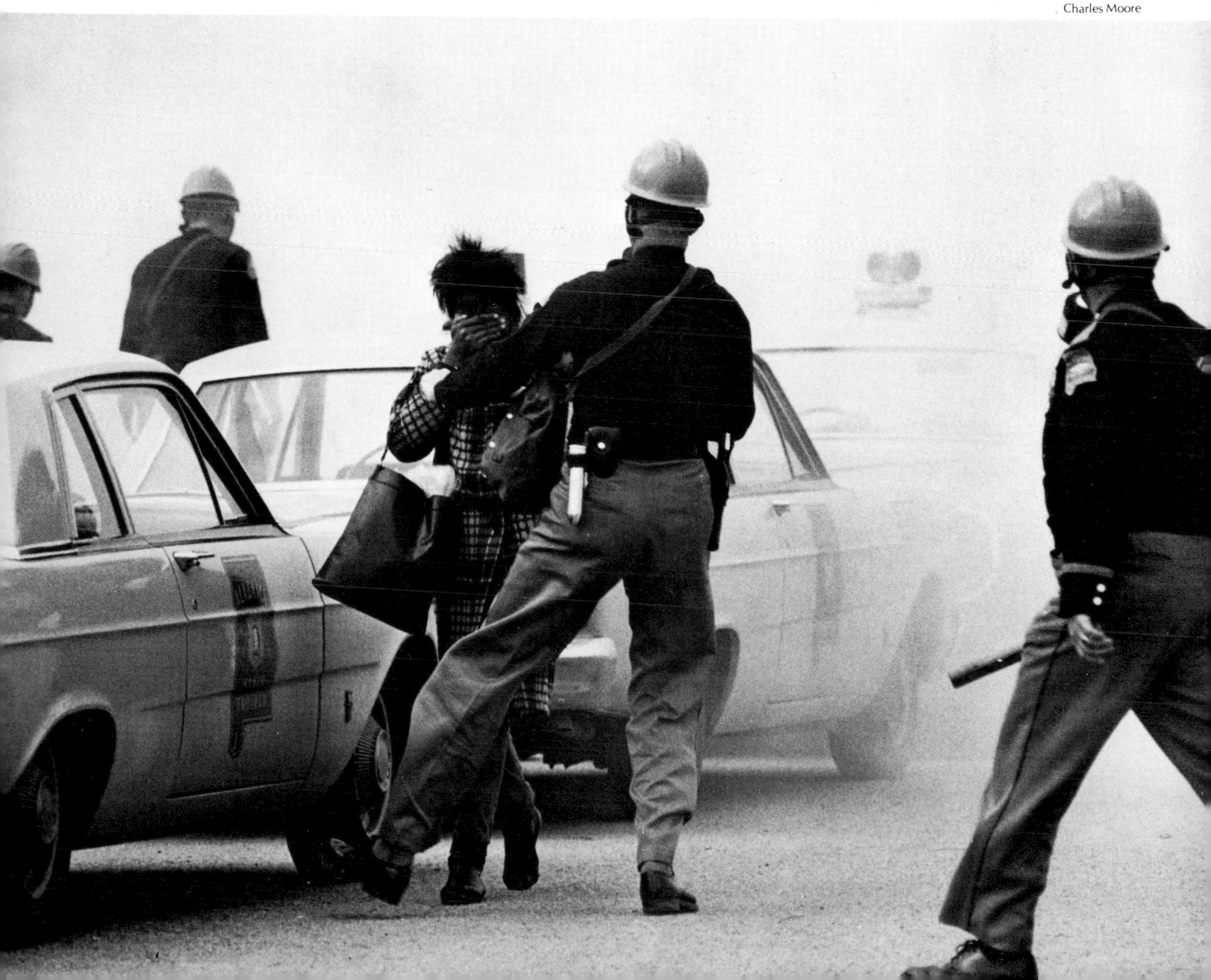

first black to register as a guest in the hundred-year-old Albert Hotel. King is also the first black since Reconstruction to eat in a white restaurant in Selma.

January 18–February 1, 1965. The first days of the demonstration are peaceful. Police protect demonstrators from white racists. The protests center around the Dallas county courthouse in Selma, where voter registration takes place. Although a few demonstrators have been arrested for breaking the law, the city police department for the most part does not interfere. A major antagonism has developed between Captain Baker and County Sheriff James G. Clark, who is in command at the courthouse. Clark disagrees with Baker's methods of noninterference with voter-registration lines outside the county courthouse in Selma. Clark orders Baker to send the crowd home.

February 2, 1965. King and Abernathy lead 265 protestors from Brown's Chapel to the courthouse to protest the slow pace at which registrars are enrolling black voters. Until now, all of the marches to the courthouse have been made by groups of fewer than twenty citizens. A larger group requires a parade permit. **"We are getting ready to move to the courthouse,"** King says. **"We're all going together today. We're going to walk together. We're going to walk together because we're not parading. We will obey every traffic law, every traffic signal we will stop for; we will not stand in the way of egress and ingress. We will not do anything to block the orderly process of movement in the community. We feel that we need to join together and move on to the courthouse."** Baker arrests the entire party. The arrest of the Nobel Prize winner makes world-wide headlines. Most of the marchers are released on bail, but knowing the publicity will help their cause, King and Abernathy choose to remain in jail for five days. From his jail cell King writes, **"This is Selma,**

Charles Moore

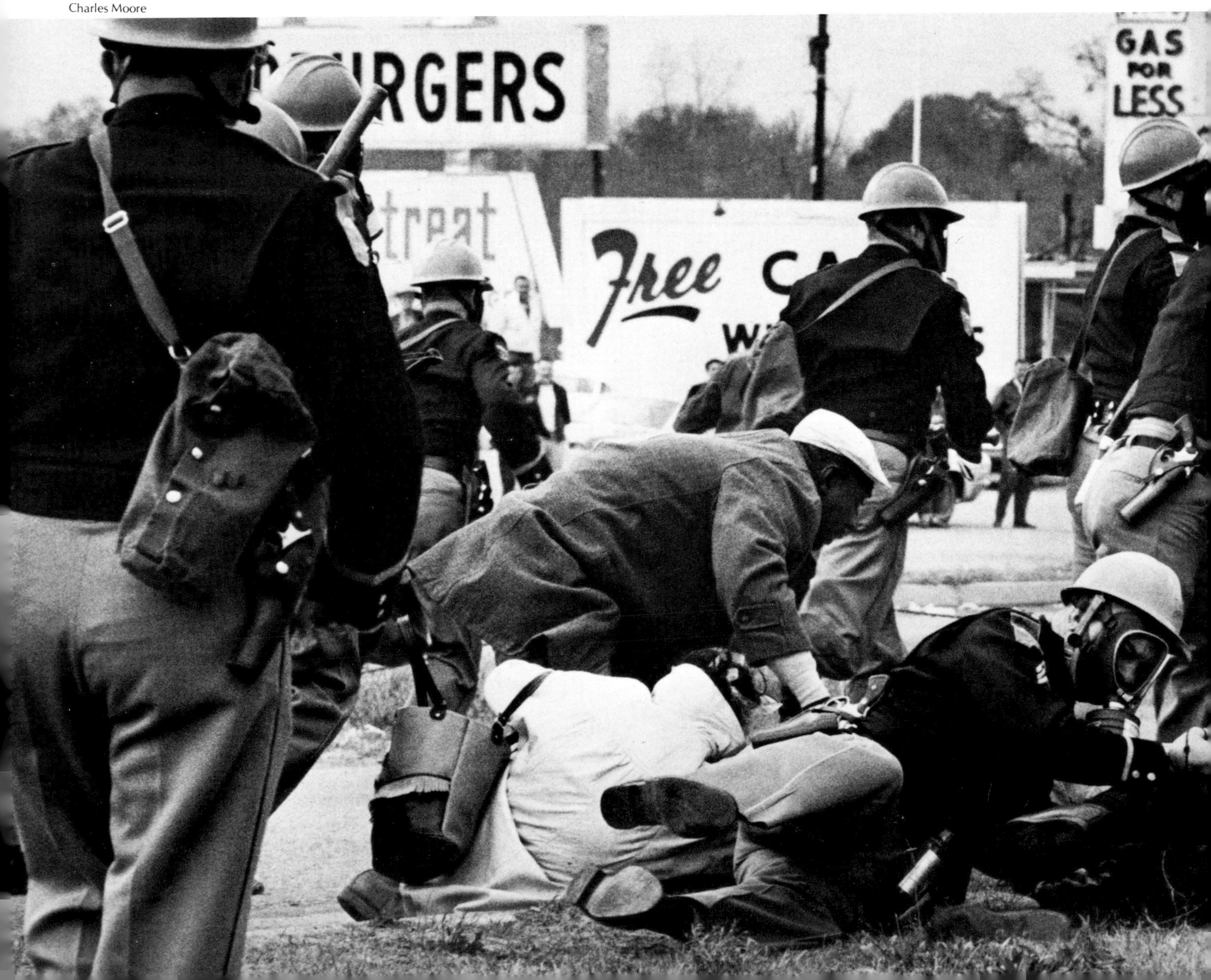
RGERS
GAS
FOR
LESS
Free

Selma becomes a headline overnight. "Bloody Sunday" is broadcast over nation-wide television. America and the world are outraged.

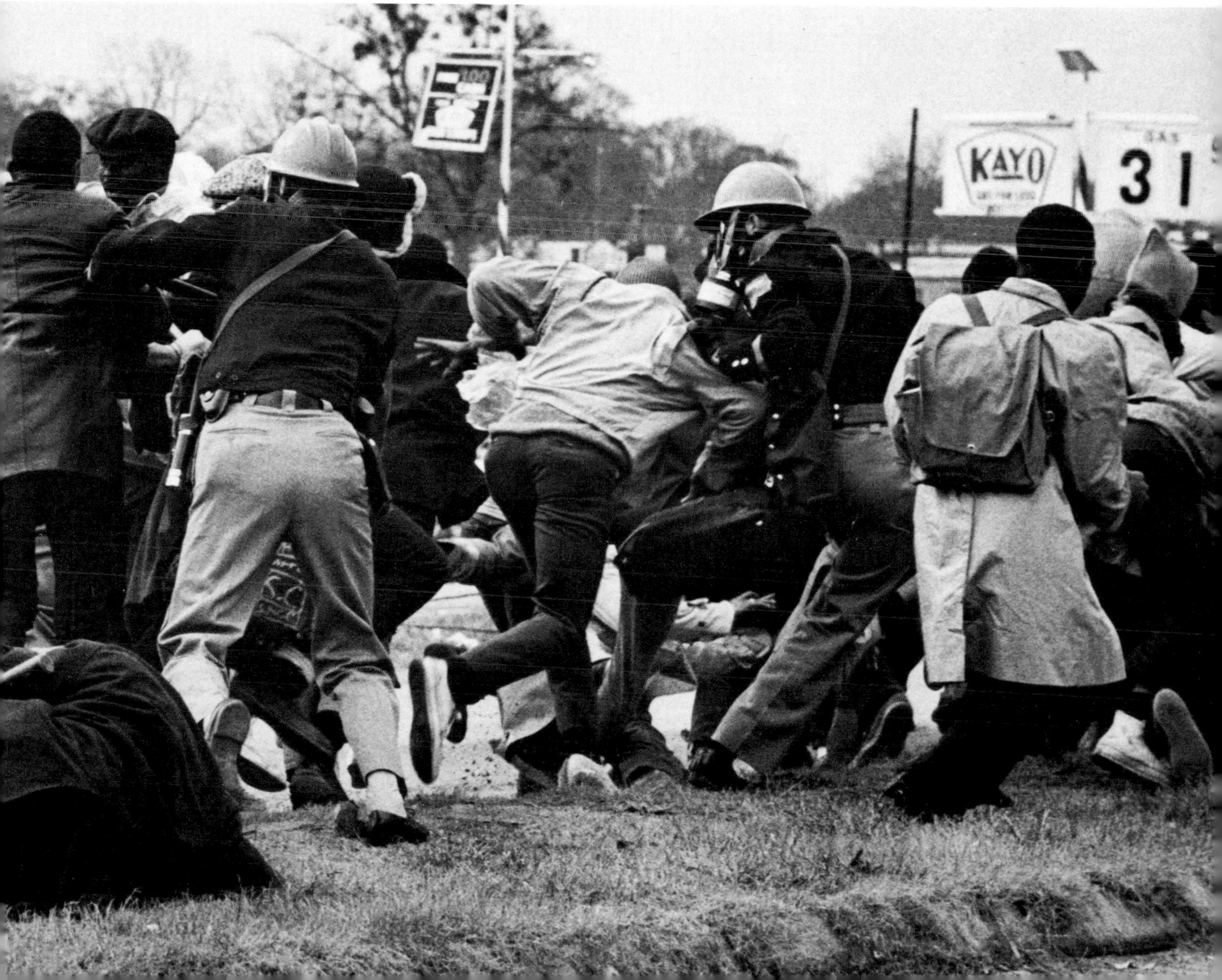
KAYO
31

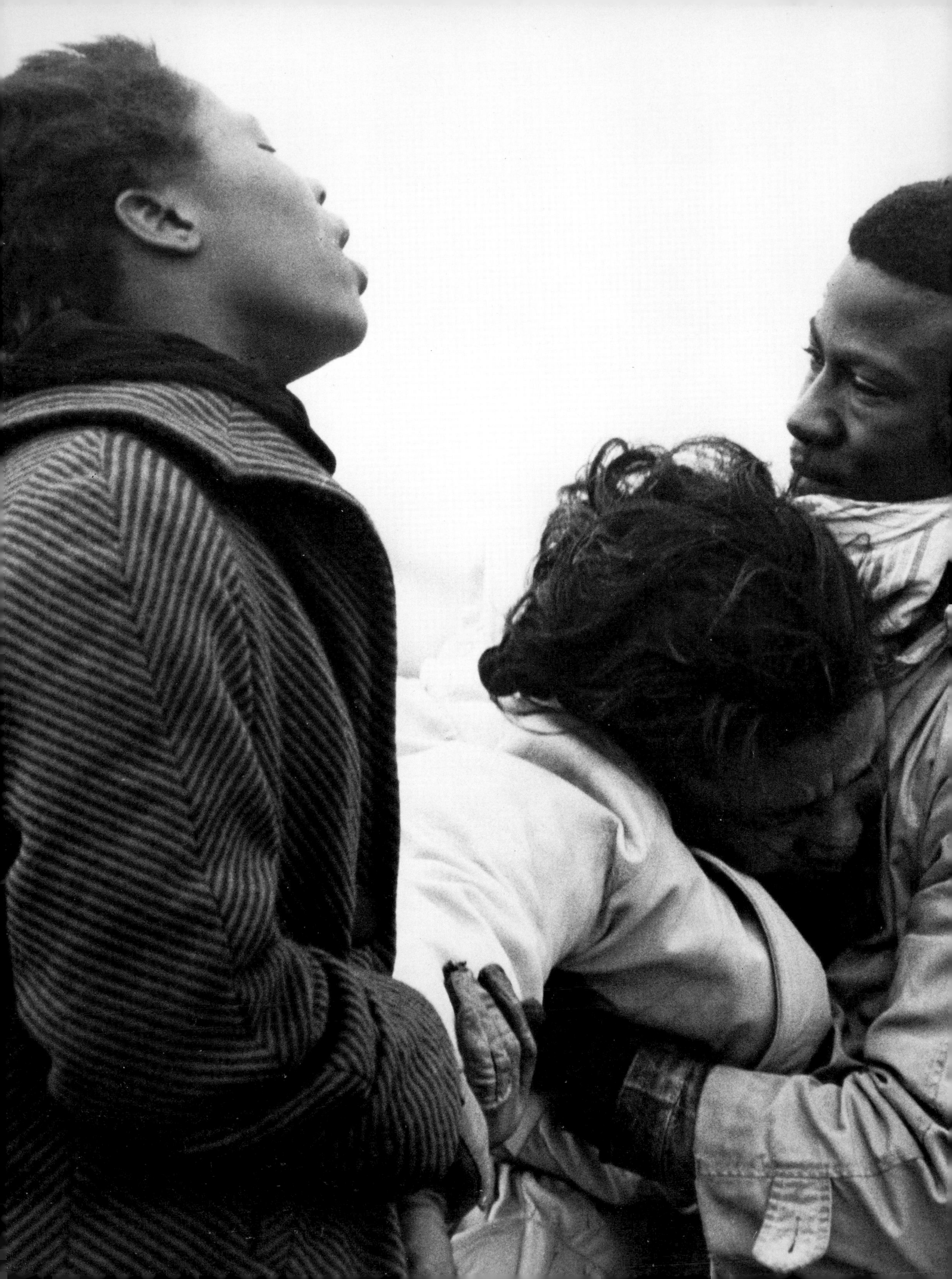

Charles Moore

Amelia Boynton, a victim of the unprovoked clubbing and tear gas attack.

Alabama. There are more Negroes in jail with me than there are on the voting rolls."

February 3, 1965. While King is in jail, militant black leader Malcolm X arrives in Selma at the invitation of two SNCC workers. Malcolm X speaks to the crowd at Brown's Chapel, emphasizing the necessity of answering violence with violence. But he later says privately to King's wife, "I want Dr. King to know that I didn't come to Selma to make his job difficult. I really did come thinking that I could make it easier. If the white people realize what the alternative is, perhaps they will be more willing to hear Dr. King."

February 10, 1965. A group of 165 children stage a protest demonstration. Sheriff Clark and his deputies encircle the youngsters inside a cordon of trucks and cars and herd them out of town. The caravan moves rapidly into the surrounding countryside, forcing the children to trot. Sobbing, out of breath, many fall behind. Some of those who cannot keep up are prodded by snickering deputies. "You kids want to march," one says, "We'll give you a good march."

February 18, 1965. The flame is reignited. Jimmie Lee Jackson, a twenty six-year-old black man, is shot by state troopers during a riot in Marion, Alabama, only thirty miles from Selma.

February 21, 1965. Malcolm X is assassinated in the Audubon Ballroom in New York City.

February 26, 1965. Jimmie Lee Jackson dies.

March 1, 1965. King leads an SCLC caravan through five Alabama counties in an effort to register voters. Wilcox and Lowndes counties do not have a single black voter on their registration lists. In Wilcox County, the civil rights leaders face a stalemate. Since a prospective voter must have two registered voters to

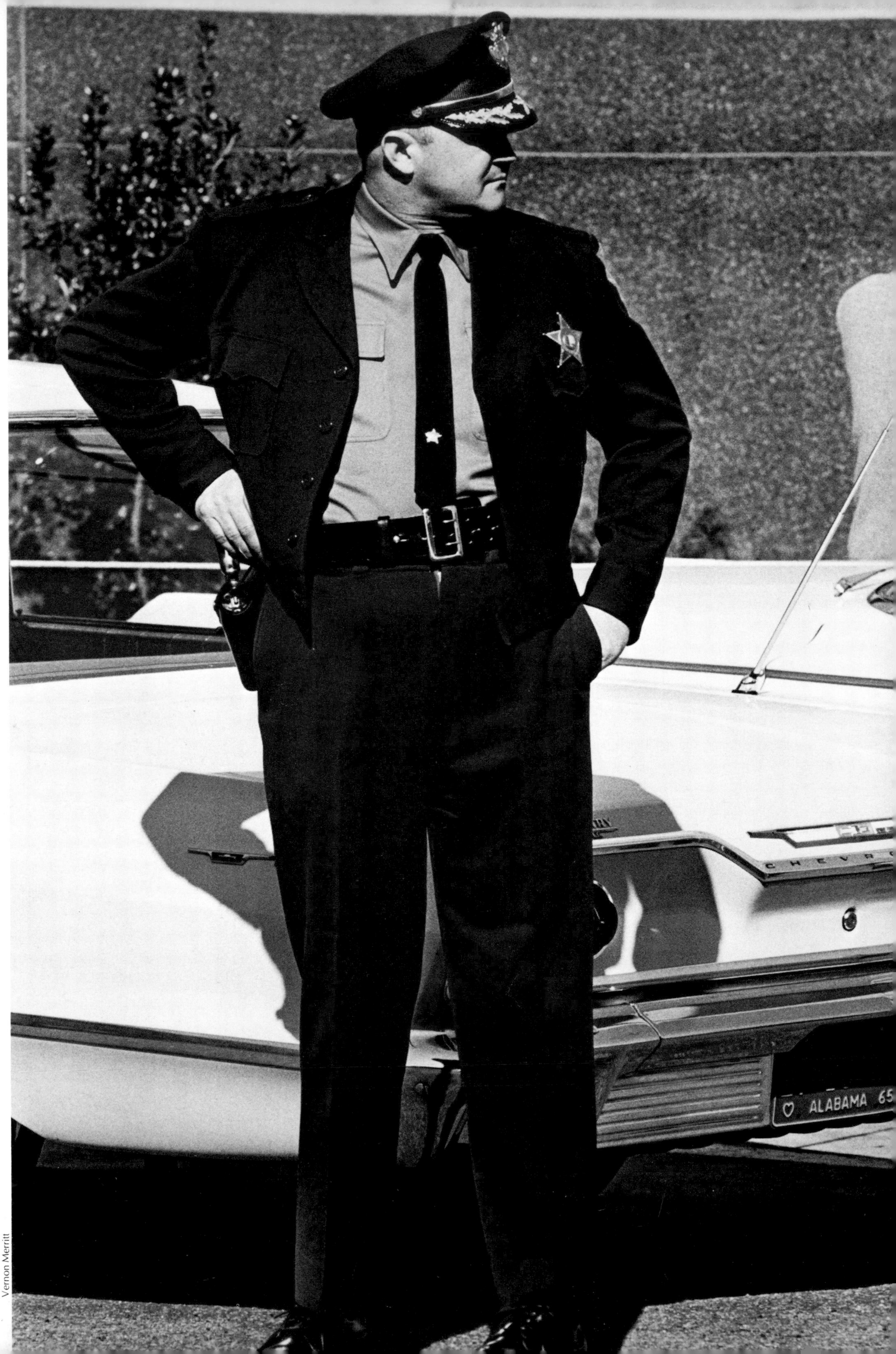
ALABAMA 65

Vernon Merritt

vouch for him and there are no blacks registered, there is no one to vouch for would-be black voters.

By the end of the day, 266 new voter applications are processed in Selma. No one can predict how many will be rejected on technicalities.

March 5, 1965. King proposes a march from Selma to Montgomery on March 7 to take their case before Governor Wallace. He warns his followers at Brown's Chapel, **"I can't promise you that it won't get you beaten."**

March 6, 1965. Wallace issues an order prohibiting the march and orders state troopers to take "whatever steps are necessary" to stop it.

March 7, 1965. Five hundred and twenty-five marchers meet at Brown's

Dallas county Sheriff James G. Clark

Below:
March 7, 1965, King meets with James Forman of SNCC, Abernathy and James Farmer of CORE in a planning session in Montgomery following the beatings on the Pettus Bridge.

Flip Schulke

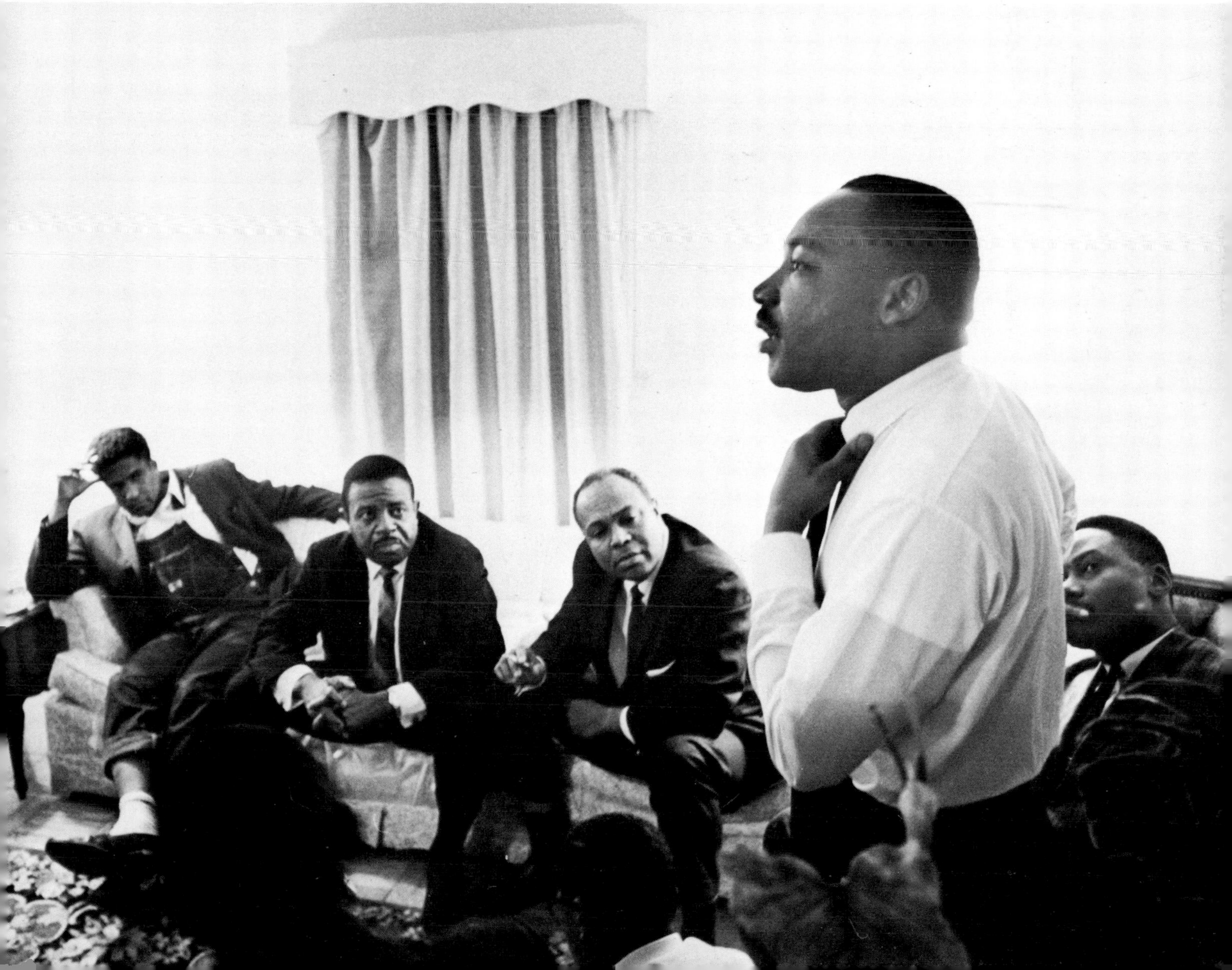

Chapel. Equipped with food, bedrolls, and blankets, they prepare to make the fifty-four-mile march to Montgomery. King has been persuaded by his associates not to lead this march, because violence is anticipated. Hosea Williams takes the lead.

The march begins quietly, as the protesters set out in pairs. They travel the first six blocks to Broad Street without incident. As the marchers turn to the Edmund Pettus Bridge, which will take them to Highway 80 and Montgomery, they pass a small posse of armed volunteers led by Sheriff Clark. Across the bridge, access to Highway 80 is blocked by state troopers standing shoulder to shoulder. As the marchers go forward, the troopers don their gas masks. When the first marchers are within fifty feet of the troopers, Major John Cloud orders them to halt. Hosea Williams asks for a word with the major, but his request is denied. The demonstrators are ordered to disperse but remain perfectly still. Within seconds the troopers advance with night sticks and tear gas, forcing the unarmed marchers to retreat back across the bridge. One trooper is observed dropping a tear gas grenade be-

On March 9, troopers again await the demonstrators at the Pettus Bridge. This time, to avoid violence, King has agreed to turn the group around before reaching the Montgomery highway.

Flip Schulke

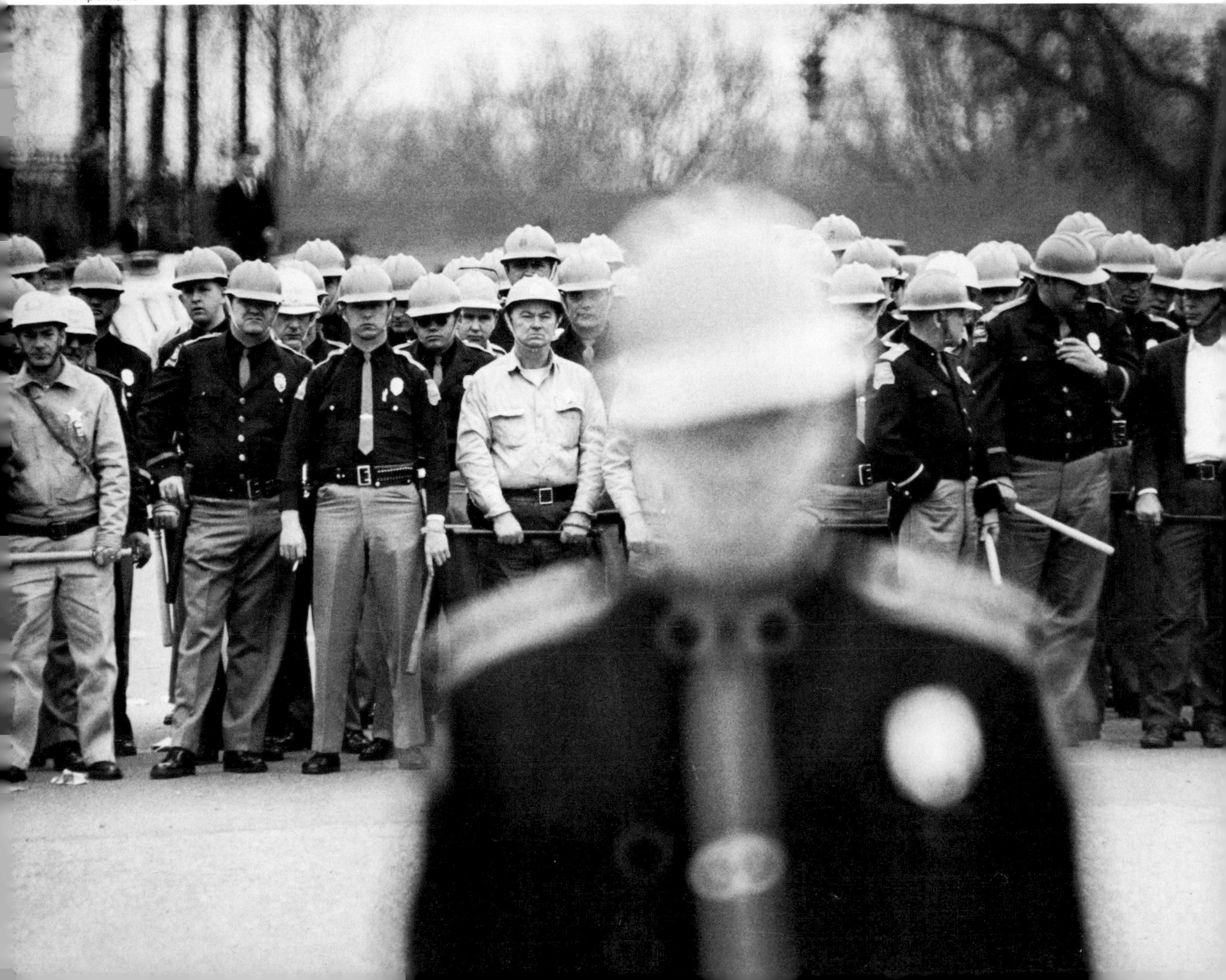

side a black woman who has been beaten to semi-consciousness.

Clark's men are waiting to add their force to the unequal struggle, chasing the helpless demonstrators back toward the church. In town, Captain Baker holds off Sheriff Clark and his posse, persuading the blacks to return to Brown's Chapel.

Emergency facilities are set up in the parsonage, where more than sixty marchers are treated for injuries. Seventeen are taken to the hospital with serious injuries.

Within hours, news of the beatings makes Selma the most publicized town in the world. People everywhere are horrified at what they see on their television screens. Newspaper headlines proclaim: "Bloody Sunday." King announces another March from Selma to Montgomery on March 9.

March 8, 1965. The United States Federal Court issues a temporary injunction against the march scheduled for the following day. President Johnson publicly asks King to postpone it. But King has put out the call to clergymen all over the nation and already more than four hundred priests, ministers, and rabbis have arrived in Selma to participate.

Singing a hymn to freedom, hundreds of clergymen from all over America answer King's call to protest the barbarism in Selma.

Flip Schulke

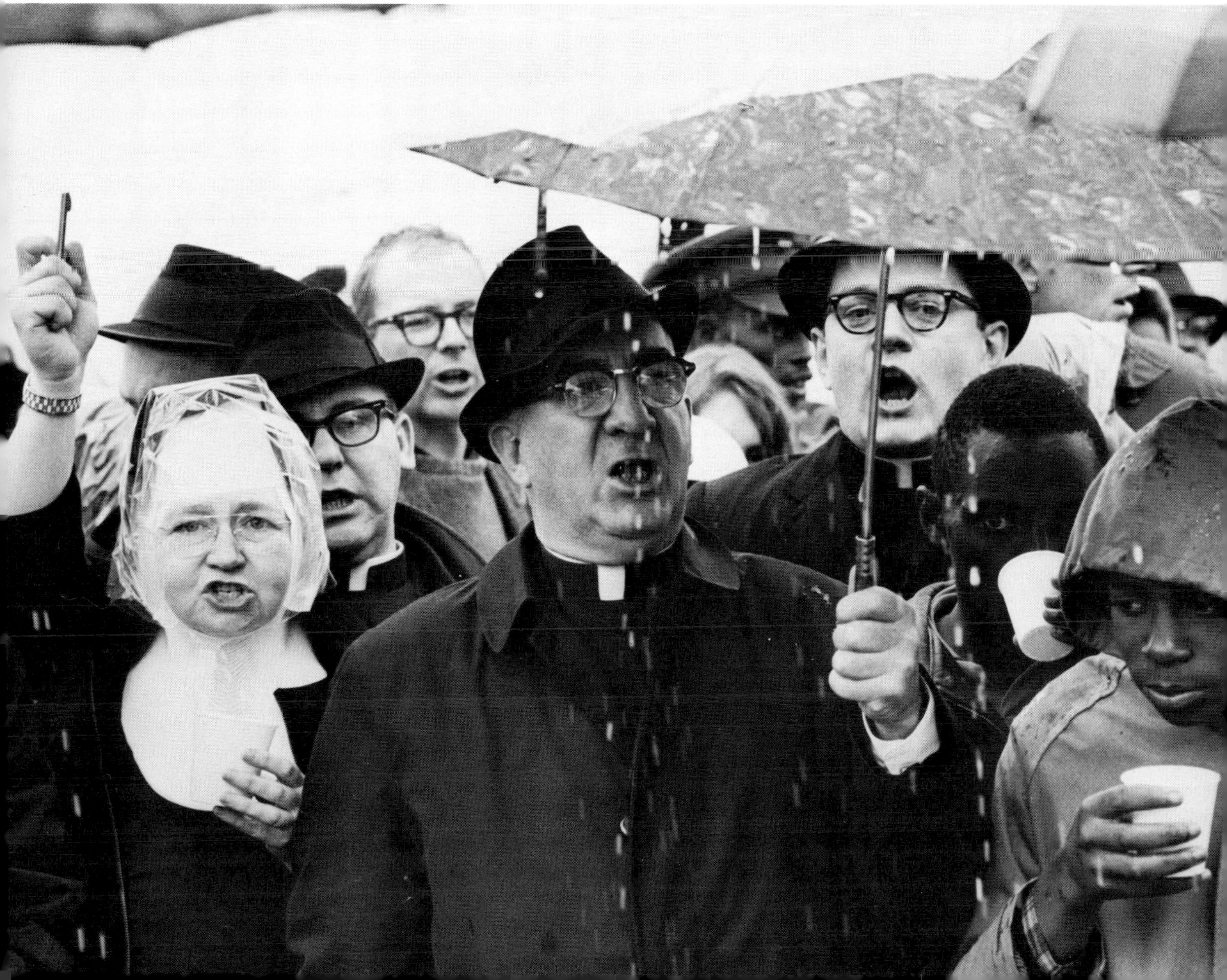

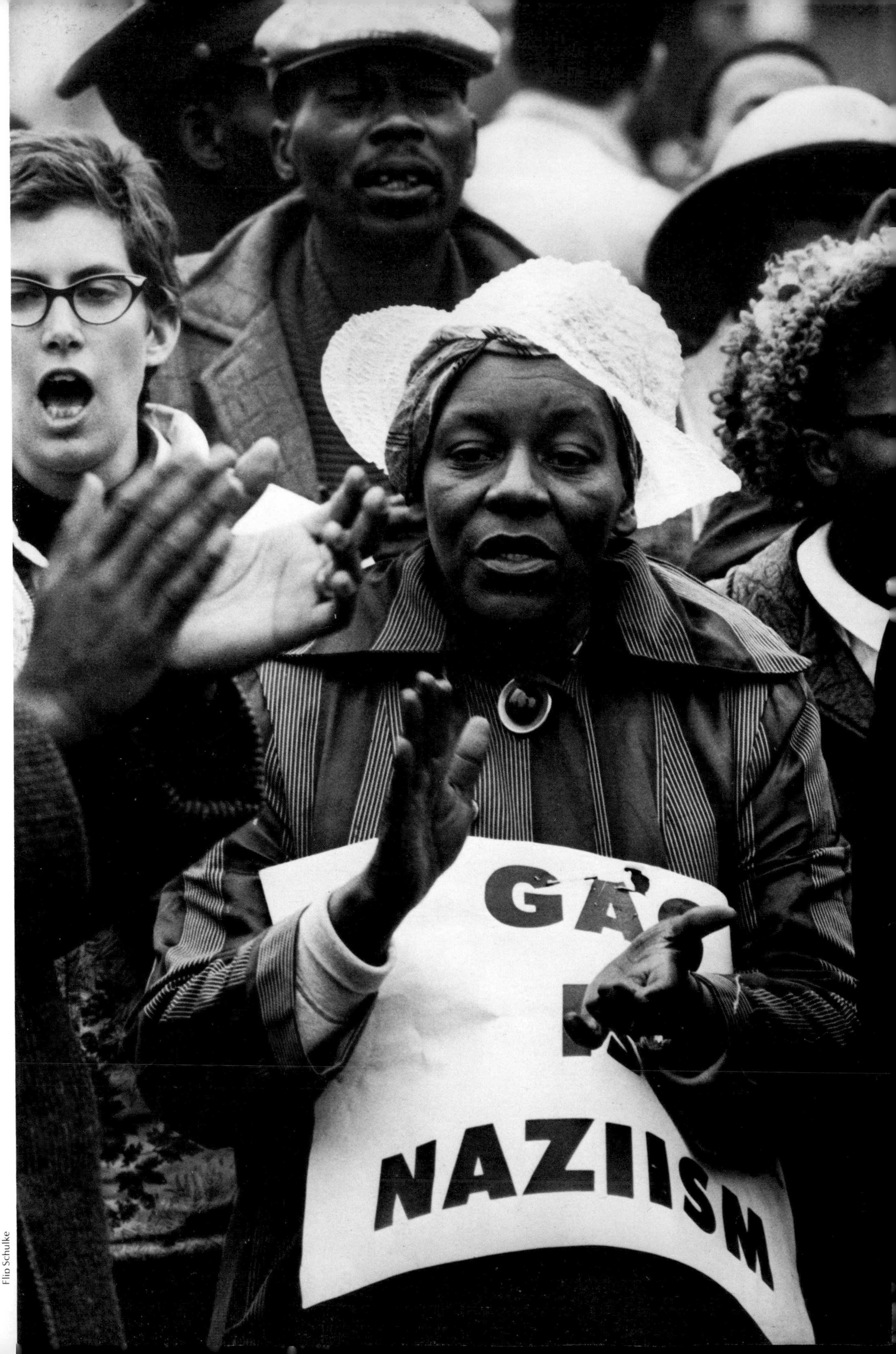
GA
NAZIISM

Flip Schulke

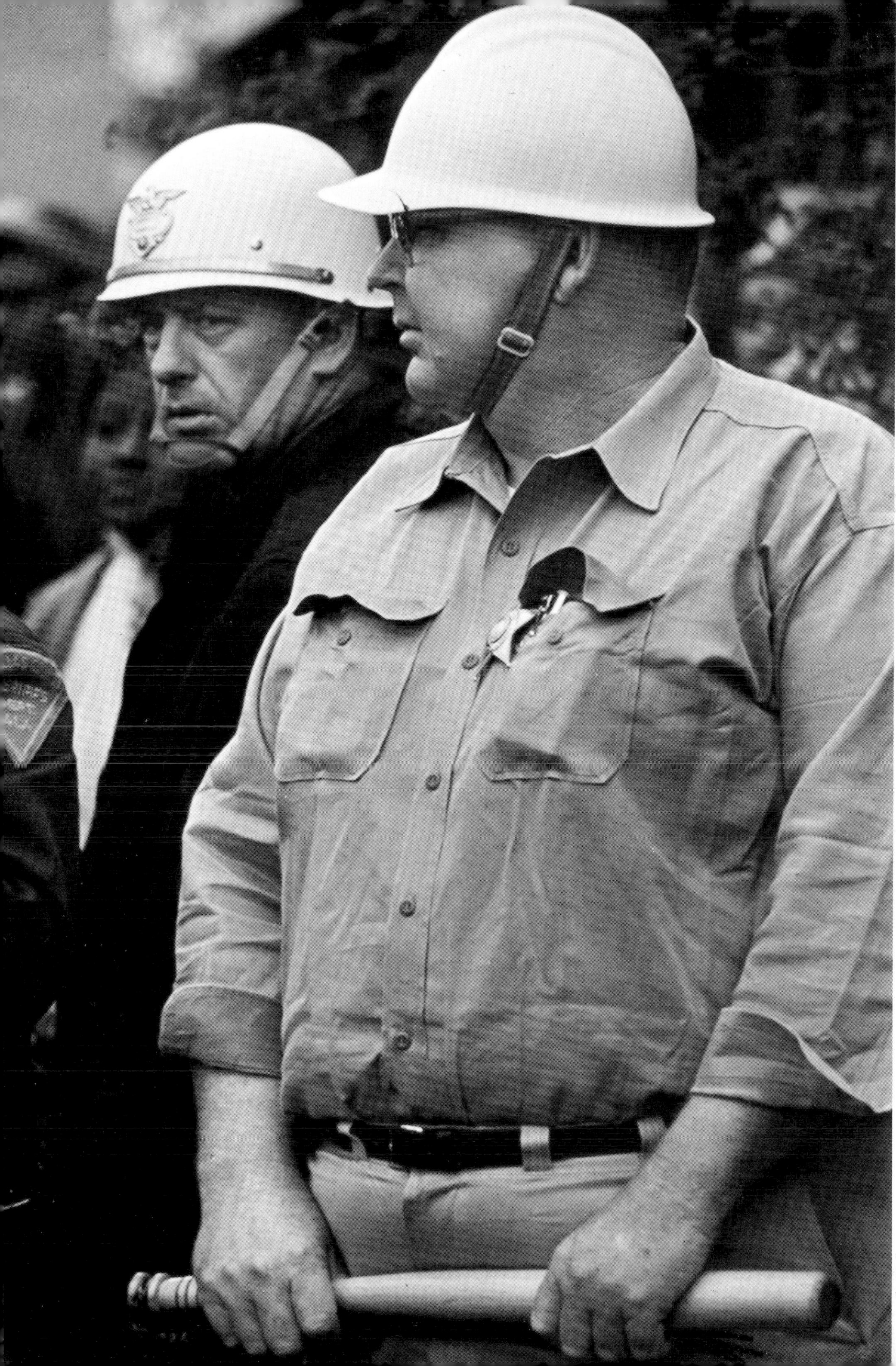
Flip Schulke

"It's better to die on the highway than make a butchery of my conscience," he says. **"I'd better go through with it."**

President Johnson sends former Florida Governor LeRoy Collins, head of the Federal Community Relations Service, to Selma to help keep the peace. Collins suggests a compromise march to the bridge, where the demonstrators can pray before returning to the church. Sheriff Clark, whose actions have been under fire, agrees and promises to control his men. King agrees without admitting to his followers that he has compromised the march.

March 9, 1965. King leads nine hundred demonstrators in prayer and says: **"We've gone too far to turn back now. We must let them know that nothing can stop us—not even death itself. We**

Archbishop Iakovos of the Greek Orthodox Church, Walter Reuther, King, and Reverend Fred Shuttlesworth are among those in attendance.

Below:
A memorial service for Reverend James Reeb is held on March 12, 1965, outside the Selma city hall.

Flip Schulke

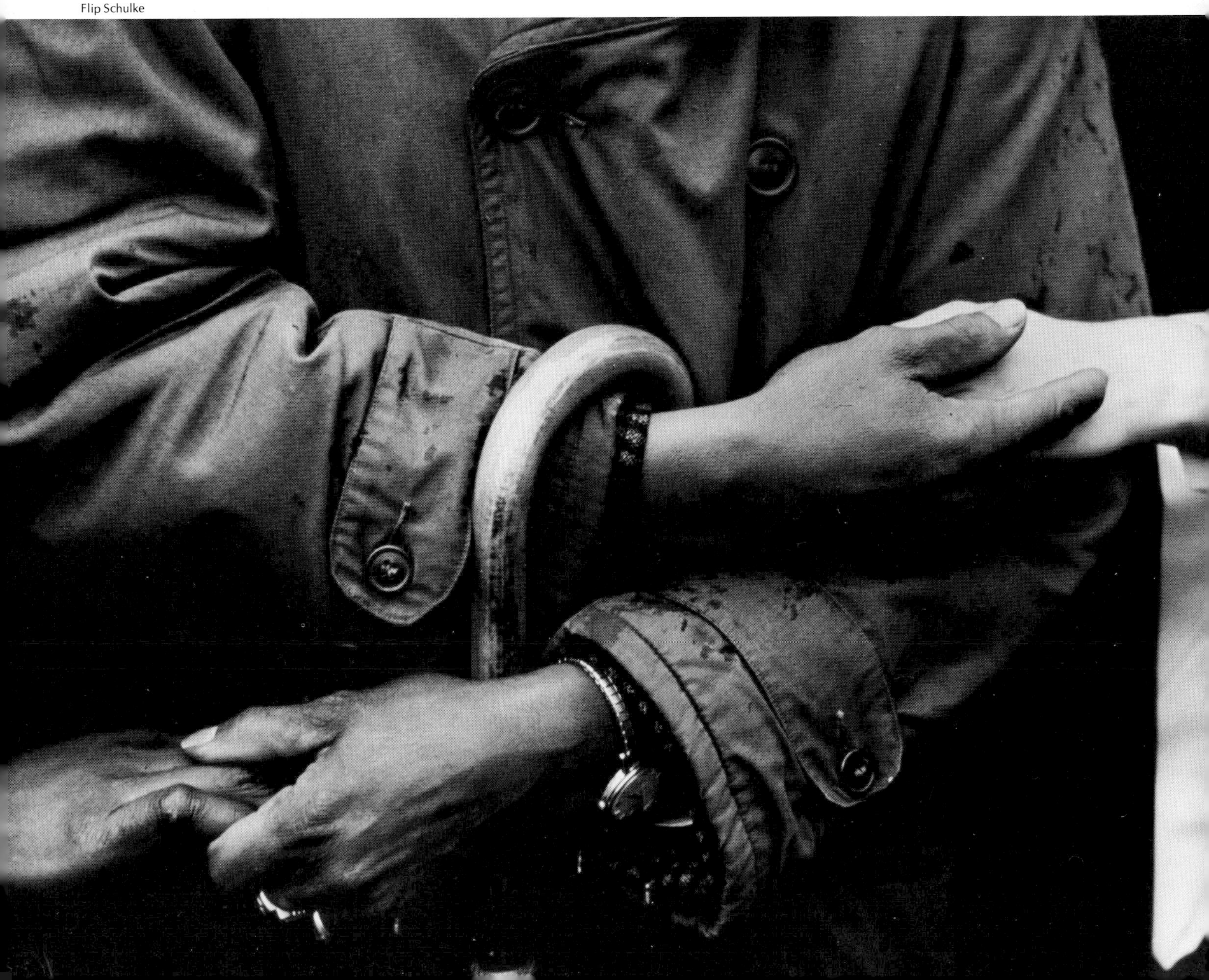

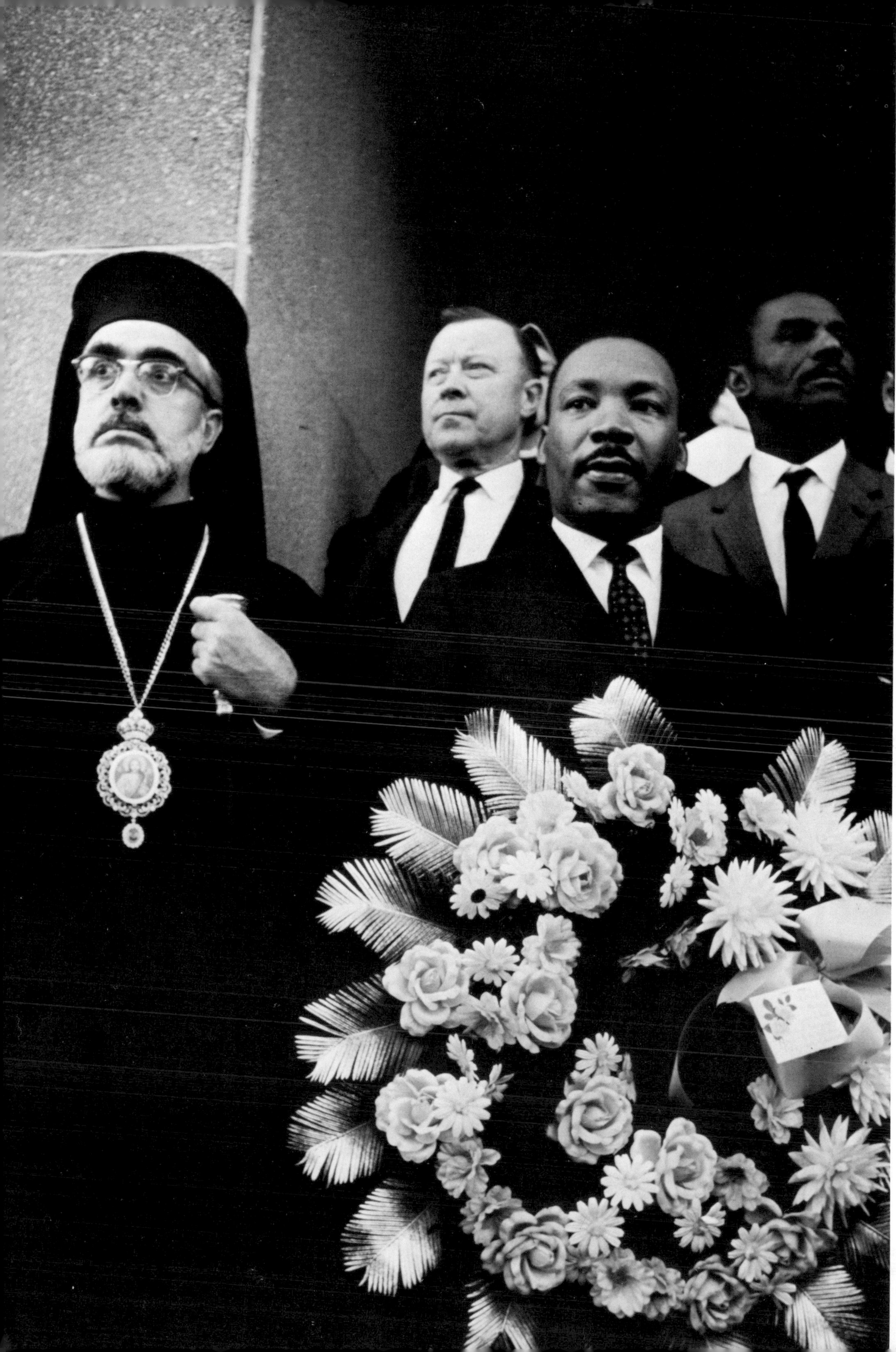

Flip Schulke

must be ready for a season of suffering." Fifteen hundred marchers, including at least 450 clergymen, follow the same route from Brown's Chapel to the Pettus Bridge. Again they are greeted by troopers, but no one reaches for a club or a canister of tear gas. As if to set a trap for King and coax him toward the Montgomery highway, the law officers open the barricade. King leads the people in prayer, then tells them to turn around and go back. Few understand; some feel betrayed; but every demonstrator obeys. The march ends without violence.

Hours later the peace is shattered. After eating dinner in a black-operated restaurant, three white Unitarian ministers who have come to Selma to march are brutally beaten by four white men, who cry, "You want to know what it's like to be a real nigger." Reverend James Reeb is bashed on the head with a two-by-four and later dies without regaining consciousness.

March 10, 1965. Seventy priests and nuns from Chicago arrive in Selma to protest the slaying. Chief Baker apprehends three of the four assailants, all members of the Ku Klux Klan. King withdraws under pressure from the forefront because of friction between the SCLC and SNCC.

March 15, 1965. A federal court overrules the city of Selma's ban on demonstrations.

President Johnson addresses a rare joint session of Congress, making a strong commitment to the black cause. "I speak tonight for the dignity of man and the destiny of democracy," he tells Congress and the nation. "At times history and fate meet at a single time in a single place to shape a turning point in man's unending search for freedom. So

Charles Moore

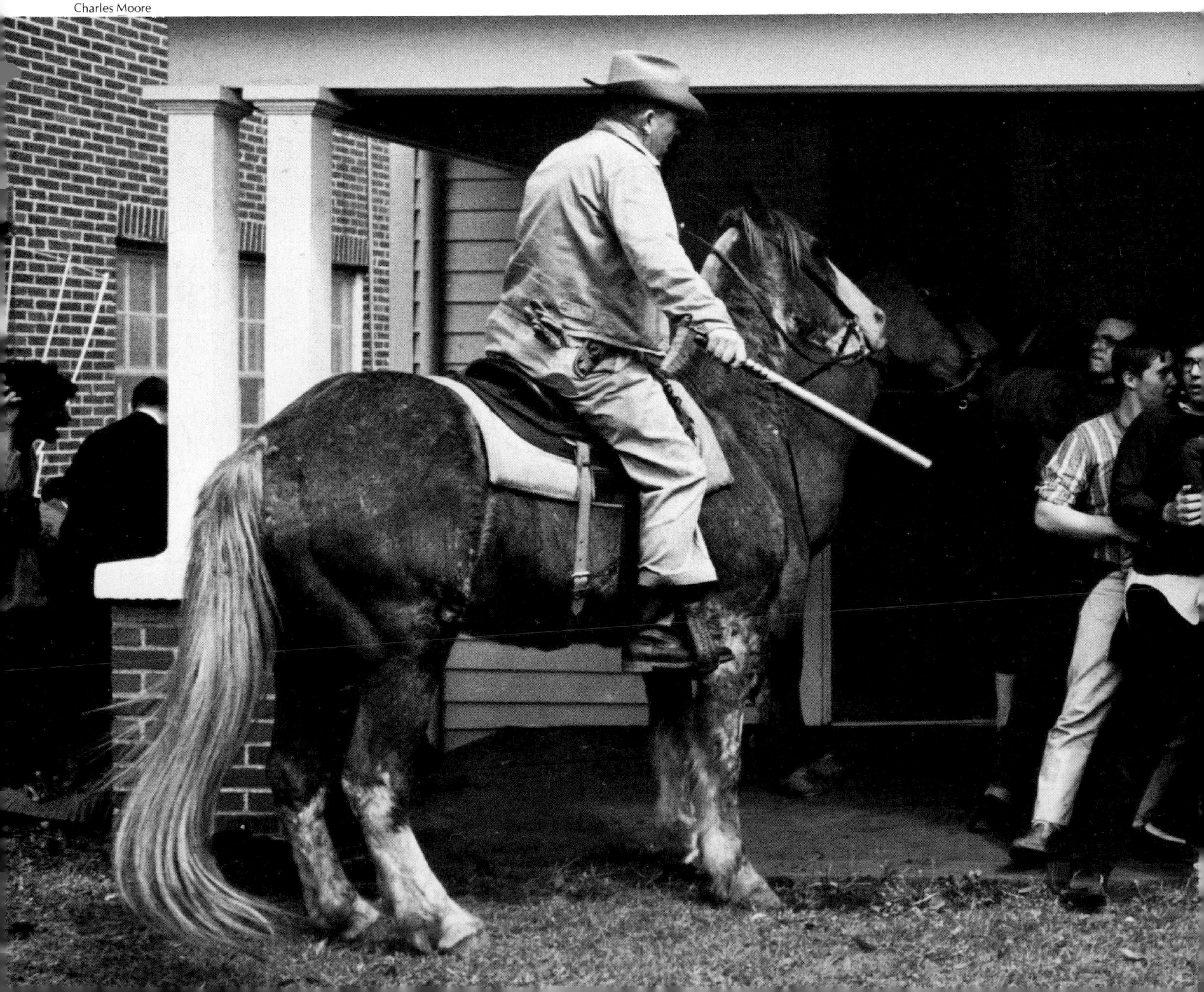

it was a century ago at Appomattox. So it was last week in Selma, Alabama. . . . What happened in Selma is part of a far larger movement which reaches into every section and state of America. It is the effort of American Negroes to secure for themselves the full blessings of American life. Their cause must be our cause too. It is not just Negroes, but all of us, who must overcome the crippling legacy of bigotry and injustice. *And we shall overcome!''* The president describes the voting rights bill which he will submit to Congress several days later and assigns it first priority.

March 16, 1965. James Forman of SNCC leads six hundred protestors in a

A group of SNCC activists protesting in Montgomery are attacked by mounted police and deputy sheriffs.

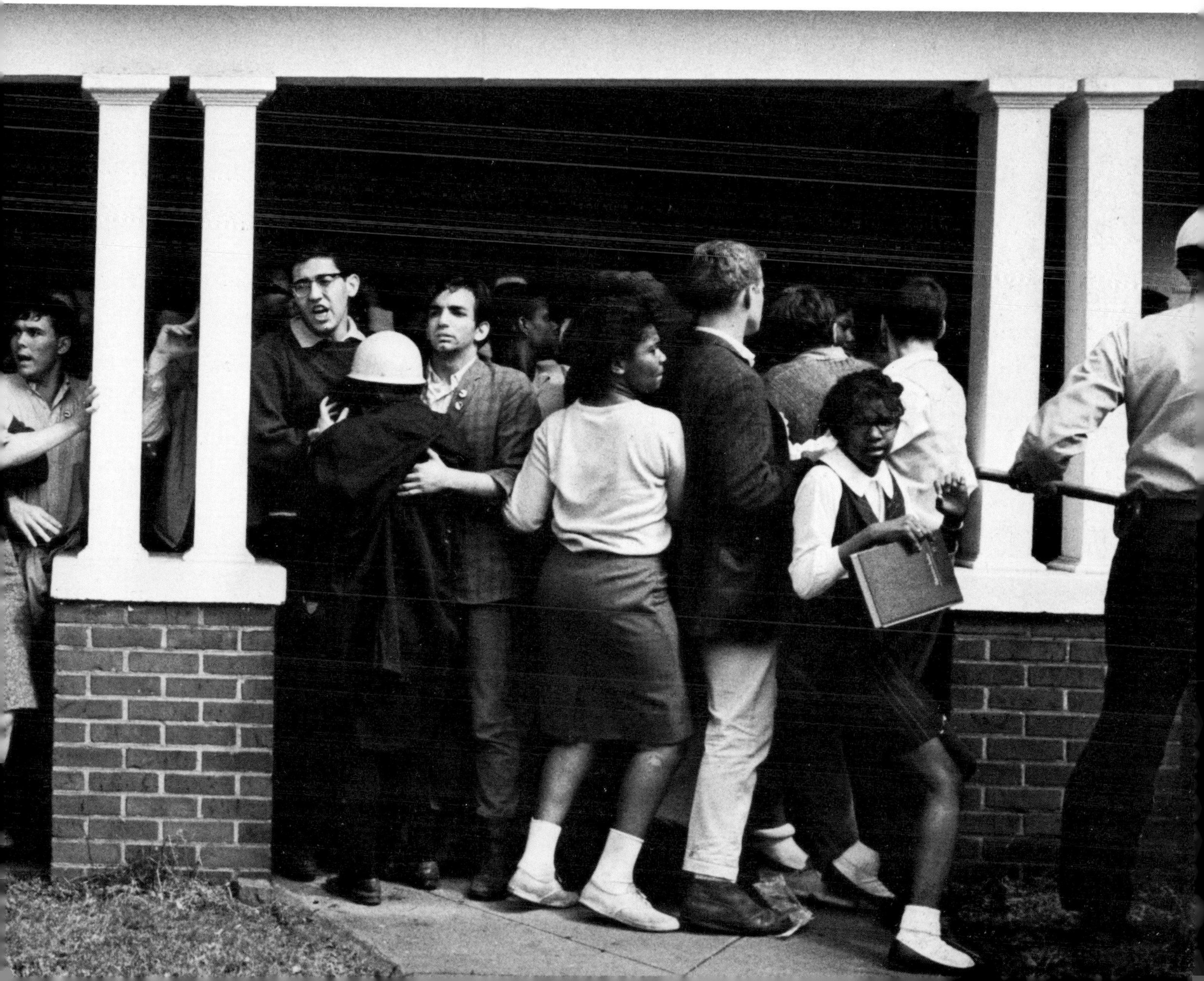

march on the county courthouse in Montgomery. Five state troopers and ten sheriff's possemen on horseback rush the crowd and injure eight demonstrators. Forman calls for massive direct action to test Johnson's sincerity. He proposes that the black community "tie up every bus, every street, and commit every act of civil disobedience ever seen."

King takes the rostrum after Forman and calls instead for a peaceful "all-out" demonstration on the county courthouse in Selma the next day. Forman agrees to the proposal.

March 17, 1965. Police provide protection as sixteen hundred marchers walk to the courthouse in Selma. It is almost exactly nine years since King and Abernathy went to trial in Montgomery. At the courthouse King speaks. **"We are here today because we do not like what happened in Montgomery yesterday. We are here to say to the white men that we will no longer let them use their clubs on us in the dark corners. We're going to make them do it in the glaring light of television."**

Charles Moore

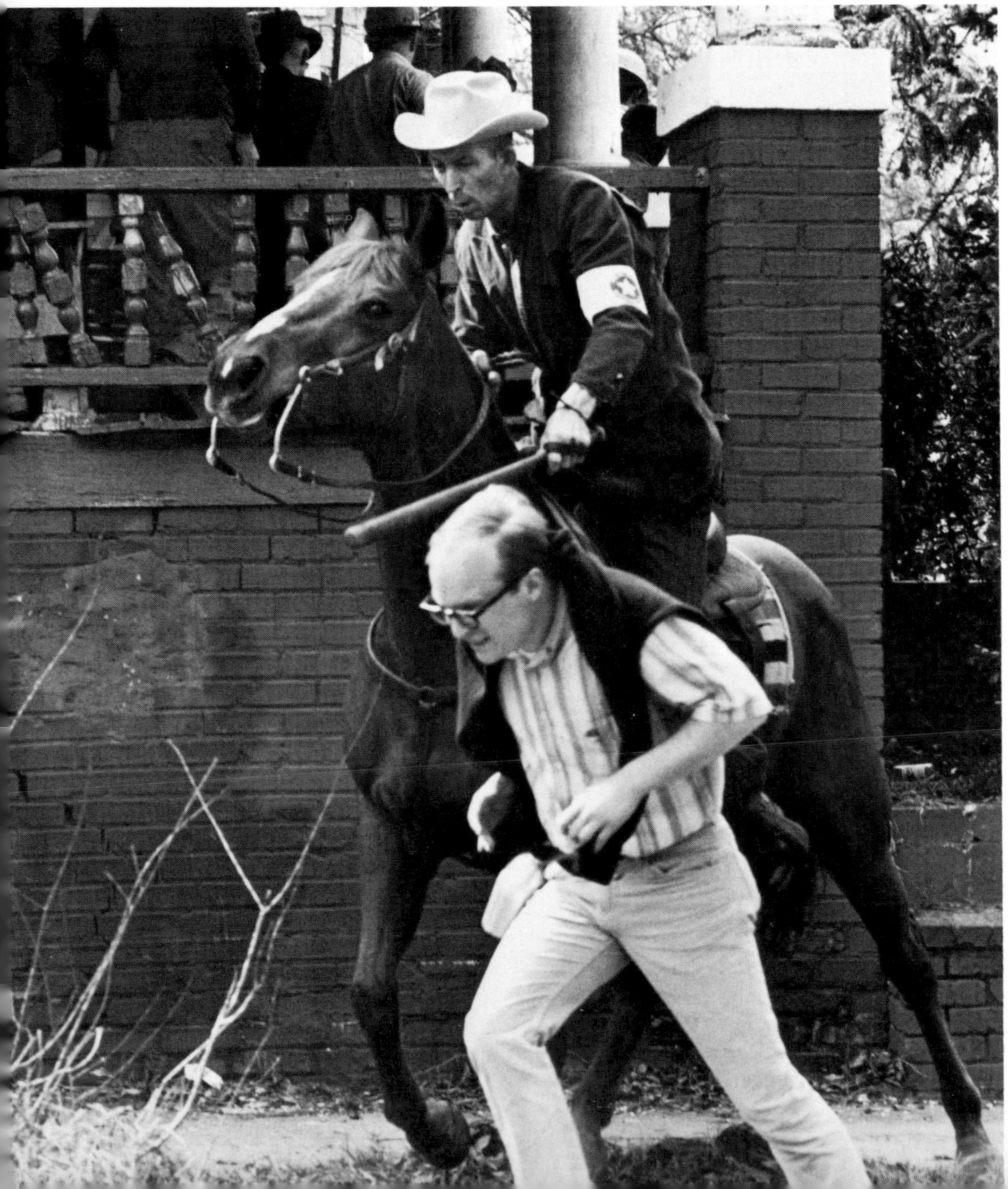

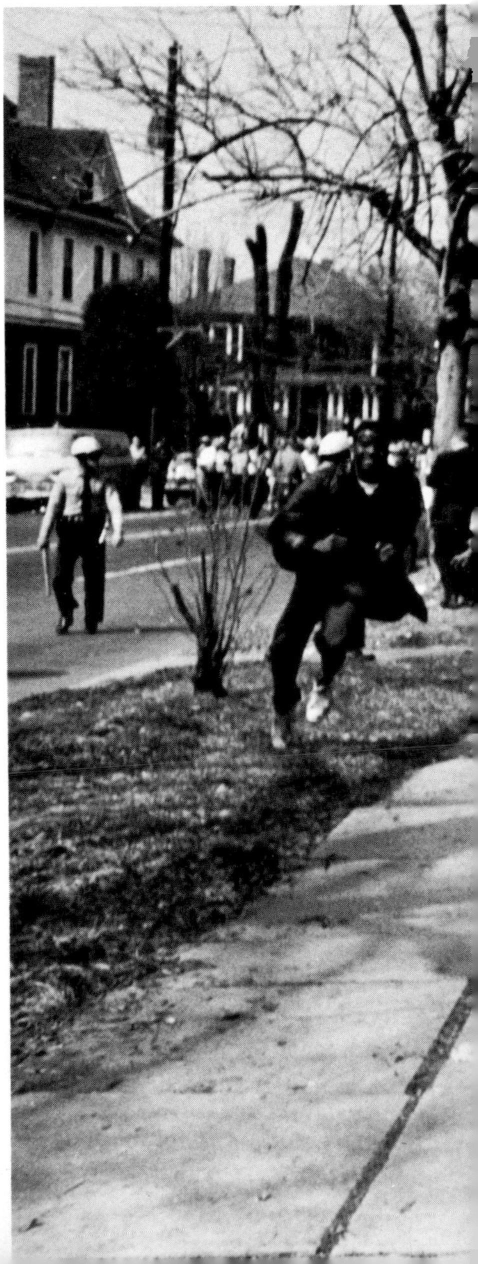

Demonstrators in Montgomery are driven from the vicinity of the state capitol by mounted police and deputy sheriffs.

King announces that a federal judge has ruled **"that we have a legal and constitutional right to march from Selma to Montgomery."**

March 18, 1965. Eighty SNCC demonstrators are arrested for sitting-in near the state capitol.

March 19, 1965. Three hundred and eighty people, mostly clergymen, are arrested in two days for picketing and praying in front of the home of the mayor of Selma.

Selma remains fairly quiet, but after two murders, numerous injuries and nearly thirty-eight hundred arrests, only fifty blacks have been added to the voting lists.

Governor Wallace claims he can't promise protection for the marchers, so President Johnson federalizes the National Guard.

March 21, 1965. The five-day march from Selma to Montgomery finally begins. Before leaving Brown's Chapel King says: **"Because of the system we don't have much education, and some of us don't know how to make our nouns and verbs agree. But thank God**

Overleaf:
The march from Selma to Montgomery finally begins.
photo by James Karales

Charles Moore

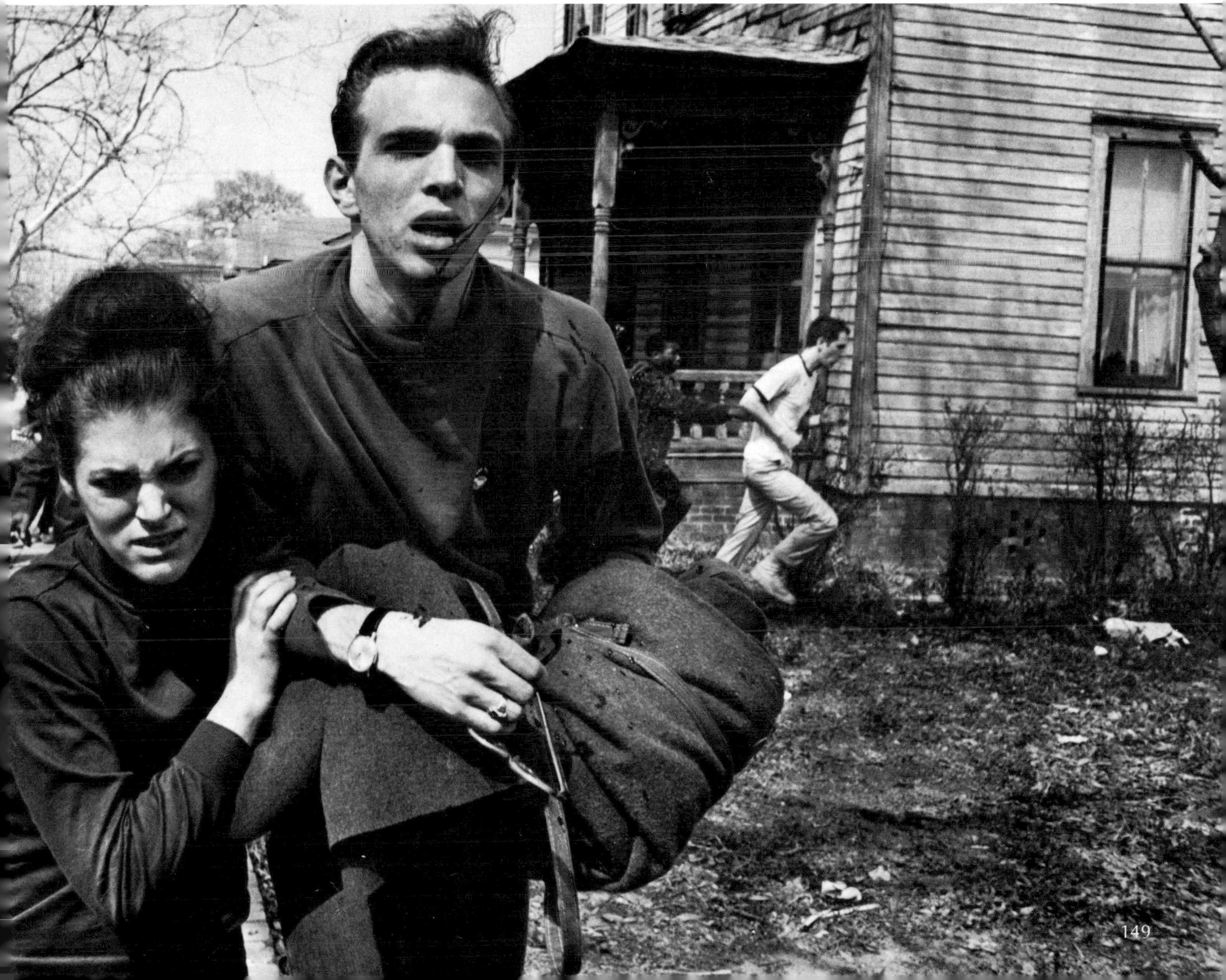

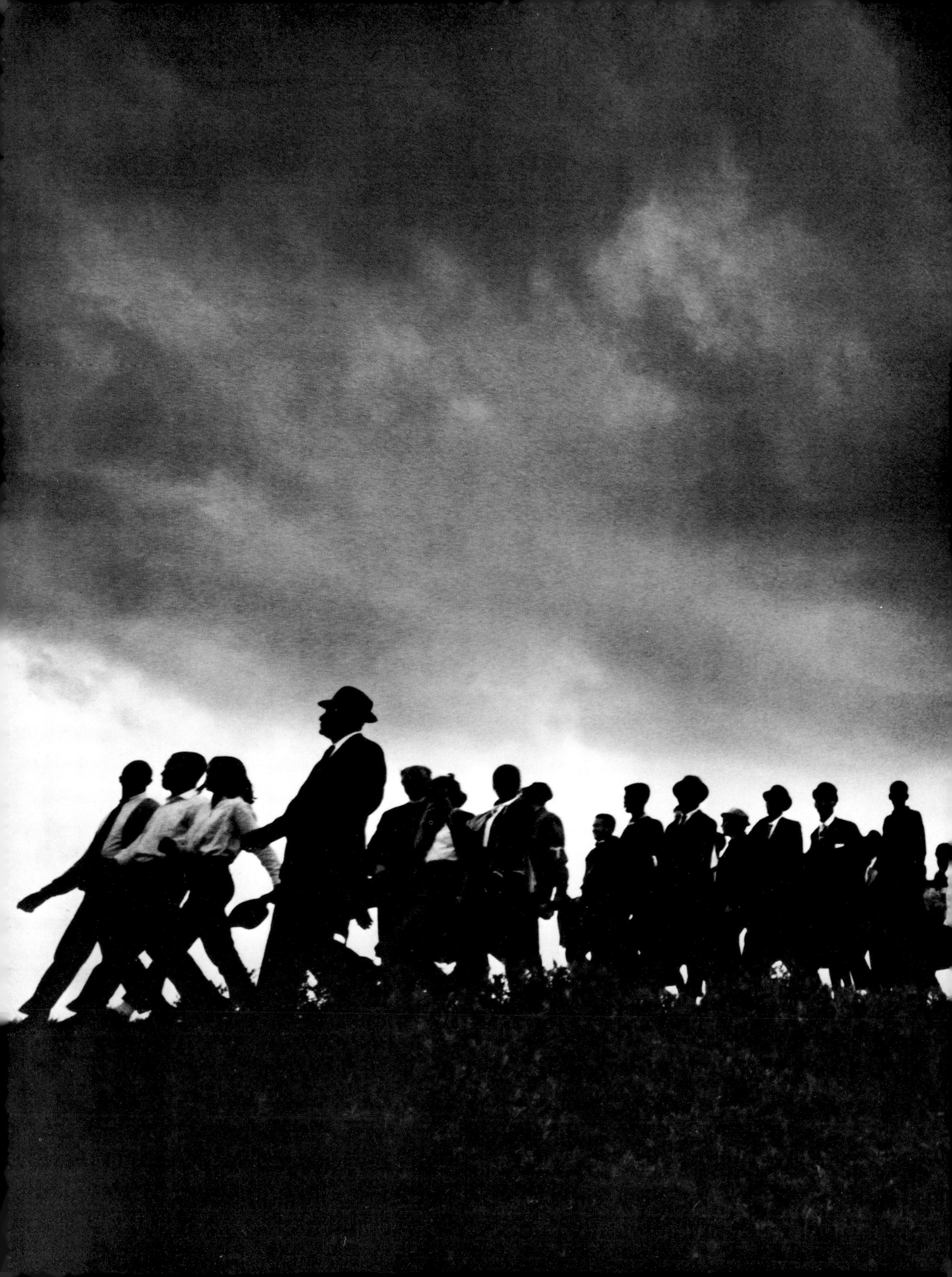

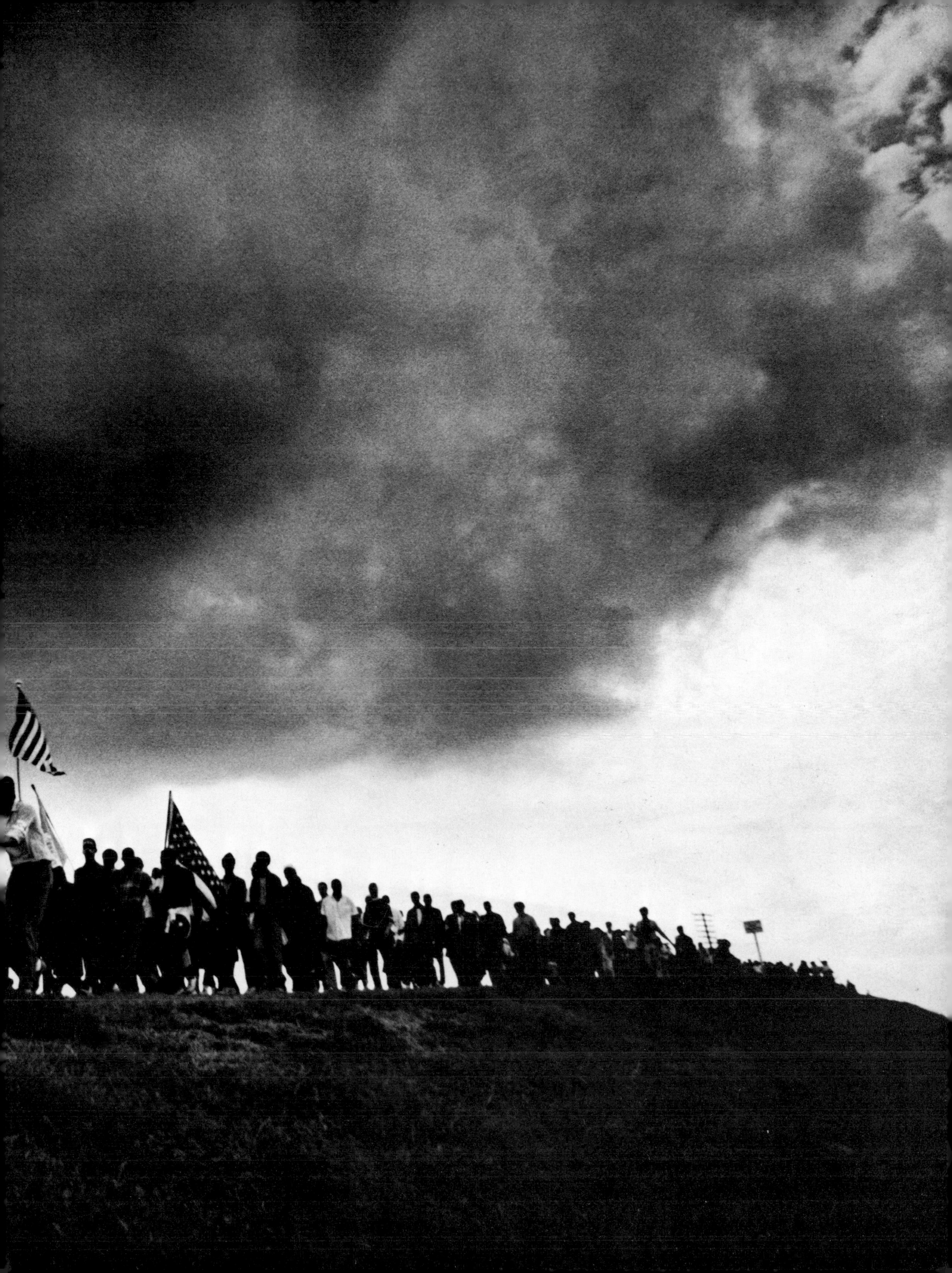

we have our bodies, our feet, and our souls." King leads three thousand marchers safely over the Pettus Bridge, only two weeks after the scene of the rout. According to the judge's ruling, only three hundred marchers will be allowed to continue after the first eight miles. Sheriff Clark stands by quietly, wearing a button in his lapel that reads "Never"—his answer to the blacks' plea for "Freedom Now."

March 25, 1965. Thousands and thousands of demonstrators from all over the country have converged on Montgomery to join the three hundred pilgrims at the end of their fifty-four mile trek. Although Governor Wallace refuses to speak to the marchers, their enthusiasm is not dampened. Civil rights

A triumphant King rests at the end of the march in Montgomery.

Below:
One of many misleading segregationist billboards observed along the road from Selma to Montgomery.

Ivan Massar

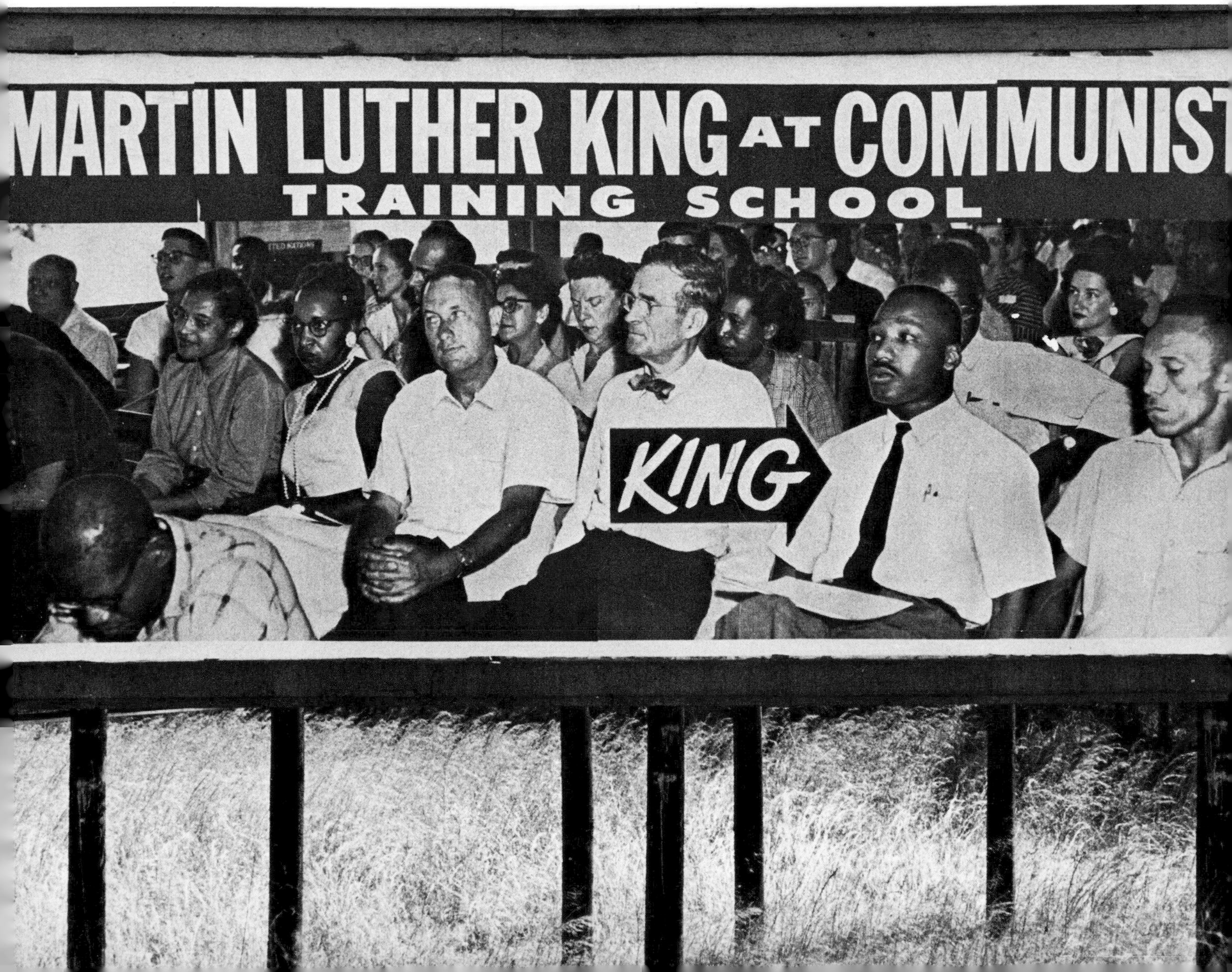
MARTIN LUTHER KING AT COMMUNIST
TRAINING SCHOOL
KING

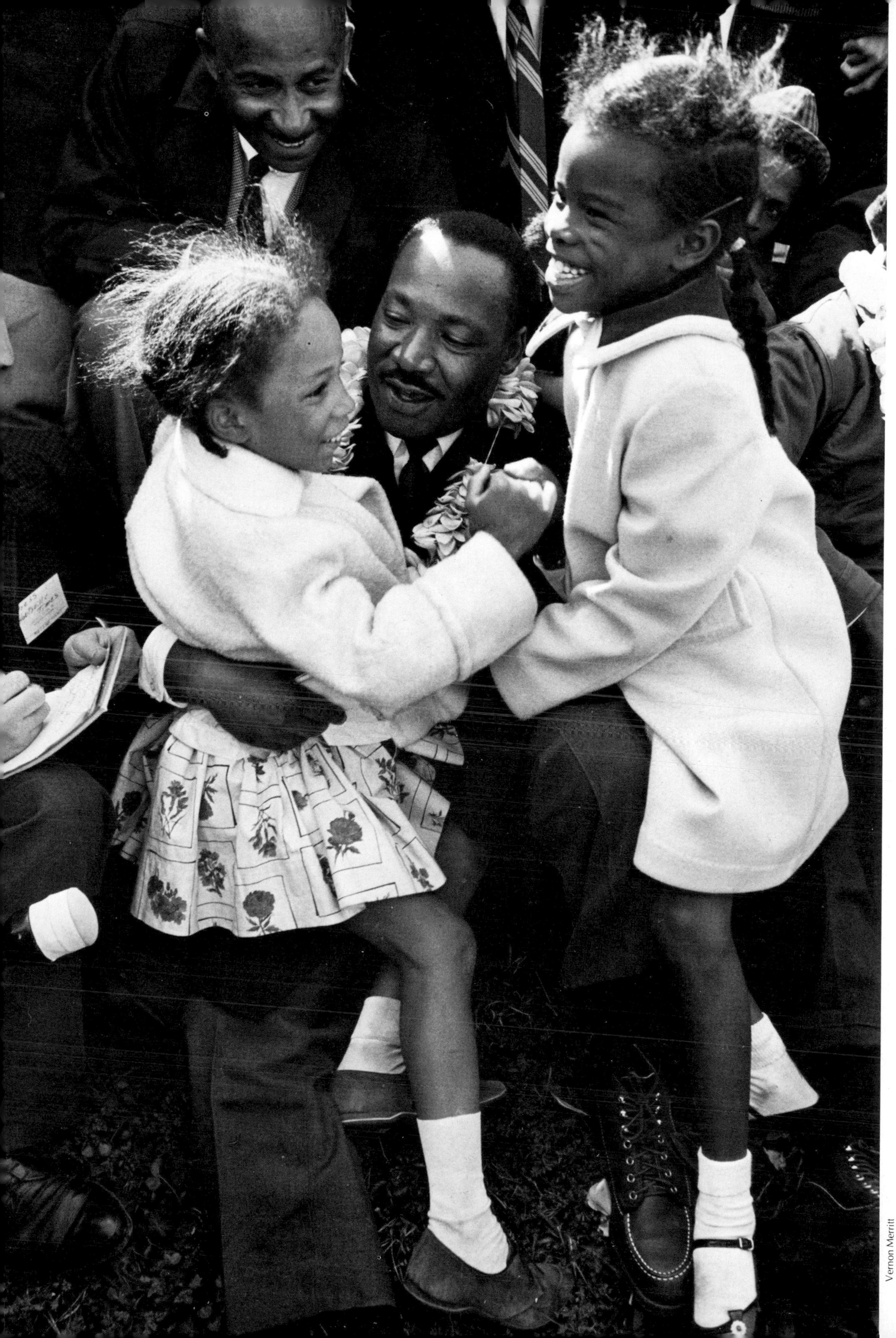

Vernon Merritt

leaders and entertainers congratulate them. "**Today,**" says King, "**I want to tell the city of Selma, today I want to say to the state of Alabama, today I want to say to the people of America and the nations of the world that we are not about to turn around. We are on the move now. Yes, we are on the move and no wave of racism can stop us. And the burning of our churches will not divert us. . . . We are on the move now. Like an idea whose time has come, not even the marching of mighty armies can halt us. We're moving to the land of freedom.**"

Once again, tragedy hastens on the heels of triumph. Mrs. Viola Liuzzo, a white volunteer from Detroit and mother of five, is shot and killed while driving from Selma to Montgomery to pick up returning marchers.

March 26, 1965. Four members of the Ku Klux Klan are arrested for the murder. President Johnson appears on nationwide television condemning the KKK. Mrs. Liuzzo, he says, "was murdered by enemies of justice, who for decades have used the rope and the gun, the tar and the feathers to terrorize their neighbors. They struck by night . . . for their purposes cannot stand the light of day."

Flip Schulke

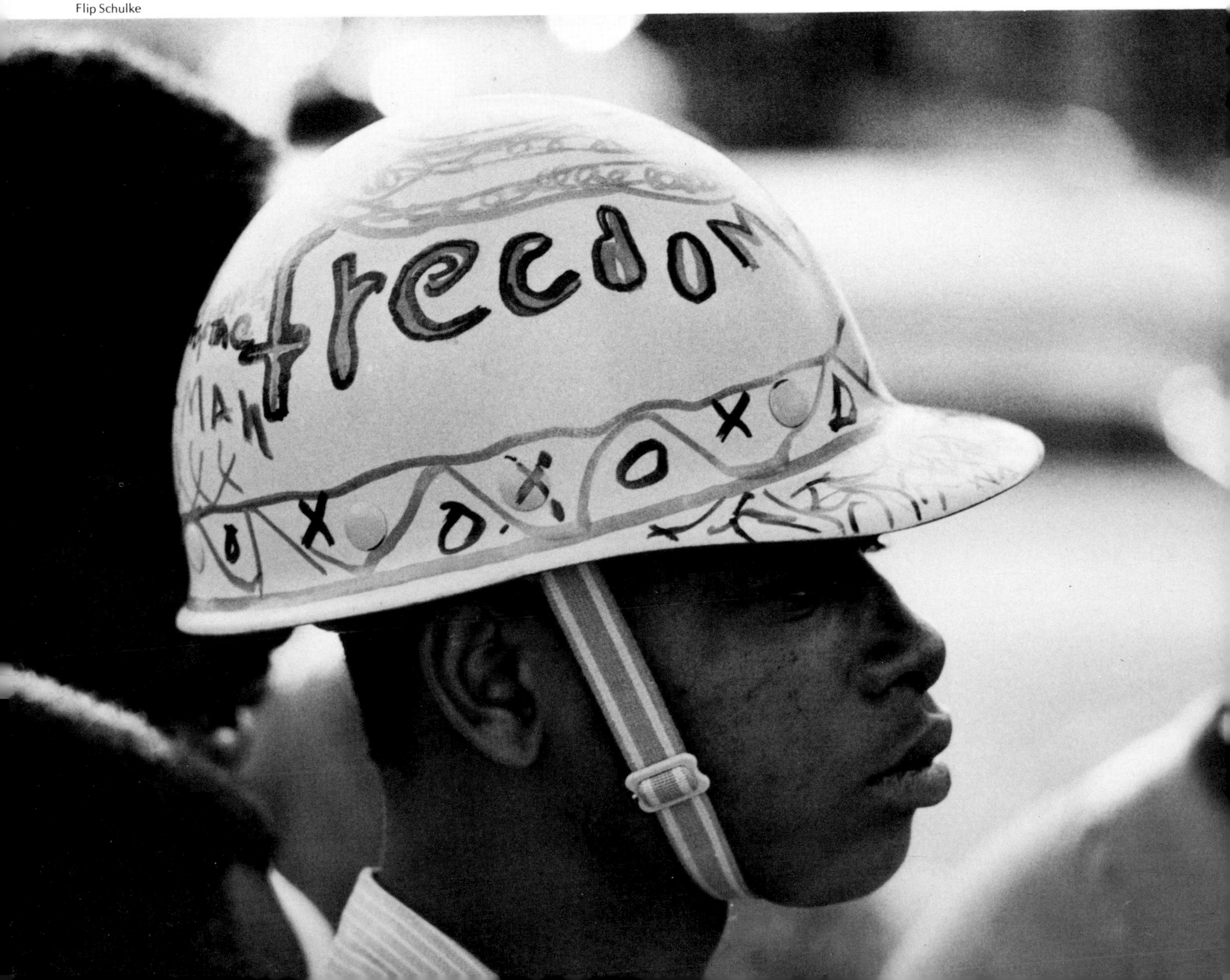
freedom

(The men are never to be convicted of murder, a state offense, but they will be convicted by the Montgomery Federal District Court of conspiring to violate the rights of persons taking part in the civil rights march. They will be sentenced to the maximum of ten years imprisonment.)

August 6, 1965. President Johnson signs the Voting Rights Act of 1965 in the room where, on August 6, 1861, President Lincoln signed a bill freeing slaves impressed into the service of the Confederacy. The bill authorizes the president to suspend literacy tests and to send federal examiners into Black Belt counties to register black voters.

President Johnson presents his voting rights bill to a joint session of Congress on March 15, insisting: "All Americans must have the right to vote. And we are going to give them that right."

Cecil Stoughton / Courtesy of Lyndon Baines Johnson Library

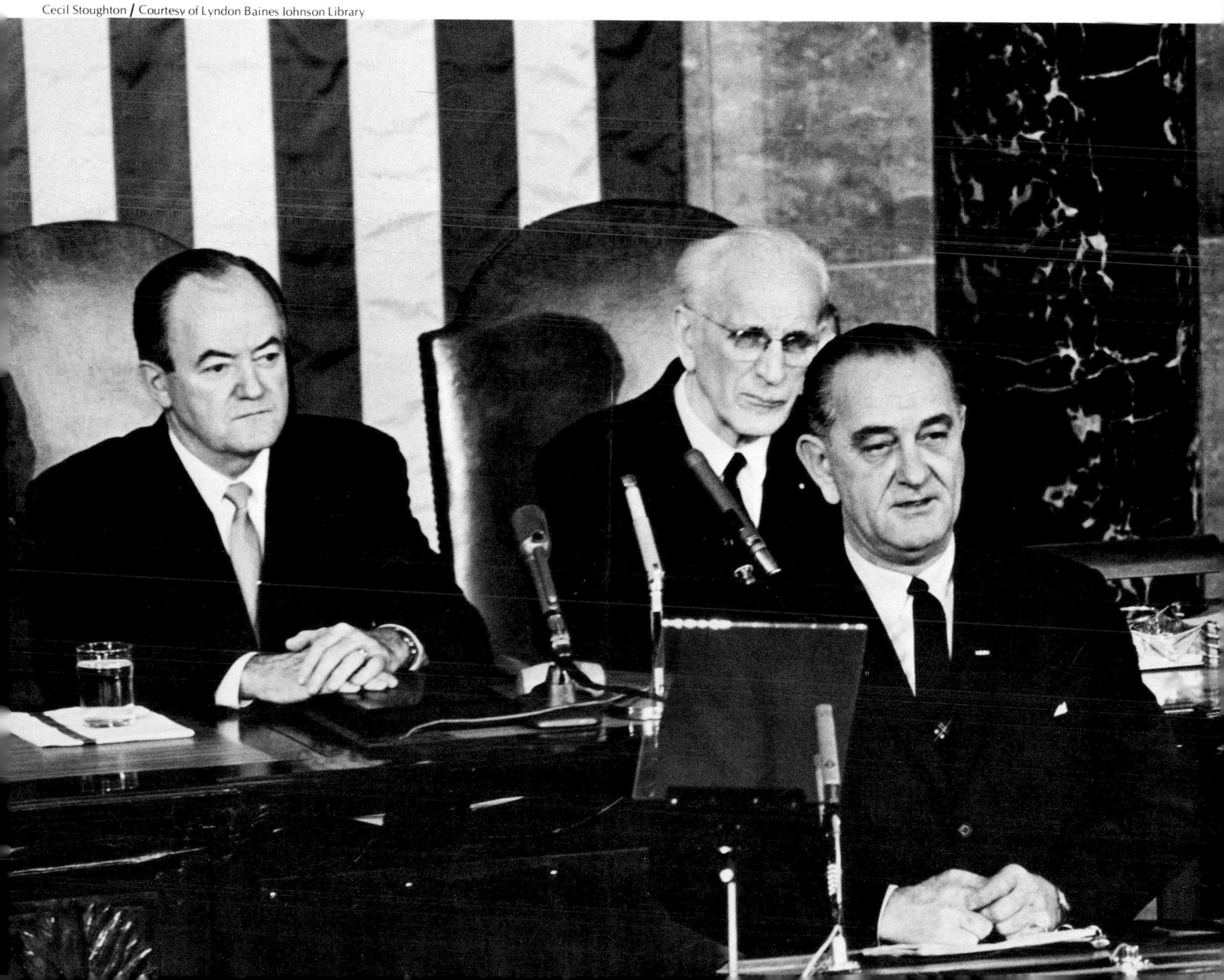

Free! RIDE to COURT HOUSE
REGIS
Citizen

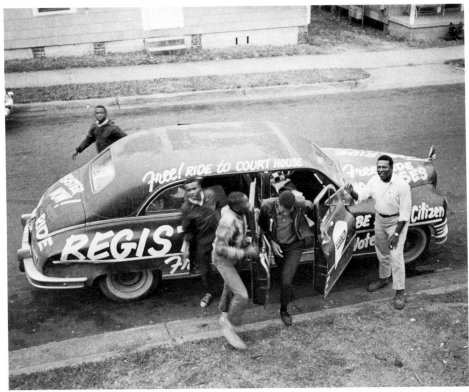

Bob Fitch

Chapter Ten

"An Idea Whose Time Has Come"

The Black Man Votes, 1966 The politics of the American South changed forever on August 6, 1965. On that day, President Johnson signed the Voting Rights Act. The new law potentially opened the voting booth to two and a half million previously disenfranchised Southern blacks. It empowered the attorney general to send federal registrars into counties where there was evidence of discrimination. It abolished poll taxes, literacy tests, and other prerequisites that had been used to disqualify black voters.

King and the leadership of the SCLC realized that the new voting legislation would be useless unless a strong campaign were mounted to raise the consciousness of southern blacks and get their names inscribed on voting rosters. They had initially expected the law to be enacted in June, 1966. When it was not, their sense of urgency only increased. Accordingly, King announced that the SCLC would organize an all-out registration drive under the direction of Hosea Williams. The campaign would concentrate on 120 rural counties across the South where blacks comprised at least 40 percent of the population. By the time the bill was finally signed, fifteen hundred volunteers from all over the country had spread into the Black Belt counties of Alabama, Georgia, Mississippi, North and South Carolina, and Florida.

In many areas, such as Dallas, Perry, Wilcox, and Greene counties in Alabama, it became necessary to request federal referees as provided for under the law. In other regions, the simple fact that the bill was now law made it possible to negotiate with state officials without requesting federal assistance.

In Alabama, Mississippi, and Louisiana federal examiners immediately opened offices in fourteen counties. In a single day they registered over a thousand new voters. By the end of 1965, federal officers had been sent into twenty-three additional counties.

The government registrars were all southerners, generally from states other than those they worked in. Some expressed belief in what they were doing as a fundamental aspect of democracy. Although they were exposed to danger, they were protected by the Justice Department as civil rights workers had

Matt Herron

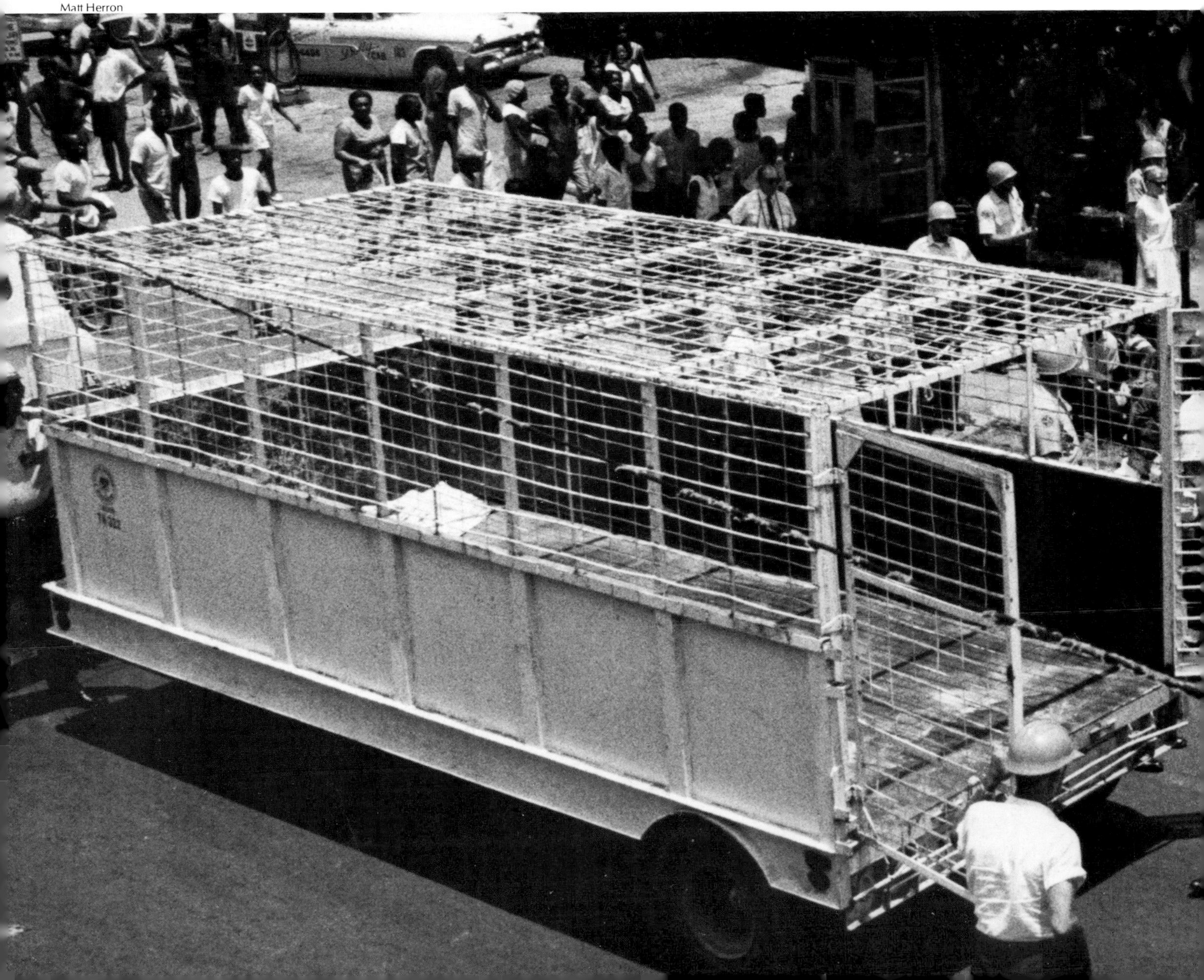

Members of the Mississippi Freedom Democratic Party are harrassed while trying to register voters in Jackson. When they march in protest on June 24, 1965, they are arrested and carted away in cage-like trucks called "nigger wagons."

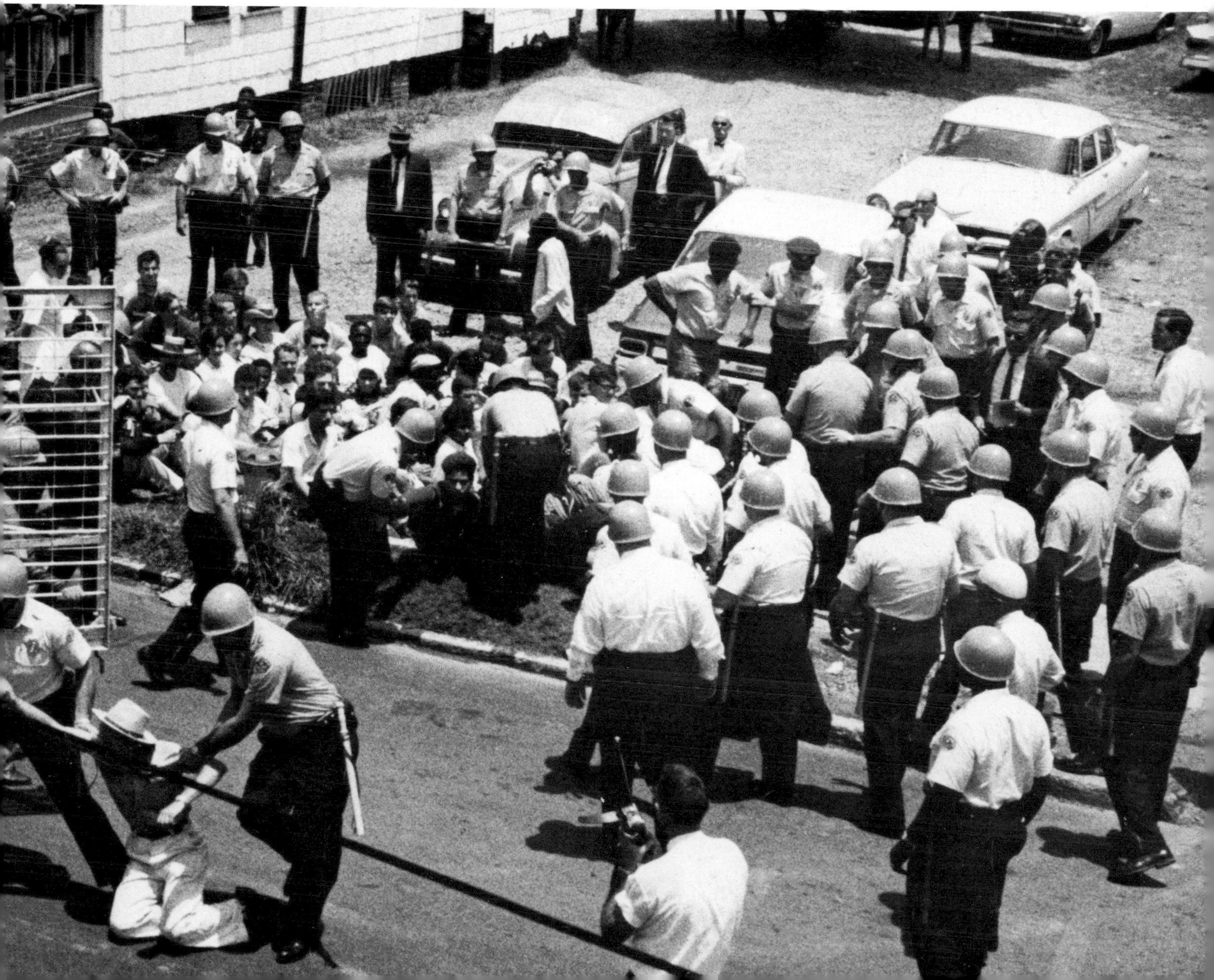

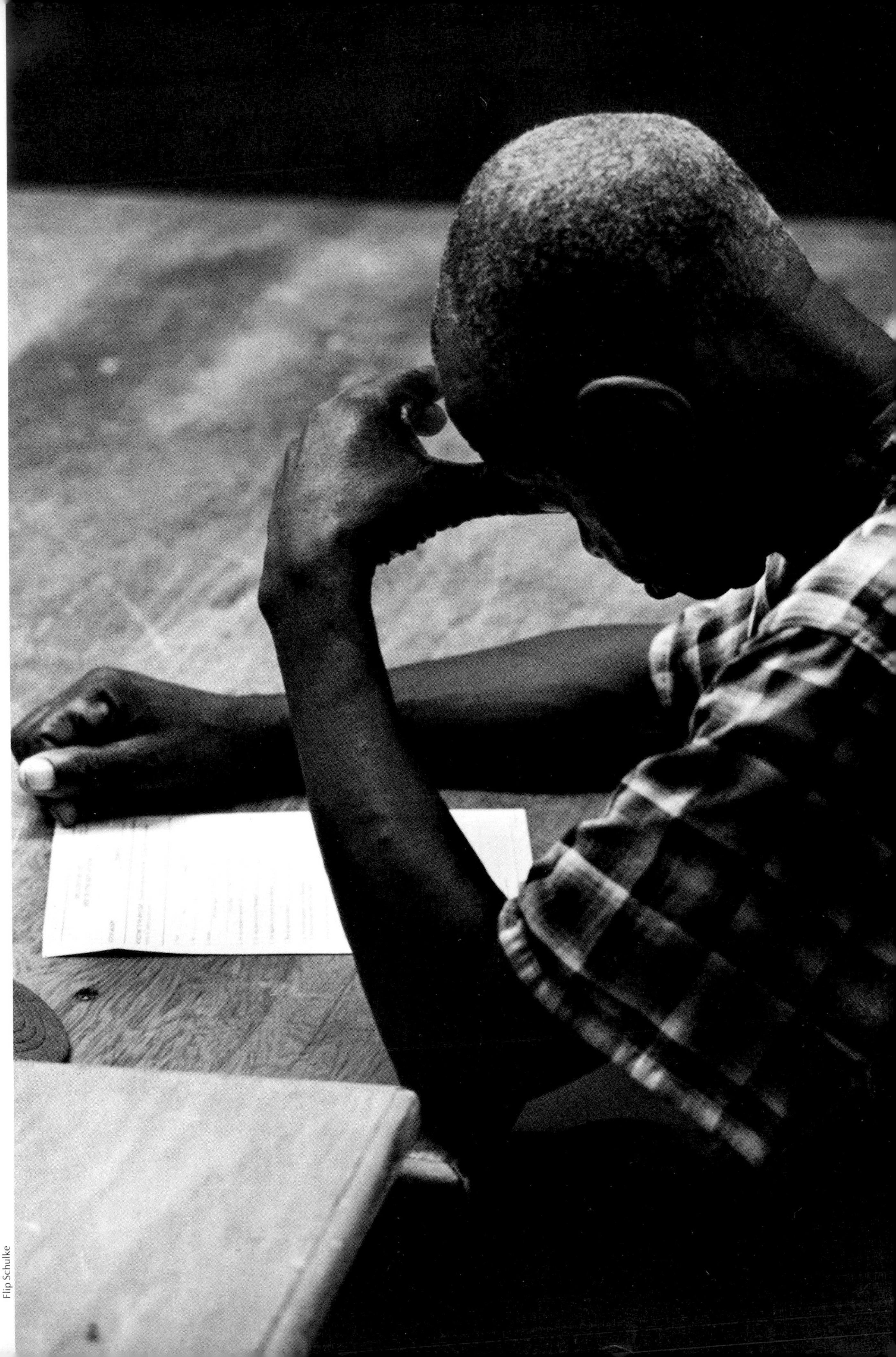

Flip Schulke

never been before. Those who maintained their segregationist views still did their job and for the most part made the bureaucratic process as easy as possible for the new voters. Many were impressed by the seriousness and sincerity of the black applicants.

The greatest gains in voter registration occurred in Alabama, where the most federal employees had been dispatched and where King and his staff had concentrated their People to People Tours to educate voters.

Although much remained to be done, the early statistics were impressive. In the seven months following the bill's passage, over 300,000 black voters were registered for the first time. All but

Left:
Filling out an application to vote in Greensboro, Alabama.

Registering to vote in Montgomery.

Bob Fitch

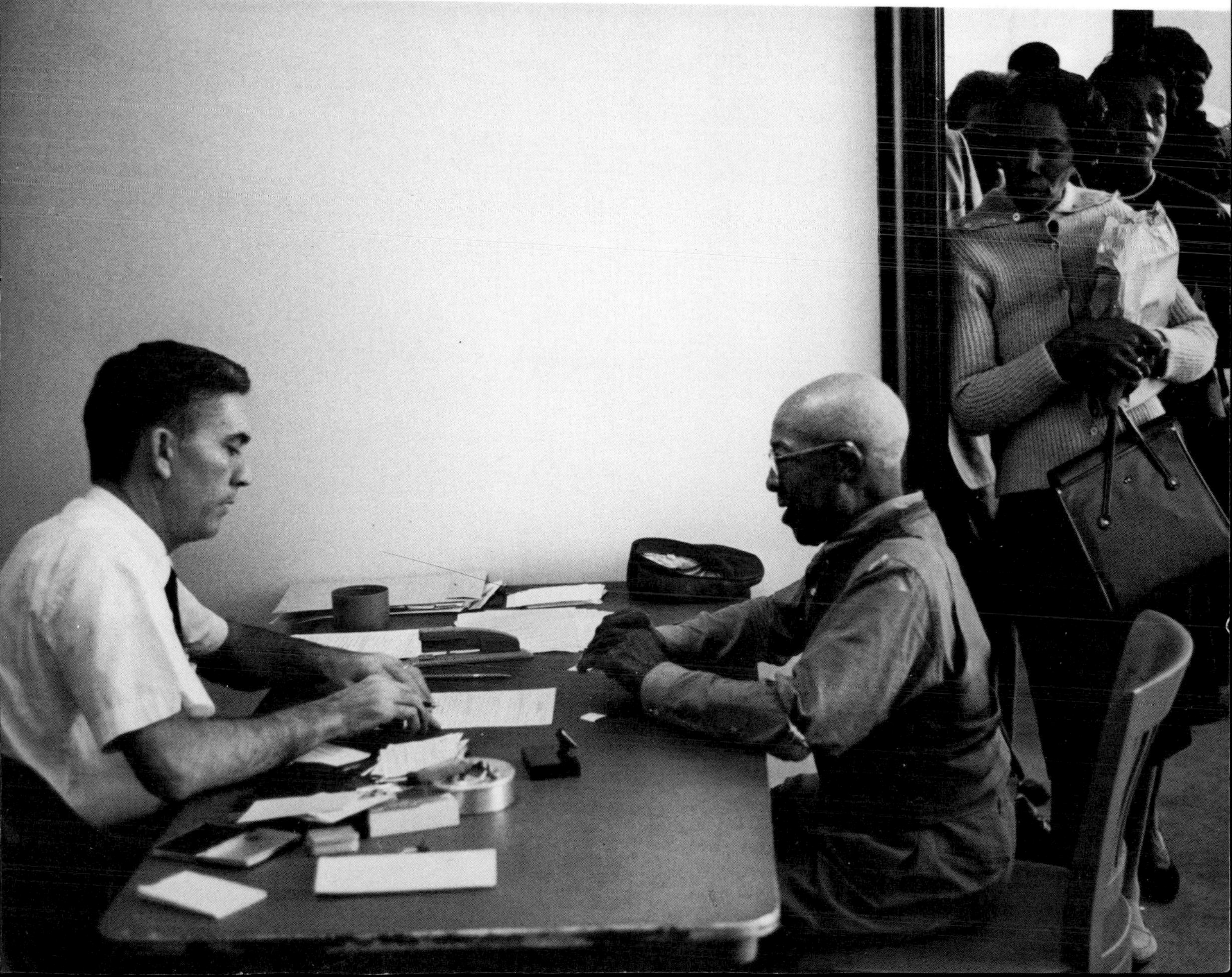

four southern states had registered over 50 percent of their eligible black voters. In Alabama, black registration increased from 23 percent to 51.2 percent within a year.

To create a viable political force, however, King realized that registered voters was only part of the task. Voter education also had to include teaching prospective voters how to read a ballot. Many of the newly enfranchised blacks were semi-literate, and, understandably, totally unfamiliar with the way in which the democratic process was supposed to work. King and his volunteers patiently explained the voting procedure and organized public meetings where blacks could meet and hear local candidates.

King makes a People to People tour, speaking to church congregations and supporting black candidates in Alabama.

Bob Fitch

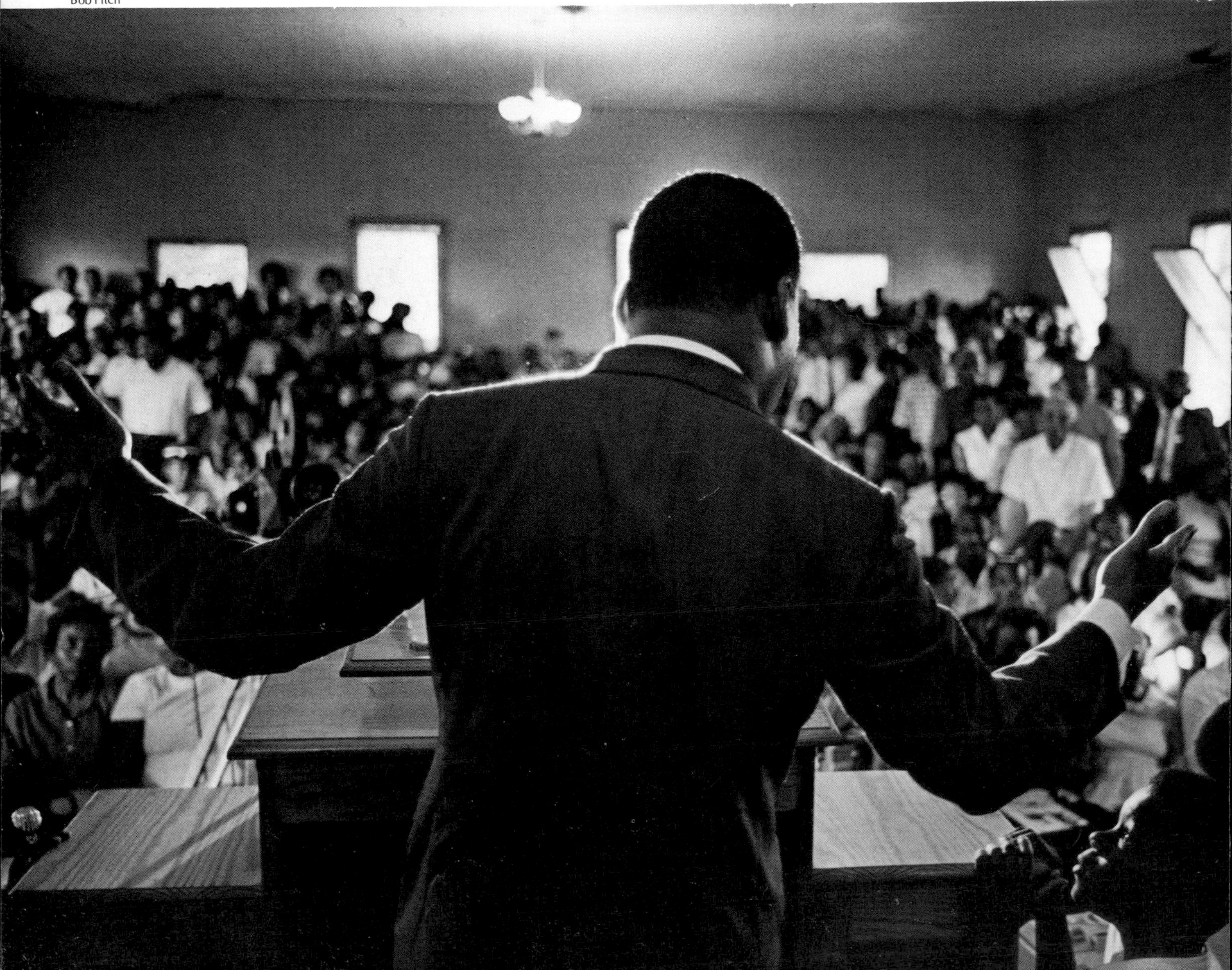

King firmly believed that the ultimate foundation of black people's power was the ballot. With the vote they could begin to control their own destinies. The Alabama primary elections of 1966 demonstrated both the underlying strength and the residual weakness of the new black voting power. Fifty-two black candidates filed for county or legislative offices in the Alabama primary. Although none won outright, twenty-four survived to the primary run-off. Only four of Alabama's black candidates were victorious in the runoff. Three of the winners were in Macon County, including Lucius Amerson, the first black to be elected sheriff in the Black Belt since Reconstruction.

At least as significant as the success of these first few candidates was the fact

Bob Fitch

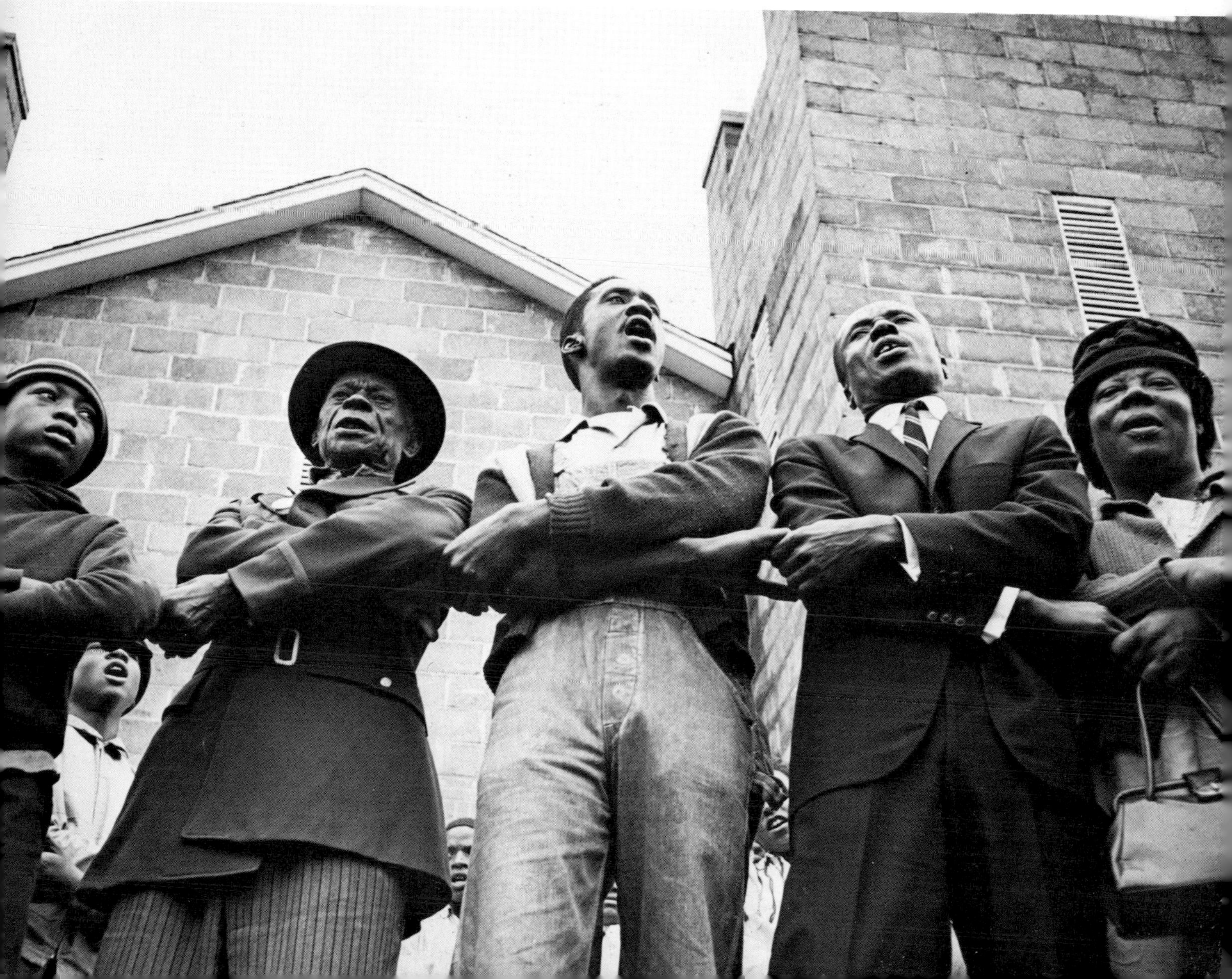

Reverend T. E. Gilmore (center) campaigns for sheriff in Greene County, Alabama. Although he lost to the white incumbent in 1966, Gilmore was eventually elected on his third attempt.

Reverend Gilmore (right) seeks the vote of an Alabama farmer.

Below:
Lucius Amerson campaigns with his family in Macon County, Alabama. Elected in 1966, he was the first black to hold the office of sheriff in the Black Belt since Reconstruction.

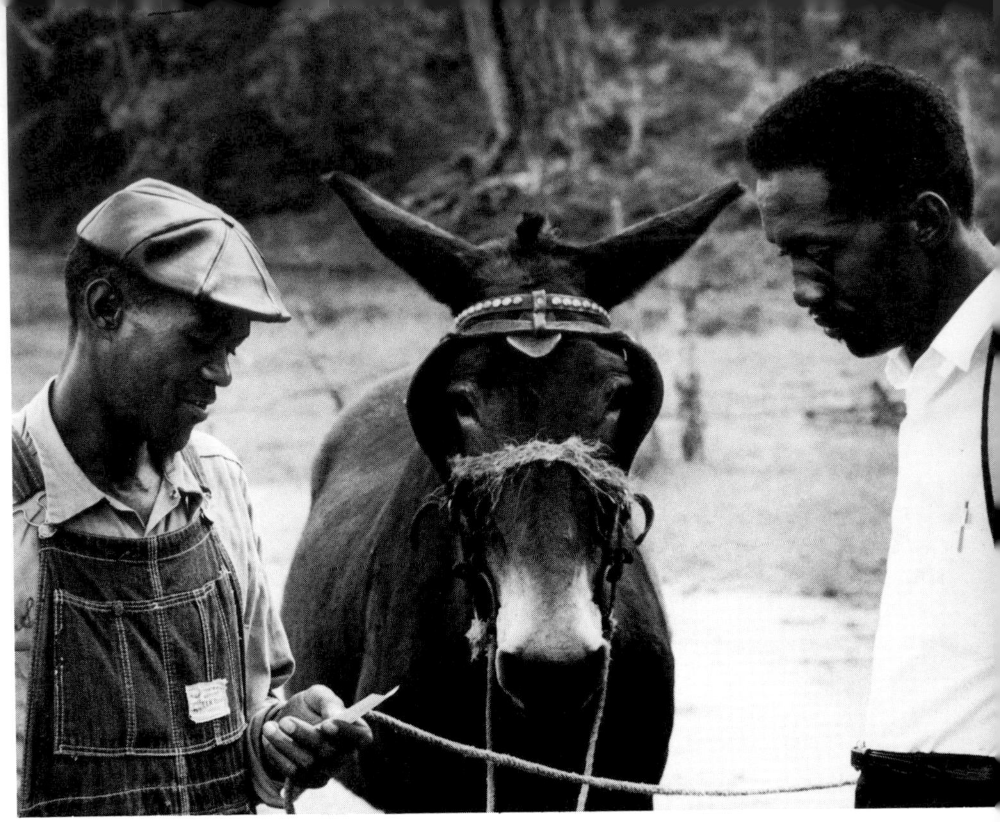

Flip Schulke

Bob Fitch

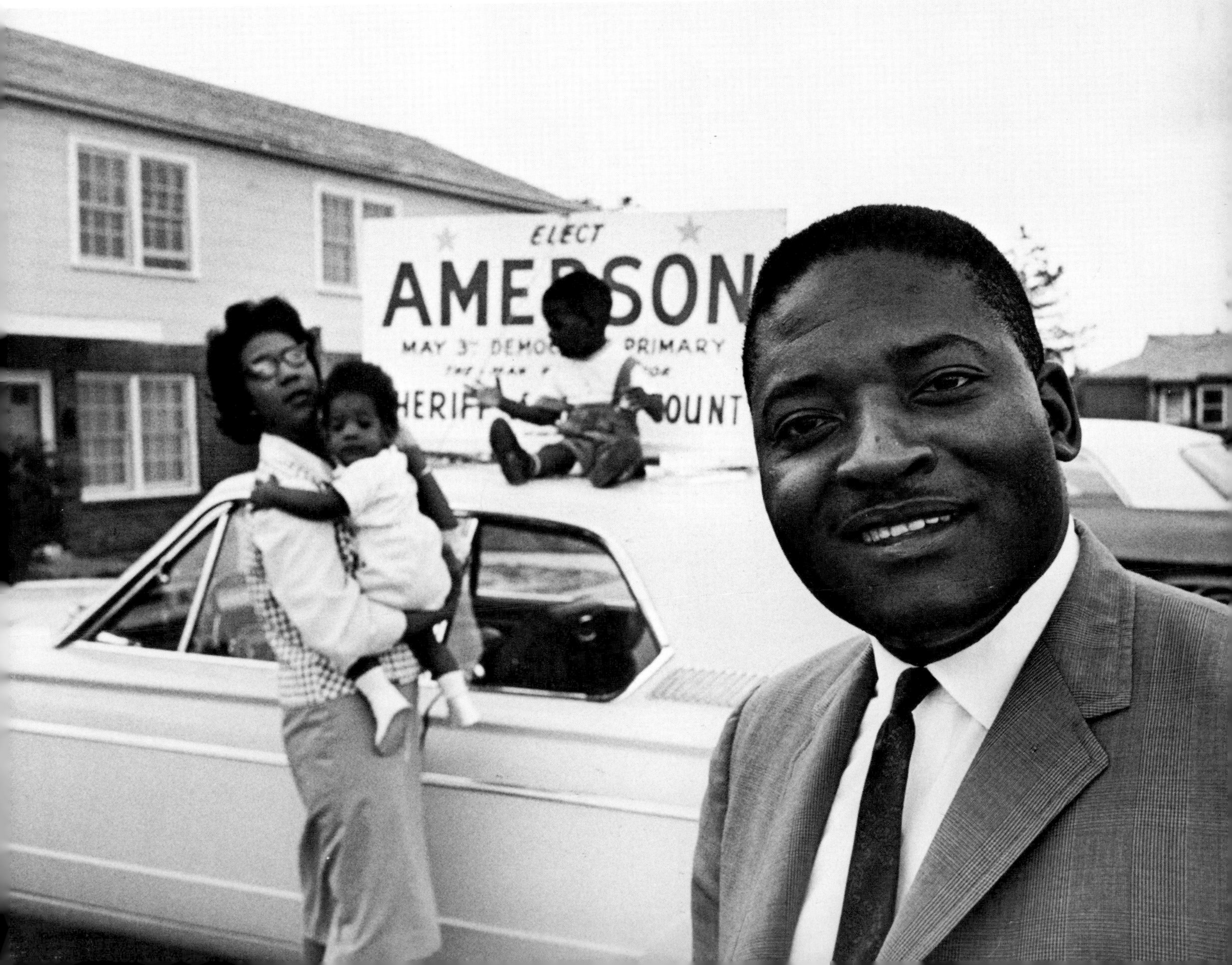
ELECT
PRIMARY

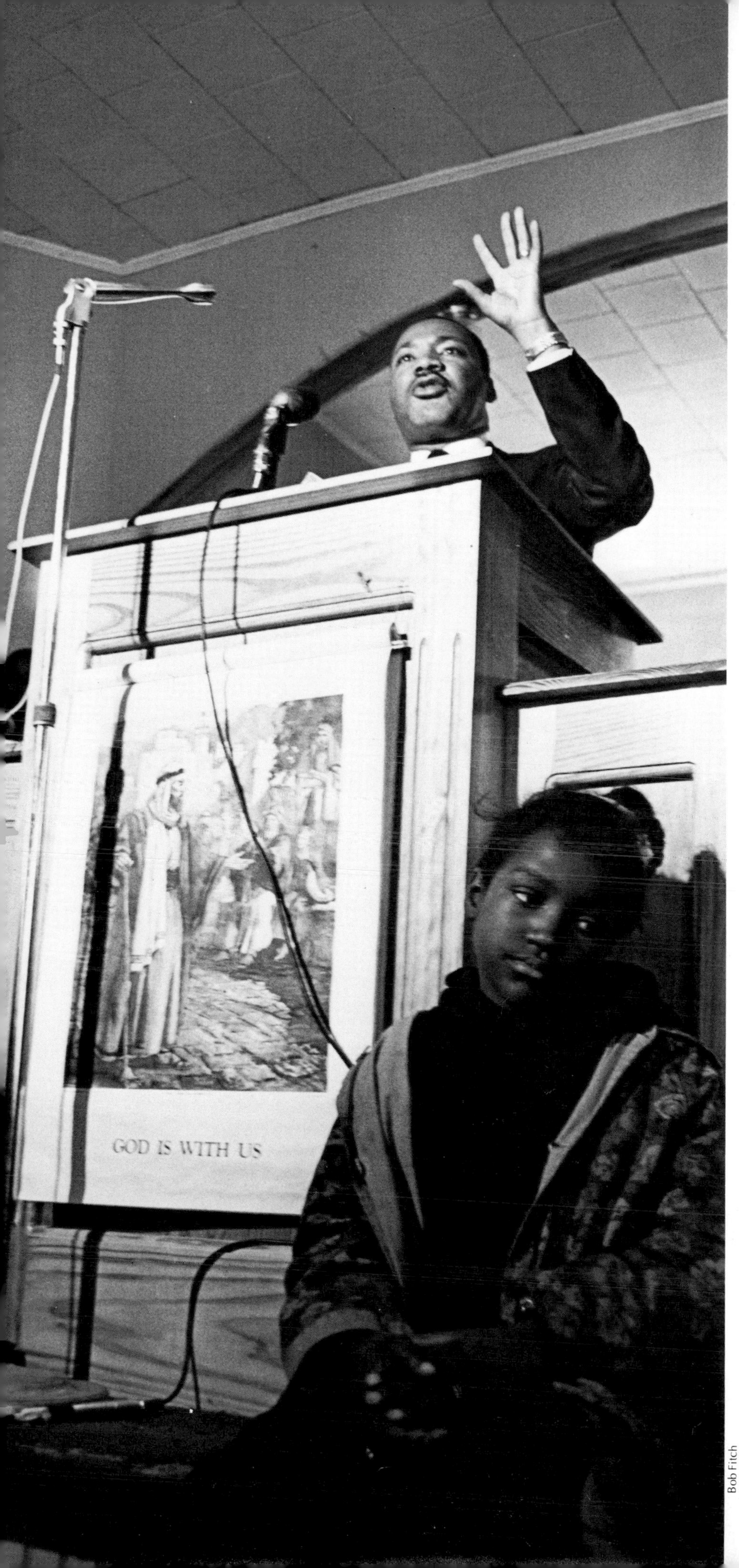
GOD IS WITH US

Bob Fitch

that the black vote brought victory for many white candidates who were racial moderates. In Dallas County the defeat of segregationist Sheriff Jim Clark by moderate Wilson Baker attested to the liberalizing influence of black voters.

While King and the SCLC were attempting to organize black and white coalitions throughout the Black Belt, Stokely Carmichael was working to establish the Lowndes County Freedom Organization in Alabama. Lowndes County, where Viola Liuzzo was slain, was 80 percent black. Nevertheless, in March 1965, not one black was listed on the voting rolls. By the time of the primary, over twenty-seven hundred blacks had been registered. Carmichael organized a protest vote, calling his new party the Black Panther Party. This first engagement in the black power movement's struggle for primacy was a failure, but from it Carmichael emerged as the head of SNCC and as the chief advocate of black power.

King continued his constant pressure on President Johnson for increasingly forceful implementation of the Voting Rights Act, and the nation witnessed the growing influence of the southern black on politics. But strong cross-currents were developing in American political thought. The war in Vietnam was raging with escalating bitterness, and the concern of liberals was diverted to attempting to halt this pointless waste of lives and resources. The forces of political activism became polarized around the issue of the Indochina war, and the struggle of blacks to take their place as voters slipped to a subordinate position. By the time of Richard Nixon's election to the presidency, federal support for voter registration had become virtually nonexistent. Under the 1965 law, nine hundred counties were eligible for federal intervention in voter registration. To

Flip Schulke

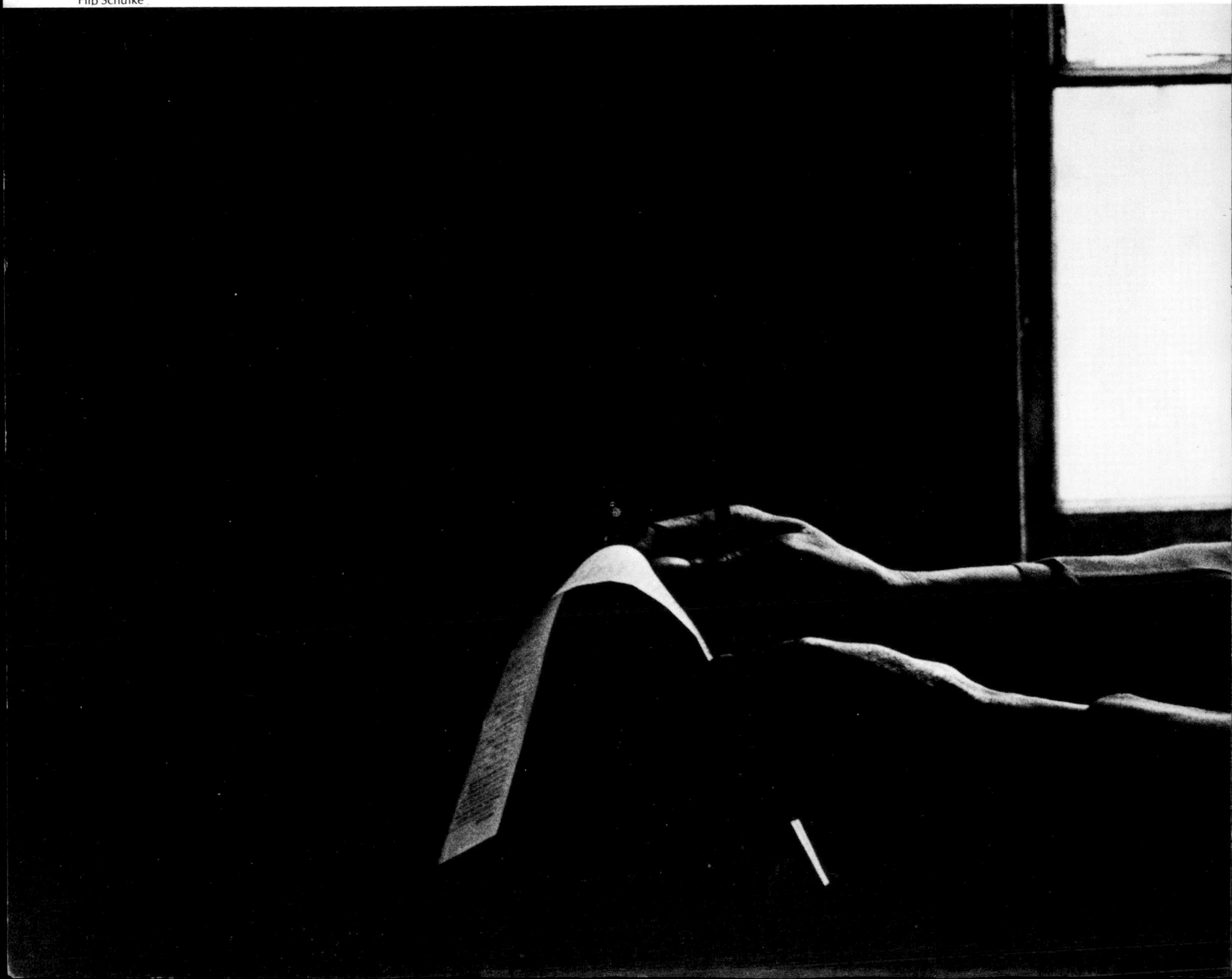

Voter education is an important aspect of the registration drive. Volunteers in Perry County, Alabama, teach new voters how to read the ballot, so that they can exercise their right to choose those who would govern them.

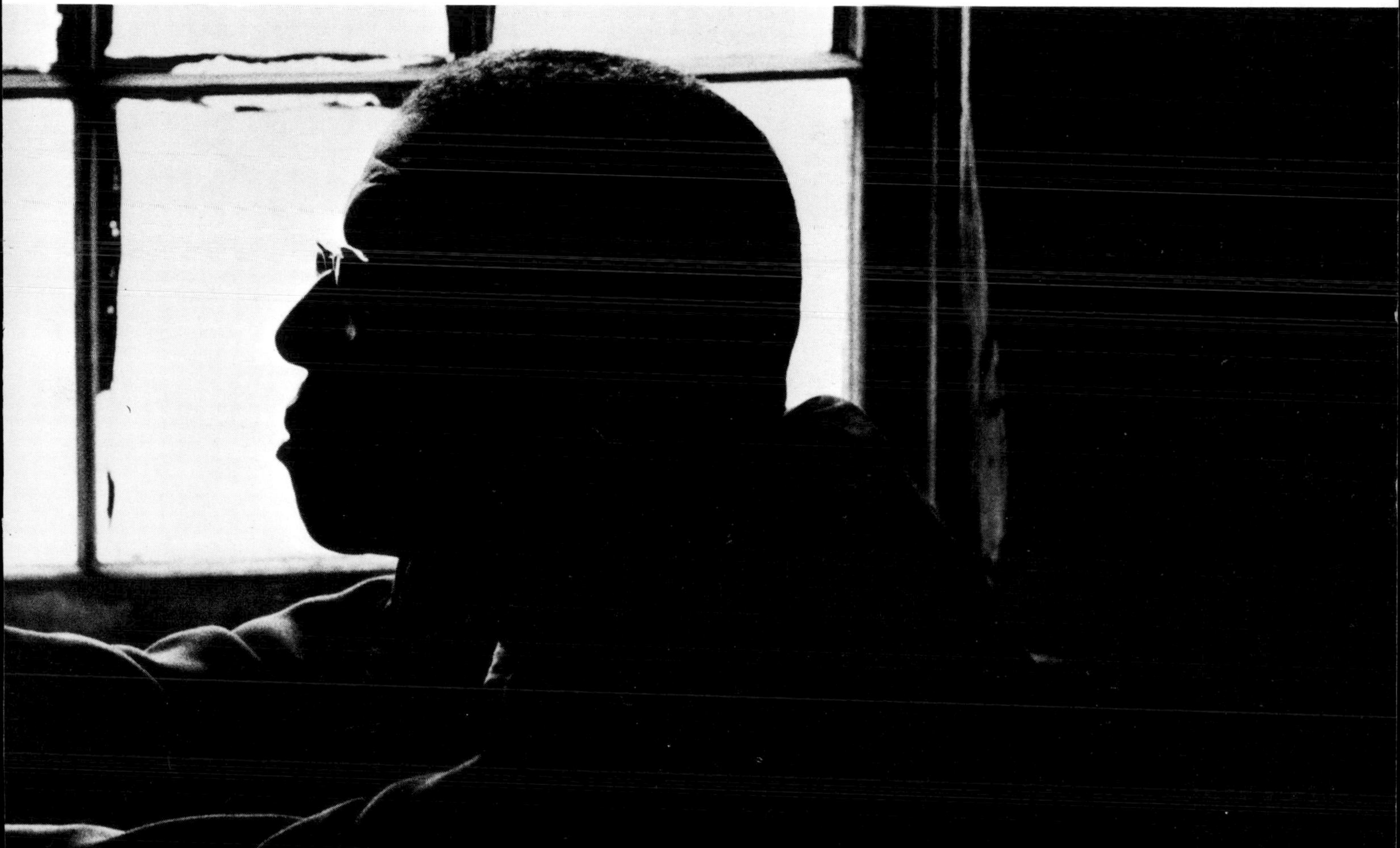

date only 103 have actually had federal assistance. And no federal referees were sent to the South during the Nixon administration.

"All through his life, every time we were demonstrating, we also registered voters," Congressman Andrew Young remembers of King. "One of the last meetings he had before his death was a meeting . . . about a black political organization to sort of serve the black community like the ADA serves the white liberal community. This was very much in his mind. This is what he wanted to see; a political advancement, because he saw that the United States would never deal with its racism and its militarism or its economic exploitation

At the polls for the first time in Perry County, Alabama.

Flip Schulke

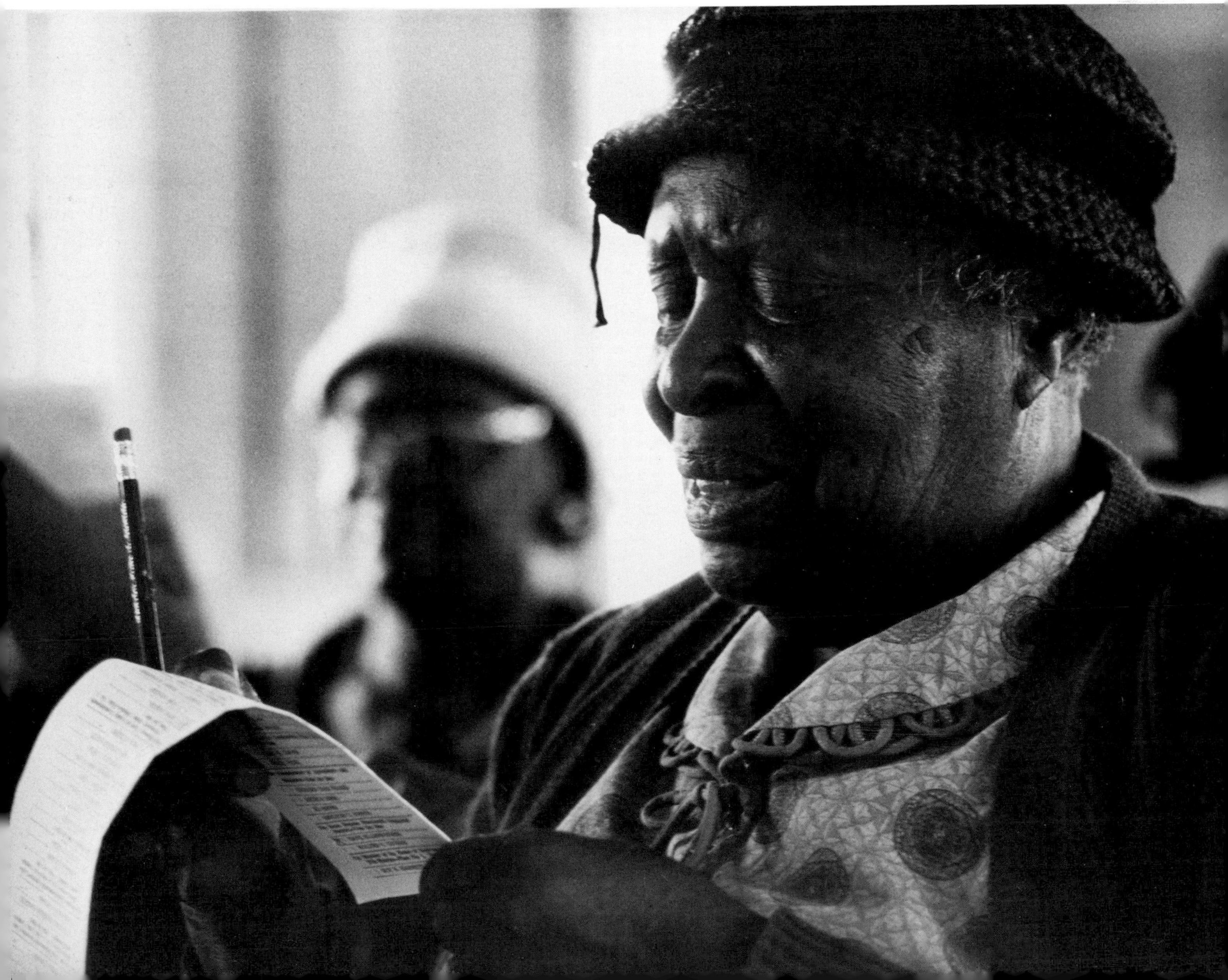

After a century of waiting, black voters stand patiently at the polls in Marion, Alabama, to cast their ballots in a state primary.

Below:
Stokely Carmichael organizes a protest vote in Lowndes County. This is the first time the symbol of the Black Panther has been used.

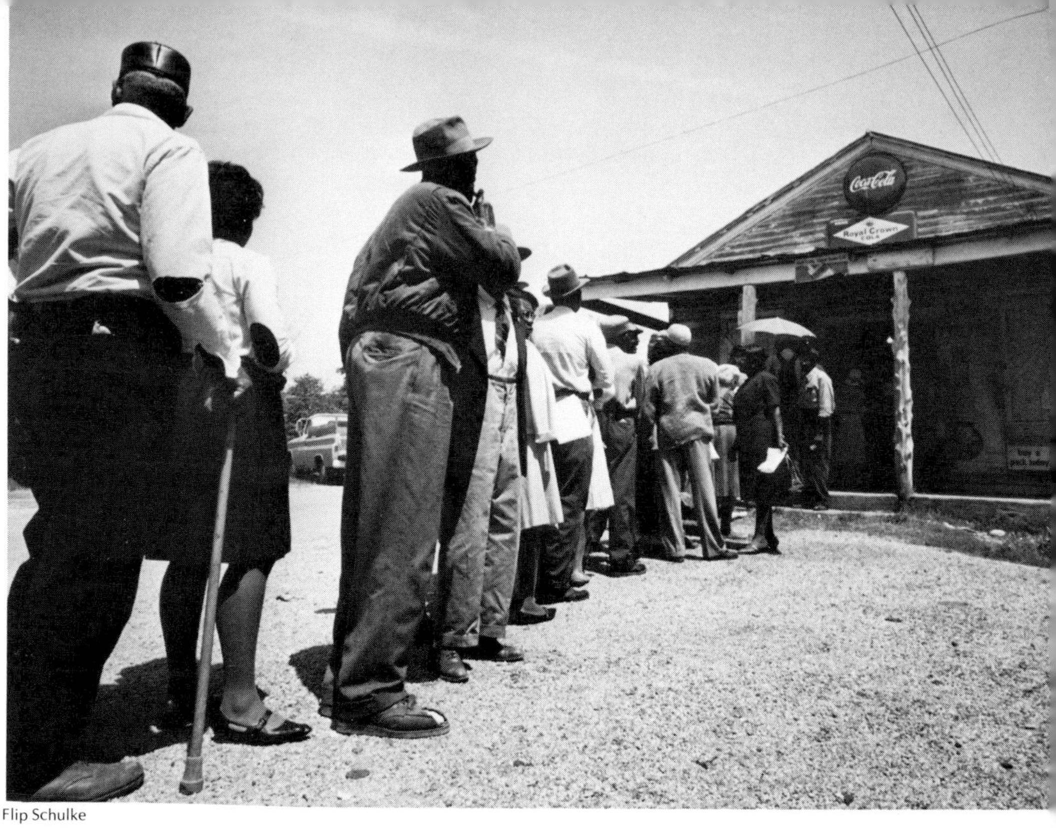
Coca-Cola
Royal Crown

Flip Schulke

Flip Schulke

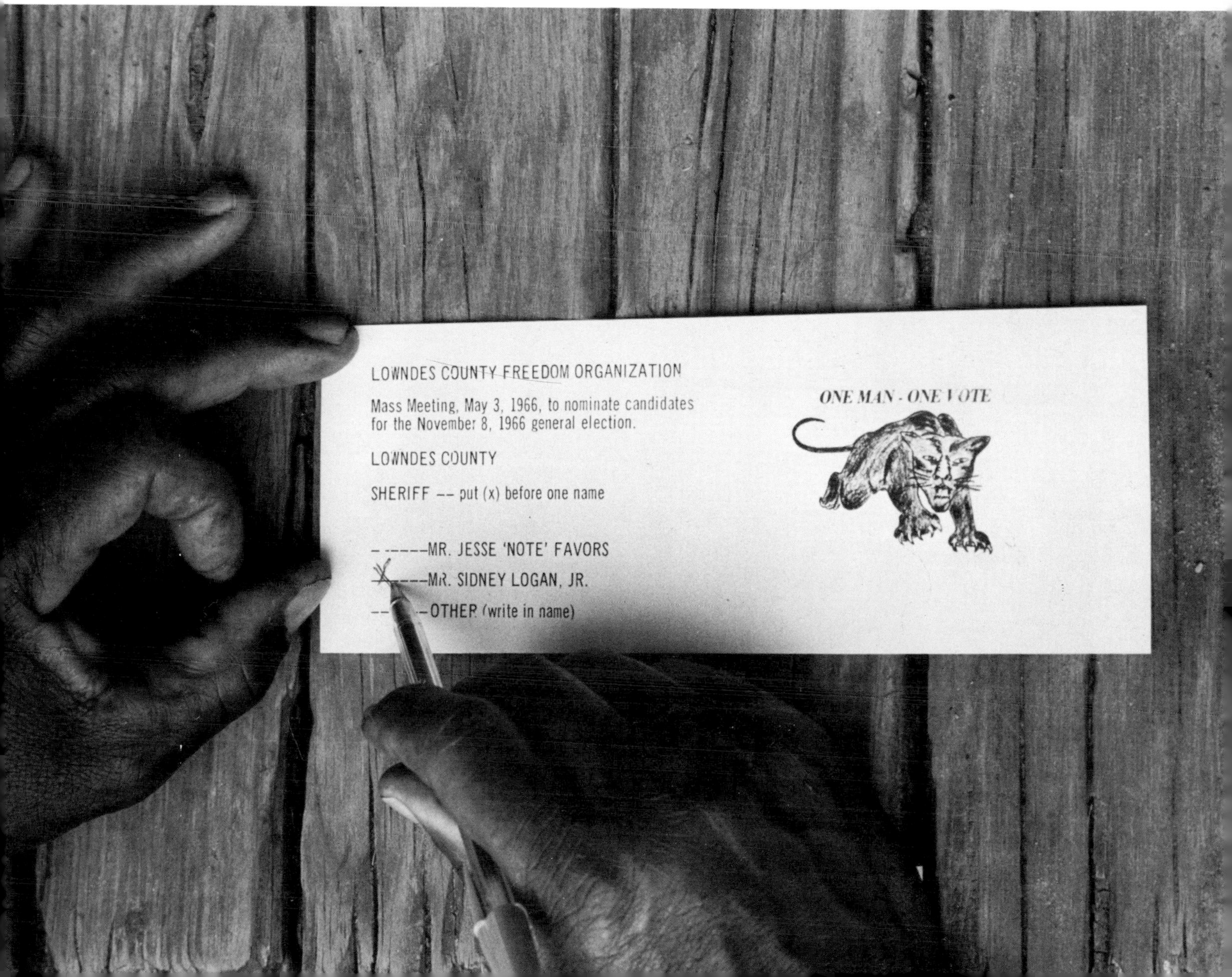
LOWNDES COUNTY FREEDOM ORGANIZATION
Mass Meeting, May 3, 1966, to nominate candidates for the November 8, 1966 general election.
LOWNDES COUNTY
SHERIFF -- put (x) before one name
------MR. JESSE 'NOTE' FAVORS
------MR. SIDNEY LOGAN, JR.
------OTHER (write in name)
ONE MAN - ONE VOTE

of the poor, whatever color they might be, until the one-party racist politics of the South was broken."

With approximately 55 percent of the black voters registered in the South, civil rights workers are continuing the voting drive today. In some areas, such as Clark County, Georgia, there are still complaints that registrars are making it difficult for blacks to register. But ten years after Selma the effects of the black vote cannot be ignored in contemporary politics.

"King said," Congressman Young continues, "'if you give us the ballot we will elect men of good will to the legislature.' . . . I think that we have seen that beginning to happen. We saw that especially in these last two elections, not only black candidates but a different kind of white southerner coming into the governor's offices and to the congressional seats. . . . With a majority of Republicans and southerners on the House Judiciary Committee, no one expected an impeachment vote [against Nixon]. But Congressmen Walter Flowers, Jim Mann, and Ray Thornton all came from areas with large black constituencies. This has an automatic liberalizing effect on officials."

These developments, gradual, evolutionary, almost geological in their slowness, represent King's kind of black power—the power that flows to blacks when they have free and open access to the ballot box. When black people speak with their votes, legislators are forced to listen. And the more votes there are, the more they pay attention.

Yoichi Okamoto / Courtesy of Lyndon Baines Johnson Library

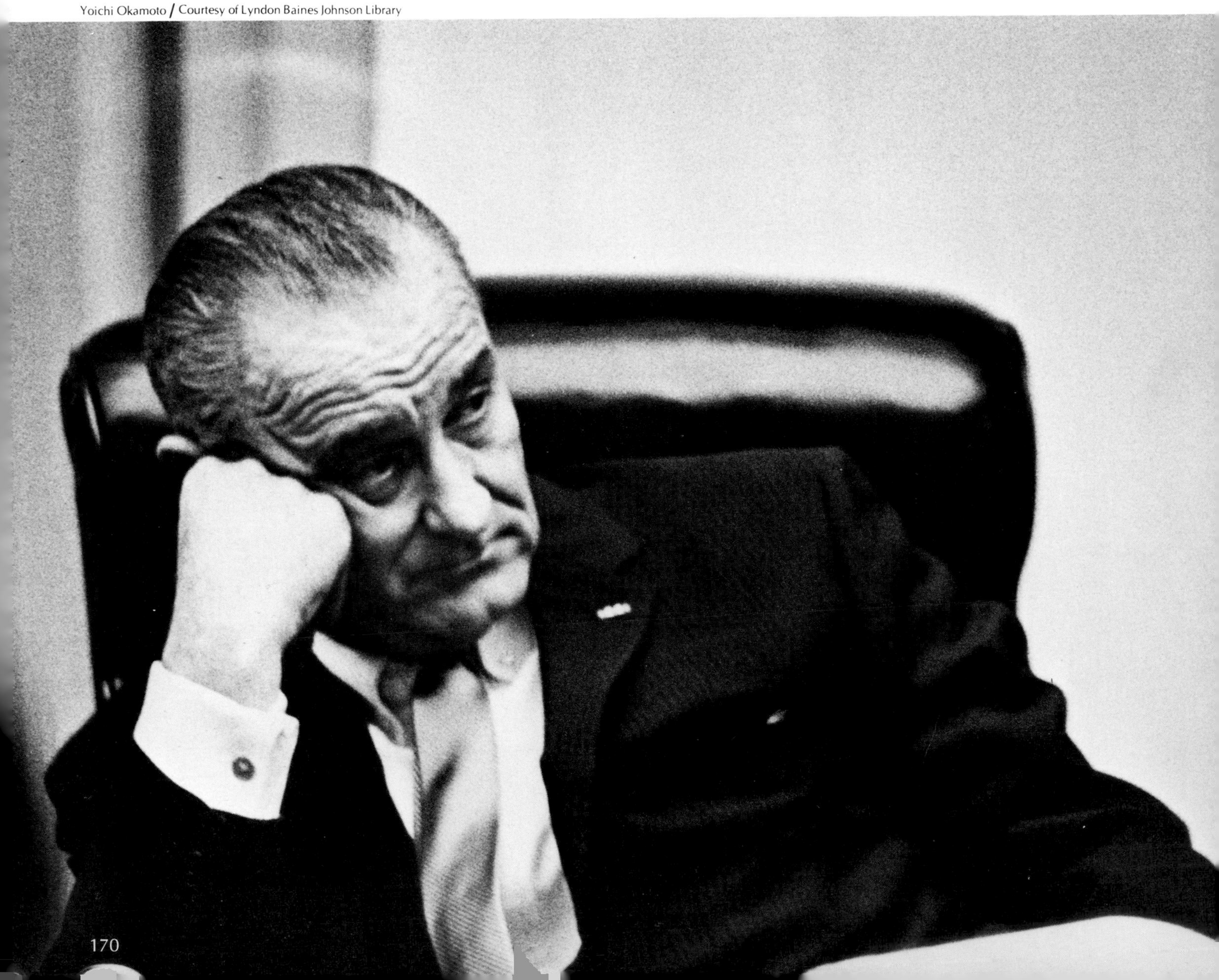

Meeting with President Johnson in March, 1966, King insists on the importance of full implementation of the Voting Rights Act.

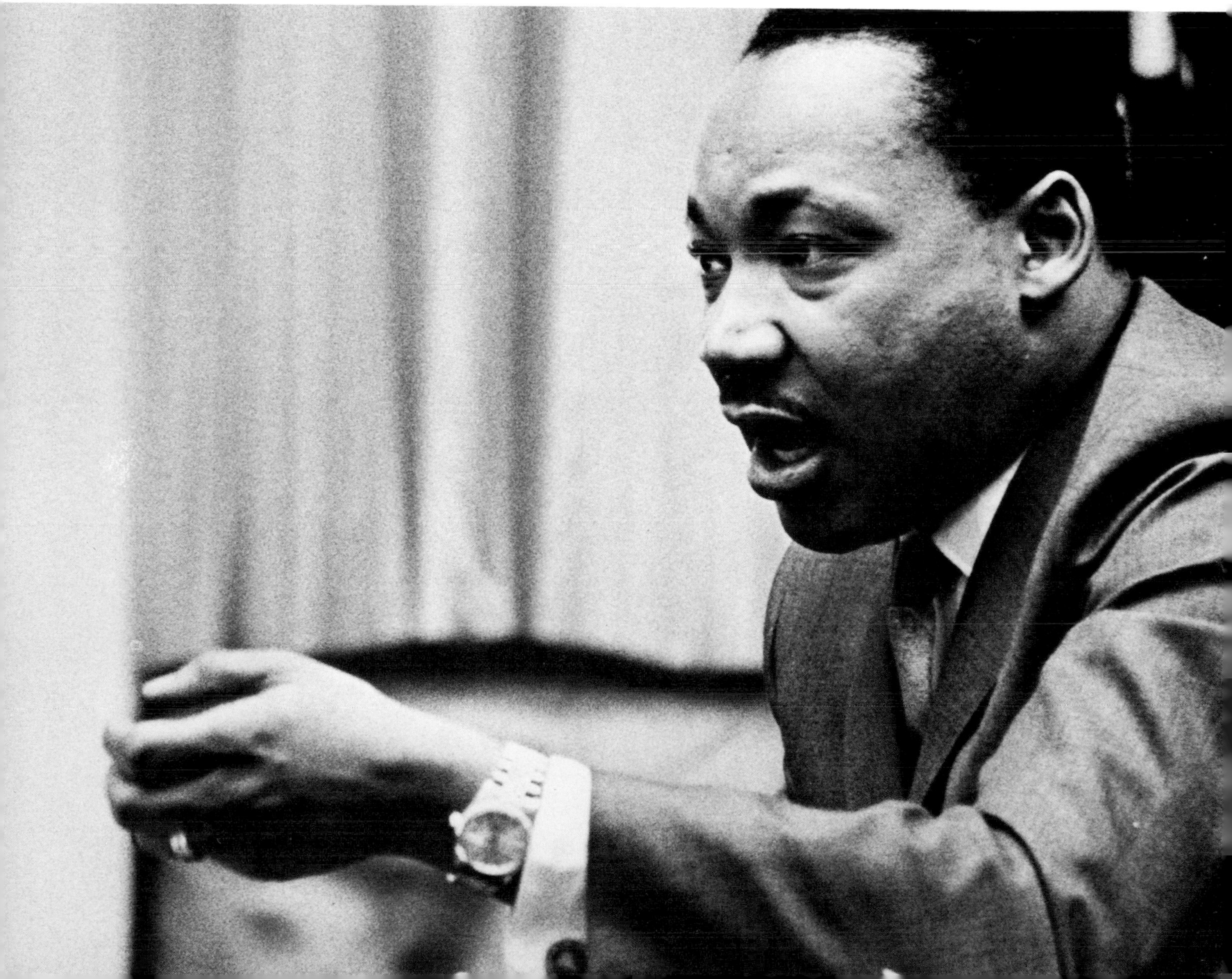

Matt Herron

Chapter Eleven

"We Have a Power"

Meredith's March Through Mississippi, June, 1966 Ever since he had entered the University of Mississippi in 1962, James Meredith had been isolated—forced to rely almost entirely on his own resources. In early June, 1966, he set off on a march through Mississippi with a handful of friends. His intention was to test the progress of his home state and to challenge his own courage.

Meredith and four friends set out from Memphis, Tennessee, just north of the Mississippi border, on June 6, 1966. Theirs was a private statement—a personal test. There was to be no press, no crowd.

The next day, as they approached Hernando, Mississippi, Meredith was shot. According to the earliest reports, he had been killed by a shotgun blast from the trees behind him. But in fact he was only superficially wounded by the sixty pellets of birdshot, and he was able to tell the police that he did not want to go to a Mississippi hospital. They took him back to Memphis.

King and other civil rights leaders hastened to his hospital bed. Like King, Floyd McKissick of CORE and Stokely Carmichael of SNCC felt the march should be continued. "We had an understanding in the movement," Andrew Young explained, "that if you let people stop you from doing something through death, then it only encouraged them to kill you whenever they wanted you to stop doing something. So we were morally obligated, we felt, to continue that march." They proposed to begin at the spot where Meredith had been shot. Meredith agreed, saying: "Yes. This thing is bigger than me."

On June 8, twenty marchers assembled on Route 51, having been grudgingly promised police protection by Governor Paul Johnson of Mississippi. The march lasted three weeks and covered two hundred miles. After the first night, the marchers slept in tents carried by a truck. As they trudged through the small towns of Mississippi, they attempted to get local blacks registered to

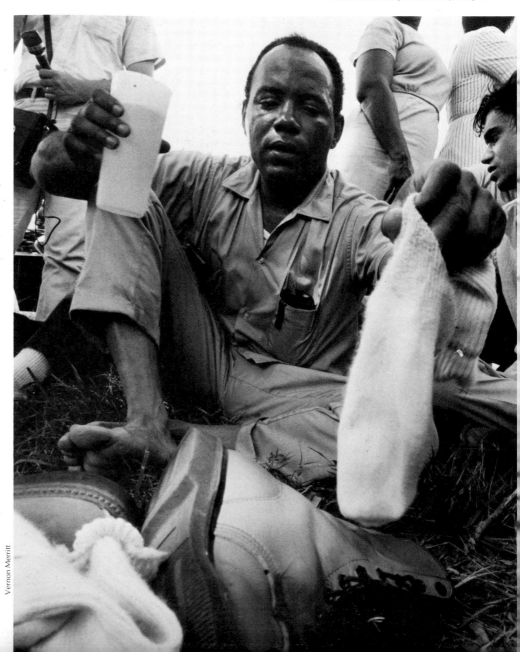

James Meredith, who had single-handedly broken the color barrier at Ole Miss four years before, sets out on a lonely march through his native state of Mississippi in June, 1966.

On the second day, he is shot by a sniper.

Vernon Merritt

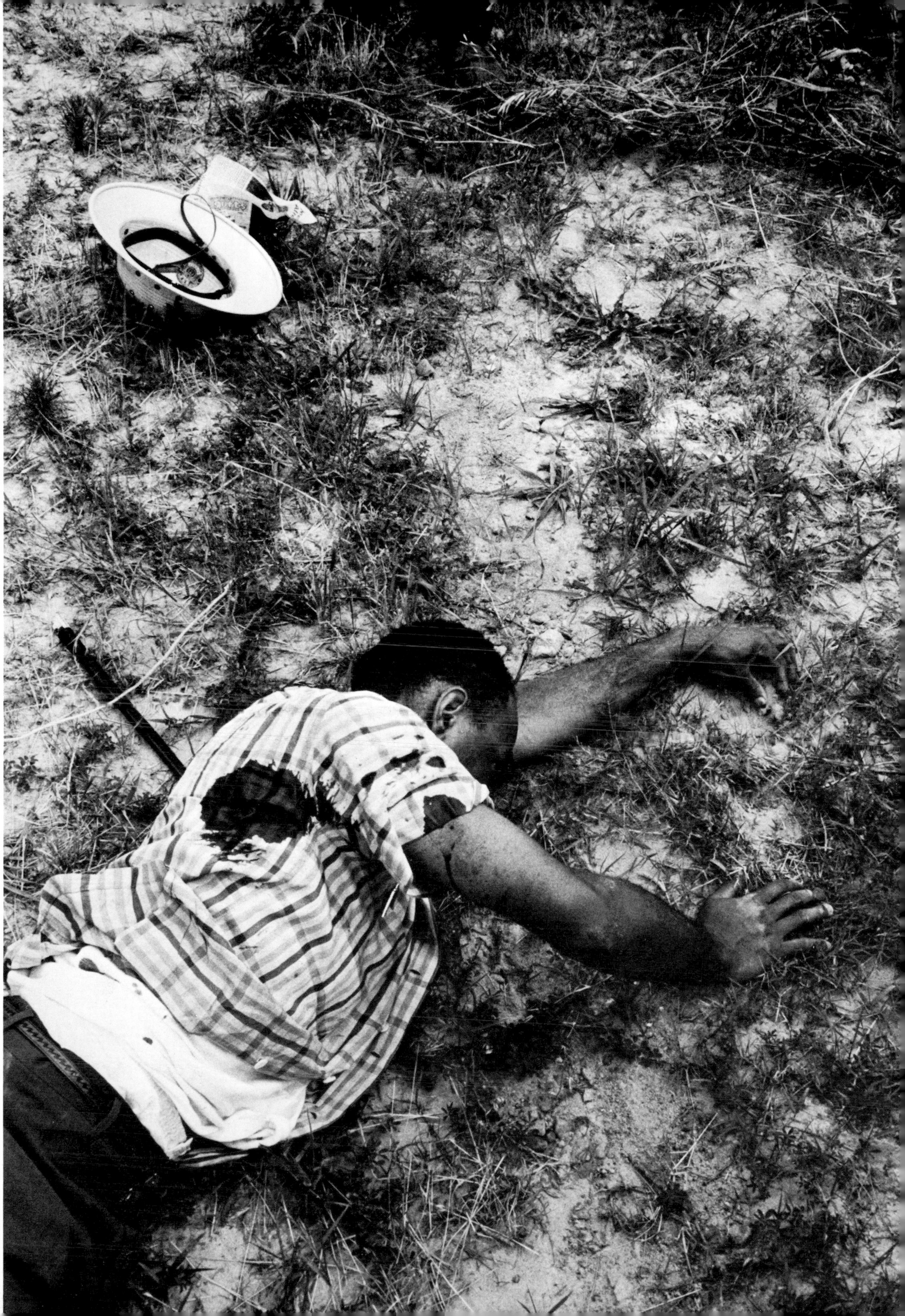

Vernon Merritt

vote. In Grenada they stopped long enough to lead thirteen hundred prospective voters to the courthouse. It was here that Carmichael started using a new slogan—"Black Power." Although it applied specifically to registering voters, King objected to the violent context in which the slogan was being placed. He suggested "Black Equality" instead, but that was unacceptable to the younger, more radical leaders.

The character of this march was different from any King had led in the past. For the first time demonstrators were questioning the effectiveness of passive resistance. Carmichael had originally urged that this be an all-black march, saying, "We don't need any more white phonies and liberals invading our movement." The marchers sang "We Shall Overcome," but when they got to the words "Black and white together," many remained silent. Others changed the lyrics to "We Shall Overrun." It required all of King's eloquence and charisma, as well as a threat to withdraw his support, to convince the activists that the march should be nonviolent and that white participants should be welcomed. Nevertheless, King was saddened by the

Hundreds take up the march where Meredith was forced to leave it. In the front row (l. to r.): Ralph Abernathy, Coretta King, King, Floyd McKissick of CORE, and Stokely Carmichael.

Bob Fitch

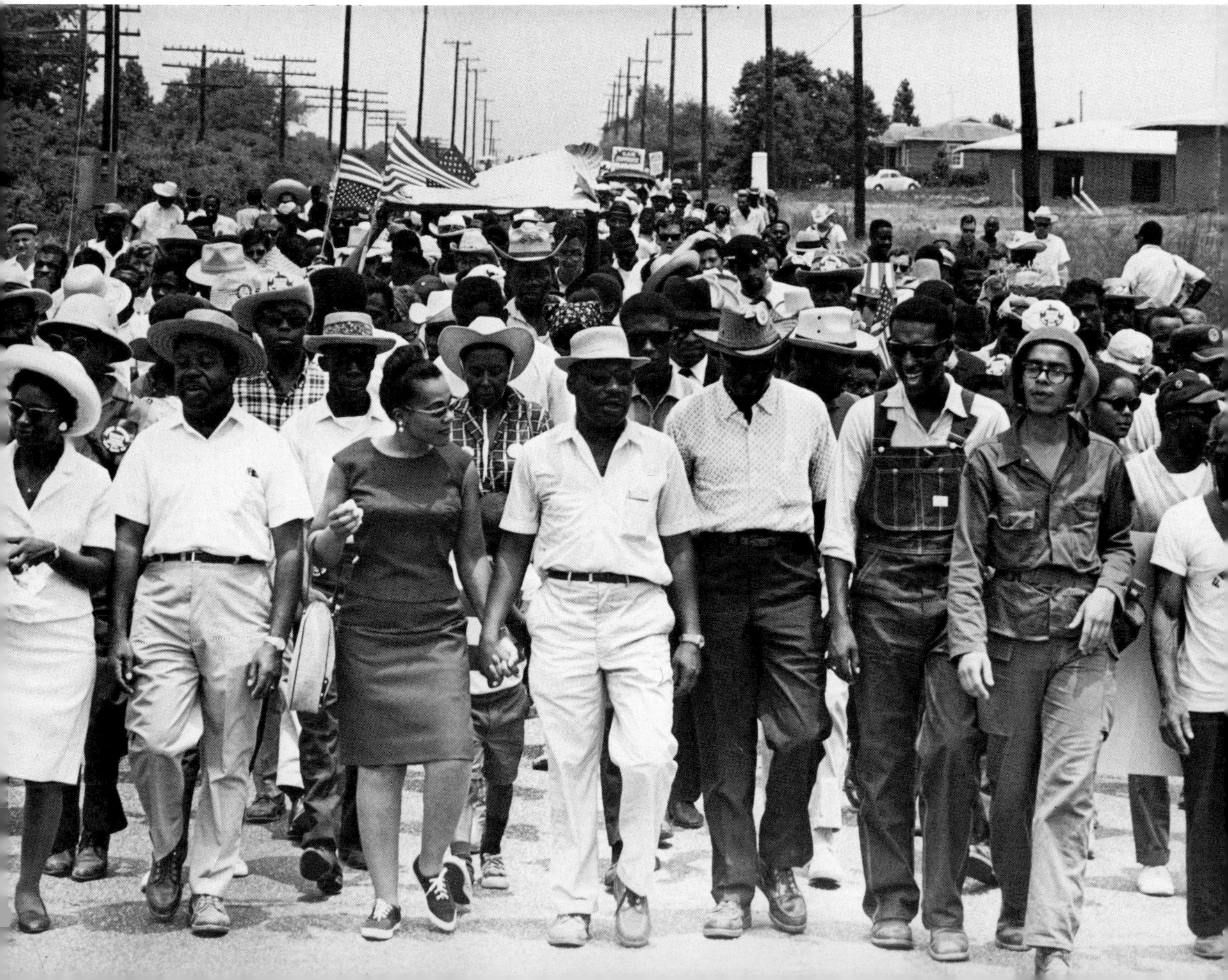

rejection of his philosophy and the seeming mockery of his life's work.

When the band of protestors reached Greenwood, Carmichael let it be known that from here on the slogan "Black Power" would be used. At a rally of six hundred demonstrators that evening, the SNCC chairman shouted, "What we need is Black Power!" His voice betrayed hatred and threatened insurrection. Taking Carmichael's lead, Hosea Williams, King's field general, grabbed the microphone and shouted, "Black Power! Get that vote and pin that badge on a black chest! Whip the policeman across the head!" At this, King jumped in: **"He means with the vote."** Sitting beside him, Carmichael smiled sarcastically, "They know what he means."

King continued to express his dismay. **"There is black power,"** he said. **"I'm all for black power, but as a slogan it is counterproductive."** For the rest of the march, no slogan was used. But as they walked together the next day, Carmichael said to King, "Martin, I deliberately decided to raise this issue on the march in order to give it a national forum and force you to take a stand for

The marchers detour through Philadelphia, Mississippi, to hold a memorial service for three dead civil rights workers. The reception is hostile.

Bob Fitch

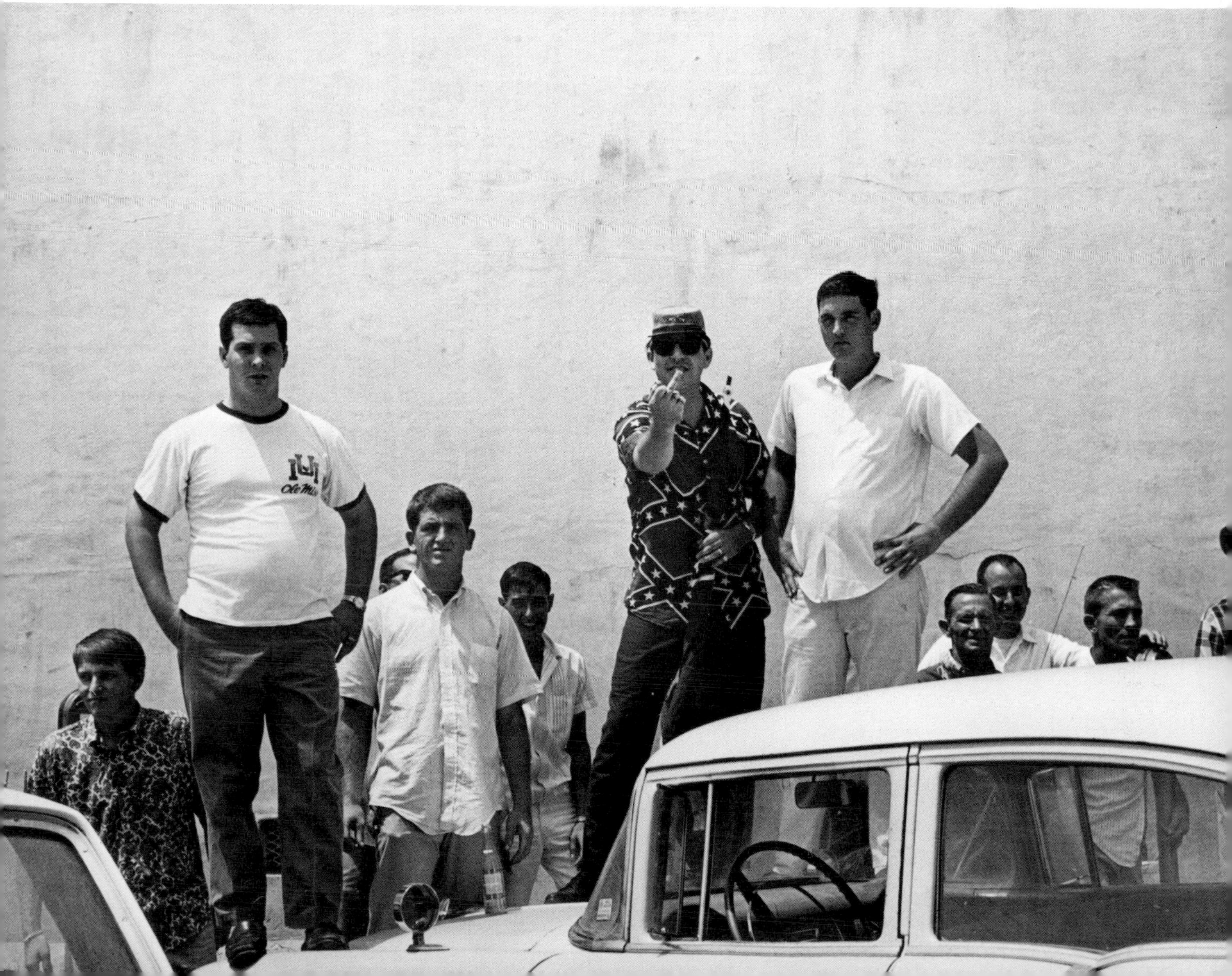

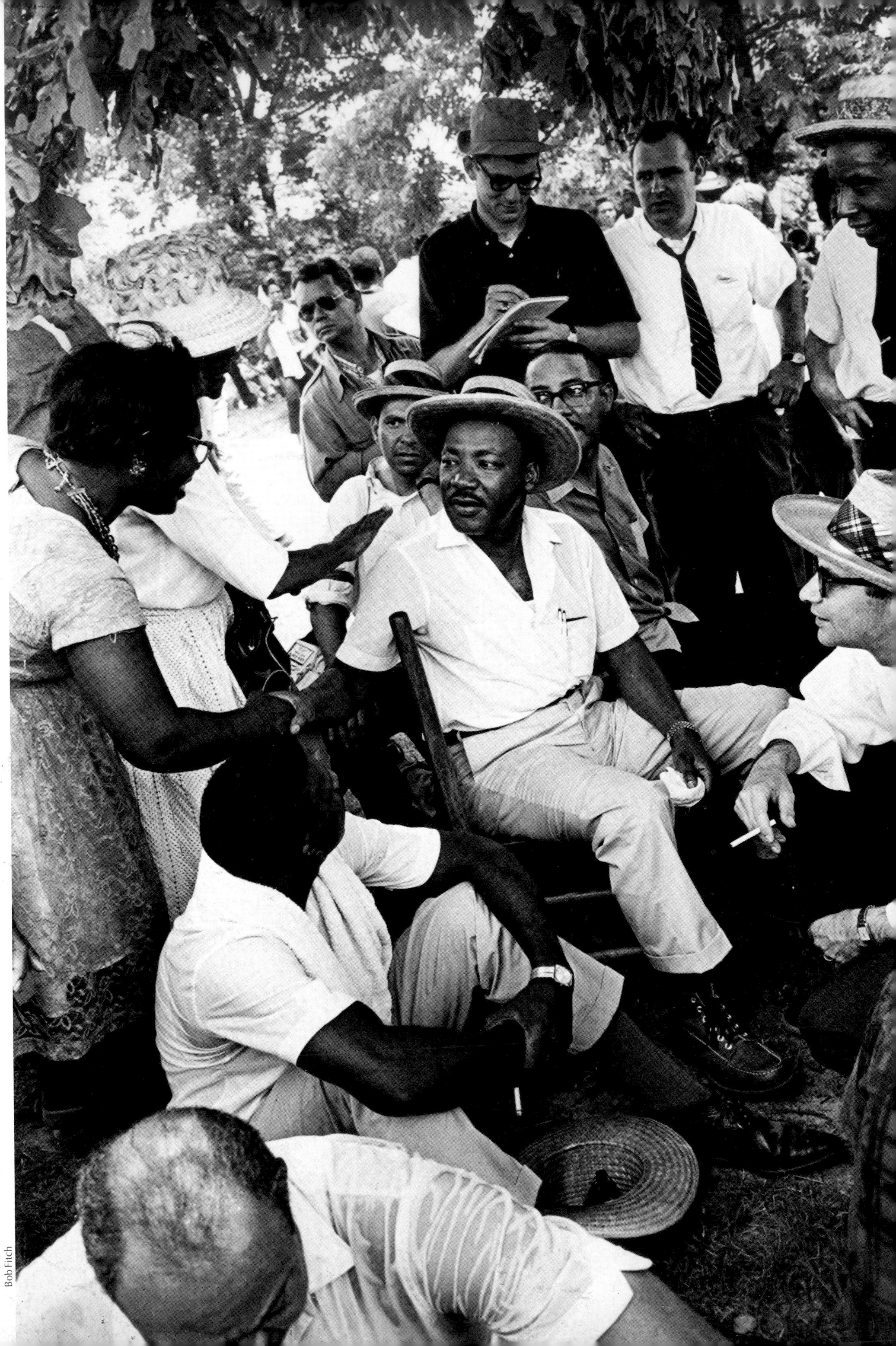

Bob Fitch

'Black Power'." **"That's all right,"** King replied, smiling. **"I've been used before. One more time won't hurt."**

Except for internal friction, the march was peaceful until the group decided to make a detour to Philadelphia, Mississippi, where civil rights workers Goodman, Chaney, and Schwerner had been murdered almost exactly two years before. Sheriff Rainey and Deputy Price, who were still on duty although under indictment for the killings, stood by and watched as white mobs hurled cherry bombs while King spoke. Police did nothing to stop the fighting that ensued. King later said the experience was one of his most frightening. **"That day in Philadelphia when I was speaking and Rainey was behind me . . . and I started saying the murderers were probably**

King rests along the route of the march.

Below:
King marching alongside Andy Young in Philadelphia, Mississippi.

Bob Fitch

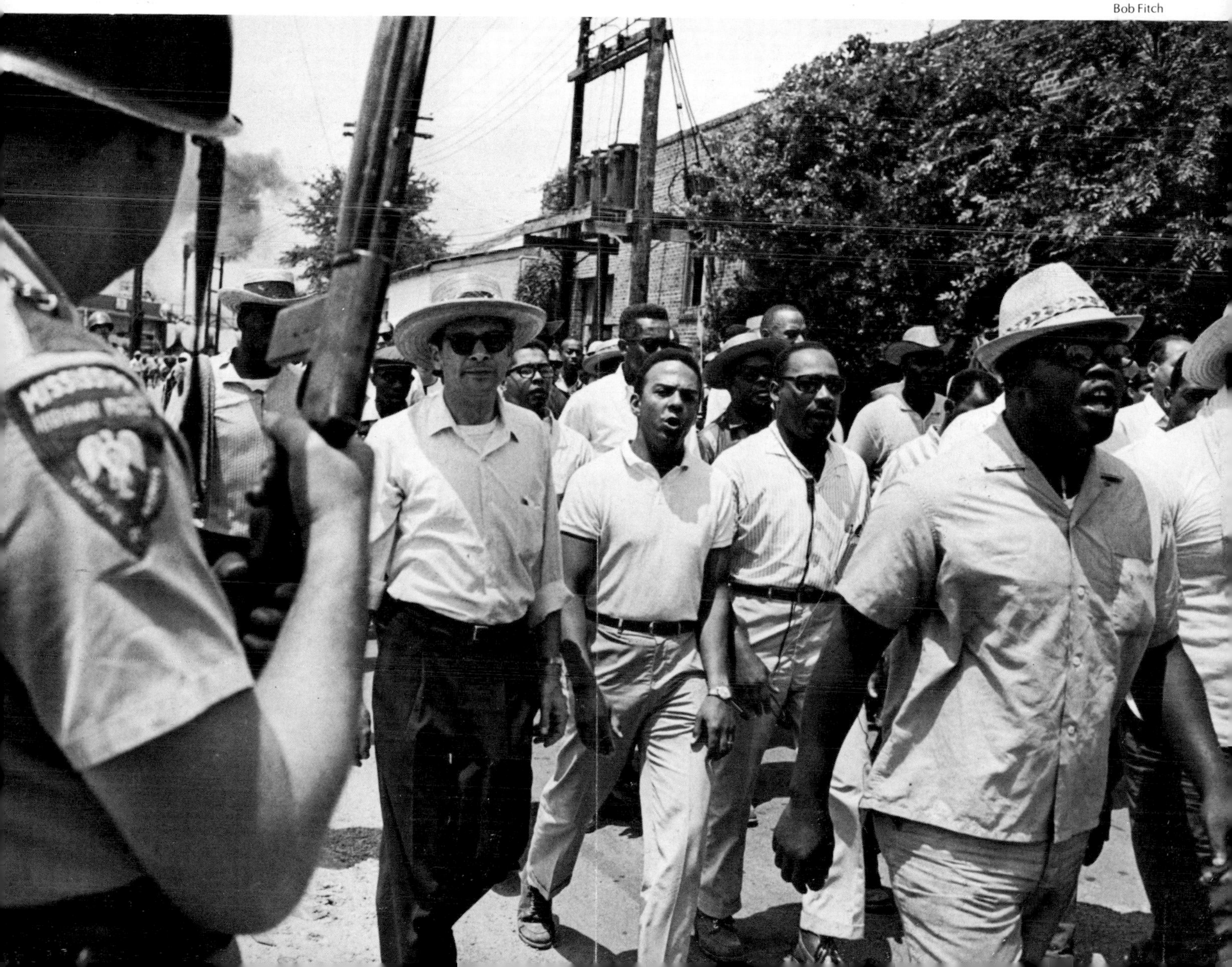

around, and some man behind me, said, 'You're damn right, they're right behind you. . . .' I was there speaking; they're all standing behind me. And I just knew I'd never see [the end of] the day."

That night as the battered marchers tried to sleep at their camp site, they were attacked by rifle fire. King announced that he would lead a second, larger march on Philadelphia later in the week, and he wired the president appealing for federal marshals to protect the demonstrators when they returned.

When the delegation reached Canton on June 24, the city denied them permission to camp on the grounds of an all-black elementary school. Summoning a large crowd from the local black community, King, Carmichael, and McKissick led the marchers to the schoolyard. As they began making camp, local and state police moved toward them hurling grenades of tear gas. The scene was all too reminiscent of the confrontation on the Edmund Pettus Bridge in Selma. The highway patrol did not arrest the black protestors; instead they beat, kicked, and clubbed them. Even those marchers who had scorned nonviolence refrained from reacting. However, King and McKissick had to calm a shaken Carmichael as the melee continued.

On the march, the growing impatience with peaceful means and gradual progress becomes increasingly apparent.

Below:
Sheriff Lawrence Rainey, Philadelphia, Mississippi.

Flip Schulke

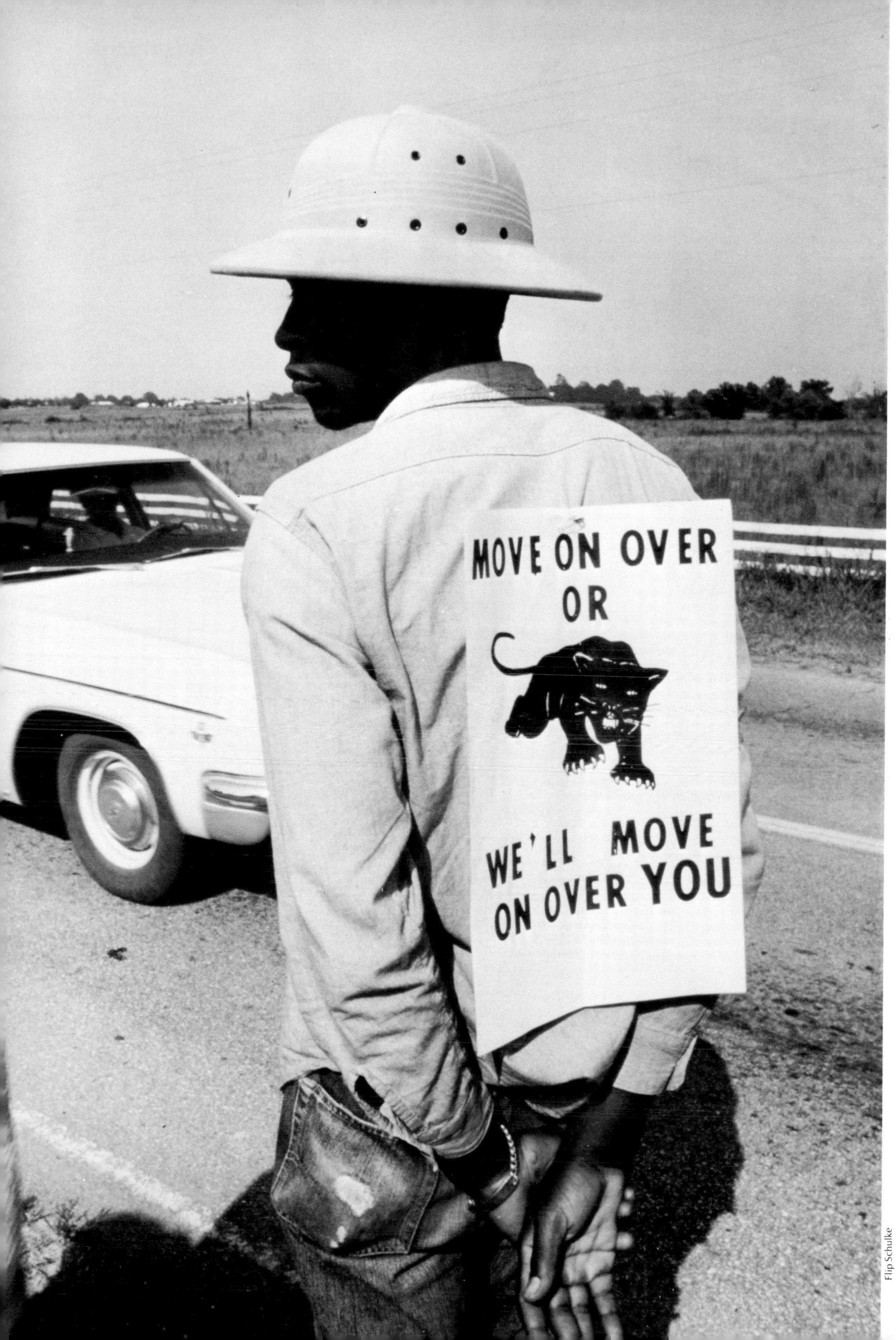
MOVE ON OVER
OR
WE'LL MOVE
ON OVER YOU

Flip Schulke

Bob Fitch

A recovered James Meredith joined the march during the last leg from Tougaloo to Jackson. The crowd had soared to fifteen thousand by the time they reached the state capital. It was the largest gathering of blacks in the history of Mississippi.

By now Carmichael and SNCC were calling the shots. They refused to allow Charles Evers, who had replaced his murdered brother Medgar as state field secretary of the NAACP, to speak. Although King was permitted to speak, he was not permitted to lead. He was dispirited when he told the marchers, **"One day, right here in this state of Mississippi, justice will become a reality for all."**

The Movement was permanently and dangerously fragmented. Within a few days CORE voted to adopt the slogan "Black Power!" and the NAACP denounced it. Roy Wilkins said "Black Power!" could only lead to "black death." Blacks were forced to choose sides, and moderate whites who had supported the peaceful Movement were left out in the cold.

King, distressed by the split, maintained his lifelong belief in nonviolence. **"I've decided that I'm going to do battle for my philosophy,"** he said. **"You ought to believe something in life, believe that thing so fervently that you will stand up with it till the end of your days. I can't make myself believe that God wants me to hate. I'm tired of violence. . . . And I'm not going to let my oppressor dictate to me what method I must use. . . . We have a power . . . a power that cannot be found in bullets and guns."**

At a rally in Greenwood, Mississippi, Stokely Carmichael calls for "Black Power!" It is the first time the slogan has been used publicly, and is widely reported by the media the next day.

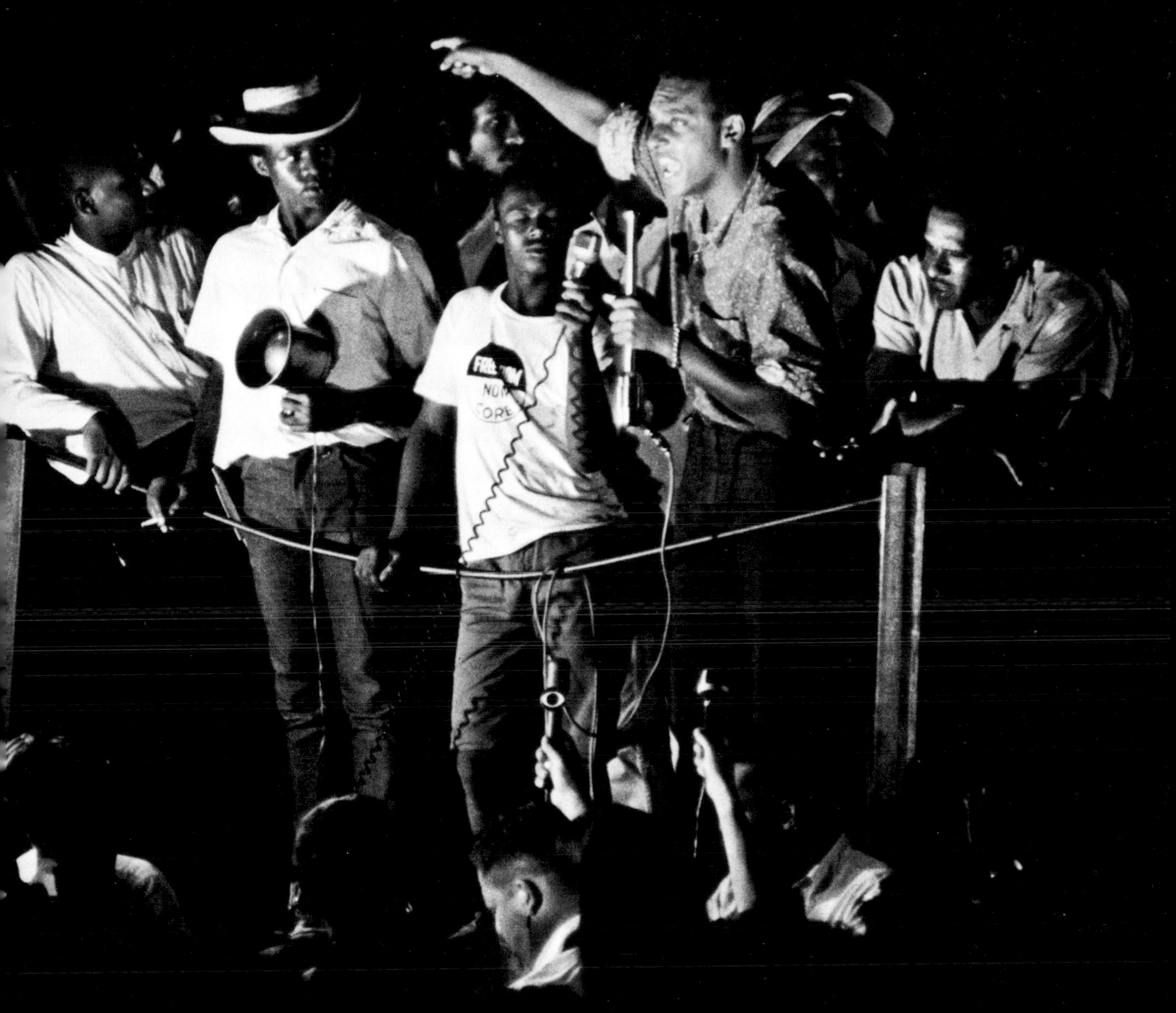

Bob Fitch

Chapter Twelve

"We Must Never Lose Infinite Hope"

Chicago, 1966 In 1966 King turned his attention to the rioting in northern cities. In Watts the previous summer he had seen the urgency of the situation in urban ghettos. He had also seen the hostility and combativeness which were far less prevalent in his native South.

AN INTERVIEW WITH JESSE JACKSON

Jesse Jackson, *currently the director of operation PUSH in Chicago, headed up SCLC in Chicago and was the architect of Operation Breadbasket, which led successful boycotts against Chicago's leading chain stores and other businesses. He managed the Poor People's Campaign Resurrection City, Washington, D.C., June, 1968.*

"The reason Dr. King chose Chicago at that time was because there was a group in Chicago called the Coordinated Council of Community Organizations (CCCO), about fifty organizations that had come together in order to fight for a better school system and to fight for a change here. Dr. King's first inclination, to my understanding, was to go to Harlem, to New York. But there was so much more organization, so much more cohesion here, and, as a result, he was lured in this direction. That combined with the fact that so many heavy supporters of the southern movements came out of Chicago. Needless to say, I am grateful that he came this way, for not only did he solidify that particular situation, but out of it Operation Breadbasket emerged as a national economic thrust, and out of that eventually emerged Operation PUSH. So in some sense the seeds that he planted here in sixty-six have now sprouted into Operation PUSH, which is a national economic organization, fighting for the very goals that he enumerated while he was alive.

"The program at that time was to prove several things. We came here with a nonviolent experiment to prove that problems in the North were just as pervasive and clear as those in the South. We found Ciceros up here and Gage Parks here, and we found Daleys here. We found that the organization was much more sophisticated and that the enemy was black and white people who were of a certain mind, as opposed say, to just the white people of the South. Here the enemy was not only the redneck, sometimes it was the black face. It was all those forces that represented the self-interest in perpetuating the evil machine. Then it was said that all black people in the North would never have the discipline to engage in this mass nonviolent movement. Well, obviously that was proven to be wrong because some of the most disciplined movements that we had were the years we marched into Gage Park and marched into Cicero, and marched into Bogen.

"The great effect of the northern movement was to wake up northern black America, that they had a problem; it wasn't just a matter of coming down south. They needed to come back home and do homework. So what some people appear to be shocked at in Boston in 1974 and 1975, we exposed in Chicago in 1966 and 1967.

"Now Dr. King said it would take from three to five years for a sustained nonviolent movement to begin to change the thing. The newspapers in their impatience wanted to make it a three-to-five-month movement. But it was a three-to-five-year movement, and as a result of raising certain basic truths in the Chicago movement, Gary, Indiana, Newark, New Jersey, Cleveland, Ohio, and other cities began to reassess their political power and political consciousness. The rock hit the water here, but the concentric circles shot right across northern America.

"So I think that the movement was successful. A number of the press people tried to create a Daley-King kind of confrontation, so that King got nothing but a promise and Daley was victorious again. That's not true. The idea that Dr. King planted, that people should have the right to live where they choose to live, led to the open housing bill, because the drive here was for open communities. We fought for open housing and we won open housing. Look at the major social legislation of the sixties; in sixty-four the Public Accommodations Bill, basically highlighted by Birmingham; sixty-five the Voting Rights Bill, highlighted by Selma, Alabama; sixty-six the open-housing drive, highlighted by Chicago. And that is the last piece of major and significant social legislation that we have gotten in nearly ten years. You can't measure the success of the movement by what has happened in Chicago even, but rather by the consciousness raised in urban America."

Reverend Jesse Jackson

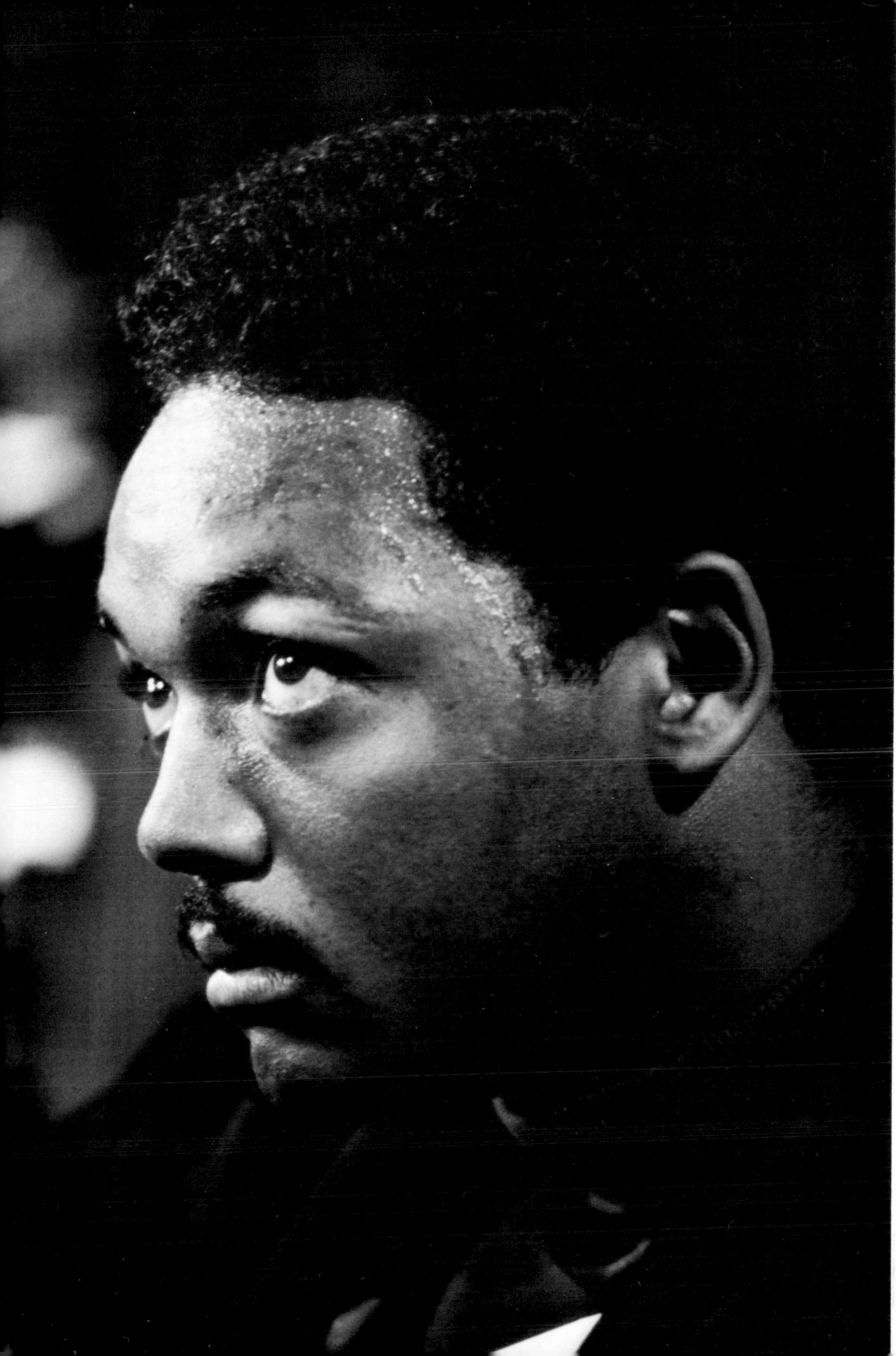

Flip Schulke

With the passage of the Voting Rights Act, poverty became the major issue of concern for King. As the war in Vietnam escalated, the president's War on Poverty lagged. On both fronts, blacks were sustaining excessive casualties.

King and his associate Reverend Jesse Jackson envisioned the coalition of the CCCO and the SCLC in Chicago as a pilot project aimed at calling attention to ghetto conditions before they exploded. Their major objectives were school desegregation and improvement, jobs, and housing.

The feeling of powerlessness that pervaded the ghetto made the creation of a cohesive movement difficult. This problem was exacerbated by Mayor Richard Daley's shrewd tactics. Instead of denouncing King's campaign, Daley ostensibly supported it. Whatever King proposed, Daley said it was already underway, giving the impression that great strides were being made in the ghetto without King or his Movement. The slight gains which resulted, King feared, were dangerous and deceptive. They would dissipate efforts for change without providing long-term solutions.

King moved his family to a ghetto tenement in Chicago's Lawndale section, and on "Freedom Sunday," July 10, he kicked off the intensive Chicago crusade which had so far been fragmented. Speaking to forty-five thousand

King makes poolroom pilgrimages in Chicago to cultivate the support of young blacks.

Bob Fitch

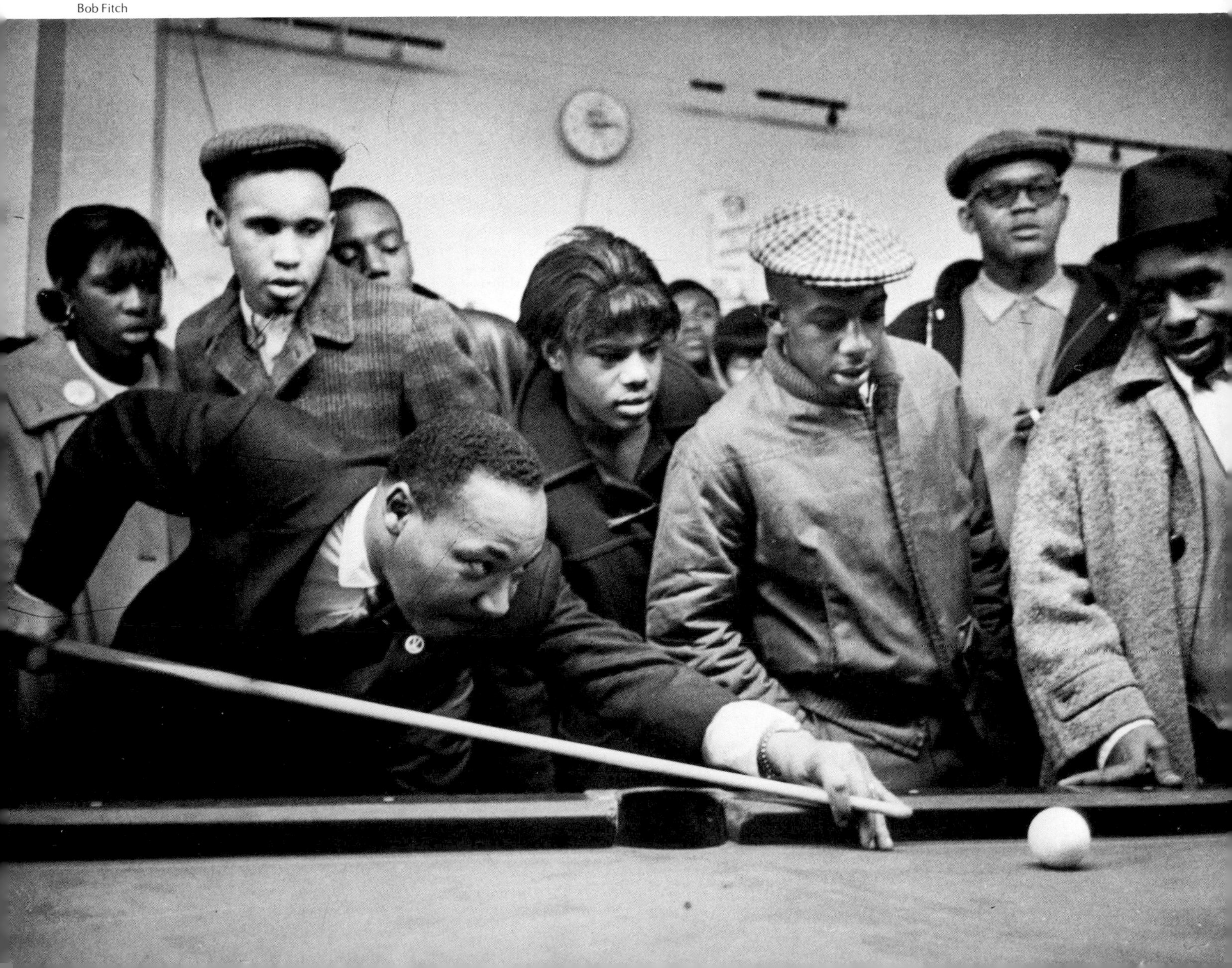

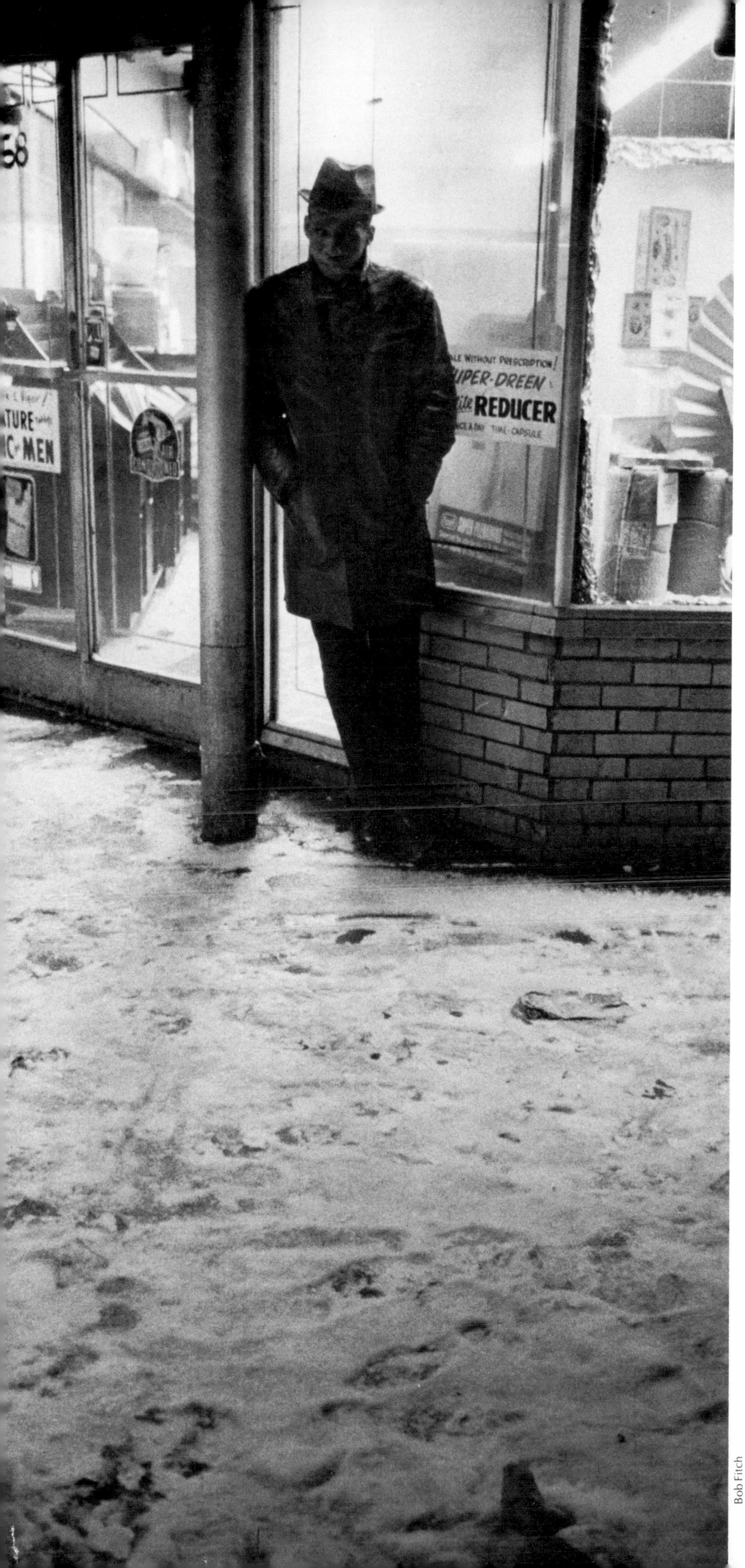
REDUCER

Bob Fitch

people at Soldier's Field, King urged blacks to go to jail, if necessary, to get rid of the slums. The crowd then marched from Soldier's Field to City Hall to present a program for change to the mayor. Finding Daley absent, King posted his demands on the door—a gesture no doubt inspired by another Martin Luther centuries before.

The program called for complete integration of public schools, doubling of the public school budget, construction of low-rent public housing throughout the city, expansion of rapid transit facilities, and support of black banks.

Several days later, rioting broke out in Chicago after police turned off a fire hydrant which black children were using to keep cool. Gangs of teenagers stoned police cars, looted white businesses, and fired on police from rooftops. Two blacks were killed and many people were injured, including six policemen. Violence continued for three days, until fifteen hundred armed National Guardsmen moved in to restore order. King and other black clergymen had risked their lives in the ghetto trying to calm the youthful rioters. On July 15 they met with Mayor Daley to request federal funds for the construction of swimming pools and recreational facilities for blacks.

The black leaders then decided to concentrate their efforts on discrimination in housing. Week after week they marched on Chicago's all-white neighborhoods. They were greeted by angry mobs hurling bricks and screaming obscenities. On one occasion the marchers were met by antagonistic whites led by American Nazi Party head George Lincoln Rockwell. Hit on the head by a brick, King quipped, **"Oh, I've been hit so many times I'm immune to it."** But he went on to say more seriously, **"I've been in many demonstrations all across the South, but I can say that I have never seen, even in Mississippi and Alabama, mobs as hostile and as hate-filled as I've seen in Chicago."**

On August 17 black leaders met for ten hours with city officials, but no agreement was forthcoming. The marches continued. Several days later black organizers informed Cook County Sheriff Richard B. Ogilvie that they planned to march on Cicero. This all-white neighborhood had become a symbol of northern discrimination. In 1951 it was the scene of a bloody riot when a black family tried to move in. Earlier in the summer of 1966 two blacks had gone job hunting there. One was beaten to death.

Ogilvie begged King to call off the march. When King refused, the prospect of a major incident provided civic leaders with the incentive to reach an agreement on black demands. Two days before the prospective march, civil rights leaders attended a hastily called meeting with Daley, Archbishop John Cody, and representatives of the Chicago Real Estate Board, the Chicago Housing Authority and the business and industrial communities.

Although basically satisfactory to King, the resulting housing agreement was a partial compromise, and militant blacks labelled it a "sellout." They decided to go through with the Cicero march. King felt, justifiably, that if the agreement was honored it would provide a strong equal housing program. Unfortunately, it never was.

On September 4, two hundred blacks, protected by ten times as many National Guardsmen, marched on Cicero. In spite of the heavy military escort, they were attacked so fiercely by flying bottles and rocks that they were forced to retreat to Lawndale.

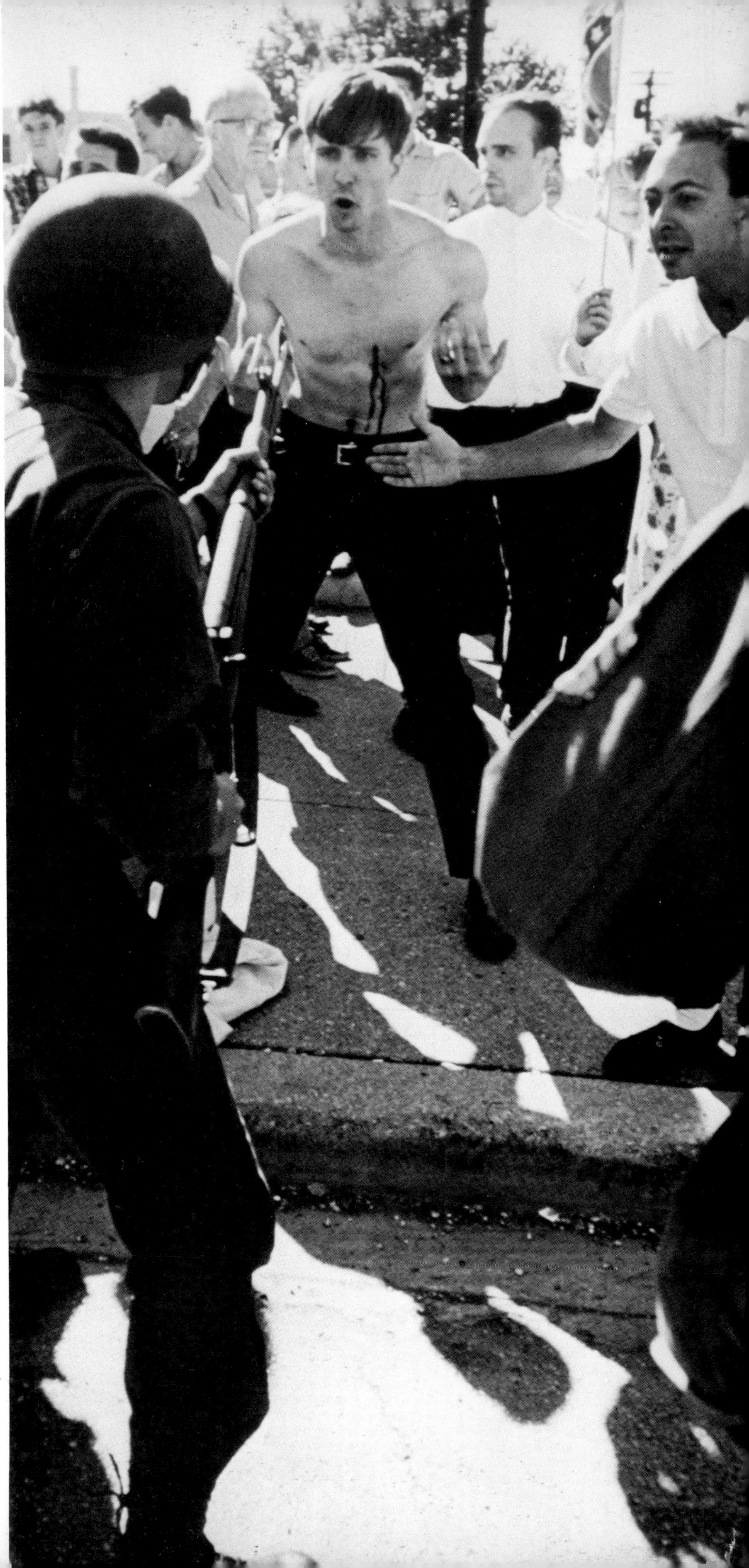

Declan Haun

A confrontation between a National Guardsman and white youth protesting against a black march through all-white Cicero, Illinois.

Opposite page:
County police officers, carrying riot sticks, haul off a young white heckler in Cicero.

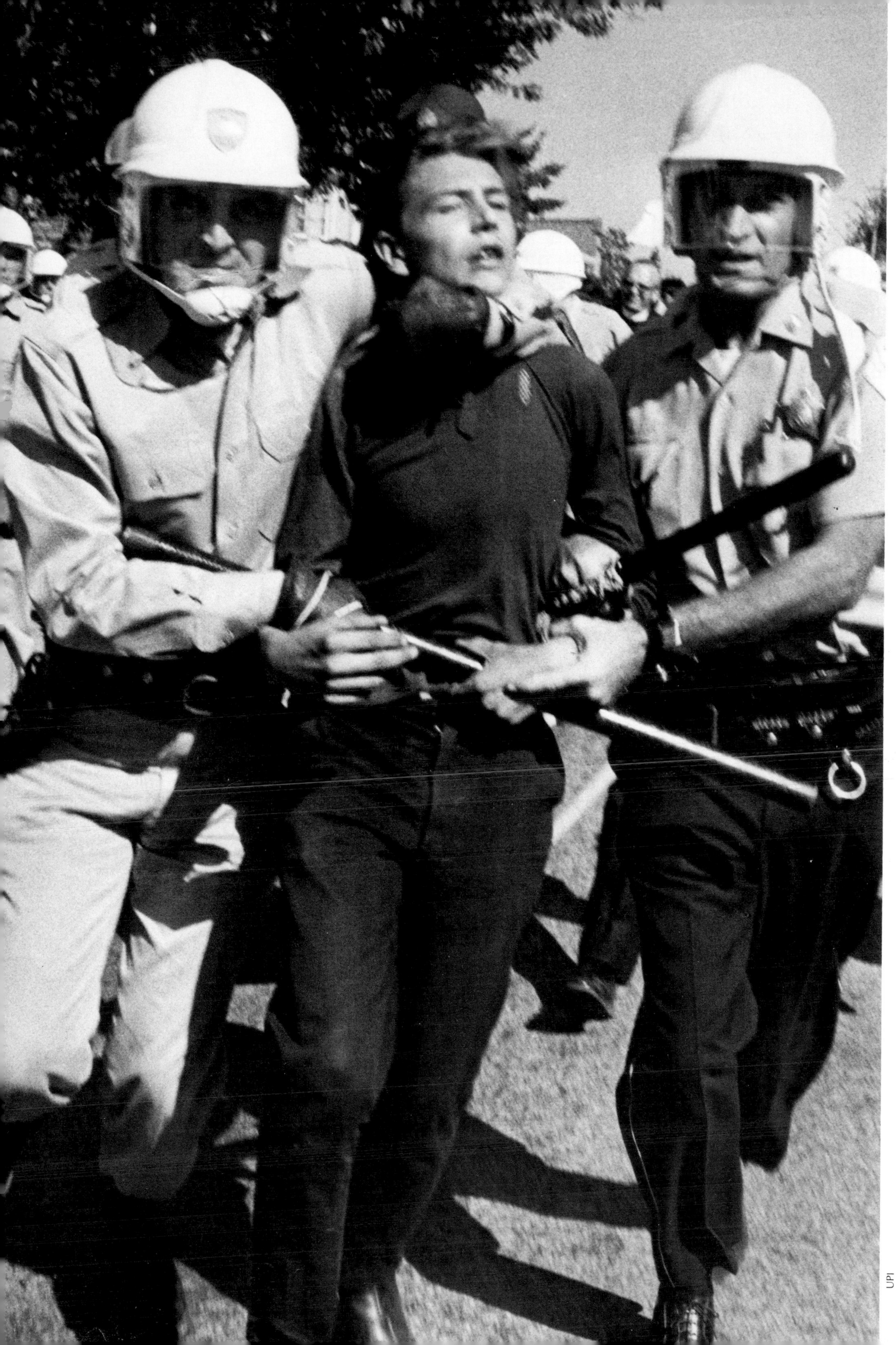

UPI

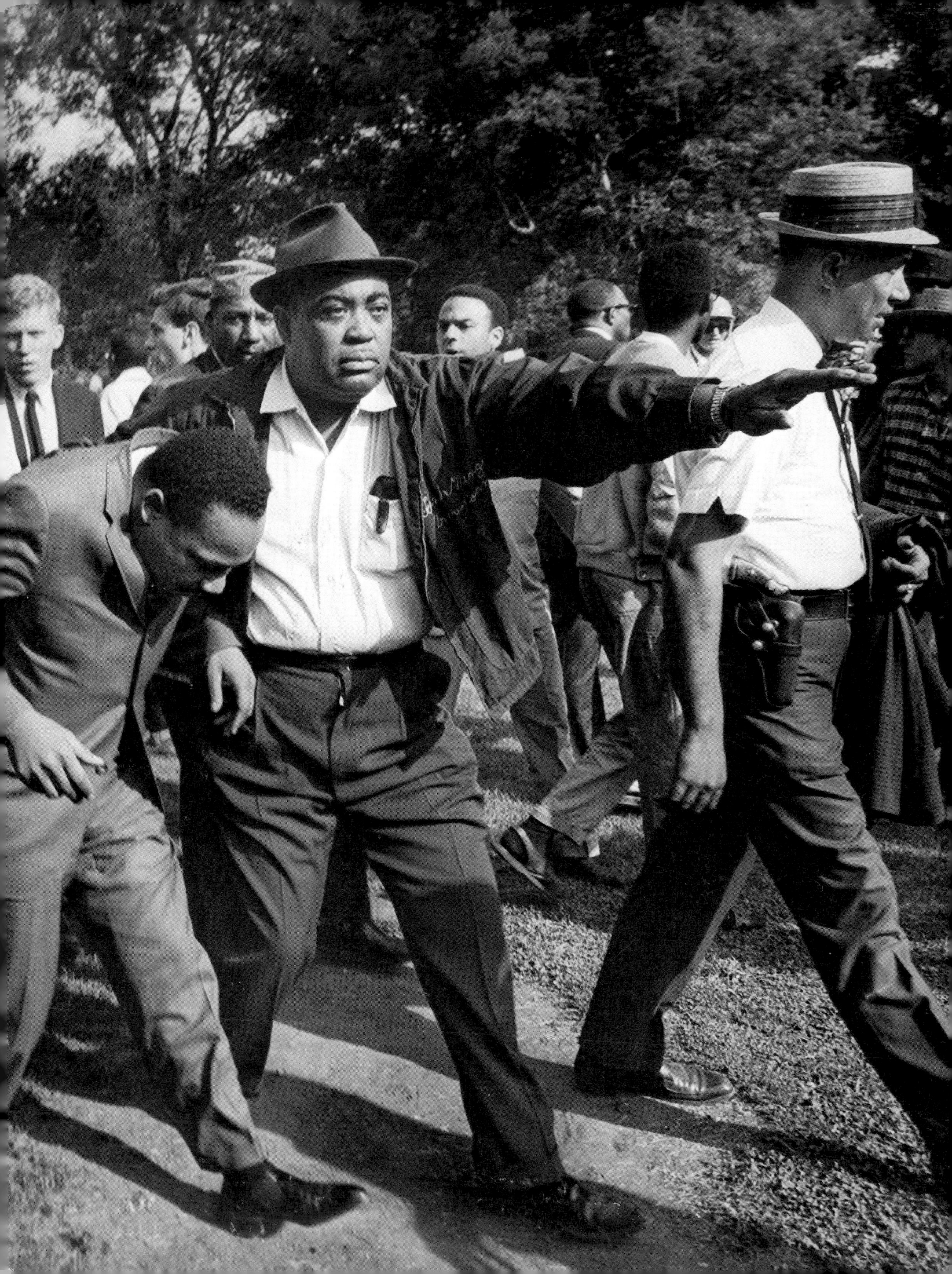

The retreat symbolized the Chicago campaign. Some progress had been made. Tenant unions had been formed, forcing slumlords to improve conditions. And Operation Breadbasket became a significant success. It boycotted businesses in black neighborhoods that did not hire blacks and created over nine hundred jobs by the end of the year. But apathy among local blacks was growing; the NAACP withdrew its support; the nation was focused on Vietnam; and there seemed no way to force the white establishment of Chicago to make good its promises.

The Black Panther Party was growing, and King felt himself losing control of the civil rights movement. Discouraged and troubled, he spoke out more fiercely against the war that was costing lives abroad and dissipating the thrust for civil liberties at home.

"Negroes and white boys will fight in brutal solidarity on the battlefield of Vietnam, but when they get back home it's doubtful that their children will be able to sit together in the same classroom. . . . Negro soldiers will die in Vietnam . . . they'll come back home to be buried in Wetumpka, Alabama, and can't even be buried there. It's time to set our own house in order."

King is struck by a rock in Cicero.

Below:
During the Chicago protests King maintains a hectic speaking schedule. Here he waits for his next plane. At his right Is Andrew Young

Bob Fitch

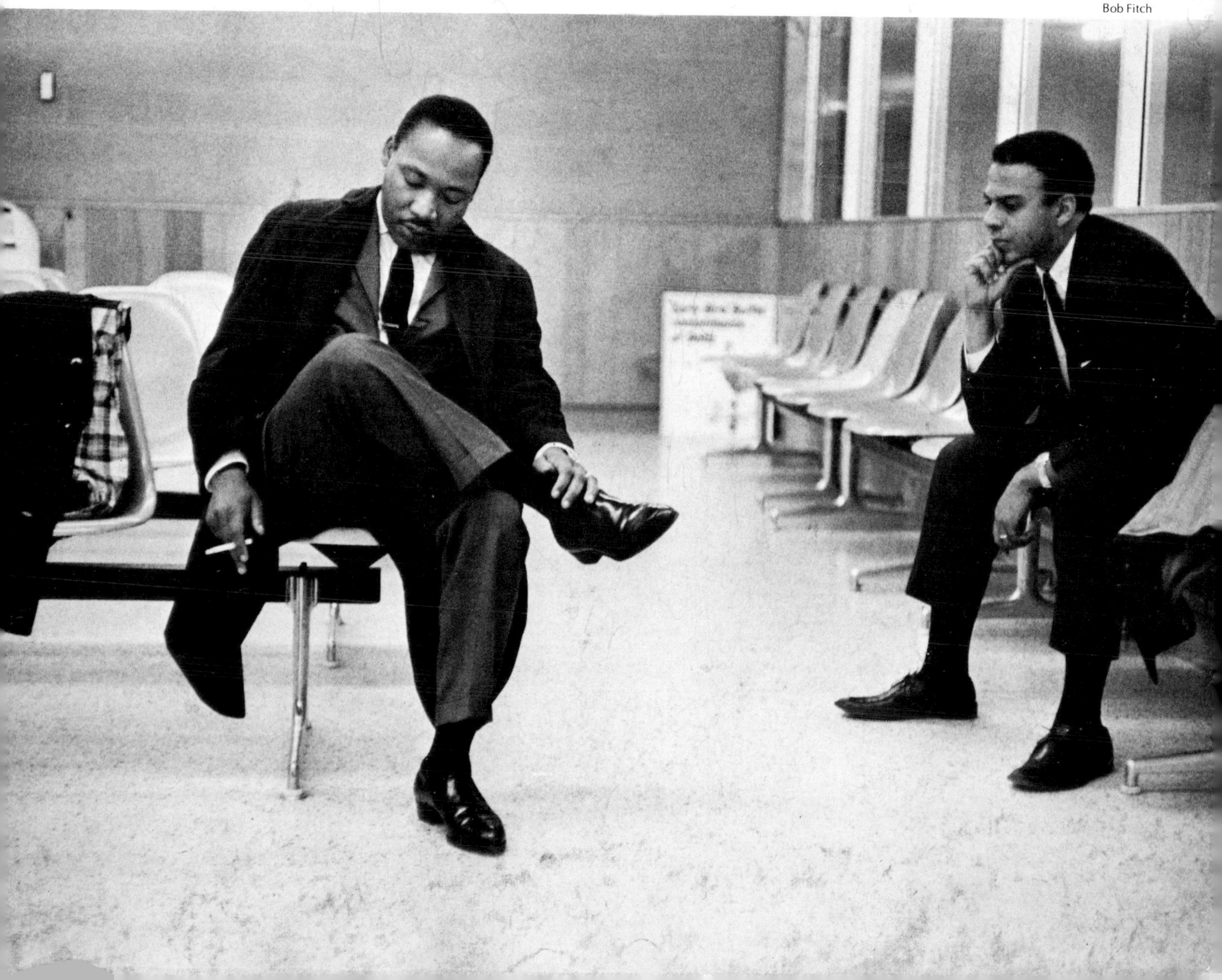

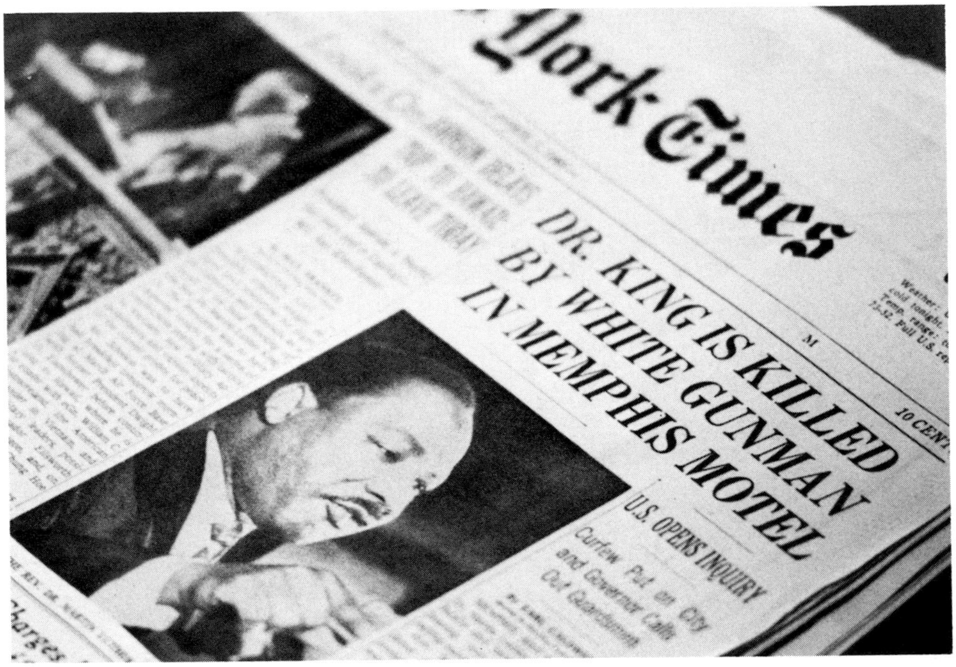
York Times
DR. KING IS KILLED
BY WHITE GUNMAN
IN MEMPHIS MOTEL
U.S. OPENS INQUIRY
Curfew Put on City
and Governor Calls
Out Guardsmen

Flip Schulke

Chapter Thirteen

"He Died to Make Me Free"

Memphis, 1968 "A man who won't die for something is not fit to live." King spoke many times of his own death. Not with fear, nor with self-pity. He was a man who had been threatened often, who had lived with danger, and who had come to terms with death.

Fear killed Martin Luther King, Jr. James Earl Ray only pulled the trigger.

It began on a rainy day in early February, 1968. The sanitation workers in Memphis reported to work but were sent home because of inclement weather. In their paychecks that week, black employees had received wages for only two hours for that day. White workers were paid for the entire day. The black union struck, sending a list of demands to newly-elected Mayor Henry Loeb. The demands were ignored.

The strike in Memphis did not initially attract King's attention. He was busy organizing his Poor People's Campaign. On April 22, he planned to walk with three thousand of the nation's needy to state their case in Washington. The marchers were to represent all races and creeds. These were the country's poor demanding notice.

But the leaders of the Memphis protest called for an all-out work stoppage on March 28, and King agreed to lead the march. When he arrived on the morning of the demonstration, King was disturbed by the presence of black power militants interspersed among the peaceful marchers whose dignified banners proclaimed, "I *AM* a Man." He was relieved to learn the youths were not to be

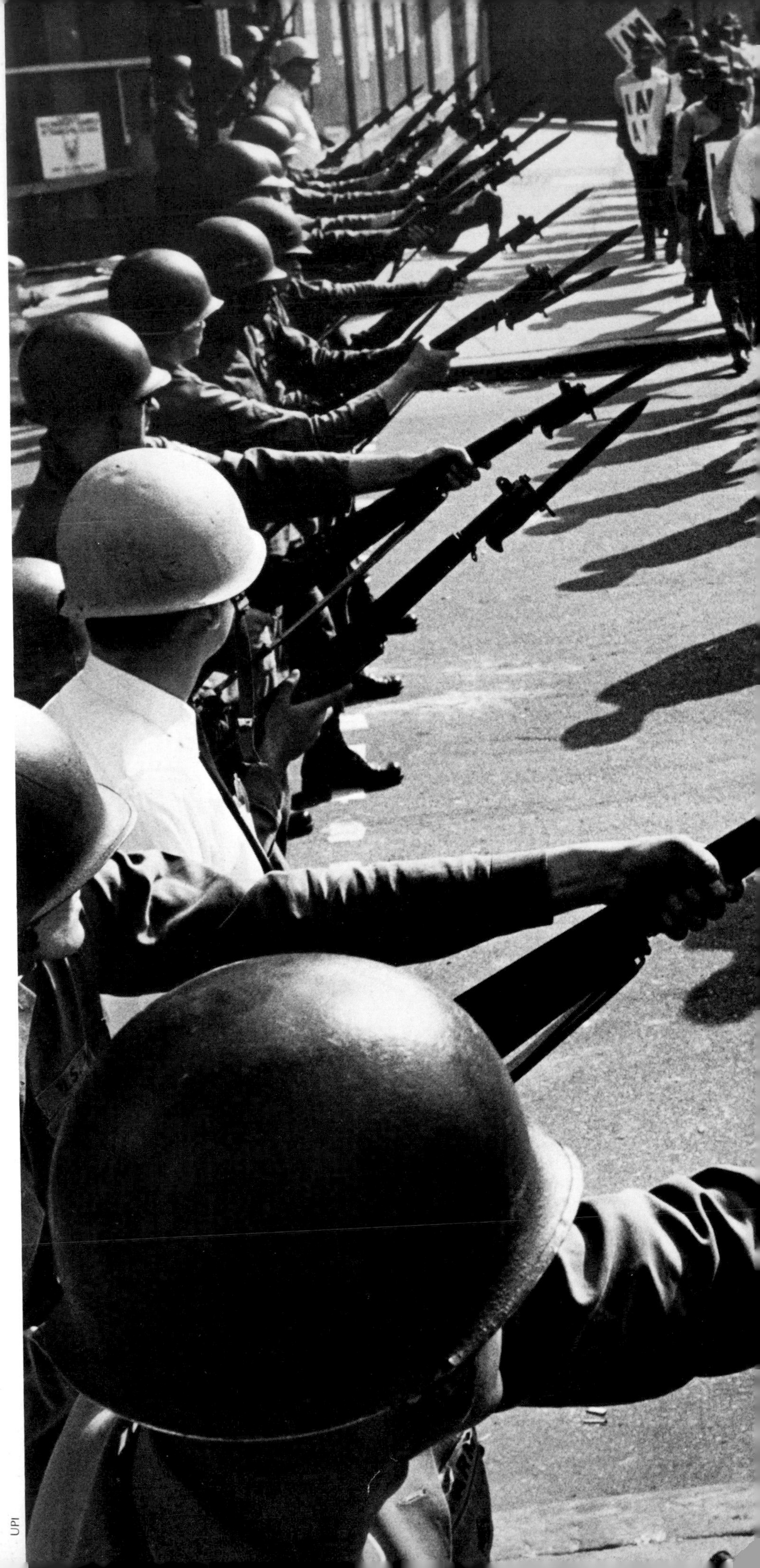

Memphis, March, 1968. National Guard bayonets line the streets as sanitation workers strike for an increase in wages and benefits irrespective of race.

UPI

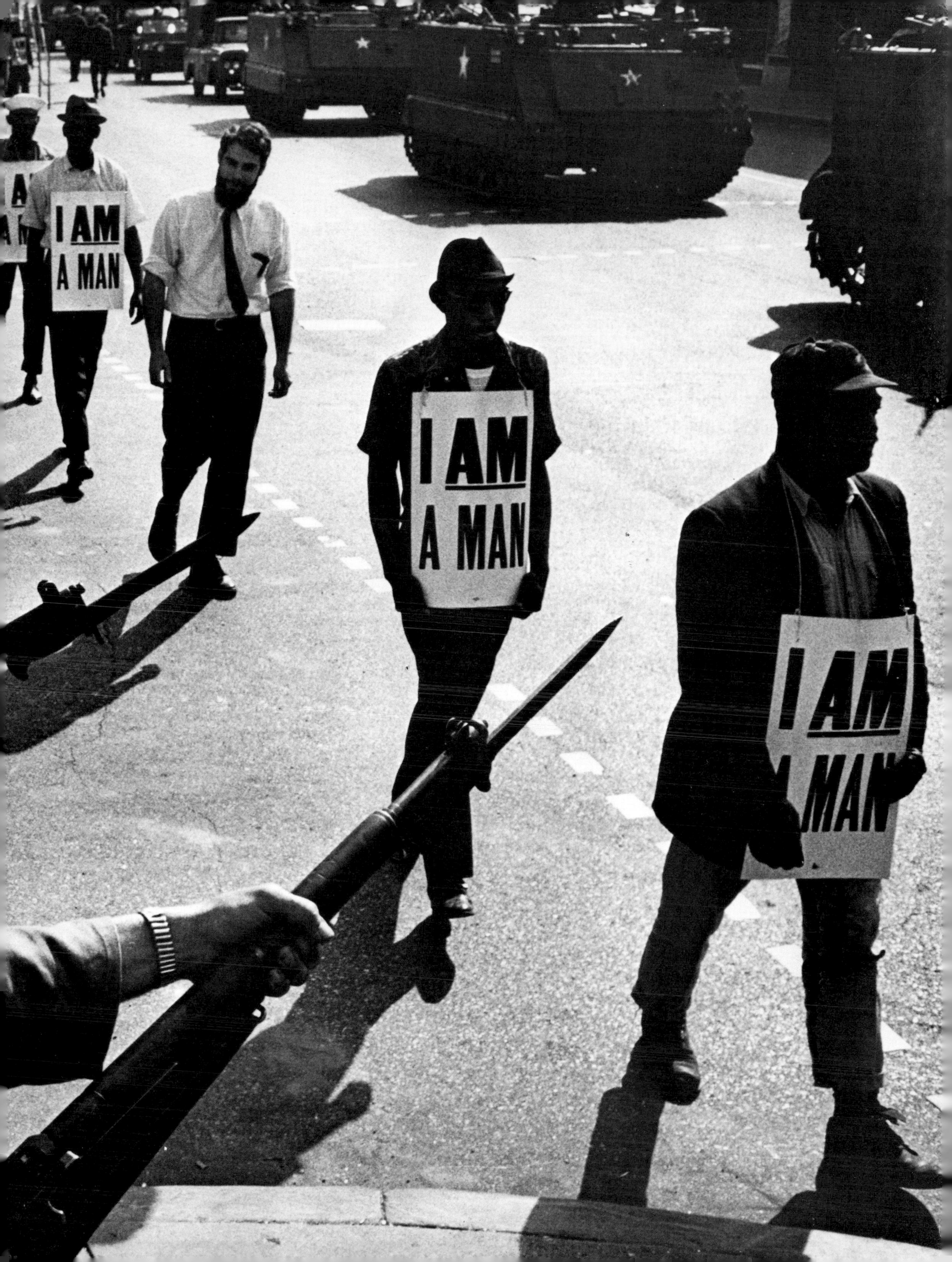

I AM A MAN
I AM A MAN
I AM A MAN

part of the assembly. The march had not advanced even three blocks, however, when it was interrupted by the sound of shattering glass.

The militants had begun breaking into stores and looting. King's aides, fearing for his life, convinced him to return to his motel. In the disorder that followed, a sixteen-year-old black was shot and killed by police; sixty others were clubbed and wounded; 280 were arrested. Looting and arson continued until the governor of Tennessee ordered four thousand National Guardsmen into the city.

King was shaken and forlorn. He partially attributed the violence to the fact that he and his associates had not planned the march and were unaware of the large militant element in Memphis. Nevertheless, he felt responsible. He felt he had failed.

Determined to prove that nonviolence was still a viable method of forcing social change, King scheduled a second march in Memphis for April 8. City officials secured a court injunction barring the demonstration. King hoped

March 28, 1968. Memphis police react as black power militants break off from the strike march to smash store windows.

UPI

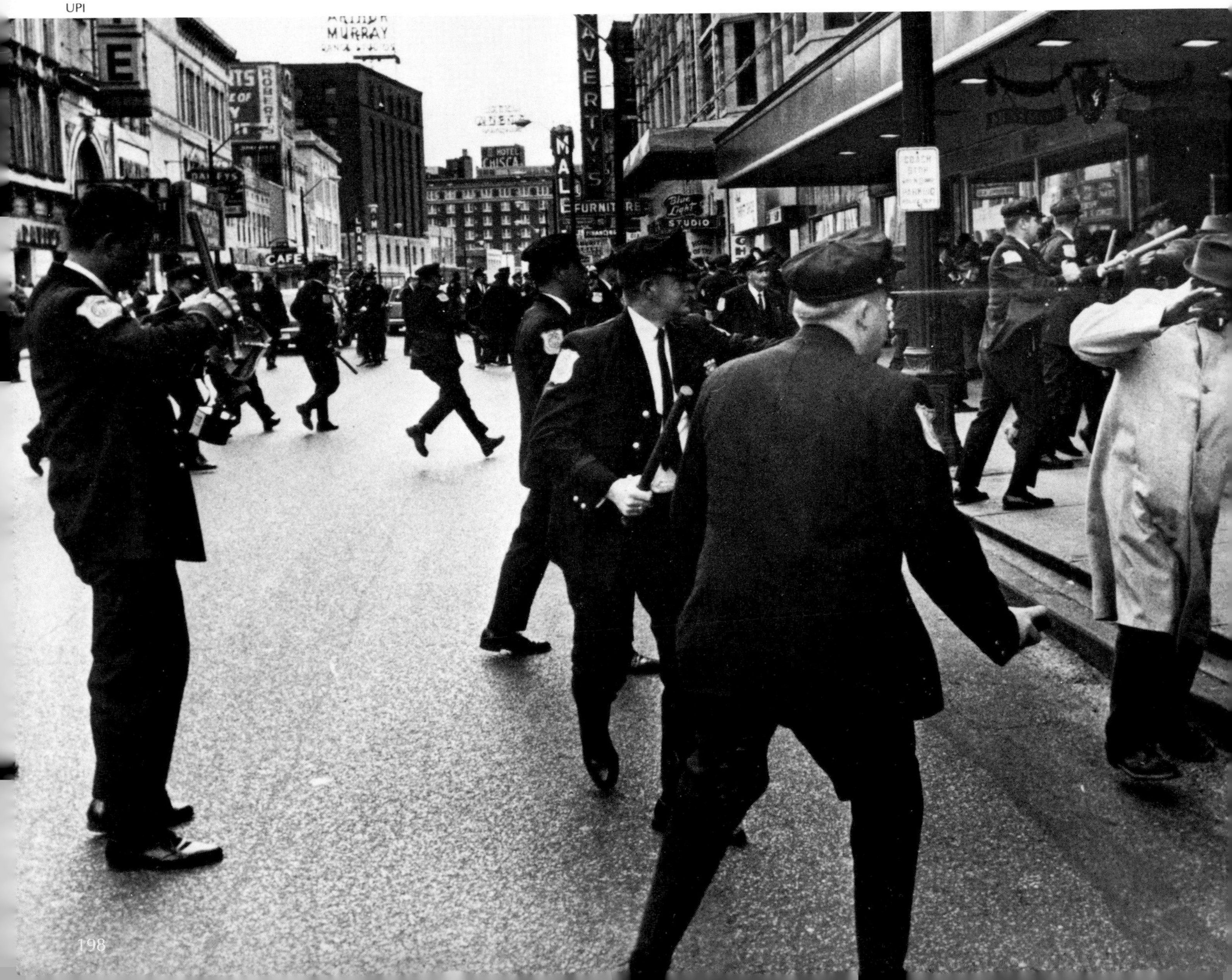

MURRAY
CAFE
STUDIO

to get the injunction set aside, but he announced his intention to lead the march regardless. He felt certain the protest would not be accompanied by violence. He never had a chance to prove it.

On April 4, King spent the day conferring with his aides in a second-floor room at the Lorraine Hotel on Mulberry Street in Memphis. He and his closest friend, Ralph Abernathy, were preparing to go to dinner when King went to the balcony outside his room and chatted with several associates in the parking lot below.

Suddenly the crack of a rifle was heard, and Martin Luther King, Jr., was dead at thirty-nine. The man whose entire life was a testament to nonviolence—the winner of the Nobel Peace Prize—had died by the assassin's bullet.

We will probably never know why James Earl Ray, a white ex-convict with no apparent motive, killed King, or who, if anyone, hired him. Those who would

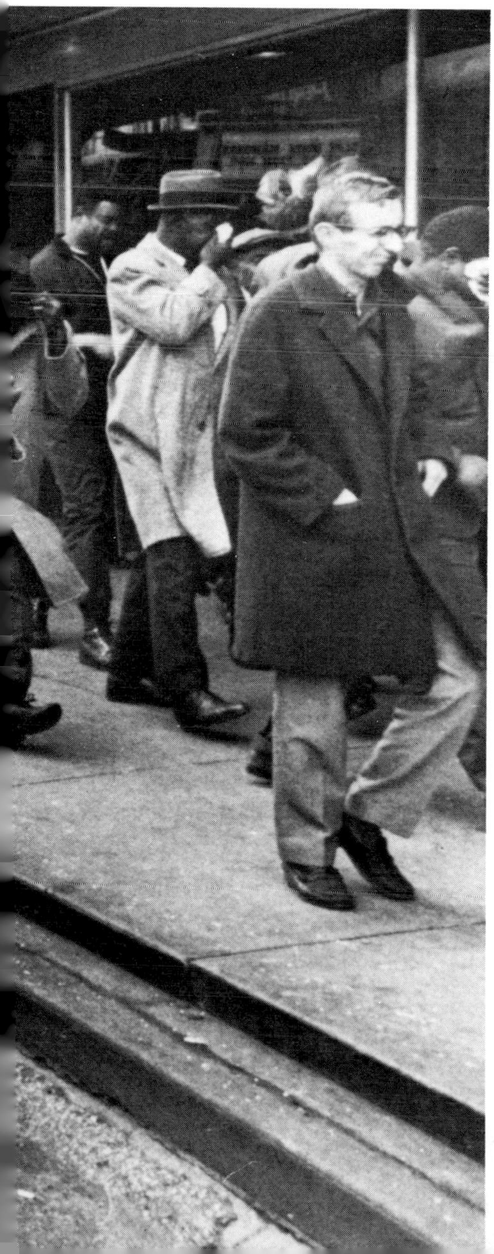

A Memphis policeman grabs a looter.

Ron McCool

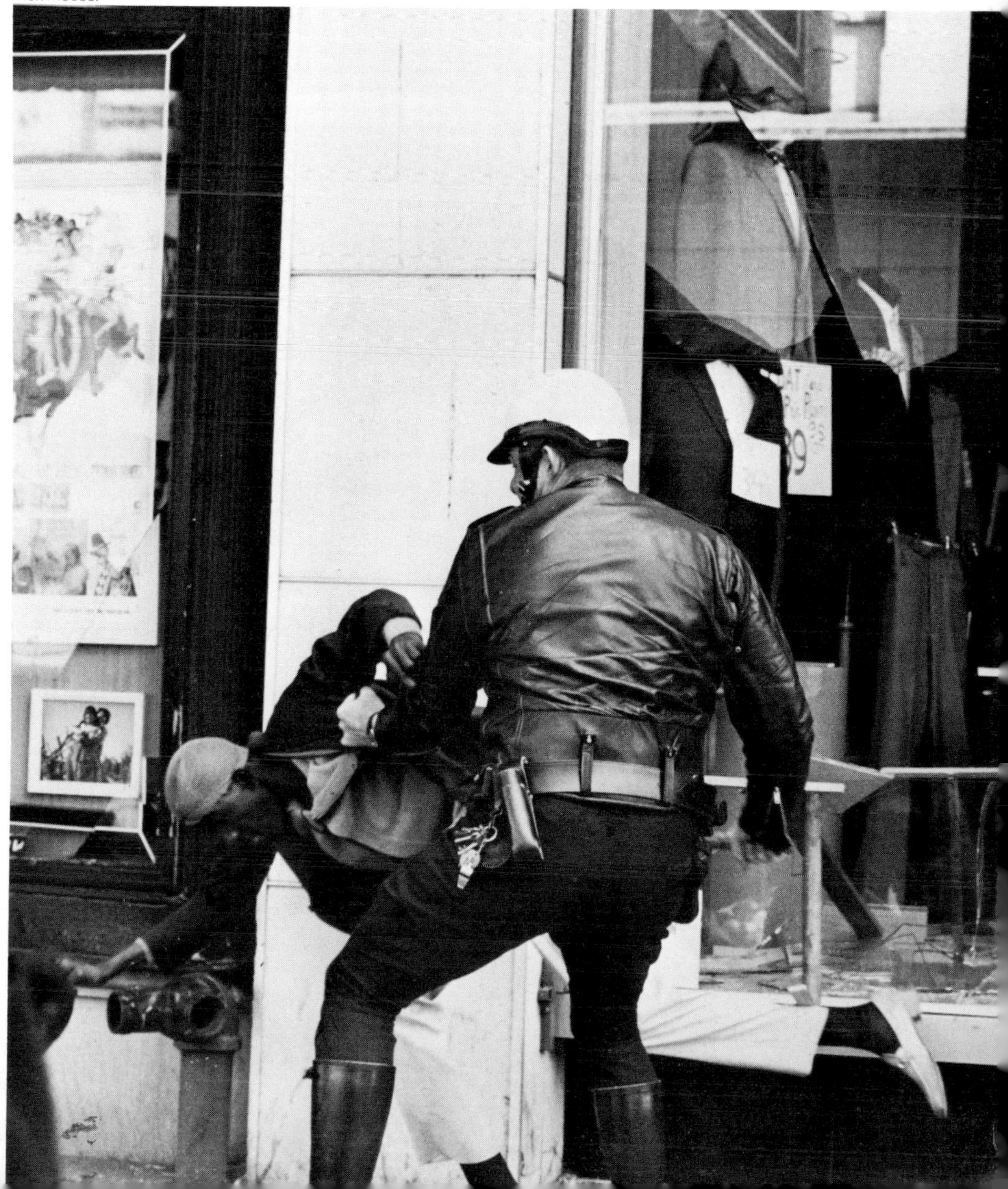

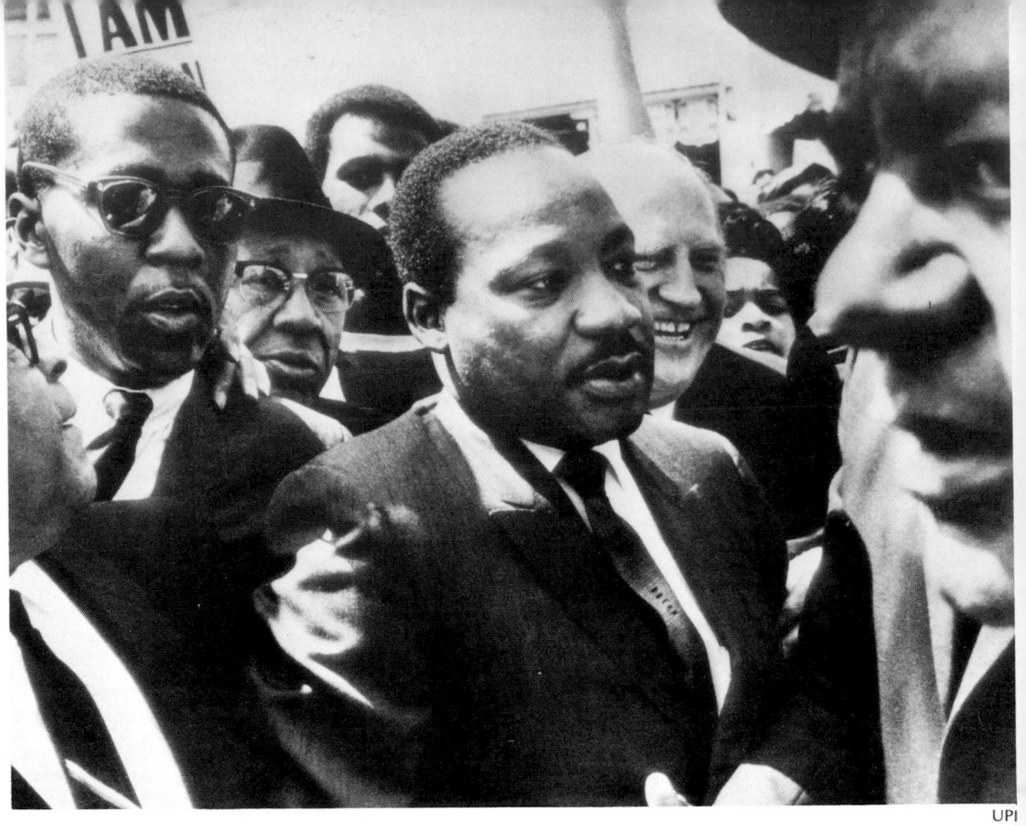
I AM

UPI

Marching with the sanitation workers on March 28, King does not expect violence.

Below:
April 4, 1968. With the body of their slain leader at their feet, members of King's entourage point to the source of the shot, from the balcony of the Lorraine Motel, Memphis.

Joseph Louw–Time-Life Picture Agency ©Time Inc.

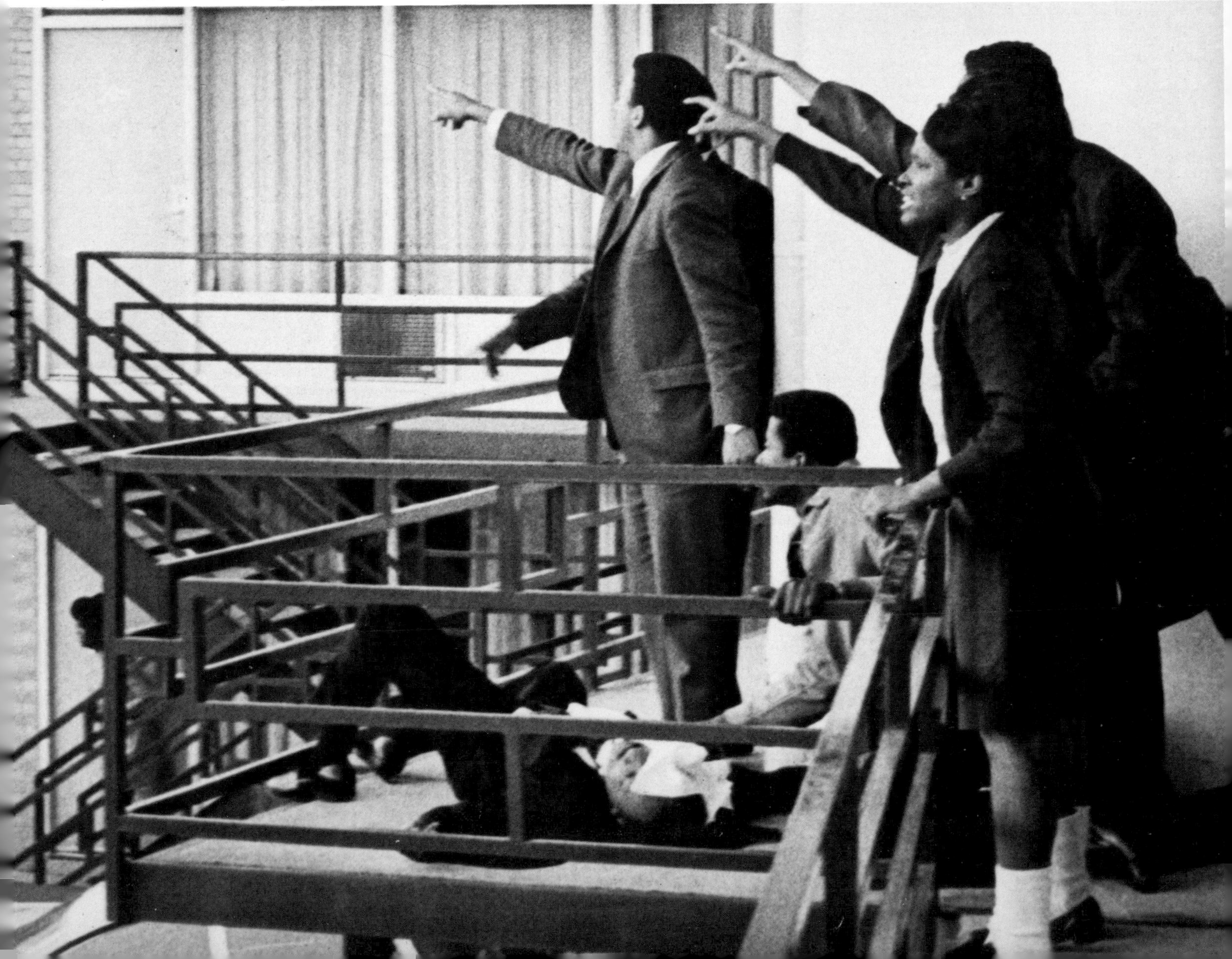

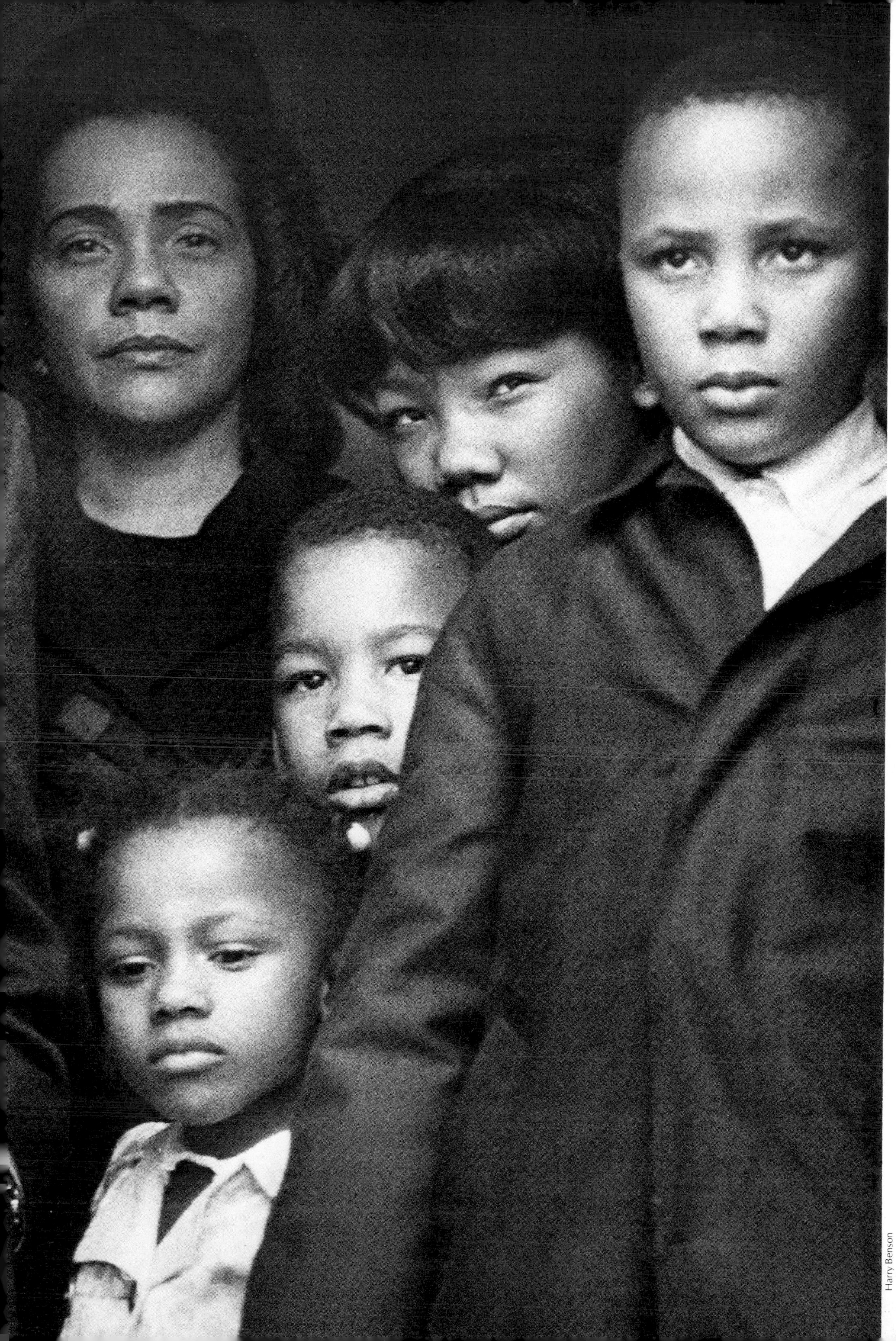

Harry Benson

demand justice must be satisfied with the sad knowledge that King's death did more to stir the conscience of the nation than all the eloquence of his life.

Ironically, rioting broke out across the nation with the news of King's death. ''When white America killed Dr. King last night she declared war on us,'' exclaimed Stokely Carmichael. ''It would have been better if she had killed Rap Brown . . . or Stokely Carmichael. But when she killed Dr. King, she lost it. . . . He was the one man in our race who was trying to teach our people to have love, compassion, and mercy for white people.''

''Dr. Martin Luther King was the last prince of nonviolence,'' reiterated Floyd McKissick. ''Nonviolence is a dead philosophy, and it was not the black people that killed it. It was the white people that killed nonviolence, and the white racists at that.''

The tributes from black and white alike began. President Johnson said the day after King's death: ''no words of

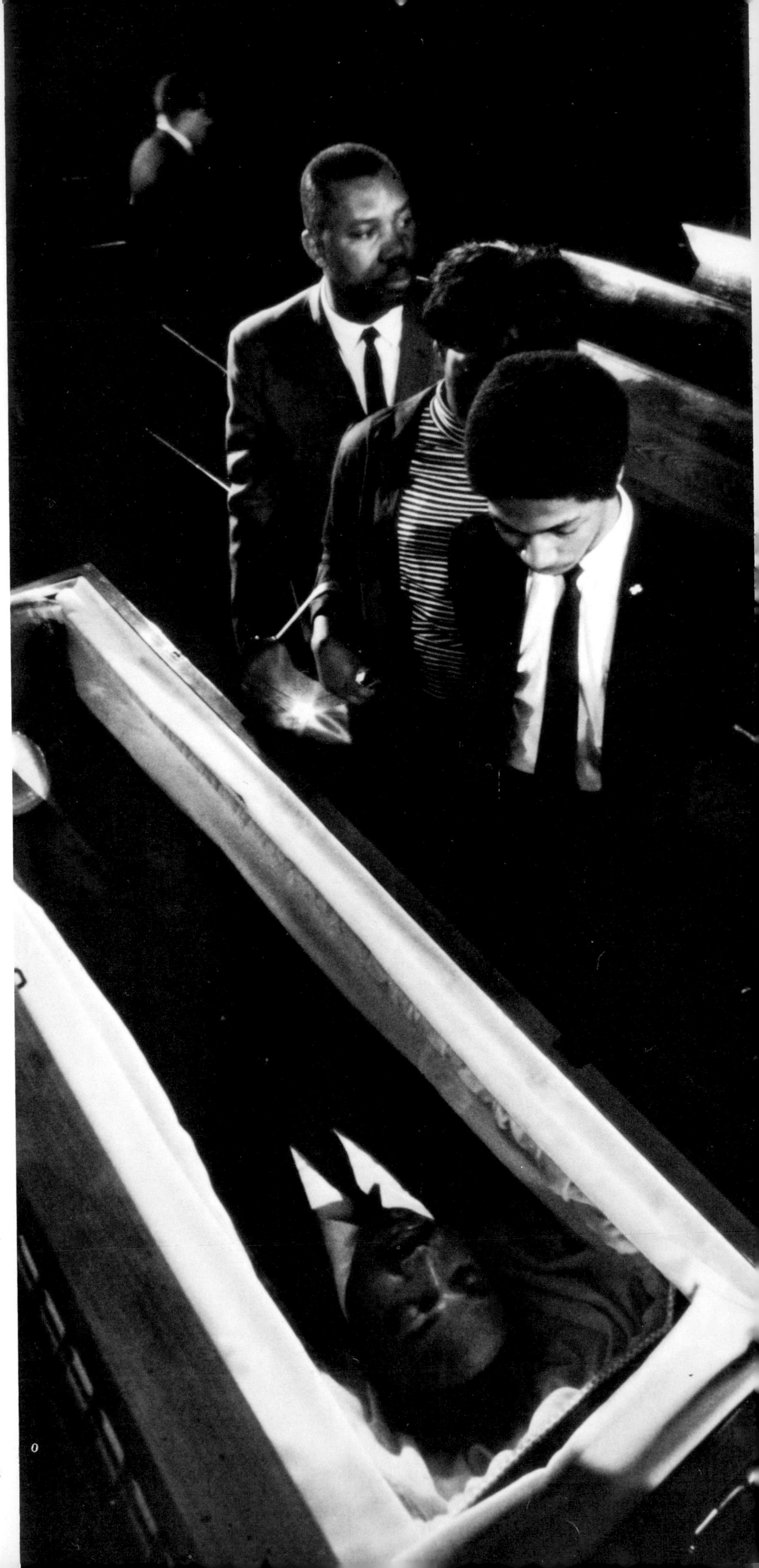

Thousands pay their last respects as King lies in state in Ebenezer Baptist Church, Atlanta.

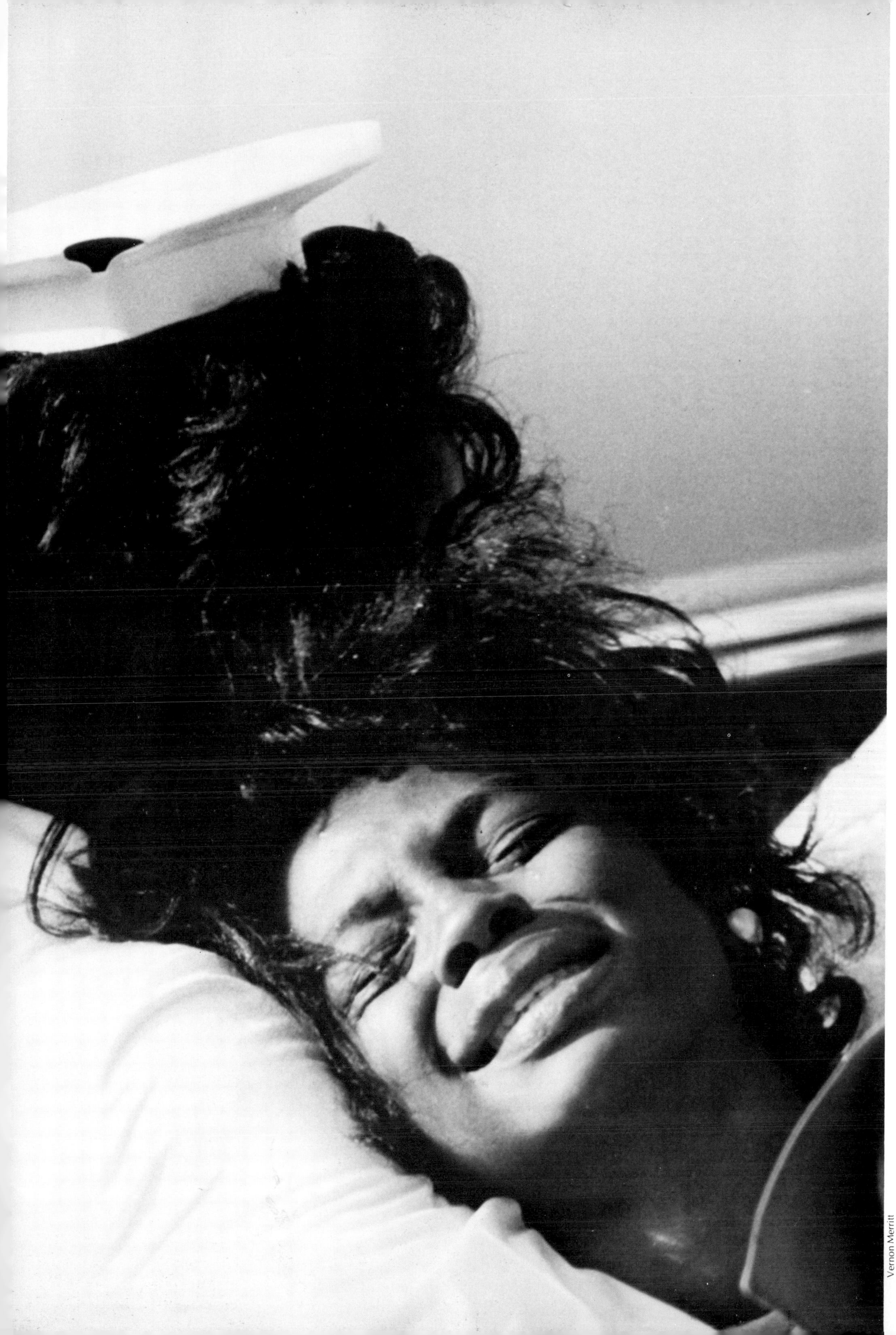

Vernon Merritt

mine can fill the void of the eloquent voice that has been stilled. But this I do believe deeply: The dream of Dr. Martin Luther King has not died with him. Men who are white, men who are black, must and will now join together as never in the past to let all the forces of divisiveness know that America shall not be ruled by the bullet, but only by the ballot of free and just men."

The president announced that Sunday, April 7 would be a day of national mourning. Flags flew at half mast. Services were held in King's honor at churches throughout America. In Washington Cathedral the congregation of four thousand included President Johnson, Vice President Humphrey, the entire Supreme Court, members of the

King's closest associates gather late into the night with Mrs. King to make arrangements for the funeral. From left: Mrs. King; Dora McDonald, King's personal secretary; Ralph Abernathy. Standing behind Abernathy is Jesse Jackson.

Bob Fitch

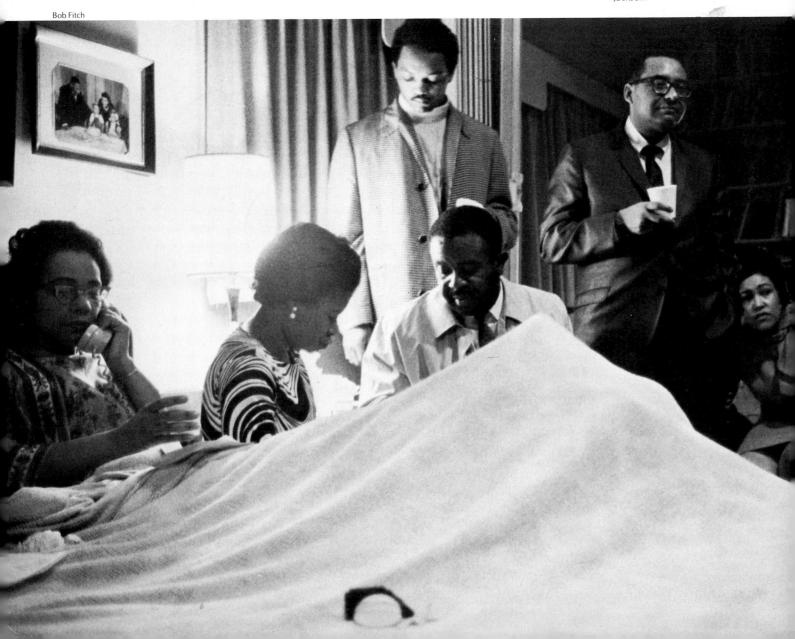

cabinet, prominent members of the legislature, and nearly every eminent black in the civil rights movement.

Tributes were paid by heads of state and world figures. Pope Paul VI said on Palm Sunday that the "cowardly and atrocious" killing "weighed on the conscience of mankind."

On April 8, King's widow, Coretta, and her three oldest children led a silent memorial march through Memphis in honor of her husband. Over fifteen thousand people took part. Many had travelled from all parts of the United States. Ralph Abernathy, who had succeeded King as head of the SCLC, marched with Mrs. King.

Coretta King addressed the crowd outside the Memphis City Hall. As she

Robert and Ethel Kennedy are among the many who have come to offer their personal condolences to Mrs. King. Two months later Robert Kennedy will be assassinated in Los Angeles.

Flip Schulke

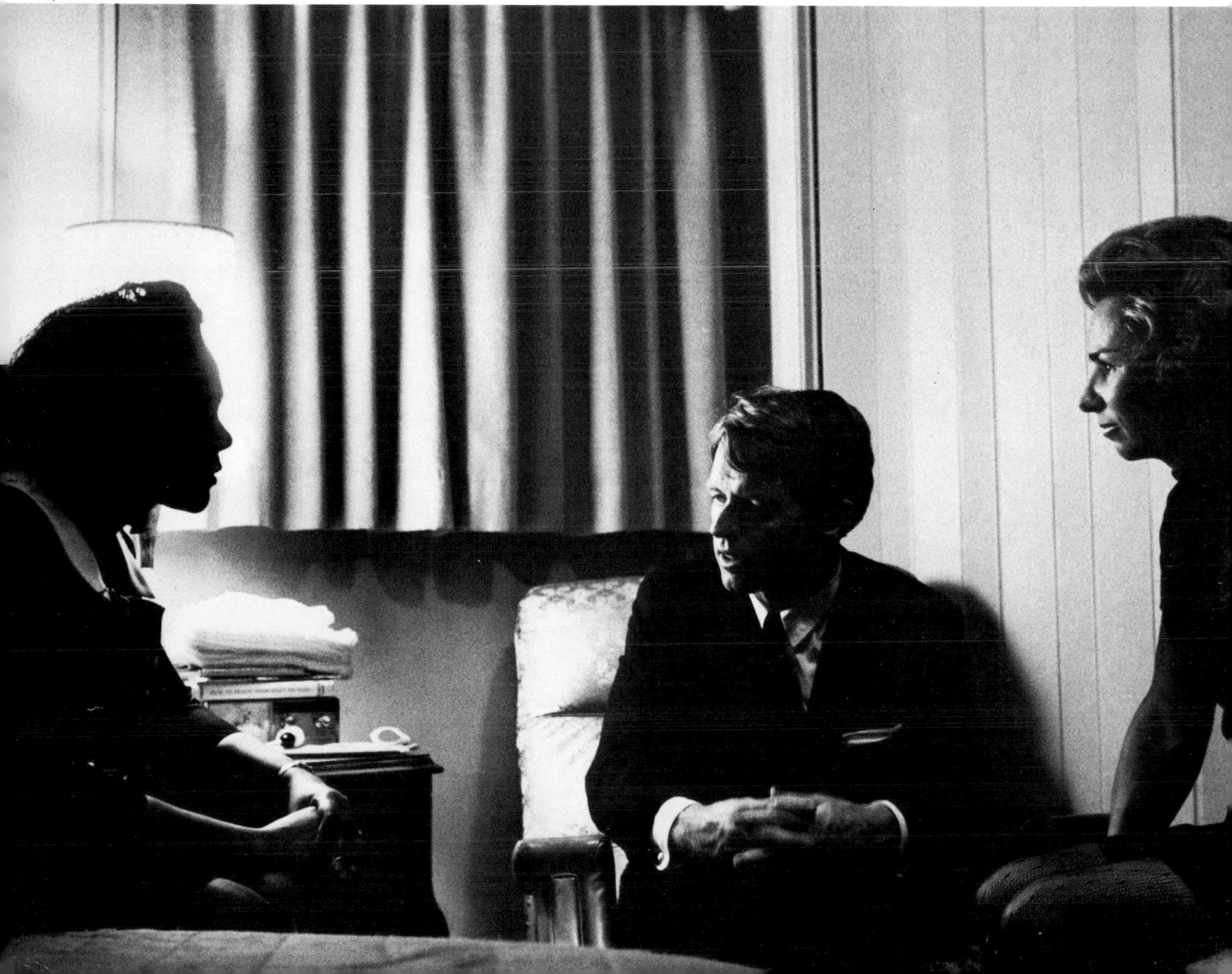

would prove many times in the future, she was prepared to take up her late husband's cause: "We must carry on because this is the way he would have wanted it to have been. . . . We are going to continue his work to make all people truly free and to make every person feel that he is a human being. His campaign for the poor must go on. . . . We are concerned about not only the Negro poor but the poor all over America and all over the world. Every man deserves a right to a job and an income so that he can pursue liberty, life, and happiness. . . ."

King's body lay in state in a chapel on the campus of Spelman College in Atlanta, and subsequently at his family's own Ebenezer Church. Mourners of all races, religions, and social classes came to pay their respects. Vast crowds, estimated at between sixty and one hundred thousand, surrounded the Ebenezer Baptist Church on April 9 during the memorial service, at which Ralph Abernathy officiated. "We gather here this morning in one of the darkest hours in the history of the black people of this nation," he said, "in one of the darkest hours in the history of all mankind."

A tape of the last sermon King had given at the Ebenezer Baptist Church was played during the service. **"If any of you are around when I have to meet my day I don't want a long speech. I'd like somebody to mention that day that Martin Luther King, Jr., tried to give his life for others. I'd like somebody to say that day that Martin Luther King, Jr., tried to love somebody. I want you to say that day that I tried to be like and to walk with them. I won't have any money to leave behind. I won't have the fine and luxurious things of life to leave behind. But I just want to leave a committed life behind. Then my living will not be in vain."**

The march that followed King's funeral epitomized the many he had made in life. Two mules pulled his casket on a flatbed farm cart from the church to Morehouse College, where his teacher and friend Dr. Benjamin Mays spoke a eulogy. In life he had fought for the poor

Coretta Scott King, Ebenezer Baptist Church

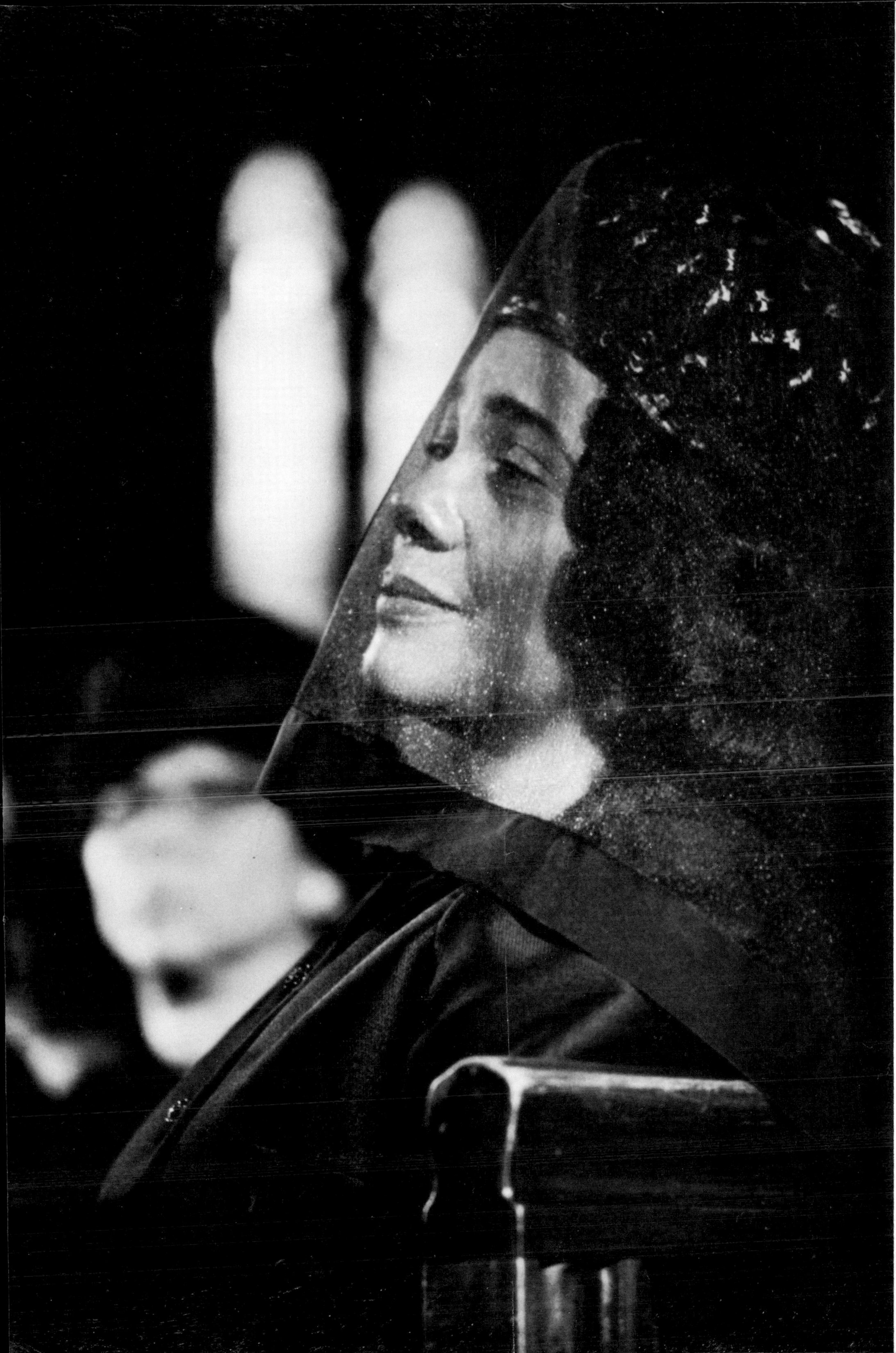

Flip Schulke

and the weak; he had died standing up for the sanitation workers of Memphis; in death he was still identified with those he had championed.

Of all the words spoken after King's death, those uttered by his colleagues who had worked with him daily, who had seen him at his heights and in his depths, have a special significance. "When he was killed," recalls Hosea Williams, "they placed the body in state in Atlanta; but I would go home to my family here, and I would have nightmares. I couldn't sleep. My wife would wake me up, I'd dress, and I'd go back over where his body was, and I stood right there. It was guarding or something, but I needed to stay near."

"Martin Luther King was not a dreamer although he had a dream," wrote Harry Belafonte and Stanley Levison, both trusted friends. "His vision of a society of justice was derived from a stirring reality. Under his leadership millions of black Americans emerged from spiritual imprisonment, from fear, from apathy, and took to the streets to proclaim their freedom. The thunder of millions of marching feet preceded the dream. Without these deeds, inspired by his awesome personal courage, the words would merely have been woven fantasy. Martin Luther King, the peaceful warrior, revealed to his people their latent power. . . ."

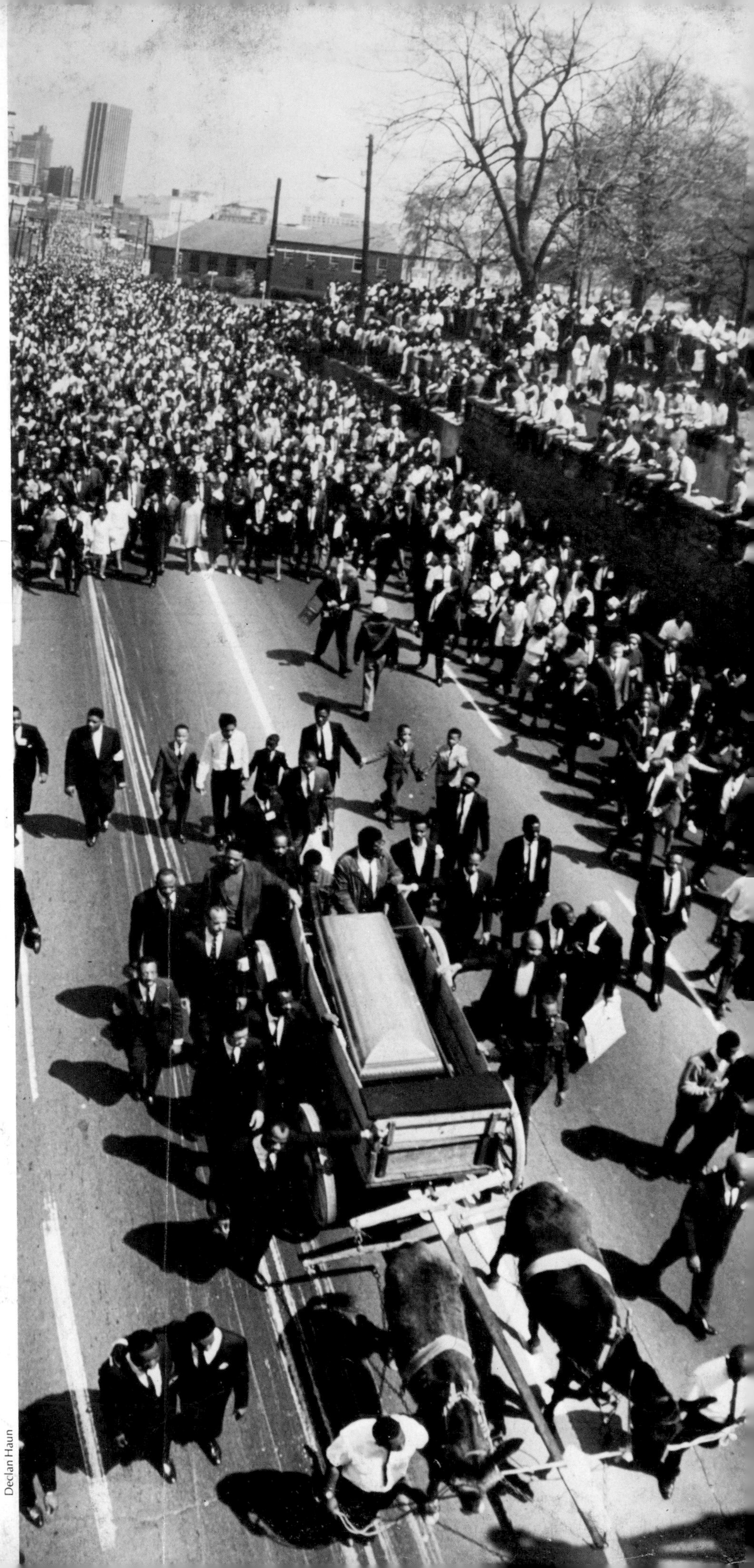

Declan Haun

The casket is carried in a wooden farm wagon through the streets of Atlanta to the grave.

Opposite page:
Solemn observers along the route of the funeral procession.

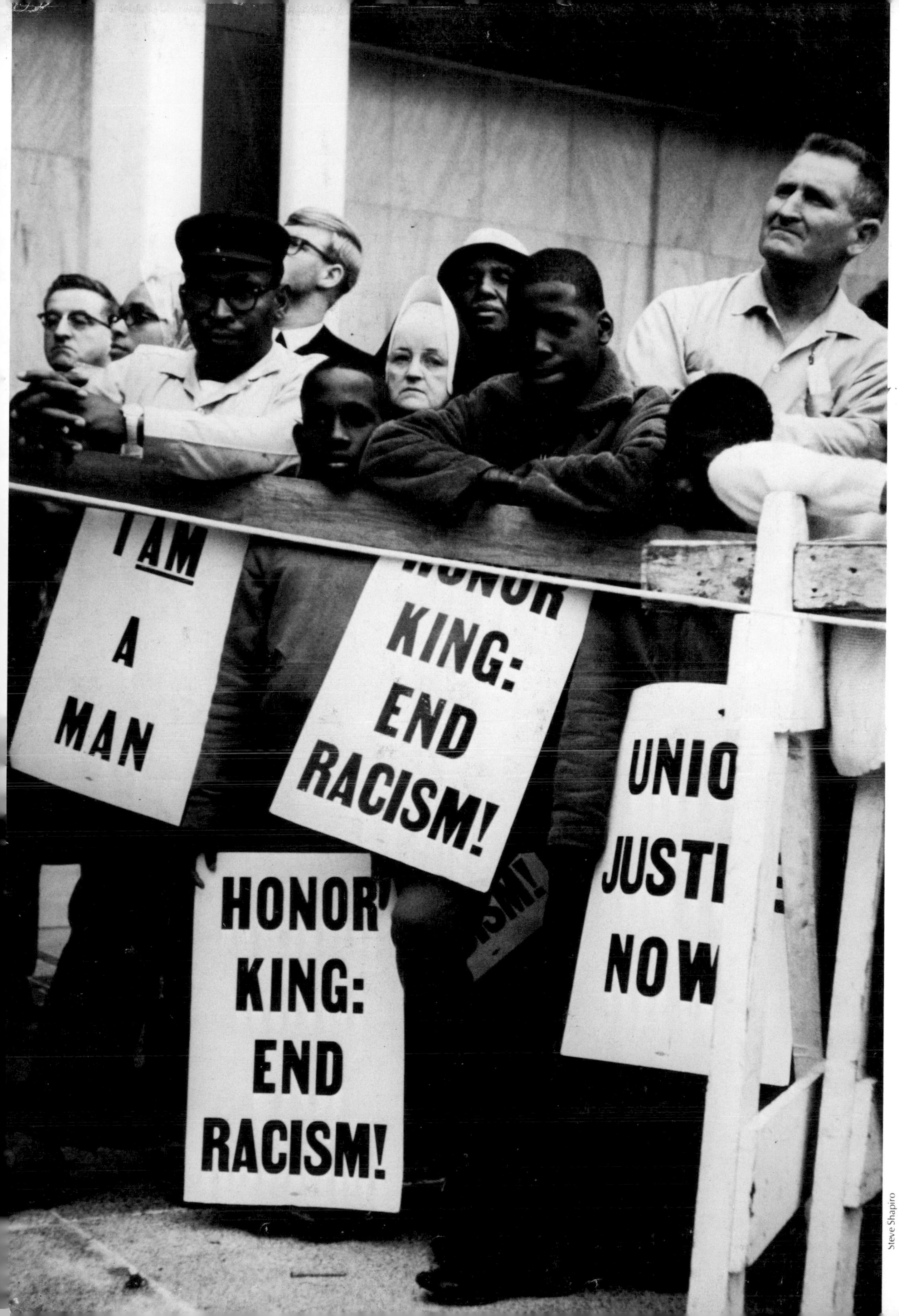
I AM
A
MAN
KING:
END
RACISM!
HONOR
KING:
END
RACISM!
UNIO
JUSTI
NOW

Steve Shapiro

"He was a man with the courage of his convictions," remarked Jesse Jackson. "There are so many people that I know now, who in order to protect their position, disregard their human or moral condition. That is to say that they know what is right, and they do what is wrong in the name of expediency, in the name of what is practical. Dr. King closed the gap between what he purported to be and what he actually was. So on that level he was a walking ball of courage and integrity which is a very rare commodity nowadays."

Harry Belafonte accompanies Mrs. King to the funeral.

Below:
Reverend and Mrs. Martin Luther King, Sr. On June 30, 1974, Mrs. King was killed by Marcus Wayne Chenault, a deranged black man, in Ebenezer Baptist Church. The bullets were intended for Reverend King, Sr.

Bob Fitch

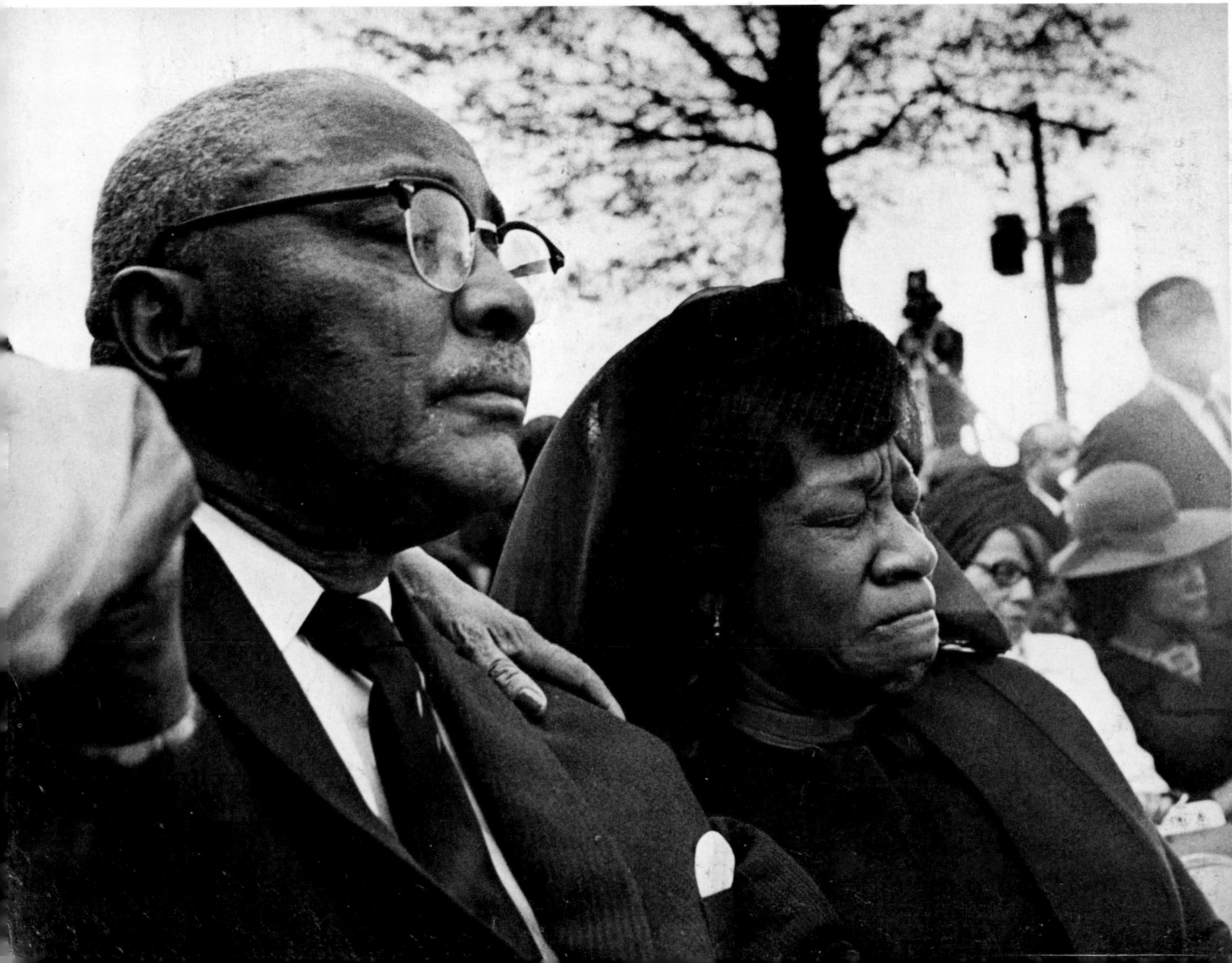

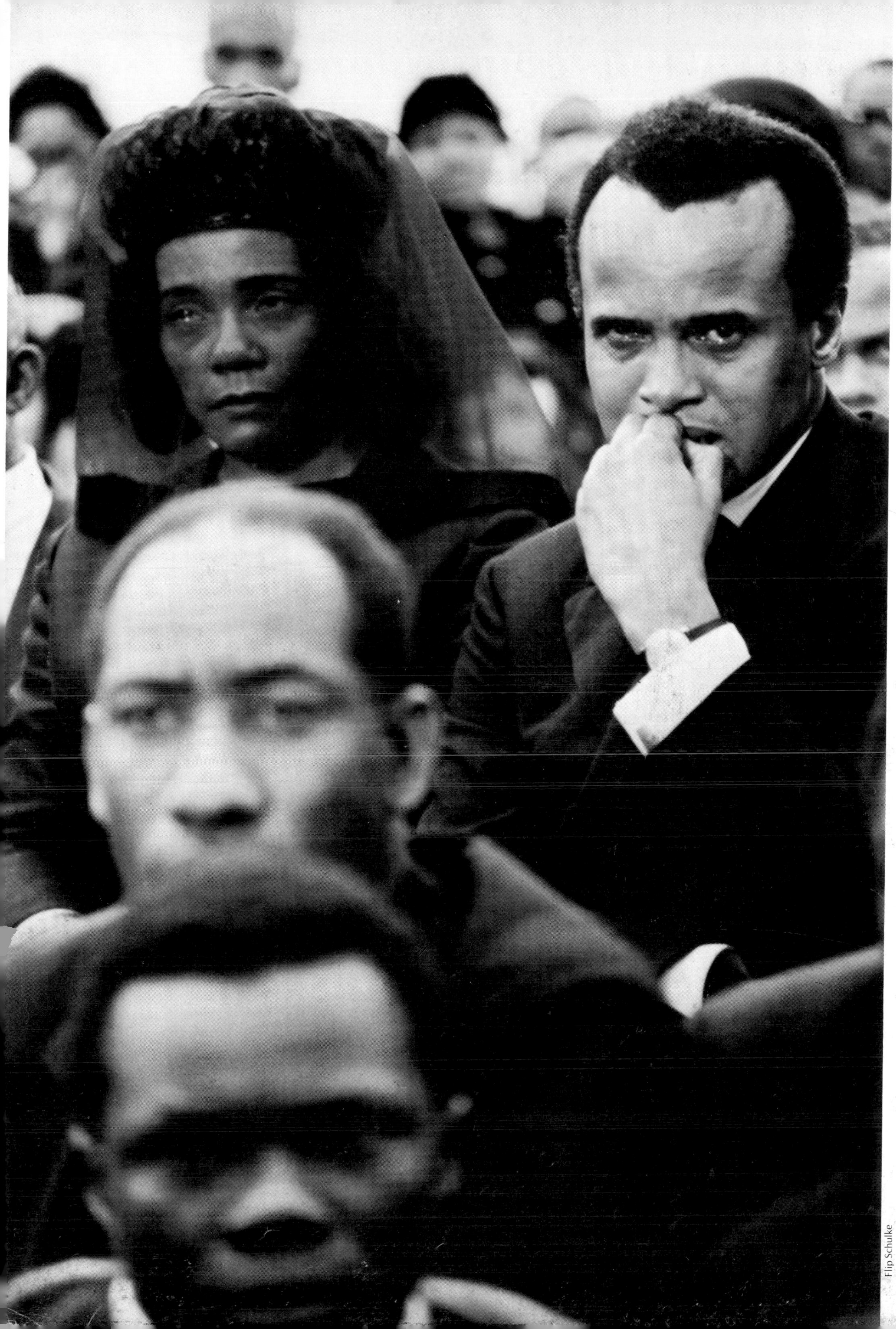

Flip Schulke

EPILOGUE

Of all the tributes paid to Dr. Martin Luther King, Jr., upon his death, time has written the most enduring eulogy. Time has corroborated King's belief that in a country beseiged by violence, nonviolence was, and is, the best weapon of black people. Time has affirmed that in a world where violence is so commonplace as to be taken for granted, it loses its power to convince.

The facts of King's life are clear. The results of his actions, his leadership, are spelled out in headlines for all the world to read. Even today, however, the meaning of his death is more ambiguous. We look at his martyrdom and ask, "What has it accomplished?" Among the major achievements since his death are two that anyone would claim with pride. That which he said was wrong has been proven wrong, and that which he believed was right has been proven right. The years have demonstrated that the strategies and philosophies in the black movement which King found morally offensive were also ineffective. Black power may have awakened the black man's consciousness, but it did nothing to spur the white man's conscience. At the core of King's conviction was the belief that people would choose good over evil, but the choice must be undeniably clear. Good must stand apart—untainted, unblemished. Without the moral superiority that King demanded, black confronts white on a common battlefield, but with vastly inferior ammunition.

The victories of black people have been tortuously slow in coming and too often incomplete. But victories there have been. From Montgomery to Memphis King left a new South behind him. Rarely has one individual, espousing so difficult a philosophy, served as the catalyst for so many significant and permanent social changes. King did not wait for evolution to occur naturally. He perpetrated it. He incited evolution. His greatness lay in his ability to analyze and attack the roots of the problem—not the symptoms. He forced people to change deeply ingrained attitudes, social customs, and convictions, not merely to change rules or laws or habits.

Even with the perspective of intervening years, it is still premature to suggest King's ultimate place in history. Locked into our own moment, we simply cannot know. In part, the passing years will inform us. In larger part, it will depend on the actions and attitudes of all of us—all those who have inherited King's dream. He has pointed the way to the promised land, never himself to reach it. If his life and death are to find a permanent place in history, we must keep marching, moving, struggling toward the land of which he dreamed.

F.S.

P.Mc P.

212

Speeches
and
Sermons

LETTER FROM BIRMINGHAM JAIL

April 16, 1963
Birmingham, Alabama

MY DEAR FELLOW CLERGYMEN:

While confined here in the Birmingham city jail, I came across your recent statement calling my present activities "unwise and untimely." Seldom do I pause to answer criticism of my work and ideas. If I sought to answer all the criticisms that cross my desk, my secretaries would have little time for anything other than such correspondence in the course of the day, and I would have no time for constructive work. But since I feel that you are men of genuine good will and that your criticisms are sincerely set forth, I want to try to answer your statement in what I hope will be patient and reasonable terms.

I think I should indicate why I am here in Birmingham, since you have been influenced by the view which argues against "outsiders coming in." I have the honor of serving as president of the Southern Christian Leadership Conference, an organization operating in every southern state, with headquarters in Atlanta, Georgia. We have some eighty-five affiliated organizations across the South, and one of them is the Alabama Christian Movement for Human Rights. Frequently we share staff, educational, and financial resources with our affiliates. Several months ago the affiliate here in Birmingham asked us to be on call to engage in a nonviolent direct-action program if such were deemed necessary. We readily consented, and when the hour came we lived up to our promise. So I, along with several members of my staff, am here because I was invited here. I am here because I have organizational ties here.

But more basically, I am in Birmingham because injustice is here. Just as the prophets of the eighth century B.C. left their villages and carried their "thus saith the Lord" far beyond the boundaries of their home towns, and just as the Apostle Paul left his village of Tarsus and carried the gospel of Jesus Christ to the far corners of the Greco-Roman world, so am I compelled to carry the gospel of freedom beyond my own home town. Like Paul, I must constantly respond to the Macedonian call for aid.

Moreover, I am cognizant of the interrelatedness of all communities and states. I cannot sit idly by in Atlanta and not be concerned about what happens in Birmingham. Injustice anywhere is a threat to justice everywhere. We are caught in an inescapable network of mutuality, tied in a single garment of destiny. Whatever affects one directly, affects all indirectly. Never again can we afford to live with the narrow, provincial "outside agitator" idea. Anyone who lives inside the United States can never be considered an outsider anywhere within its bounds.

You deplore the demonstrations taking place in Birmingham. But your statement, I am sorry to say, fails to express a similar concern for the conditions that brought about the demonstrations. I am sure that none of you would want to rest content with the superficial kind of social analysis that deals merely with effects and does not grapple with underlying causes. It is unfortunate that demonstrations are taking place in Birmingham, but it is even more unfortunate that the city's white power structure left the Negro community with no alternative.

In any nonviolent campaign there are four basic steps: collection of the facts to determine whether injustices exist; negotiation; self-purification; and direct action. We have gone through all these steps in Birmingham. There can be no gainsaying the fact that racial injustice engulfs this community. Birmingham is probably the most thoroughly segregated city in the United States. Its ugly record of brutality is widely known. Negroes have experienced grossly unjust treatment in the courts. There have been more unsolved bombings of Negro homes and churches in Birmingham than in any other city in the nation. These are the hard, brutal facts of the case. On the basis of these conditions, Negro leaders sought to negotiate with the city fathers. But the latter consistently refused to engage in good-faith negotiation.

Then, last September, came the opportunity to talk with leaders of Birmingham's economic community. In the course of the negotiations, certain promises were made by the merchants—for example, to remove the stores' humiliating racial signs. On the basis of these promises, the Reverend Fred Shuttlesworth and the leaders of the Alabama Christian Movement for Human Rights agreed to a moratorium on all demonstrations. As the weeks and months went by, we realized that we were the victims of a broken promise. A few signs, briefly removed, returned; the others remained.

As in so many past experiences, our hopes had been blasted, and the shadow of deep disappointment settled upon us. We had no alternative except to prepare for direct action, whereby we would present our very bodies as a means of laying our case before the conscience of the local and the national community. Mindful of the difficulties involved, we decided to undertake a process of self-purification. We began a series of workshops on nonviolence, and we repeatedly asked ourselves: "Are you able to accept blows without retaliation?" "Are you able to endure the ordeal of jail?" We decided to schedule our direct-action program for the Easter season, realizing that except for Christmas, this is the main shopping period of the year. Knowing that a strong economic-withdrawal program would be the by-product of direct action, we felt that this would be the best time to bring pressure to bear on the merchants for the needed change.

Then it occurred to us that Birmingham's mayoral election was coming up in March, and we speedily decided to postpone action until after election day. When we discovered that the Commissioner of Public Safety, Eugene "Bull" Connor, had piled up enough votes to be in the run-off, we decided again to postpone action until the day after the run-off so that the demonstrations could not be used to cloud the issues. Like many others, we waited to see Mr. Connor defeated, and to this end we endured postponement after postponement. Having aided in this community need, we felt that our direct-action program could be delayed no longer.

You may well ask, "Why direct action? Why sit-ins, marches, and so forth? Isn't negotiation a better path?" You are quite right in calling for negotiation. Indeed, this is the very purpose of direct action. Nonviolent direct action seeks to create such a crisis and foster such a tension that a community which has constantly refused to negotiate is forced to confront the issue. It seeks so to dramatize the issue that it can no longer be ignored. My citing the creation of tension as part of the work of the nonviolent-resister may sound rather shocking. But I must confess that I am not afraid of the word "tension." I have earnestly opposed violent tension, but there is a type of constructive, nonviolent tension which is necessary for growth. Just as Socrates felt that it was necessary to create a tension in the mind so that individuals could rise from the bondage of myths and half-truths to the unfettered realm of creative analysis and objective appraisal, so must we see the need for nonviolent gadflies to create the kind of tension in society that will help men rise from the dark depths of prejudice and racism to the majestic heights of understanding and brotherhood.

The purpose of our direct-action program is to create a situation so crisis-packed that it will inevitably open the door to negotiation. I therefore concur with you in your call for negotiation. Too long has our beloved Southland been bogged down in a tragic effort to live in monologue rather than dialogue.

One of the basic points in your statement is that the action that I and my associates have taken in Birmingham is untimely. Some have asked: "Why didn't you give the new city administration time to act?" The only answer that I can give to this query is that the new Birmingham administration must be prodded about as much as the outgoing one, before it will act. We are sadly mistaken if we feel that the election of Albert Boutwell as mayor will bring the millennium to Birmingham. While Mr. Boutwell is a much more gentle person than Mr. Connor, they are both segregationists, dedicated to maintenance of the status quo. I have hoped that Mr. Boutwell will be reasonable enough to see the futility of massive resistance to desegregation. But he will not see this without pressure from devotees of civil rights. My friends, I must say to you that we have not made a single gain in civil rights without determined legal and nonviolent pressure. Lamentably, it is an historical fact that privileged groups seldom give up their privileges voluntarily. Individuals may see the moral light and voluntarily give up their unjust posture; but, as Reinhold Niebuhr has reminded us, groups tend to be more immoral than individuals.

We know through painful experience that freedom is never voluntarily given by the oppressor; it must be demanded by the oppressed. Frankly, I have yet to engage in a direct-action campaign that was "well timed" in view of those who have not suffered unduly from the disease of segregation. For years now I have heard the word "Wait!" It rings in the ear of every Negro with piercing familiarity. This "Wait" has almost always meant "Never." We must come to see, with one of our distinguished jurists, that "justice too long delayed is justice denied."

We have waited for more than 340 years for our constitutional and God-given rights. The nations of Asia and Africa are moving with jetlike speed toward gaining political independence, but we still creep at horse-and-buggy

NOBEL PRIZE ACCEPTANCE SPEECH

December 10, 1964
Oslo, Norway

Your Majesty, your Royal Highness, Mr. President, excellencies, ladies and gentlemen:

I accept the Nobel Prize for Peace at a moment when twenty-two million Negroes of the United States of America are engaged in a creative battle to end the long night of racial injustice. I accept this award in behalf of a civil rights movement which is moving with determination and a majestic scorn for risk and danger to establish a reign of freedom and a rule of justice.

I am mindful that only yesterday in Birmingham, Alabama, our children, crying out for brotherhood, were answered with fire hoses, snarling dogs and even death. I am mindful that only yesterday in Philadelphia, Mississippi, young people seeking to secure the right to vote were brutalized and murdered.

I am mindful that debilitating and grinding poverty afflicts my people and chains them to the lowest rung of the economic ladder.

Therefore, I must ask why this prize is awarded to a movement which is beleaguered and committed to unrelenting struggle: to a movement which has not won the very peace and brotherhood which is the essence of the Nobel Prize.

After contemplation, I conclude that this award which I received on behalf of that movement is profound recognition that nonviolence is the answer to the crucial political and moral question of our time—the need for man to overcome oppression and violence without resorting to violence and oppression.

Civilization and violence are antithetical concepts. Negroes of the United States, following the people of India, have demonstrated that nonviolence is not sterile passivity, but a powerful moral force which makes for social transformation. Sooner or later, all the people of the world will have to discover a way to live together in peace, and thereby transform this pending cosmic elegy into a creative psalm of brotherhood.

If this is to be achieved, man must evolve for all human conflict a method which rejects revenge, aggression and retaliation. The foundation of such a method is love.

The tortuous road which has led from Montgomery, Alabama, to Oslo bears witness to this truth. This is the road over which millions of Negroes are traveling to find a new sense of dignity. This same road has opened for all Americans a new era of progress and hope. It has led to a new civil rights bill, and it will, I am convinced, be widened and lengthened into a superhighway of justice as Negro and white men in increasing numbers create alliances to overcome their common problems.

I accept this award today with an abiding faith in America and an audacious faith in the future of mankind. I refuse to accept the idea that the "isness" of man's present nature makes him morally incapable of reaching up for the eternal "oughtness" that forever confronts him.

I refuse to accept the idea that man is mere flotsam and jetsam in the river of life which surrounds him. I refuse to accept the view that mankind is so tragically bound to the starless midnight of racism and war that the bright daybreak of peace and brotherhood can never become a reality.

I refuse to accept the cynical notion that nation after nation must spiral down a militaristic stairway into the hell of thermonuclear destruction. I believe that unarmed truth and unconditional love will have the final word in reality. This is why right temporarily defeated is stronger than evil triumphant.

I believe that even amid today's mortar bursts and whining bullets, there is still hope for a brighter tomorrow. I believe that wounded justice, lying prostrate on the blood-flowing streets of our nations, can be lifted from this dust of shame to reign supreme among the children of men.

I have the audacity to believe that peoples everywhere can have three meals a day for their bodies, education and culture for their minds, and dignity, equality and freedom for their spirits. I believe that what self-centered men have torn down, other-centered can build up. I still believe that one day mankind will bow before the altars of God and be crowned triumphant over war and bloodshed, and nonviolent redemptive goodwill will proclaim the rule of the land. "And the lion and the lamb shall lie down together and every man shall sit under his own vine and fig tree and none shall be afraid." I still believe that we shall overcome.

This faith can give us courage to face the uncertainties of the future. It will give our tired feet new strength as we continue our forward stride toward the city of freedom. When our days become dreary with low-hovering clouds and our nights become darker than a thousand midnights, we will know that we are living in the creative turmoil of a genuine civilization struggling to be born.

Today I come to Oslo as a trustee, inspired and with renewed dedication to humanity. I accept this prize on behalf of all men who love peace and brotherhood. I say I come as a trustee, for in the depths of my heart I am aware that this prize is much more than an honor to me personally.

Every time I take a flight I am always mindful of the many people who make a successful journey possible, the known pilots and the unknown ground crew.

So you honor the dedicated pilots of our struggle who have sat at the controls as the freedom movement soared into orbit. You honor, once again, Chief Luthuli of South Africa, whose struggles with and for his people, are still met with the most brutal expression of man's inhumanity to man.

You honor the ground crew without whose labor and sacrifices the jet flights to freedom could never have left the earth.

Most of these people will never make the headlines and their names will not appear in Who's Who. Yet, the years have rolled past and when the blazing light of truth is focused on this marvelous age in which we live—men and women will know and children will be taught that we have a finer land, a better people, a more noble civilization—because these humble children of God were willing to suffer for righteousness' sake.

I think Alfred Nobel would know what I mean when I say that I accept this award in the spirit of a curator of some precious heirloom which he holds in trust for its true owners—all those to whom beauty is truth and truth beauty—and in whose eyes the beauty of genuine brotherhood and peace is more precious than diamonds or silver or gold.

THE DRUM MAJOR INSTINCT

February 4, 1968
Ebenezer Baptist Church, Atlanta, Georgia

This morning I would like to use as a subject from which to preach "The Drum Major Instinct." And our text for the morning is taken from a very familiar passage in the tenth chapter as recorded by Saint Mark; beginning with the thirty-fifth verse of that chapter, we read these words: "And James and John the sons of Zebedee came unto him saying, 'Master, we would that thou shouldest do for us whatsoever we shall desire.' And he said unto them, 'What would ye that I should do for you?' And they said unto him, 'Grant unto us that we may sit one on thy right hand, and the other on thy left hand in thy glory.' But Jesus said unto them, 'Ye know not what ye ask. Can ye drink of the cup that I drink of, and be baptized with the baptism that I am baptized with?' And they said unto him, 'We can.' And Jesus said unto them, 'Ye shall indeed drink of the cup that I drink of, and with the baptism that I am baptized with all shall ye be baptized. But to sit on my right hand and on my left hand is not mine to give, but it shall be given to them for whom it is prepared.' "

And then, Jesus goes on toward the end of that passage to say, "But so shall it not be among you, but whosoever will be great among you, shall be your servant; and whosoever of you will be the chiefest, shall be servant of all." The setting is clear. James and John are making a specific request of the master. They had dreamed, as most Hebrews dreamed, of a coming king of Israel who would set Jerusalem free. And establish his kingdom on Mount Zion, and in righteousness rule the world. And they thought of Jesus as this kind of king, and they were thinking of that day when Jesus would reign supreme as this new king of Israel. And they were saying now, 'when you establish your kingdom, let one of us sit on the right hand, and the other on the left hand of your throne.'

Now very quickly, we would automatically condemn James and John, and we would say they were selfish. Why would they make such a selfish request? But before we condemn them too quickly, let us look calmly and honestly at ourselves, and we will discover that we too have those same basic desires for recognition, for importance, that same desire for attention, that same desire to be first. Of course the other disciples got mad with James and John, and you could understand why, but we must understand that we have some of the same James and John qualities. And there is, deep down within all of us, an instinct. It's a kind of drum major instinct—a desire to be out front, a desire to lead the parade, a desire to be first. And it is something that runs a whole gamut of life.

And so before we condemn them, let us see that we all have the drum major instinct. We all want to be important, to surpass others, to achieve distinction, to lead the parade. Alfred Adler, the great psycho-analyst, contends that this is the dominant impulse. Sigmund Freud used to contend that sex was the dominant impulse, and Adler came with a new argument saying that this quest for recognition, this desire for attention, this desire for distinction is the basic impulse, the basic drive of human life—this drum major instinct.

And you know, we begin early to ask life to put us first. Our first cry as a baby was a bid for attention. And all through childhood the drum major impulse or instinct is a major obsession. Children ask life to grant them first place. They are a little bundle of ego. And they have innately the drum major impulse, or the drum major instinct.

Now in adult life, we still have it, and we really never get by it. We like to do something good. And you know, we like to be praised for it. Now if you don't believe that, you just go on living life, and you will discover very soon that you like to be praised. Everbody likes it, as a matter of fact. And somehow this warm glow we feel when we are praised, or when our name is in print, is something of the vitamin A to our ego. Nobody is unhappy when they are praised, even if they know they don't deserve it, and even if they don't believe it. The only unhappy people about praise is when that praise is going too much toward somebody else. But everybody likes to be praised, because of this real drum major instinct.

Now the presence of the drum major instinct is why so many people are joiners. You know there are some people who just join everything. And it's really a quest for attention, and recognition, and importance. And they get names that give them that impression. So you get your groups, and they become the grand patron, and the little fellow who is henpecked at home needs a chance to be the most worthy of the most worthy of something. It is the drum major impulse and longing that runs the gamut of human life. And so we see it everywhere, this quest for recognition. And we join things, over-join really, that we think that we will find that recognition in.

Now the presence of this instinct explains why we are so often taken by advertisers. You know those gentlemen of massive verbal persuasion. And they have a way of saying things to you that kind of gets you into buying. In order to be a man of distinction, you must drink this whiskey. In order to make your neighbors envious, you must drive this type of car. In order to be lovely to love you must wear this kind of lipstick or this kind of perfume. And you know, before you know it you're just buying that stuff. That's the way the advertisers do it.

I got a letter the other day. It was a new magazine coming out. And it opened up, "Dear Dr. King. As you know, you are on many mailing lists. And you are categorized as highly intelligent, progressive, a lover of the arts, and the sciences, and I know you will want to read what I have to say." Of course I did. After you said all of that and explained me so exactly, of course I wanted to read it.

But very seriously, it goes through life, the drum major instinct is real. And you know what else it causes to happen? It often causes us to live above our means. It's nothing but the drum major instinct. Do you ever see people buy cars that they can't even begin to buy in terms of their income? You've seen people riding around in Cadillacs and Chryslers who don't earn enough to have good T-Model Ford. But it feeds a repressed ego.

You know economists tell us that your automobiles should not cost more than half of your annual income. So if you're making an income of five thousand dollars, your car shouldn't cost more than about twenty-five hundred. That's just good economics. And if it's a family of two, and both members of the family make ten thousand dollars, they would have to make out with one car. That would be good economics, although it's often inconvenient. But so often . . . haven't you seen people making five thousand dollars a year and driving a car that costs six thousand. And they wonder why their ends never meet. That's a fact.

Now the economists also say that your house shouldn't cost, if you're buying a house, it shouldn't cost more than twice your income. That's based on the economy, and how you would make ends meet. So, if you have an income of five thousand dollars, it's kind of difficult in this society. But say it's a family with an income of ten thousand dollars, the house shouldn't cost more than twenty thousand. But I've seen folk making ten thousand dollars, living in a forty and fifty thousand dollar house. And you know they just barely make it. They get a check every month somewhere, and they owe all of that out before it comes in; never have anything to put away for rainy days.

But now the problem is, it is the drum major instinct. And you know, you see people over and over again with the drum major instinct taking them over. And they just live their lives trying to outdo the Joneses. They got to get this coat because this particular coat is a little better, and a little better looking than Mary's coat. And I got to drive this car because it's something about this car that makes my car a little better than my neighbor's car. I know a man who used to live in a thirty-five thousand dollar house. And other people started building thirty-five thousand dollar houses, so he built a seventy-five thousand dollar house, and he built a hundred thousand dollar house. And I don't know where he's going to end up if he's going to live his life trying to keep with the Joneses.

There comes a time that the drum major instinct can become destructive. And that's where I want to move now. I want to move to the point of saying that if this instinct is not harnessed, it becomes a very dangerous, pernicious instinct. For instance, if it isn't harnessed, it causes one's personality to become distorted. I guess that's the most damaging aspect of it—what it does to the personality. If it isn't harnessed, you will end up day in and day out trying to deal with your ego problem by boasting.

Have you ever heard people that—you know, and I'm sure you've met them—that really become sickening because they just sit up all the time talking about themselves. And they just boast, and boast, and boast, and that's the person who has not harnessed the drum major instinct.

And then it does other things to the personality. It causes you to lie about who you know sometimes. There are some people who are influence peddlers. And in their attempt to deal with the drum major instinct, they have to try to identify with the so-called big name people. And if you're not careful, they will make you think they know somebody that they don't really know. They know them well, they sip tea with them. And they . . . this and that. That . . . that happens to people.

And the other thing is that it causes one to engage ultimately in activities that are merely used to get attention. Criminologists tell us that some people are driven to crime because of this drum major instinct. They don't feel that they are getting enough attention through the normal channels of social behavior, and others turn to anti-social behavior in order to get attention, in order to feel important. And so they get that gun. And before they know it they rob the bank in a quest for recognition, in a quest for importance.

And then the final great tragedy of the distorted personality is the fact that when one fails to harness this instinct, he ends by trying to push others down in order to push himself up. And whenever you do that, you engage in some of the most vicious activities. You will spread evil, vicious, lying gossip on people, because you are trying to pull them down in order to push yourself up.

And the great issue of life is to harness the drum major instinct.

Now the other problem is when you don't harness the drum major instinct, this uncontrolled aspect of it, is that it leads to snobbish exclusivism. Now you know, this is the danger of social clubs, and fraternities. I'm in a fraternity; I'm in two or three. For sororities, and all of these, I'm not talking against them, I'm saying it's the danger. The danger is that they can become forces of classism and exclusivism where somehow you get a degree of satisfaction because you are in something exclusive, and that's fulfilling something, you know. And I'm in this fraternity, and it's the best fraternity in the world and everybody can't get in this fraternity. So it ends up, you know, a very exclusive kind of thing.

And you know, that can happen with the church. I've known churches get in that bind sometimes. I've been to churches you know, and they say, "We have so many doctors and so many school teachers, and so many lawyers, and so many businessmen in our church." And that's fine, because doctors need to go to church, and lawyers, and businessmen, teachers—they ought to be in church. But they say that, even the preacher sometime will go on through it, they say that as if the other people don't count. And the church is the one place where a doctor ought to forget that he's a doctor. The church is the one place where a Ph.D. ought to forget that he's a Ph.D. The church is the one place that the schoolteacher ought to forget the degree she has behind her name. The church is the one place where the lawyer ought to forget that he's a lawyer. And any church that violates the 'whosoever will, let him come' doctrine is a dead, cold church, and nothing but a little social club with a thin veneer of religiosity.

When the church is true to its nature, it says, "Whosoever will, let him come." And it does not propose to satisfy the perverted uses of the drum major instinct. It's the one place where everybody should be the same standing before a common master and savior. And a recognition grows out of this—that all men are brothers because they are children of a common father.

The drum major instinct can lead to exclusivism in one's thinking, and can lead one to feel that because he has some training, he's a little better than that person that doesn't have it, or because he has some economic security, that he's a little better than the person who doesn't have it. And that's the uncontrolled, perverted use of the drum major instinct.

Now the other thing is that it leads to tragic—and we've seen it happen so often—tragic race prejudice. Many have written about this problem—Lillian Smith used to say it beautifully in some of her books. And she would say it to the point of getting men and women to see the source of the problem. Do you know that a lot of the race problem grows out of the drum major instinct? A need that some people have to feel superior. A need that some people have to feel that they are first, and to feel that their white skin ordained them to be first. And they have said it over and over again in ways that we see with our own eyes. In fact, not too long ago, a man down in Mississippi said that God was a charter member of the White Citizens Council. And so God being the charter member means that everybody who's in that has a kind of divinity, a kind of superiority.

And think of what has happened in history as a result of this perverted use of the drum major instinct. It has led to the most tragic prejudice, the most tragic expressions of man's inhumanity to man.

I always try to do a little converting when I'm in jail. And when we were in jail in Birmingham the other day, the white wardens all enjoyed coming around to the cell to talk about the race problem. And they were showing us where we were so wrong demonstrating. And they were showing us where segregation was so right. And they were showing us where intermarriage was so wrong. So I would get to preaching, and we would get to talking—calmly, because they wanted to talk about it. And then we got down on day to the point—that was the second or third day—to talk about where they lived, and how much they were earning. And when those brothers told me what they were earning, I said, now, "You know what? You ought to be marching with us. You're just as poor as Negroes." And I said, "You are put in the position of supporting your oppressor. Because through prejudice and blindness, you fail to see that the same forces that oppress Negroes in American society oppress poor white people. And all

you are living on is the satisfaction of your skin being white, and the drum major instinct of thinking that you are somebody big because you are white. And you're so poor you can't send your children to school. You ought to be out here marching with every one of us every time we have a march."

Now that's a fact. That the poor white has been put into this position—where through blindness and prejudice, he is forced to support his oppressors, and the only thing he has going for him is the false feeling that he is superior because his skin is white. And can't hardly eat and make his ends meet week in and week out.

And not only does this thing go into the racial struggle, it goes into the struggle between nations. And I would submit to you this morning that what is wrong in the world today is that the nations of the world are engaged in a bitter, colossal contest for supremacy. And if something doesn't happen to stop this trend I'm sorely afraid that we won't be here to talk about Jesus Christ and about God and about brotherhood too many more years. If somebody doesn't bring an end to this suicidal thrust that we see in the world today, none of us are going to be around, because somebody's going to make the mistake through our senseless blundering of dropping a nuclear bomb somewhere, and then another one is going to drop. And don't let anybody fool you, this can happen within a matter of seconds. They have twenty-megaton bombs in Russia right now that can destroy a city as big as New York in three seconds with everybody wiped away, and every building. And we can do the same thing to Russia and China.

But this is where we are drifting, and we are drifting there, because nations are caught up with the drum major instinct. I must be first. I must be supreme. Our nation must rule the world. And I am sad to say that the nation in which we live is the supreme culprit. And I'm going to continue to say it to America, because I love this country too much to see the drift that it has taken.

God didn't call America to do what she's doing in the world now. God didn't call America to engage in a senseless, unjust war, [such] as the war in Vietnam. And we are criminals in that war. We have committed more war crimes almost than any nation in the world, and I'm going to continue to say it. And we won't stop it because of our pride, and our arrogance as a nation.

But God has a way of even putting nations in their place. The God that I worship has a way of saying, "Don't play with me." He has a way of saying, as the God of the Old Testament used to say to the Hebrews, "Don't play with me, Israel. Don't play with me, Babylon. Be still and know that I'm God. And if you don't stop your reckless course, I'll rise up and break the backbone of your power." And that can happen to America. Every now and then I go back and read Gibbons' *Decline and Fall of the Roman Empire*. And when I come and look at America, I say to myself, the parallels are frightening.

And we have perverted the drum major instinct. But let me rush on to my conclusion, because I want you to see what Jesus was really saying. What was the answer that Jesus gave these men? It's very interesting. One would have thought that Jesus would have said, "You are out of your place. You are selfish. Why would you raise such a question?"

But that isn't what Jesus did. He did something altogether different. He said in substance, 'Oh I see, you want to be first. You want to be great. You want to be important. You want to be significant. Well you ought to be. If you're going to be my disciple, you must be.' But he reordered priorities. And he said, "Yes, don't give up this instinct. It's a good instinct if you use it right. It's a good instinct if you don't distort it and pervert it. Don't give it up. Keep feeling the need for being important. Keep feeling the need for being first. But I want you to be first in love. I want you to be first in moral excellence. I want you to be first in generosity. That is what I want you to do."

And he transformed the situation by giving a new definition of greatness. And you know how he said it? He said now, "Brethren, I can't give you greatness. And really, I can't make you first." This is what Jesus said to James and John. You must earn it. True greatness comes not by favoritism, but by fitness. And the right hand and the left are not mine to give, they belong to those who are prepared.

And so Jesus gave us a new norm of greatness. If you want to be important—wonderful. If you want to be recognized—wonderful. If you want to be great—wonderful. But recognize that he who is greatest among you shall be your servant. That's your new definition of greatness. And this morning, the thing that I like about it . . . by giving that definition of greatness, it means that everybody can be great. Because everybody can serve. You don't have to have a college degree to serve. You don't have to make your subject and your verb agree to serve. You don't have to know about Plato and Aristotle to serve. You don't have to know Einstein's theory of relativity to serve. You don't have to know the second theory of thermo-dynamics in physics to serve. You only need a heart full of grace. A soul generated by love. And you can be that servant.

I know a man, and I just want to talk about him a minute, and maybe you will discover who I'm talking about as I go down the way, because he was a great one. And he just went about serving. He was born in an obscure village, the child of a poor peasant woman. And then he grew up in still another obscure village, where he worked as a carpenter until he was thirty years old. Then for three years, he just got on his feet, and he was an itinerant preacher. And then he went about doing some things. He didn't have much. He never wrote a book. He never held an office. He never had a family. He never owned a house. He never went to college. He never visited a big city. He never went two hundred miles from where he was born. He did none of the usual things that the world would associate with greatness. He had no credentials but himself.

He was thirty-three when the tide of public opinion turned against him. They called him a rabble-rouser. They called him a troublemaker. They said he was an agitator. He practiced civil disobedience; he broke injunctions. And so he was turned over to his enemies, and went through the mockery of a trial. And the irony of it all is that his friends turned him over to them. One of his closest friends denied him. Another of his friends turned him over to his enemies. And while he was dying, the people who killed him gambled for his clothing, the only possession that he had in the world. When he was dead, he was buried in a borrowed tomb, through the pity of a friend.

Nineteen centuries have come and gone, and today, he stands as the most influential figure that ever entered human history. All of the armies that ever marched, all the navies that ever sailed, all the parliaments that ever sat, and all the kings that ever reigned put together have not affected the life of man on this earth as much as that one solitary life. His name may be a familiar one. But today I can hear them talking about him. Every now and then somebody says, "He's king of kings." And again I can hear somebody saying, "He's lord of lords." Somewhere else I can hear somebody saying, "In Christ there is no east nor west." And they go on and talk about . . ." In him there's no north and south, but one great fellowship of love throughout the whole wide world." He didn't have anything. He just went around serving, and doing good.

This morning, you can be on his right hand and his left hand if you serve. It's the only way in.

Every now and then I guess we all think realistically about that day when we will be victimized with what is life's final common denominator—that something we call death. We all think about it. And every now and then I think about my own death, and I think about my own funeral. And I don't think of it in a morbid sense. Every now and then I ask myself, "What is it that I would want said?" And I leave the word to you this morning.

If any of you are around when I have to meet my day, I don't want a long funeral. And if you get somebody to deliver the eulogy, tell them not to talk too long. Every now and then I wonder what I want them to say. Tell them not to mention that I have a Nobel Peace Prize, that isn't important. Tell them not to mention that I have three or four hundred other awards, that's not important. Tell him not to mention where I went to school.

I'd like somebody to mention that day, that Martin Luther King, Jr., tried to give his life serving others. I'd like for somebody to say that day, that Martin Luther King, Jr., tried to love somebody. I want you to say that day, that I tried to be right on the war question. I want you to be able to say that day, that I did try to feed the hungry. And I want you to be able to say that day, that I did try, in my life, to clothe those who were naked." I want you to say, on that day, that I did try, in my life, to visit those who were in prison. I want you to say that I tried to love and serve humanity.

Yes, if you want to say that I was a drum major, say that I was a drum major for justice; say that I was a drum major for peace; I was a drum major for righteousness. And all of the other shallow things will not matter. I won't have any money to leave behind. I won't have the fine and luxurious things of life to leave behind. But I just want to leave a committed life behind.

And that's all I want to say . . . if I can help somebody as I pass along, if I can cheer somebody with a word or song, if I can show somebody he's travelling wrong, then my living will not be in vain. If I can do my duty as a Christian ought, if I can bring salvation to a world once wrought, if I can spread the message as the master taught, then my living will not be in vain.

Yes, Jesus, I want to be on your right side or your left side, not for any selfish reason. I want to be on your right or your best side, not in terms of some political kingdom or ambition, but I just want to be there in love and in justice and in truth and in commitment to others, so that we can make of this old world a new world.

"I'VE BEEN TO THE MOUNTAINTOP"

April 3, 1968
Masonic Temple, Memphis, Tennessee

Thank you very kindly, my friends. As I listened to Ralph Abernathy in his eloquent and generous introduction and then thought about myself, I wondered who he was talking about. It's always good to have your closest friend and associate to say something good about you. And Ralph is the best friend that I have in the world.

I'm delighted to see each of you here tonight in spite of a storm warning. You reveal that you are determined to go on anyhow. Something is happening in Memphis, something is happening in our world.

As you know, if I were standing at the beginning of time, with the possibility of general and panoramic view of the whole human history up to now, and the Almighty said to me, "Martin Luther King, which age would you like to live in?"—I would take my mental flight by Egypt through, or rather across the Red Sea, through the wilderness on toward the promised land. And in spite of its magnificence, I wouldn't stop there. I would move on by Greece, and take my mind to Mount Olympus. And I would see Plato, Aristotle, Socrates, Euripides and Aristophanes assembled around the Parthenon as they discussed the great and eternal issues of reality.

But I wouldn't stop there. I would go on, even to the great hey-day of the Roman Empire. And I would see developments around there, through various emperors and leaders. But I wouldn't stop there. I would even come up to the day of the Renaissance, and get a quick picture of all that the Renaissance did for the cultural and esthetic life of man. But I wouldn't stop there. I would even go by the way that the man for whom I'm named had his habitat. And I would watch Martin Luther as he tacked his ninety-five theses on the door at the church in Wittenberg.

But I wouldn't stop there. I would come on up even to 1863, and watch a vacillating President by the name of Abraham Lincoln finally come to the conclusion that he had to sign the Emancipation Proclamation. But I wouldn't stop there. I would even come up to the early thirties, and see a man grappling with the problems of the bankruptcy of his nation. And come with an eloquent cry that we have nothing to fear but fear itself.

But I wouldn't stop there. Strangely enough, I would turn to the Almighty, and say, "If you allow me to live just a few years in the second half of the Twentieth Century, I will be happy." Now that's a strange statement to make, because the world is all messed up. The nation is sick. Trouble is in the land. Confusion all around. That's a strange statement. But I know, somehow, that only when it is dark enough, can you see the stars. And I see God working in this period of the Twentieth Century in a way that men, in some strange way, are responding—something is happening in our world. The masses of people are rising up. And wherever they are assembled today, whether they are in Johannesburg, South Africa; Nairobi, Kenya; Accra, Ghana; New York City; Atlanta, Georgia; Jackson, Mississippi; or Memphis, Tennessee—the cry is always the same—"We want to be free."

And another reason that I'm happy to live in this period is that we have been forced to a point where we're going to have to grapple with the problems that men have been trying to grapple with through history, but the demands didn't force them to do it. Survival demands that we grapple with them. Men, for years now, have been talking about war and peace. But now, no longer can they just talk about it. It is no longer a choice between violence and non-violence in this world, it's non-violence or non-existence.

That is where we are today. And also in the human rights revolution, if something isn't done, and in a hurry, to bring the colored peoples of the world out of their long years of poverty, their long years of hurt and neglect, the whole world is doomed. Now, I'm just happy that God has allowed me to live in this period, to see what is unfolding. And I'm happy that He's allowed me to be in Memphis.

I can remember, I can remember when Negroes were just going around as Ralph has said, so often, scratching where they didn't itch, and laughing when they were not tickled. But that day is all over. We mean business now, and we are determined to gain our rightful place in God's world.

And that's all this whole thing is about. We aren't engaged in any negative protest and in any negative arguments with anybody. We are saying that we are determined to be men. We are determined to be people. We are saying, that we are God's children. And that we don't have to live like we are forced to live.

Now, what does all of this mean in this great period of history? It means that we've got to stay together. We've got to stay together and maintain unity. You know, whenever Pharoah wanted to prolong the period of slavery in Egypt, he had a favorite, favorite formula for doing it. What was that? He kept the slaves fighting among themselves. But whenever the slaves get together, something happens in Pharoah's court, and he cannot hold the slaves in slavery. When the slaves get together, that's the beginning of getting out of slavery. Now let us maintain unity.

Secondly, let us keep the issues where they are. The issue is injustice. The issue is the refusal of Memphis to be fair and honest in its dealings with its public servants, who happen to be sanitation workers. Now, we've got to keep attention on that. That's always the problem with a little violence. You know what happened the other day, and the press dealt only with the window breaking. I read the articles. They very seldom got around to mentioning the fact that one thousand, three hundred sanitation workers were on strike, and that Memphis is not being fair to them, and that Mayor Loeb is in dire need of a doctor. They didn't get around to that.

Now we're going to march again, and we've got to march again, in order to put the issue where it is supposed to be. And force everybody to see that there are thirteen hundred of God's children here suffering, sometimes going hungry, going through dark and dreary nights wondering how this thing is going to come out. That's the issue. And we've got to say to the nation: we know it's coming out. For when people get caught up with that which is right and they are willing to sacrifice for it, there is no stopping point short of victory.

We aren't going to let any Mace stop us. We are masters in our non-violent movement in disarming police forces, they don't know what to do. I've seen them so often. I remember in Birmingham, Alabama, when we were in that majestic struggle there we would move out of the 16th Street Baptist Church day after day; by the hundreds we would move out. And Bull Connor would tell them to send the dogs forth and they did come; but we just went before the dogs singing, "Ain't gonna let nobody turn me round." Bull Connor next would say, "Turn the fire hoses on." And as I said to you the other night, Bull Connor didn't know history. He knew a kind of physics that somehow didn't relate to the transphysics that we knew about. And that was the fact that there was a certain kind of fire that no water could put out. And we went before the fire hoses; we had known water. If we were Baptist or some other denomination, we had been immersed. If we were Methodist, and some others, we had been sprinkled, but we knew water.

That couldn't stop us. And we just went on before the dogs and we would look at them; and we'd go on before the water hoses and we would look at it, and we'd just go on singing "Over my head I see freedom in the air." And then we would be thrown in the paddy wagons, and sometimes we were stacked in there like sardines in a can. And they would throw us in, and old Bull would say, "Take them off," and they did; and we would just go in the paddy wagon singing, "We Shall Overcome." And every now and then we'd get in the jail, and we'd see the jailers looking through the windows being moved by our prayers, and being moved by our words and our songs. And there was a power there which Bull Connor couldn't adjust to; and so we ended up transforming Bull into a steer, and we won our struggle in Birmingham.

Now we've got to go on to Memphis just like that. I call upon you to be with us Monday. Now about injunctions: We have an injunction and we're going into court tomorrow morning to fight this illegal, unconstitutional injunction. All we say to America is, "Be true to what you said on paper." If I lived in China or even Russia, or any totalitarian country, maybe I could understand the denial of certain basic First Amendment privileges, because they hadn't committed themselves to that over there. But somewhere I read of the freedom of assembly. Somewhere I read of the freedom of speech. Somewhere I read of the freedom of the press. Somewhere I read that the greatness of America is the right to protest for right. And so just as I say, we aren't going to let any injunction turn us around. We are going on.

We need all of you. And you know what's beautiful to me, is to see all of these ministers of the Gospel. It's a marvelous picture. Who is it that is supposed to articulate the longings and aspirations of the people more than the preacher? Somehow the preacher must be an Amos, and say, "Let justice roll down like waters and righteousness like a mighty stream." Somehow, the preacher must say with Jesus, "The spirit of the Lord is upon me, because he hath annointed me to deal with the problems of the Poor."

And I want to commend the preachers, under the leadership of these noble men: James Lawson, one who has been in this struggle for many years; he's been to jail for struggling; but he's still going on, fighting for the rights of his people. Rev. Ralph Jackson, Billy Kyles. I could just go right on down the list, but time will not permit. But I want to thank them all. And I want you to thank them, because so often, preachers aren't concerned about anything but themselves. And I'm always happy to see a relevant ministry.

It's alright to talk about "long white robes over yonder," in all of its symbolism. But ultimately people want some suits and dresses and shoes to wear down here. It's alright to talk about "streets flowing with milk and honey," but God has commanded us to be concerned about the slums down here, and his children who can't eat three square meals a day. It's alright to talk about the new Jerusalem, but one day, God's preacher must talk about the New York, the new Atlanta, the new Philadelphia, the new Los Angeles, the new Memphis, Tennessee. This is what we have to do.

Now the other thing we'll have to do is this: Always anchor our external direct action with the power of economic withdrawal. Now, we are poor people, individually, we are poor when you compare us with white society in America. We are poor. Never stop and forget that collectively, that means all of us together, collectively we are richer than all the nations in the world, with the exception of nine. Did you ever think about that? After you leave the United States, Soviet Russia, Great Britain, West Germany, France, and I could name the others, the Negro collectively is richer than most nations of the world. We have an annual income of more than thirty billion dollars a year, which is more than all of the exports of the United States, and more than the national budget of Canada. Did you know that? That's power right there, if we know how to pool it.

We don't have to argue with anybody. We don't have to curse and go around acting bad with our words. We don't need any bricks and bottles, we don't need any Molotov cocktails, we just need to go around to these stores, and to these massive industries in our country, and say, "God sent us by here, to say to you that you're not treating his children right. And we've come by here to ask you to make the first item on your agenda—fair treatment, where God's children are concerned. Now, if you are not prepared to do that, we do have an agenda that we must follow. And our agenda calls for withdrawing economic support from you."

And so, as a result of this, we are asking you tonight, to go out and tell your neighbors not to buy Coca-Cola in Memphis. Go by and tell them not to buy Sealtest Milk. Tell them not to buy—what is the other bread?—Wonder Bread. And what is the other bread company, Jesse? Tell them not to buy Hart's Bread. As Jesse Jackson has said, up to now, only the garbage men have been feeling pain, now we must kind of redistribute the pain. We are choosing these companies because they haven't been fair in their hiring policies; and we are choosing them because they can begin the process of saying, they are going to support the needs and the rights of these men who are on strike. And then they can move on downtown and tell Mayor Loeb to do what is right.

But not only that, we've got to strengthen black institutions. I call upon you to take your money out of the banks downtown and deposit your money in Tri-State bank—We want a "bank-in" movement in Memphis. So go by the Savings and Loan Association. I'm not asking you something that we don't do ourselves at SCLC. Judge Hooks and others will tell you that we have an account here in the savings and loan association from the Southern Christian Leadership Conference. We're just telling you to follow what we're doing. Put your money there. You have six or seven black insurance companies in Memphis. Take out your insurance there. We want to have an "insurance-in."

Now these are some practical things we can do. We begin the process of building a greater economic base. And at the same time, we are putting pressure where it really hurts. I ask you to follow through here.

Now, let me say as I move to my conclusion that we've got to give ourselves to this struggle until the end. Nothing would be more tragic than to stop at this point, in Memphis. We've got to see it through. And when we have our march, you need to be there. Be concerned about your brother. You may not be on strike. But either we go up together, or we go down together.

Let us develop a kind of dangerous unselfishness. One day a man came to Jesus; and he wanted to raise some questions about some vital matters in life. At points, he wanted to trick Jesus, and show him that he knew a little more than Jesus knew, and through this, throw him off base. Now that question could have easily ended up in a philosophical and theological debate. But Jesus immediately pulled that question from mid-air, and placed it on a dangerous curve between Jerusalem and Jericho. And He talked about a certain man, who fell among thieves. You remember that a Levite and a priest passed by on the other side. They didn't stop to help him. And finally a man of another race came by. He got down from his beast, decided not to be compassionate by proxy. But he got down with him, administered first aid, and helped the man in need. Jesus ended up saying, this was the good man, this was the great man, because he had the capacity to project the "I" into the "thou," and to be concerned about his brother. Now you know, we use our imagination a great deal to try to determine why the priest and the Levite didn't stop. At times we say they were busy going to church meetings—an ecclesiastical gathering—and they had to get on down to Jerusalem so they wouldn't be late for their meeting. At other times we would speculate that there was a religious law that "One who was engaged in religious ceremonials was not to touch a human body twenty-four hours before the ceremony." And every now and then we begin to wonder whether maybe they were not going down to Jerusalem, or down to Jericho, rather to organize a "Jericho Road Improvement Association." That's a possibility. Maybe they felt that it was better to deal with the problem from the casual root, rather than to get bogged down with an individual effort.

But I'm going to tell you what my imagination tells me. It's possible that these men were afraid. You see, the Jericho road is a dangerous road. I remember when Mrs. King and I were first in Jerusalem. We rented a car and drove from Jerusalem down to Jericho. And as soon as we got on that road, I said to my wife, "I can see why Jesus used this as a setting for his parable." It's a winding, meandering road. It's really conducive for ambushing. You start out in Jerusalem, which is about 1200 miles, or rather 1200 feet above sea level. And by the time you get down to Jericho, fifteen or twenty minutes later, you're about 2200 feet below sea level. That's a dangerous road. In the days of Jesus it came to be known as the 'Bloody Pass'. And you know, it's possible that the priest and the Levite looked over that man on the ground and wondered if the robbers were still around. Or it's possible that they felt that the man on the ground was merely faking. And he was acting like he had been robbed and hurt, in order to seize them over there, lure them there for quick and easy seizure. And so the first question that the Levite asked was, "If I stop to help this man, what will happen to me? But then the good Samaritan came by. And he reversed the question: "If I do not stop to help this man, what will happen to him?"

That's the question before you tonight. Not, "If I stop to help the sanitation workers, what will happen to all of the hours that I usually spend in my office every day and every week as a pastor?" The question is not, "If I stop to help this man in need, what will happen to me?" If I do not stop to help the sanitation workers, what will happen to them?" That's the question.

Let us rise up tonight with a greater readiness. Let us stand with a greater determination. And let us move on in these powerful days, these days of challenge to make America what it ought to be. We have an opportunity to make America a better nation. And I want to thank God, once more, for allowing me to be here with you.

You know, several years ago, I was in New York City autographing the first book that I had written. And while sitting there autographing books, a demented black woman came up. The only question I heard from her was, "Are you Martin Luther King?"

And I was looking down writing, and I said yes. And the next minute I felt something beating on my chest. Before I knew it I had been stabbed by this demented woman. I was rushed to Harlem Hospital. It was a dark Saturday afternoon. And that blade had gone through, and the X-rays revealed that the tip of the blade was on the edge of my aorta, the main artery. And once that's punctured, you drown in your own blood—that's the end of you.

It came out in the New York Times the next morning, that if I had sneezed, I would have died. Well, about four days later, they allowed me, after the operation, after my chest had been opened, and the blade had been taken out, to move around in the wheel chair in the hospital. They allowed me to read some of the mail that came in, and from all over the states, and the world, kind letters came in. I read a few, but one of them I will never forget. I had received one from the President and the Vice-President. I've forgotten what those telegrams said. I'd received a visit and a letter from the Governor of New York, but I've forgotten what the letter said. But there was another letter that came from a little girl, a young girl who was a student at the White Plains High School. And I looked at that letter, and I'll never forget it. It said simply, "Dear Dr. King: I am a ninth-grade student at the White Plains High School." She said, "While it should not matter, I would like to mention that I'm a white girl. I read in the paper of your misfortune, and of your suffering. And I read that if you had sneezed, you would have died. And I'm simply writing you to say that I'm so happy that you didn't sneeze."

And I want to say tonight, I want to say that I, am happy that I didn't sneeze. Because if I had sneezed, I wouldn't have been around here in 1960, when students all over the South started sitting-in at lunch counters. And I knew that as they were sitting in, they were really standing up for the best in the American dream. And taking the whole nation back to those great walls of democracy which were dug deep by the founding fathers in the Declaration of Independence and the Constitution. If I had sneezed, I wouldn't have been around here in 1961, when we decided to take a ride for freedom, and ended segregation in the interstate travel. If I had sneezed, I wouldn't have been around in 1962, when Negroes in Albany, Georgia, decided to straighten their backs up. And whenever men and women straighten their backs up, they are going somewhere, because a man can't ride your back unless it is bent. If I had sneezed, I wouldn't have been here in 1963, when the black people in Birmingham, Alabama, aroused the conscience of this nation, and brought into being the Civil Rights Bill. If I had sneezed, I wouldn't have had a chance later that year, in August, to try to tell America about a dream that I had had. If I had sneezed, I wouldn't have been down in Selma, Alabama, to see the great movement there. If I had sneezed, I wouldn't have been in Memphis to see a community rally around those brothers and sisters who are suffering. I'm so happy that I didn't sneeze.

And they were telling me, now it doesn't matter now. It really doesn't matter what happens now. I left Atlanta this morning, and as we got started on the plane, there were six of us, the pilot said over the public address system, "We are sorry for the delay, but we have Dr. Martin Luther King on the plane. And to be sure that all of the bags were checked, and to be sure that nothing would be wrong with the plane, we had to check out everything carefully. And we've had the plane protected and guarded all night."

And then I got into Memphis. And some began to say the threats, or talk about the threats that were out. What would happen to me from some of our sick white brothers?

Well, I don't know what will happen now. We've got some difficult days ahead. But it doesn't matter with me now. Because I've been to the mountain-top. And I don't mind. Like anybody, I would like to live a long life. Longevity has its place. But I'm not concerned about that now. I just want to do God's will. And He's allowed me to go up to the mountain. And I've looked over. And I've seen the promised land. I may not get there with you. But I want you to know tonight, that we, as a people will get to the promised land. And I'm happy, tonight. I'm not worried about anything. I'm not fearing any man. Mine eyes have seen the glory of the coming of the Lord.